Master of Wisdom

Ārya Nāgārjuna

Master of Wisdom

Writings of the Buddhist Master Nāgārjuna

Translations and Studies
by Chr. Lindtner

Yeshe De Project

Dharma Publishing

Tibetan Translation Series

Buddha's Lions
Calm and Clear
Elegant Sayings
Golden Zephyr
Kindly Bent to Ease Us
Legend of the Great Stupa
Life and Liberation of Padmasambhava
Marvelous Companion
Master of Wisdom
Mind in Buddhist Psychology
Mother of Knowledge
Voice of the Buddha

This book is issued in cooperation with the Yeshe De Buddhist Research and Translation Project. Founded in 1983, the Yeshe De Project draws its inspiration from Ye-shes-sde, a direct disciple of Padmasambhava, whose works establish him as a translator without parallel in the history of Dharma transmission.

Library of Congress Cataloging-in-Publication Data

Nāgārjuna, 2nd cent.
Master of Wisdom.

(Tibetan Translation Series)
Bibliography: p.
Includes index.
1. Mādhyamika (Buddhism)–Collected Works.
I. Lindtner, Chr. II. Title. III. Series.
BQ2751.L56A2513 1986 294.3'85 86-29111
ISBN 0-89800-139-0

Typeset in Mergenthaler Palatino. Printed and bound in the United States of America by Dharma Press, Oakland, CA.

9 8 7 6 5 4 3 2 1

Publisher's Preface

Homage to the Buddha, Dharma, and Sangha

In the history of Buddhism, the great master Nāgārjuna stands out with a splendor matched by few others. His teaching and activity on behalf of the Dharma are virtually unparalleled, and his writings have had enormous influence not only within the Buddhist tradition, but also on the other philosophical traditions of India. Today that influence is beginning to be felt in Western thought as well.

Several Buddhist scriptures contain prophecies stating that Nāgārjuna would appear five hundred years after the time of the Buddha. Based on Western scholarship, this would place him in the first century of the Christian era, a time when the Mahāyāna was first becoming widely known. His impact on the Dharma and on the Buddhist community in this time of transition and transformation was incalculable.

Nāgārjuna was an early abbot of Nālandā, and he laid the groundwork for the later flourishing of Buddhist universities at Nālandā, Vikramaśīla, and elsewhere. In founding the śāstra tradition, he showed the role that human intelligence could play in attaining inner realization. Largely through his efforts, the exploration of the highest forms of knowledge became a central focus of Buddhist practice.

At the same time, Nāgārjuna explored more esoteric paths to realization, transmitting to his students methods and attainments of the deepest significance. He supported preservation of the stūpa built at the site of the Buddha's enlightenment in Bodh Gayā, and constructed temples and erected stūpas throughout all of India. He is said to have traveled to non-human realms as well, including the realm of the nāgas, from which he returned with the text of the Prajñāpāramitā in 100,000 lines. His writings, which span the range of human knowledge, spread from India to Tibet and China, where they were quickly translated from the Sanskrit. Commentaries on his works abounded in both India and Tibet, shaping centuries of philosophical inquiry.

Nāgārjuna devoted himself to understanding the Buddha. He sought to determine how the Enlightened One had come to be and how he had attained realization. He explored and celebrated the beauty and special qualities of this exemplary being, who transcended the conventional human realm, yet epitomized the perfection of human possibilities.

Nāgārjuna's investigations into the Buddha's special understanding led him to the Prajñāpāramitā, known as the mother of the Tathāgatas. Turning to the study of the Prajñāpāramitā with all his energy and insight, Nāgārjuna came to know the inner heart of reality as śūnyatā. Cutting through all extremes and dichotomies, he became one of the first to systematically establish the Madhyamaka, or Middle Way, thereby founding a firm philosophical basis for the Mahāyāna. His exploration of the two truths, the validity of conceptual knowledge, and the interdependence of all phenomena established a framework used by generations of leading thinkers and countless meditators.

Modern Western scholars have suggested that there may have been several Nāgārjunas, whom the tradition has mistakenly treated as one. They have also cast doubt on the authenticity of many of the works ascribed to Nāgārjuna by the Tibetan and the Chinese canonical traditions. Such theories have their origin in the great love that scholars have always had for speculation. While they certainly raise important questions, they have also had an unfortunate tendency to create confusion. It will require much continuing effort by new generations of dedicated scholars to set these issues straight once and for all.

The present work contains translations and editions of a number of key works by Ārya Nāgārjuna, together with a wide range of useful studies by Dr. Lindtner. At this early stage in our knowledge of the Buddhist tradition, it would be unrealistic to expect definitive treatments. However, Dr. Lindtner's efforts reflect extensive study and care, and we are most grateful to be able to present them. There remain many additional works by Nāgārjuna that are not yet available: works of beauty, sophistication, and depth that speak to the concerns of modern thought and to the issues that daily confront those who seek to walk the path of realization. We hope that in the future we will be able to present more such works in translation.

In preparing the present edition, we have had excellent cooperation throughout from Dr. Lindtner. An earlier version of this work was published by Dr. Lindtner himself in Denmark. In order to make the work accessible to a wider audience, we have substantially rearranged the materials presented. Dr. Lindtner has provided a list of corrections to his earlier edition, which we have incorporated in the text, and he has been kind enough to translate specially for this edition some of the Sanskrit and Tibetan passages cited in his concluding essay. He has also given us permission to include among the editions presented here his critical edition of the Śūnyatāsaptativṛtti, a commentary by Ārya Nāgārjuna on his own root text.

In addition, we have added to this edition a glossary, index, and other finding aids as well. The glossary is based almost exclusively on terms that Dr. Lindtner had originally presented parenthetically in the translations, and thus cannot be considered complete. However, it should still prove useful to students interested in further Madhyamaka studies. We hope that the other materials presented will also encourage further study, together with an ever-deepening appreciation for Nāgārjuna's writings.

Finally, we have made numerous minor editorial changes in the translations (as well as a few elsewhere in the book) for the sake of clarity and simplicity in the design and in the language, or for students who would like to see how the Tibetan has been rendered into English. Some of the changes are also intended to maintain consistency, either internally or else with terminology and usage adopted in some of our previous books (for example, we have treated 'samsara' and 'nirvana' throughout as English words). Dr. Lindtner kindly gave us considerable leeway in this regard. Of course, working with texts of such difficulty, we have sought to change the translations only in ways that would not affect the meaning, and have consulted with Dr. Lindtner whenever we believed this to be an issue. Nonetheless, the responsibility for any inaccuracies that may have resulted is ours.

For readers who wish to compare the translations with the facing transliterated Tibetan, it should be noted that Tibetan and English may not always correspond, because Dr. Lindtner drew on the original Sanskrit wherever that was available. Interested readers can consult the Sanskrit editions presented in Part II of the book. (For the Śūnyatāsaptati, readers should also compare the Tibetan verses as they are presented in Nāgārjuna's commentary, also reprinted in Part II—in some cases there are significant differences.) The following list presents a few instances of verses for which Dr. Lindtner's translation follows the Sanskrit rather than the Tibetan: CS I, 2, 14; CS III, 32, 42, 56.

For many years now we have wanted to focus more effort on the publication in English of works from the śāstra tradition, works which offer a wealth of teachings in a form well-suited to certain characteristics of the Western mind. For some time we had to put this project aside while we worked on preparing a complete edition of the Tibetan Buddhist

Canon. Now, however, we are ready to begin anew. This book is a suitable starting point, for Nāgārjuna can be regarded as the founder of the śāstra tradition. He and the later master Asaṅga are known in Tibet as the two excellent ones, or the two great lions, while Asaṅga's brother Vasubandhu is considered the greatest of the śāstra interpreters.

Among other leading figures of the śāstra tradition are Nāgārjuna's disciple Āryadeva and the Mādhyamika masters Bhāvaviveka and Candrakīrti. Dignāga and Dharmakīrti are the greatest among those who explored epistemology and logic, while Guṇaprabha and Śākyaprabha revealed the depths of the Vinaya, and Candragomin and Śāntideva are chief among those who established the vision of the Bodhisattva path. Their works, together with those of dozens of other masters, offer an unsurpassed wealth of teachings that we hope will become increasingly available to the West in the years to come.

With this project in mind, we express our sincere wish that the present work be the forerunner of many more, and that each in turn mark an improvement in form and content over those that have come before. Anyone interested in joining us in making that goal a reality is invited to contact Dharma Publishing for more information.

In readying this book for publication, Jack Petranker provided technical editing, prepared the glossary and index, and supervised other aspects of production. Several other staff members gave generously of their time and energy to make publication possible. We extend to all of them our thanks, and in particular wish to express our appreciation to Dr. Lindtner for his unfailing courtesy and flexibility.

Dedicated to all who are working for the continuing revelation of the Buddhadharma

Preface

These studies in the writings and philosophy of the Buddhist Patriarch Nāgārjuna could not have achieved their present form had I not been able to benefit from the co-operation and support of a number of friends, students, colleagues and library staffs here and abroad. To all of them, too numerous to mention individually, it is a pleasure to acknowledge my sincere gratitude and tender my best thanks.

In particular I would like to mention the names of four svyūthyas; namely, Per K. Sørenson, Ole Holten Pind, Harish Gaonkar, and Torvald Olsson, with all of whom I have enjoyed indulging in the study of Madhyamaka texts and in discussions concerning problems of Indian philology and philosophy. Professors J.W. de Jong, V.V. Gokhale and M. Hahn, Dr. M. Hara and Mr. A. Saito all provided me with indispensable suggestions, papers, or copies of manuscripts.

I most heartily thank Mrs. Else Pauly, who read the proofs, and above all Dr. Eric Grinstead, who, readily and generously as always, *inter alia* rendered unfailing support *in rebus sinicis* and in reading my manuscript.

Finally, I cannot be reticent about the deep and obvious debt my work owes to that of scholars who have done so much, in various respects, to clear the perilous madhyamā pratipad before me. Suffice it to mention the names of Erich Frauwallner, Poul Tuxen, Jacques May, Étienne Lamotte, and Louis de La Vallée Poussin, still the unsurpassed master of Buddhist studies.

C.L.

Contents

Introduction

Even though a steadily increasing number of papers and books about Nāgārjuna and the Madhyamaka school testify to a widespread interest in this branch of Mahāyāna Buddhism,[1] Indologists have still not laid the solid foundation required for real progress in these studies. Only a small, though important, fraction of his works is available in modern editions and reliable translations,[2] while more than one hundred of the most varied texts transmitted under Nāgārjuna's name still lie in Chinese and Tibetan versions, and even in Sanskrit manuscripts, without having been analyzed, let alone critically edited.[3]

It is only when a genuine and intelligible kernel of text has been extracted from this poorly digested mass that the two main tasks awaiting the scholar in this field may be taken up. The first will be the endeavor to understand the ideas and the personality of Nāgārjuna from his own works against his own background (mainly Buddhist); the next, to trace the immense impact — for I am certain that it will prove to have been so — that his efforts exercised on subsequent developments, not only inside but also outside the Buddhist fold.[4]

A unanimous tradition regards the Mūlamadhyamakakārikā as Nāgārjuna's magnum opus. In a previous work, I have attempted to determine which other works can be regarded as indisputably genuine. Some comments on the criteria I have employed can be found in Part III of this book and the accompanying notes.

In summary, I found that apart from the Mūlamadhyamakakārikā, twelve other texts must be considered genuine. These twelve are as follows: Śūnyatāsaptati, Vigrahavyāvartanī, Vaidalyaprakaraṇa, *Vyavahārasiddhi, Yuktiṣaṣṭikā, Catuḥstava, Ratnāvalī, Pratītyasamutpādahṛdayakārikā, Sūtrasamuccaya, Bodhicittavivaraṇa, Suhṛllekha, and *Bodhisaṁbhāra[ka]. They will be translated, edited, or analyzed on the following pages.

My desire to treat all the works definitely to be ascribed to Nāgārjuna in one way or another has made the present work rather wide in its scope. Inevitably this entails that numerous details or points of minor significance are tacitly passed by. This could not be otherwise. Nobody could be more aware of how much still remains to be done by future research than I am. However, I have done my best to clarify or at least indicate all points affording genuine problems, textual or philosophical. For misunderstandings and omissions I can, of course, only crave the reader's indulgence.

It will be convenient for the reader if I provide a synthetic survey (saṁkṣepa) of Nāgārjuna's chief religious and philosophical persuasions.[5]

The best starting point for such an exposition is the theory of two truths (satyadvaya): a relative or conventional truth (saṁvṛtisatya) that serves as the means for obtaining the absolute or ultimate truth (paramārthasatya).[6]

The ultimate goal of all endeavors is the highest good of oneself and of others: abolition of rebirth, or nirvana.[7] It implies the attainment of Buddhahood, or a twofold body (kāyadvaya).[8] This may be considered from four perspectives:

Ontologically: All phenomena (dharma) are empty (śūnya) since they lack own-being (svabhāva), inasmuch as empirically and logically they only occur in mutual dependence (pratītyasamutpanna).[9]

Epistemologically: The ultimate truth (tattva) is the object of a cognition without an object (advayajñāna),[10] and thus only an object metaphorically speaking (upādāya prajñapti).[11]

Psychologically: It is the abolition of all the passions (kleśa), primarily desire (rāga), hatred (dveṣa) and delusion (moha).[12]

Ethically: It implies freedom from the bonds of karma but subjection to the altruistic imperatives of compassion (karuṇā).[13]

The conventional Buddhist means ([saṁ]vyavahāra) devised for the fulfillment of this objective may be classified variously, but fit most briefly and comprehensively under the heading of the two accumulations for enlightenment (bodhisaṁbhāra):[14]

Accumulation of merit (puṇyasaṁbhāra). This comprises the four perfections (pāramitā): Liberality (dāna) and good morals (śīla),[15] which are mainly for the benefit of others, and patience (kṣānti) and energy (vīrya), which are for one's own good.[16] Their practice presupposes faith (śraddhā) in the 'law' of karma and results in the attainment of the physical body (rūpakāya) of a Buddha.[17] Along with the pursuit of meditation (dhyāna), the fifth pāramitā, this constitutes temporal happiness (abhyudaya).[18]

Accumulation of cognition (jñānasaṁbhāra). This consists in ecstatic meditation (dhyāna) surpassed by insight into the emptiness (śūnyatā) of all phenomena (dharmas), or wisdom (prajñā).[19] This is the *non plus ultra* or ultimate good (naiḥśreyasa) of all living beings.[20] It amounts to the attainment of a 'spiritual body' (Dharmakāya).[21]

In other words, cognition of emptiness and display of acts of compassion are — to the chosen few — the two means of realizing enlightenment.[22]

With this scheme in mind I trust the reader will be able to interpret each of Nāgārjuna's statements within their proper context.

Like other Indian hagiographers the ancient anonymous authors of Nāgārjuna legends did not share our curiosity to understand the personality of this remarkable individual. For a portrayal of the man we must refer to the conclusions we may draw from investigating his works.[23]

Only blurred outlines of a shadowy figure are still visible, at least to my eye. Nāgārjuna was first of all an ardently devoted Mahāyānist and a staunch propagator of his faith (especially evidenced by the Sūtrasamuccaya, Catuḥstava and Ratnāvalī).[24] His learning was extensive and not confined to the various branches of Buddhist lore.[25] Though he even attempted to make converts of Brahmin logicians (Vaidalya-prakaraṇa),[26] his main concern was to reform the dogmatic attitude (dṛṣṭiparāmarśa) of Abhidharma by propagating his conviction of the emptiness of all phenomena. This was the scope of his fundamental work, the Mūlamadhyamaka-kārikā, and its supplements, the Śūnyatāsaptati and Vigraha-vyāvartanī (which meet some of the objections that inevitably rain down upon a radical innovator).[27]

His commitment to the cause of instructing the lay public had several outcomes. The Suhṛllekha and Ratnāvalī are, each in its own way, introductions to Buddhism. They are addressed to a monarch.[28] His *Bodhisaṁbhāra[ka] and Bodhicittavivaraṇa are manuals in the theory and practice of Mahāyāna for the benefit of monks and laymen. These facts tally well with the tradition that Nāgārjuna had close connections at court and held responsible monastic offices.[29] It is thus quite probable that he played a decisive role in the foundation of monasteries and the like in Nāgārjunakoṇḍā.[30]

Of his character we only catch occasional glimpses of self-assurance and sarcasm as well as humility and compassion. His writings are, on the whole, characterized by a lucid and elegant diction, thus differing significantly, for example, from those of his pupil Āryadeva.[31]

Throughout this book, I have sometimes used abbreviations in referring to the principal works under discussion, as follows:

BS	*Bodhisaṁbhāra[ka]
BV	Bodhicittavivaraṇa
CS	Catuḥstava
	CS I = Lokātītastava; CS III = Acintyastava
MK	Mūlamadhyamakakārikā
PK	Pratītyasamutpādahṛdayakārikā
RĀ	Ratnāvalī
SL	Suhṛllekha
ŚS	Śūnyatāsaptati
SS	Sūtrasamuccaya
VP	Vaidalyaprakaraṇa
VS	*Vyavahārasiddhi
VV	Vigrahavyāvartanī
YṢ	Yuktiṣaṣṭikā

TRANSLATIONS

Lokātītastava

'Jig rten las 'das par bstod pa ||

1

| dben pa'i ye shes rig gyur pa | | 'jig rten 'das khyod phyag 'tshal 'dud | | gang khyod 'gro la phan pa'i phyir | | yun ring thugs rjes ngal bar gyur |

2

| phung po tsam las grol ba yi | | sems can med par khyod bzhed la | | sems can don la'ang mchog gzhol bar | | thub pa chen po khyod nyid bzhugs |

3

| blo ldan khyod kyis phung de 'ang | | sgyu ma smig rgyu dri za yi | | grong khyer rmi lam ji bzhin du | | blo ldan rnams la rab tu bstan |

4

| gang dag rgyu las byung ba rnams | | de med par ni yod min pas | | gzugs brnyan nyid dang mtshungs pa ru | | gsal bar ci yi phyir mi 'dod |

5

| 'byung ba mig gi gzung min pas | | de dngos mig gi ji ltar yin | | gzugs nyid gzung bar rab bkag pa | | gzugs nyid khyod kyis de ltar gsungs |

Hymn to [the Buddha] Transcending the World

1

O You who are beyond the world! Obeisance to You versed in the knowledge of the void. Solely for the benefit of the world You have long shown untiring compassion!

2

You maintain that apart from the mere skandhas no living being exists, and yet, great sage, You have exhausted yourself for the sake of living beings!

3

You who are a sage! To the sages You have declared that the skandhas also are comparable to an illusion, a mirage, a city of gandharvas, and dreams!

4

[The skandhas] occur due to a cause and do not exist in the absence of such: Because of this, have You not clearly maintained that they are like reflections?

5

The [four great] elements are imperceptible to the eye, so how can the 'visible' consist of them? Speaking thus of form You rejected the belief in form.

6

| tshor bya med par de med pas | | tshor ba nyid ni bdag med pas | | tshor bya de yang rang bzhin gyis | | yod pa med par khyod nyid bzhed |

7

| ming dang don dag tha dad min | | me yis kha nyid 'tshig par 'gyur | | gzhan na'ang rtogs pa med 'gyur zhes | | bden pa gsung ba khyod kyis bstan |

8

| byed po rang dbang las nyid kyang | | tha snyad du ni khyod kyis bstan | | phan tshun bltos pa can nyid du | | grub par khyod ni bzhed pa lags |

9

| byed po yod min spyod pa'ang med | | bsod nams de min rten 'brel skyes | | brten nas skyes gang ma skyes zhes | | tshig gi bdag po khyod kyis gsungs |

10

| shes pa med par shes bya min | | de med rnam par shes pa'ang med | | de phyir shes dang shes bya dag | | rang dngos med ces khyod kyis gsungs |

11

| mtshan nyid mtshon bya gzhan nyid na | | mtshon bya mtshan nyid med par 'gyur | | tha dad min na'ang de med par | | khyod kyis gsal po nyid du bstan |

6

As it does not exist without an object to be felt, feeling is without self. And You maintain that the object of feeling does not exist by own-being either.

7

If a concept [= name: ming] and its object [=meaning: don] were not different, [the word] 'fire' would burn the mouth. If [they] were different, there would be no comprehension [of anything]. Thus have You spoken as a speaker of truth.

8

That an agent is self-dependent and [his] action is also You have [only] expressed conventionally. Actually You maintain that both are established in mutual dependence.

9

[In the ultimate sense] no agent [of an action] exists and no experiencer either. Merit and demerit originate dependently. You have declared, O Master of words, that what originates dependently is unoriginated!

10

[There is] no object of knowledge unless it is being known. But the knowing consciousness does not exist without [its object]! Thus You have said that knowledge and the object of knowledge do not exist by own-being.

11

If a mark were different from the marked, the marked would exist [as such] without the mark! And you have clearly demonstrated that if [mark and marked] are conceived of as not different, neither exists.

12

| mtshan nyid mtshon bya rnam bral zhing | | tshig gis brjod pa rnam spangs par | | khyod kyis ye shes spyan nyid kyis | | 'gro ba 'di dag zhi bar mdzad |

13

| dngos po yod pa nyid mi skye | | med pa'ang ma yin yod med min | | bdag las ma yin gzhan las min | | gnyis min skye ba ji lta bu |

14

| yod pa gnas par rigs 'gyur gyi | | 'jig par 'gyur ba ma yin no | | med pa mi gnas par rigs pas | | 'jig par 'gyur ba ma yin no |

[Translated from Sanskrit]

17

| re zhig zhig pa'i rgyu las kyang | | 'bras bu 'byung bar mi rigs la | | ma zhig las min rmi lam dang | | 'dra ba'i skye ba khyod nyid bzhed |

12

With your eye of knowledge You view as calm this world that is devoid of marked and mark and free from the utterances of words.

13

An existent thing does not arise, nor does a non-existent, nor an existent and non-existent: either from itself, [from something] else, or from both. [So] how can it be born [at all]?

14

It is not reasonable that an existent, [which must be] linked to duration, should be destroyed. [And] how can something non-existent, like the horns of a horse, be extinguished?

15

Destruction is not different from the entity; nor can it be thought of as something not-different. If it were different [from the entity to be destroyed, it] would be permanent. If it were not-different, it could not occur.

16

Certainly destruction is not reasonable if the thing is a unity; certainly destruction is not reasonable if the thing is manifold.

17

First of all, it is not logical that the effect should arise either from a cause that has been destroyed or from one that has not [yet] been destroyed. [Therefore,] You maintain that origination is like a dream.

18

| sa bon zhig dang ma zhig las | | myu gu 'byung ba ma yin pas | | khyod kyis skye ba thams cad ni | | sgyu ma 'byung ba bzhin du gsungs |

19

| de phyir khyod kyis 'gro 'di dag | | yongs su brtags pa las byung bar | | kun tu shes bya 'byung ba na'ang | | skye ba med cing 'gag med gsungs |

20

| rtag la 'khor ba yod ma yin | | mi rtag pa la'ang 'khor ba med | | de nyid rig pa'i mchog khyod kyis | | 'khor ba rmi lam 'dra bar gsungs |

21

| sdug bsngal rang gis byas pa dang | | gzhan gyis byas dang gnyis kas byas | | rgyu med par ni rtog ge 'dod | | khyod kyis brten nas 'byung bar gsungs |

22

| rten cing 'brel par gang byung ba | | de nyid khyod ni stong par bzhed | | dngos po rang dbang yod min zhes | | mnyam med khyod kyi seng ge'i sgra |

23

| kun rtog thams cad spangs pa'i phyir | | stong nyid bdud rtsi ston mdzad na | | gang zhig de la zhen gyur pa | | de nyid khyod kyis shin tu smad |

18

Neither from the destroyed nor the non-destroyed seed can the sprout possibly arise. You have stated that all arising is like the arising of an illusion.

19

Therefore You have fully understood that this world has arisen due to imagination. It is unreal, [and] not having originated it cannot be destroyed.

20

There is no permanent wandering in samsara; there is no impermanent wandering in samsara. You, the best among knowers of truth, have declared samsara to be like a dream.

21

Dialecticians maintain that suffering is created by itself, created by another, created by both, [or created] without a cause; but You have stated that it arises dependently.

22

What arises dependently is exactly what You regard as śūnyatā. O, your incomparable lion's roar is that no independent thing exists!

23

The ambrosial teaching of śūnyatā aims at abolishing all conceptions. But if someone believes in śūnyatā You [have declared that] he is lost!

24

| bems po gzhan dbang stong pa nyid | | sgyu ma bzhin du rkyen 'byung bar | | mgon po khyod kyis chos kun gyi | | dngos med goms par mdzad pa lags |

25

| khyod kyis cung zhig ma bskyed cing | | 'ga' yang bkag pa ma mchis la | | sngon gyi ji ltar phyis de bzhin | | de bzhin nyid ni thugs su chud |

26

| 'phags pa rnams kyis brten pa yi | | bsgoms ma zhugs par mtshan med 'di | | rnam par shes par 'gar 'gyur ram | | .... |

27

| mtshan ma med la ma zhugs par | | thar pa med ces gsungs pa'i phyir | | de phyir khyod kyis theg chen la | | ma lus par ni de nyid bstan |

28

| bstod pa'i snod khyod bstod pa las | | bdag gis bsod nams gang thob pa | | des ni 'gro ba ma lus rnams | | mtshan ma'i 'ching las grol gyur cig |

| 'jig rten las 'das pa bstod pa slob dpon 'phags pa klu sgrub kyis mdzad pa rdzogs so |

24

O Protector! [Since they] are inactive, dependent, and empty, dependently arisen like an illusion, You have made it clear that all phenomena are without own-being.

25

You have put forward nothing and denied nothing. Now as then You are fully aware of Suchness.

26

Unless one resorts to the development practiced by the noble ones, consciousness will certainly never become signless here [in this world].

27

You have proclaimed that there is no liberation unless one resorts to the signless. Therefore You have demonstrated it comprehensively in the Mahāyāna.

28

By the merit which I have obtained by praising You, a fit vessel of praise, may the entire world become free from the bondage of signs.

Acintyastava

bSam gyis mi khyab par bstod pa ||

1

| gang zhig dngos po rten 'byung rnams | | ngo bo med pa nyid du gsungs | | ye shes mnyam med bsam mi khyab | | dpe med de la phyag 'tshal lo |

2

| ji ltar khyod kyis theg chen la | | nyid kyis chos la bdag med rtogs | | de bzhin blo dang ldan rnams la | | thugs rje'i dbang gis bstan pa mdzad |

3

| rkyen rnams las ni 'brel 'byung ba | | ma skyes lags par khyod kyis gsungs | | ngo bo nyid kyis de ma skyes | | de phyir stong par rab tu bstan |

4

| ji ltar 'di na sgra brten nas | | brag ca kun tu 'byung ba ltar | | sgyu ma smig rgyu bzhin du dang | | de bzhin srid pa kun tu 'byung |

5

| sgyu ma dang ni smig rgyu dang | | dri za'i grong khyer gzugs brnyan dang | | rmi lam gal te ma skyes na | | mthong ba la sogs dpe med 'gyur |

Hymn to the Inconceivable [Buddha]

1

I bow down to the inconceivable, incomparable [Buddha] whose knowledge is unequaled, who has declared that [all] dependently arising things lack own-being.

2

Just as You personally understood the selflessness of phenomena in the Mahāyāna, so, swayed by compassion, You have demonstrated it to the wise [Bodhisattvas].

3

You have stated that [whatever] arises from conditions is unoriginated. You have clearly shown that it is not born through own-being and thus is empty.

4

Just as here in this world an echo arises in dependence on a sound, so also [all] existence arises like an illusion or mirage.

5

If illusions, mirages, cities of gandharvas, and reflections are unborn, along with dreams, [then as to] them there can be no [real] vision or any other [forms of sense knowledge].

6

| ji ltar rgyu rkyen las byung ba | | de dag byas pa can du bzhed | | de bzhin rkyen las byung ba kun | | mgon po khyod kyis kun rdzob gsungs |

7

| byis pa gang dag ci brjod pa | | bgyis pa zhes 'brid de mchis te | | chang pa stong pa 'dra ba lags | | don bzhin ma lags rab tu bstan |

8

| gang tshe byas pa'i dngos ma skyes | | de tshe da ltar byung ba ci | | gang zhig pas na 'das par 'gyur | | ma 'ongs pa yang ji ltar bltos |

9

| rang las dngos po skye ba med | | gzhan dang gnyis ka las ma yin | | yod min med min yod med min | | de tshe gang las gang zhig 'byung |

10

| ma skyes pa la rang bzhin med | | ci phyir rang las kun tu 'byung | | rang bzhin dngos po med grub pas | | gzhan las kyang ni 'byung ba med |

11

| rang nyid yod na gzhan yod 'gyur | | gzhan nyid yod na rang nyid yod | | de dag bltos pa can du grub | | pha rol tshu rol bzhin du gsungs |

6

Just as [things] arising from causes and conditions are handed down as composite, O Protector, You have said that the entire conditionally born [world exists only] by convention.

7

It is a meaningless [statement] enticing the simple-minded [that] something created exists as a whole! It is a false statement, [delusive] like an empty fist.

8

If a composite thing is not born, how then can it be present? If a thing [i.e., the cause] has been destroyed, it is done with; how then can it relate to what is about to arise?

9

A thing is not born from itself, [something] else, or both, whether it be existent, non-existent, or existent and non-existent. How then can anything arise?

10

The unborn has no own-being, [so] how could it arise from itself? Nor can it arise from [something] else, since it is definitely established that there is no own-being.

11

If there were own-being there would be other-being; if other-being, own-being [could be] maintained. Establishment of those two has been stated [by You] to be correlative, like the far shore and the near.

12

| gang tshe ci la'ang mi bltos pa | | de tshe gang la gang zhig 'byung | | gang tshe ring la mi bltos pa | | de tshe thung sogs ga la mchis |

[Translated from Sanskrit]

14

| ji ltar gcig du ma mchis pa | | 'das dang ma 'ongs la sogs pa | | nyon mong rnam byang de bzhin te | | yang dag log pa'ang rang las ci |

15

| dngos gang rang las ma mchis na | | de tshe thams cad ci zhig mchis | | gzhan zhes brjod pa gang lags te | | rang gi rang bzhin med na min |

16

| gang tshe gzhan gyi dngos med pa | | de tshe dngos rnams rang bzhin med | | de tshe gzhan dbang dngos 'dzin pa | | gdon gyi theg pa ci zhig mchis |

17

| gdod ma nyid nas mnyam gyur pa | | rang bzhin gyis kyang mya ngan 'das | | yang dag par ni ma skyes lags | | de slad chos rnams khyod kyis gsungs |

12

When something is not related to anything, how then can that thing exist? For example, when it is not related to 'long', how can 'short' exist?

13

When there is existence there is non-existence, as there is short when there is long. Since there is existence when there is non-existence, each of the two does not exist.

14

Unity and multiplicity, past and future and the like, defilement and purification, true and false — how [can they exist] by themselves?

15

When an entity does not exist entirely by itself, it certainly cannot exist as an [independent] whole. What is called 'other' does not exist without its own own-being.

16

When there are no 'other' things, there are no things with self-nature. Then what [kind of] seizure of materialism is [the concept of an independent] dependent [nature]!

17

[Since all things] are from the beginning born the same and pass into nirvana by their own nature, You have said that phenomena are in reality unborn.

18

| blo ldan khyod kyis gzugs la sogs | | ngo bo nyid med par bstan pa | | dbu ba chu bur sgyu la sogs | | smig rgyu chu shing 'dra ba lags |

19

| dbang po rnams kyis gang dmigs de | | gal te yang dag mchis gyur na | | byis pas yang dag rig par 'gyur | | de tshe yang dag shes pas ci |

20

| dbang po rnams ni bems po dang | | tshad ma nyid kyang ma yin dang | | lung ma bstan pa nyid dang ni | | log par yongs shes khyod kyis gsungs |

21

| gang gis ci zhig ma rtogs pa | | yang dag ji bzhin thugs chud nas | | des na 'jig rten mi shes pas | | bsgribs pa zhes kyang khyod kyis gsungs |

22

| yod ces pa ni rtag par lta | | med ces pa ni chad par lta | | des na mtha' gnyis bral ba yi | | chos de khyod kyis bstan pa mdzad |

23

| des na chos rnams mu bzhi dang | | bral bar khyod kyis bka' stsal lags | | rnam shes bya ba'am ma lags la | | . . . . |

18

You have, O Sage, shown that form and [the remaining skandhas] lack own-being, like foam, bubbles, illusions, clouds, mirages, and plantains.

19

If that which is perceived with the senses were real, the simple-minded would already have knowledge of reality. What then would knowledge of reality be worth?

20

You have stated that the senses are dull, unreliable, imprecise, and [sources of] wrong understanding.

21

Having deeply understood that no one has access to the truth, You have stated that this is why the world is shrouded in ignorance.

22

'Exists' is the dogma of eternalism. 'Exists not' is the dogma of annihilation. [But] You have revealed the Dharma [of dependent co-origination], free from the two extremes.

23

Therefore You have said that phenomena are beyond the four categories. They are not knowable to consciousness, much less within the sphere of words.

24

| rmi lam mig 'phrul las byung dang | | zla ba gnyis la sogs mthong bzhin | | 'gro ba 'byung ba de dngos su | | ma byung de bzhin khyod kyis gzigs |

[Translated from Sanskrit]

26

| ji ltar rgyu las rmi lam na | | 'byung ba mthong ba de bzhin du | | dngos po thams cad 'byung ba bzhin | | 'jig pa'ang de bzhin bzhed pa lags |

27

| de bzhin chags sogs sdug bsngal dang | | 'khor ba sdug bsngal kun nyon mongs | | tshogs rdzogs pa dang thar pa yang | | rmi lam 'dra bar khyod kyis gsungs |

28

| de bzhin skyes dang ma skyes dang | | 'ongs pa dang ni song ba yang | | de bzhin bcings grol ye shes la | | gnyis 'dod yang dag rig ma lags |

29

| gang la skyes pa yod ma lags | | de la mya ngan 'das gang yod | | sgyu ma'i glang po 'dra bas na | | don du gzod nas zhi ba nyid |

24

Like a dream, an illusion, [or] seeing two moons: Thus have You seen the world, as a creation not created as real.

25

Like a son who is born, established, and dies in a dream, the world, You have said, is not really born, does not endure, and is not destroyed.

26

In a dream, whatever arises is experienced as resulting from causality. You maintain that all things are like this, both in their origination and their dissolution.

27

You have proclaimed that suffering born from desire and the other [poisons], as well as the kleśas, the suffering of samsara, the completing of the [two] accumulations, and even liberation are like a dream.

28

When [someone] understands [something] as born or unborn, present or gone, bound or liberated, he maintains duality [and consequently] does not know the truth.

29

How can what does not arise pass into nirvana? Since it is like an illusory elephant it is in truth originally at peace.

30

| skyes pa nyid na'ang ma skyes pa | | sgyu ma'i glang po ji bzhin bzhed | | de bzhin thams cad skyes pa 'am | | yang dag par ni ma skyes lags |

31

| 'jig rten mgon po dpag med kyis | | sems can dpag tu ma mchis pa | | so sor mya ngan 'das mdzad kyang | | de dag gis kyang gang ma bkrol |

32

| thub chen gang phyir sems can rnams | | rang las ma skyes de yi phyir | | gang yang gang gis ma bkrol zhes | | de skad khyod kyis gsal bar gsungs |

33

| ji ltar sgyu ma mkhan gyis byas | | dngos po stong pa de bzhin du | | byas pa thams cad dngos stong gzhan | | khyod gsungs de bzhin byed pa po |

34

| byed pa po yang gzhan gyis bgyis | | byas pa can du 'gyur ba lags | | yang na de yi bya ba byed | | byed pa por ni thal bar 'gyur |

35

| 'di dag thams cad ming tsam zhes | | khyod kyis gsung ni bstod de gsungs | | brjod pa las ni gzhan gyur pa | | brjod par bgyi ba yod ma mchis |

30

Just as [we] assert that an illusory elephant, though [apparently] born, is not born, thus everything [apparently] born is in reality unborn.

31

Countless world-protectors have [apparently] led innumerable beings one by one into nirvana, but [in reality] not one [being] has been liberated by them!

32

Have you not clearly stated, O great Sage, that when those beings who attain nirvana are [in fact] not born [at all, then] no one is liberated by anyone?

33

Just as the work of a magician is empty of substance, all the rest of the world — including a creator — has been said by You to be empty of substance.

34

A creator created by another [creator] cannot avoid being created [and so is impermanent]. But [to say he creates himself] implies that the creator is the agent of the activity that affects him!

35

You have proclaimed everything merely a name. Nothing expressible is found apart from the expression.

36

| de phyir chos rnams thams cad ni | | rtog pa tsam zhes khyod kyis gsungs | | gang gis stong par rnam rtog pa'i | | rtog pa yang ni med ces gsungs |

37

| dngos dang dngos med gnyis 'das pa | | la lar ma 'das pa yang lags | | shes pa med cing shes bya'ang med | | med min yod min gang lags dang |

38

| gang yang gcig min du ma'ang min | | gnyis ka ma yin gcig kyang med | | gzhi med pa dang mi gsal dang | | bsam mi khyab dang dpe med dang |

39

| gang yang mi skye mi 'gag dang | | chad pa med cing rtag med pa | | de ni nam mkha' 'dra ba lags | | yi ge ye shes spyod yul min |

40

| de ni rten cing 'brel par 'byung | | de ni stong par khyod bzhed lags | | dam pa'i chos kyang de lta bu | | de bzhin gshegs pa'ang de dang mtshungs |

41

| de ni de nyid don dam ni | | de bzhin nyid dang rdzas su bzhed | | de ni yang dag mi bslu ba | | de rdzogs pas na sangs rgyas brjod |

36

Therefore You have declared that all phenomena are merely abstractions. Even the abstraction through which śūnyatā is conceived You have declared non-existent.

37–39

[That which] has transcended the duality of being and non-being, without however having transcended anything at all; that which is not knowledge or knowable, not existent or non-existent, not one or many, not both or neither; [that which is] without foundation, unmanifest, inconceivable, incomparable; that which arises not, disappears not, is not to be annihilated, and is not permanent—that is [reality], like space, not within the range of words [or] knowledge.

40

Just that is dependent co-origination; just that is what You maintain to be śūnyatā. The true principle (saddharma) is of that kind, and the Tathāgata is like that also.

41

It is also accepted as the truth, the ultimate meaning, suchness, and the real. It is the indisputable. Whoever awakens to this is called Buddha.

42

| sangs rgyas rnams dang chos dbyings dang | | des na don du tha mi dad | | bdag nyid dang ni gzhan rnams dang | | des na mnyam par khyod bzhed lags |

43

| dngos po rnams las stong gzhan min | | de med par yang dngos po med | | de phyir rten cing 'byung ba'i chos | | stong pa lags par khyod kyis bstan |

44

| rgyu dang rkyen las byung ba'ang lags | | gzhan gyi dbang las kun rdzob ste | | gzhan gyi dbang zhes rab tu gsungs | | dam pa'i don ni bcos ma yin |

45

| ngo bo nyid dang rang bzhin dang | | yang dag rdzas dngos yod pa'ang lags | | brtags pa'i dngos po med pa nyid | | gzhan gyi dbang ni yod ma lags |

46

| brtags pa'i dngos po yod ces pa | | sgro 'dogs lags par khyod kyis gsungs | | byas pa chad nas med ces pa | | chad pa lags par khyod kyis gsungs |

47

| yang dag shes pas chad pa med | | rtag pa nyid kyang med par bzhed | | 'gro ba dngos pos stong pa lags | | de slad smig rgyu 'dra bar bzhed |

42

Therefore there is really no difference between the world of living beings and Buddhas. Hence You maintain the identity of yourself and others.

43

Śūnyatā is not different from things and there is no thing without it. Therefore You have declared that dependently arising things are empty.

44

The conventional arises from causes and conditions and is relative. Thus have [You] spoken of the relative. The ultimate meaning, however, is not fabricated.

45

It is also termed own-being, nature, truth, substance, the real, [and the] true. [Conventionally] an imagined thing does not exist but a relative is found [to exist].

46

You have stated that [affirmative] attribution is to say about an imaginary entity that it exists. [You] have also declared that cutting off [i.e., negation] is to say that a compound [entity] does not exist, because it is annihilated.

47

According to cognition of truth, [however], You maintain that there is no annihilation or permanence. [You] assert that the entire world is empty of substance, like a mirage.

48

| ji ltar ri dwags skom chu ni | | chad med rtag pa yod ma yin | | de bzhin 'gro ba thams cad kyang | | chad med rtag pa med par gsungs |

49

| gang la rdzas shig ste 'gyur ba | | de la chad sogs 'jigs pa 'byung | | de la 'jig rten mtha' yod dang | | mtha' med par yang 'gyur ba lags |

50

| shes pa yod pas shes bya bzhin | | shes bya yod pas de shes bzhin | | gang tshe gnyis ka ma skyes par | | rtogs pa de tshe ci zhig yod |

51

| de ltar sgyu ma la sogs dpe | | sman pa'i mchog gis gsal bstan nas | | lta ba thams cad 'gog byed pa'i | | dam pa'i chos ni bstan pa lags |

52

| ngo bo med pa nyid bstan pa | | de ni yang dag dam pa lags | | dngos po'i gdon gyis zin rnams kyi | | gso ba de ni bla na med |

53

| des na chos kyi mchod sbyin pa | | mchod sbyin rim pas rtag rgyun du | | 'jig rten gsum po sbyin sreg mdzad |
| .... |

48

Just as a mirage is neither annihilated nor permanent, thus all existence is said to be neither annihilated nor permanent.

49

One to whom things present themselves has [the dogmas of] annihilation and [permanence] imposed upon him and accepts implicitly that the world is finite or infinite.

50

Just as there is the knowable when there is knowing, there is knowing when there is the knowable. When both are unborn, what is [there to be] understood?

51

By thus teaching clearly through analogies — such as illusion and so forth — the Supreme Physician has taught the Holy Dharma, which cures all dogmas.

52

The ultimate truth is the teaching that things are without own-being. This is the unsurpassed medicine for those consumed by the fever of positivism.

53

Precisely therefore, O Offering-Priest of the Dharma, You have repeatedly made Dharma Offerings in the three worlds that are unsurpassed, unhindered, and unimpeded.

54

| dngos 'dzin 'jigs pa gcod bgyid cing | | mu stegs ri dwags 'jigs bgyid pa | | bdag med seng ge'i nga ro'i sgra | | rmad byung de ni khyod kyis gsungs |

55

| stong pa nyid dang chos zab pa'i | | chos kyi rnga chen brdung ba lags | | ngo bo nyid med sgra bo che'i | | chos kyi dung ni bus pa lags |

56

| sangs rgyas bstan pa bdud rtsi yi | | chos kyi rdzas ni gsungs pa lags | | chos rnams kyi ni ngo bo nyid | | nges pa'i don no zhes kyang bstan |

57

| gang yang skye dang 'gag la sogs | | sems can srog la sogs bstan pa | | de ni bkri don kun rdzob tu | | mgon po khyod kyis bstan pa lags |

58

| shes rab pha rol phyin mtsho yi | | pha rol gang gis gtan phyin te | | bsod nams yon tan rin chen phyug | | mgon khyod yon tan pha rol phyin |

59

| de ltar dpe med bsam mi khyab | | 'gro ba'i mgon po bstod pa yis | | bdag gis bsod nams gang thob des | | 'gro ba khyod dang mtshungs par shog |

| bsam gyis mi khyab par bstod pa slob dpon chen po klu sgrub kyi zhal snga nas mdzad pa rdzogs so |

54

You have uttered this wonderful lion's roar of not-self, which cuts off the fear [caused by] belief in things [and] terrifies the [timid] deer — the tīrthikas!

55

[You] have beaten the Dharma Drum [that resounds with the] deep truth of śūnyatā. [You] have blown the Dharma Conch, with its clear note of no own-being.

56

[You] have proclaimed the gift of Dharma: the nectar of the Buddha's teaching. The final meaning has been indicated — that is, of course, that phenomena are empty.

57

But the teaching regarding origination, cessation, and so forth; regarding the lives of sentient beings and the like, has meaning requiring interpretation. O Protector, you have also called it convention.

58

One who has finally reached the far shore of the ocean of perfect wisdom dwells amidst the jewels of the virtues of merit, fully conversant with the ocean of your virtues.

59

By virtue of the merit I have obtained by thus praising [You], the inconceivable [and] incomparable Leader of beings, may beings become like You!

Bodhicittavivaraṇa

Byang chub sems kyi 'grel pa ||

| dngos po thams cad dang bral ba | | phung po khams dang skye mched kyi | | gzung dang 'dzin pa rnam spangs pa | | chos bdag med pas mnyam nyid pas | | rang sems gdod nas ma skyes pa | | stong pa nyid kyi rang bzhin no | | zhes bya ba 'byung ngo || sangs rgyas bcom ldan 'das rnams dang | byang chub sems dpa' chen po de rnams kyis ji ltar byang chub chen por thugs bskyed pa de bzhin du | bdag gis kyang sems can ma bsgral ba rnams bsgral ba dang | ma grol ba rnams grol ba dang | dbugs ma byung ba rnams dbugs dbyung ba dang | yongs su mya ngan las ma 'das pa rnams yongs su mya ngan las bzla ba'i phyir dus 'di nas bzung nas byang chub snying po la mchis kyi bar du byang chub chen por sems bskyed par bgyi'o | | byang chub sems dpa' gsang sngags kyi sgor spyad pa spyod pa rnams kyis de ltar kun rdzob kyi rnam pas byang chub kyi sems smon pa'i rang bzhin can bskyed nas | don dam pa'i byang chub kyi sems bsgom pa'i stobs kyis bskyed par bya ba yin pas de'i phyir de'i rang bzhin bshad par bya'o ||

1

| byang chub sems kyi bdag nyid dngos | | dpal ldan rdo rje rnams btud de | | byang chub sems kyi bsgom pa ni | | srid pa 'jig de bdag gis bshad |

2

| sangs rgyas rnams kyi byang chub sems | | bdag dang phung sogs rnam rig gi | | rtog pa rnams kyis ma bsgribs pa | | rtag tu stong nyid mtshan nyid bzhed |

Exposition of Bodhicitta

It has been stated: "Due to the sameness [or] selflessness of phenomena, one's own mind — devoid of all entities, exempt from the skandhas, elements, sense-fields, and subject and object — is originally unborn; in essence empty."

Just as the Buddhas, our Lords, and the great Bodhisattvas have produced the thought of Great Enlightenment (mahābodhicitta), thus I shall also, from now until [I dwell] in the heart of enlightenment, produce the thought of Great Enlightenment in order to save living beings unsaved, liberate those not liberated, console those not consoled, and lead to nirvana those who have not arrived at nirvana.

When a Bodhisattva, having practiced a course by way of mantras, has thus produced the bodhicitta that in its relative aspect has the nature of aspiration, he must by means of meditational development produce the absolute bodhicitta. Therefore I will reveal its nature.

1

Bowing to the glorious Vajrasattvas embodying the mind of enlightenment, I shall expound the development of the bodhicitta that abolishes [the three kinds of] existence [in samsara].

2

The Buddhas maintain that bodhicitta is not enveloped in notions conscious of a self, skandhas, and so forth, [but] is always marked by being empty [of any such notions].

3

| snying rjes brlan pa'i sems kyis ni | | 'bad pas bsgom par bya ba yin | | thugs rje'i bdag nyid sangs rgyas kyis | | byang chub sems 'di rtag tu bsgoms |

4

| mu stegs can gyis gang brtags pa | | bdag de rigs pas rnam dpyad na | | phung rnams kun gyi nang rnams na | | gang zhig gnas kyang rnyed ma yin |

5

| phung rnams yod kyi de rtag min | | de yang bdag gi ngo bo min | | gang yang rtag dang mi rtag gnyis | | rten dang brten pa'i dngos po med |

6

| bdag ces bya ste yod min na | | byed po zhes bya ga la rtag | | chos can yod na chos rnams la | | 'jig rten na ni spyod pa 'jug |

7

| gang phyir rtag pas don byed pa | | rim dang cig car gyis min pa | | de phyir phyi rol nang du ni | | rtag pa'i dngos de med pa nyid |

8

| gal te nus na ci de ltos | | de ni cig car dngos 'byin 'gyur | | gang zhig dngos gzhan la ltos la | | de ni rtag dang nus ldan min |

3

[Those] with minds [only] tinged by compassion must develop [bodhicitta] with particular effort. This bodhicitta is constantly developed by the compassionate Buddhas.

4

When the self imagined by the tīrthikas is analyzed logically, it obtains no place within the [five] skandhas.

5

If it were [identical with] the skandhas [the self] would not be permanent, but the self has no such nature. And between things permanent and impermanent a container-content relationship is not [possible].

6

When there is no so-called self how can the so-called creator be permanent? [Only] if there were a subject might one begin investigating its attributes in the world.

7

Since a permanent [creator] cannot create things, whether gradually or all at once, there are no permanent things, whether external or internal.

8

Why [would] an efficacious [creator] be dependent? He would of course produce things all at once. A [creator] who depends on something else is neither eternal nor efficacious.

9

| gal te dngos na rtag min te | | dngos rnams rtag tu skad cig phyir | | gang phyir mi rtag dngos po la | | byed pa po nyid bkag pa med |

10

| bdag sogs bral ba'i 'jig rten 'di | | phung po khams dang skye mched dang | | gzung dang 'dzin pa nyid dag gi | | blo yis rnam par 'joms par 'gyur |

11

| phan par bzhed pa rnams kyis ni | | gzugs dang tshor ba 'du shes dang | | 'du byed rnam shes phung po lnga | | de ltar nyan thos rnams la gsungs |

12

| rkang gnyis mchog gis rtag tu yang | | gzugs di dbu ba rdos dang 'dra | | tshor ba chu yi chu bur 'dra | | 'du shes smig rgyu dang mtshungs shing |

13

| 'du byed chu shing dang 'dra la | | rnam shes sgyu ma lta bu zhes | | phung po bstan pa 'di lta bu | | byang chub sems dpa' rnams la gsungs |

14

| 'byung chen bzhi yi rang bzhin can | | gzugs kyi phung por rab tu bshad | | lhag ma gzugs med nyid du ni | | med na mi 'byung phyir na 'grub |

9

If [he] were an entity he [would] not be permanent, for things are perpetually instantaneous (since [you] do not deny that impermanent things have a creator).

10

This [empirical] world, free from a self and the rest, is vanquished by the [Śrāvakas'] understanding of the skandhas, elements, sense-fields, and subject and object.

11

Thus the benevolent [Buddhas] have spoken to the Śrāvakas of the five skandhas: form, feeling, apprehension, karma-formations and consciousness.

12–13

But to the Bodhisattvas [the Buddha], the best among those who walk on two legs, has always taught this doctrine about the skandhas: "Form is like a mass of foam, feeling is like bubbles, apprehension is like a mirage, karma-formations are like the plantain, and consciousness is like an illusion."

14

The form skandha is declared to have the four great elements as its nature. The remaining [four skandhas] are inseparably established as immaterial.

15

| de dag rnams kyi mig gzugs sogs | | khams rnams bshad pa de dag nyid | | skye mched dag ni gzung ba dang | | 'dzin par yang ni shes par bya |

16

| gzugs rdul med gzhan dbang po med | | byed po'i dbang po shin tu med | | skyod pa po dang skyed pa dag | | yang dag bskyed par rigs ma yin |

17

| gzugs rdul dbang shes skyed min te | | de ni dbang po las 'das yin | | 'dus pa de rnams skyed byed na | | tshogs pa de yang mi 'dod do |

18

| phyogs kyi dbye bas phye ba yis | | rdul phran la yang dbye ba mthong | | gang la cha shas kyis brtags pa | | der ni rdul phran ji ltar 'thad | |

19

| phyi rol don ni rnam gcig la | | tha dad shes pa 'jug par 'gyur | | yid 'ong gzugs ni gang yin pa | | de nyid gzhan la gzhan du 'gyur |

20

| bud med gzugs ni gcig pu la | | ro dang 'dod bya bza' ba la | | kun rgyu chags can khyi rnams bzhin | | rnam par rtog pa gsum yin no |

15

Among these eye, form, and so forth are classified as [the eighteen] elements. Again, as subject-object these are to be known as the [twelve] sense-fields.

16

Form is not the atom, nor is it the [organ] of sense. It is absolutely not the active sense [of consciousness]. [Thus] an instigator and a creator are not suited to producing [form].

17

The form atom does not produce sense consciousness, [because] it passes beyond the senses. If [empirical forms are supposed to] be created by an assemblage [of atoms], this accumulation is unacceptable.

18

If you analyze by spatial division, even the atom is seen to possess parts. That which is analyzed into parts — how can it logically be an atom?

19

Concerning one single external object divergent judgments may prevail. Precisely that form which is pleasant [to one person] may appear differently to others.

20

Regarding the same female body, an ascetic, a lover and a wild dog entertain three different notions: "A corpse!" "A mistress!" "A tasty morsel!"

21

| don mtshungs pa yis don byed pa | | rmi lam gnod pa bzhin min nam | | rmi lam sad pa'i gnas skabs la | | don byed pa la khyad par med |

22

| gzung dang 'dzin pa'i ngo bo yis | | rnam shes snang ba gang yin pa | | rnam shes las ni tha dad par | | phyi rol don ni 'ga' yang med |

23

| de phyir dngos po'i ngo bor ni | | phyi don rnam pa kun tu med | | rnam shes so sor snang ba 'di | | gzugs kyi rnam par snang bar 'gyur |

24

| ji ltar skye bo sems rmongs pas | | sgyu ma smig rgyu dri za yi | | grong khyer la sogs mthong ba ltar | | de bzhin gzugs sogs snang ba yin |

25

| bdag tu 'dzin pa bzlog pa'i phyir | | phung po khams sogs bstan pa yin | | sems tsam po la gnas nas ni | | skal chen rnams kyis de yang spangs |

26

| rnams par shes par smra ba la | | sna tshogs 'di ni sems su grub | | rnam shes rang bzhin gang zhe na | | da ni de nyid bshad bya ste |

21

Things are efficacious due to being *like* objects. Is it not like an offense while dreaming [i.e., nocturnal emission]? Once awakened from the dream the net result is the same.

22

As to the appearance of consciousness under the form of subject and object, [one must realize] that there exists no external object apart from consciousness.

23

In no way at all is there an external thing in the mode of an entity. This particular appearance of consciousness appears under the aspect of form.

24

The deluded see illusions, mirages, cities of gandharvas, and so forth. Form manifests in the same way.

25

The purpose of the [Buddha's] teachings about the skandhas, elements, and so forth is [merely] to dispel the belief in a self. By establishing [themselves] in pure consciousness the greatly blessed [Bodhisattvas] abandon that as well.

26

According to Vijñānavāda, this manifold [world] is established to be mere consciousness. What the nature of this consciousness might be we shall analyze now.

27

| 'di dag thams cad sems tsam zhes | | thub pas bstan pa gang mdzad de | | byis pa rnams kyi skrag pa ni | | spang ba'i phyir yin de nyid min |

28

| kun brtags dang ni gzhan dbang dang | | yongs su grub pa 'di nyid ni | | stong nyid bdag nyid gcig pu yi | | ngo bo sems la brtags pa yin |

29

| theg chen dga' ba'i bdag nyid la | | chos la bdag med mnyam pa nyid | | sems ni gdod nas ma skyes te | | sangs rgyas kyis ni mdor bsdus gsungs |

30

| rnal 'byor spyod pa pa rnams kyis | | rang gi sems kyi dbang byas te | | gnas yongs gyur nas dag pa'i sems | | so sor rang gi spyod yul brjod |

31

| 'das pa gang yin de ni med | | ma 'ongs pa ni thob pa min | | gnas phyir gnas ni yongs gyur pa | | da lta ba la ga la yod |

32

| de ji ltar de ltar snang min | | ji ltar snang de de ltar min | | rnam shes bdag med ngo bo ste | | rten gzhan rnam par shes pa med |

27

The Muni's teaching that "The entire [world] is mere mind" is intended to remove the fears of the simple-minded. It is not a [teaching] concerning reality.

28

[The three natures]—the imagined, the dependent, and the absolute—have only one nature of their own: śūnyatā. They are the imaginations of mind.

29

To [Bodhisattvas] who rejoice in the Mahāyāna the Buddhas present in brief the selflessness and equality of [all] phenomena [and the teaching] that mind is originally unborn.

30

The Yogācārins give predominance to mind in itself. [They] claim that mind purified by a transformation in position [becomes] the object of its own specific [knowledge].

31

[But mind] that is past does not exist, [while] that which is future is nowhere discovered. [And] how can the present [mind] shift from place [to] place?

32

[The ālayavijñāna] does not appear the way it is. As it appears—it is not like that. Consciousness essentially lacks substance; it has no other basis [than insubstantiality].

33

| ji ltar khab len dang nye bas | | lcags ni myur du yongs su 'khor | | de la sems ni yod min te | | sems dang ldan bzhin snang bar 'gyur |

34

| de bzhin kun gzhi rnam shes ni | | bden min bden pa bzhin du ni | | gang tshe 'gro 'ong g·yo bar 'gyur | | de tshe srid pa 'dzin par byed |

35

| ji ltar rgya mtsho dang ni shing | | sems ni med kyang g·yo bar 'gyur | | de bzhin kun gzhi rnam shes ni | | lus brten nas ni g·yo ba yin |

36

| lus med na ni rnam par shes | | yod pa min zhes yongs rtog na | | de yi so so rang rig nyid | | ci 'dra zhes kyang brjod par gyis |

37

| so so rang rig nyid brjod pas | | de ni dngos po nyid du brjod | | 'di de yin zhes brjod pa ni | | nus min zhes kyang brjod pa yin |

38

| rang la de bzhin gzhan dag la | | nges pa bskyed par bya ba'i phyir | | rtag tu 'khrul pa med par ni | | mkhas rnams rab tu 'jug pa yin |

33

When a lodestone is brought near, iron turns swiftly around; [though] it possesses no mind, [it] appears to possess mind. In just the same way,

34

The ālayavijñāna appears to be real though it is not. When it moves to and fro it [seems to] retain the [three] existences.

35

Just as the ocean and trees move though they have no mind, the ālayavijñāna is active [only] in dependence on a body.

36

Considering that without a body there is no consciousness, you must also state what kind of specific knowledge of itself this [consciousness] possesses!

37

By saying that a specific knowledge of itself [exists] one says it is an entity. But one also says that it is not possible to say, "This is it!"

38

To convince themselves as well as others, those who are intelligent [should] always proceed without error!

39

| shes pas shes bya rtogs pa ste | | shes bya med par shes pa med | | de ltar na ni rig bya dang | | rig byed med ces cis mi 'dod |

40

| sems ni ming tsam yin pa ste | | ming las gzhan du 'ga' yang med | | ming tsam du ni rnam rig blta | | ming yang rang bzhin med pa yin |

41

| nang ngam de bzhin phyi rol lam | | yang na gnyis ka'i bar dag tu | | rgyal ba rnams kyis sems ma rnyed | | de phyir sgyu ma'i rang bzhin sems |

42

| kha dog dbyibs kyi dbye ba 'am | | gzung ba dang ni 'dzin pa 'am | | skyes pa bud med ma ning sogs | | ngo bo sems ni gnas pa min |

43

| mdor na sangs rgyas rnams kyis ni | | gzigs par ma gyur gzigs mi 'gyur | | rang bzhin med pa'i rang bzhin can | | ji lta bur na gzigs par 'gyur |

44

| dngos po zhes bya rnam rtog yin | | rnam rtog med pa stong pa yin | | gang du rnam rtog snang gyur pa | | der ni stong nyid ga la yod |

39

The knowable is known by a knower. Without the knowable no knowing [is possible]. So why not accept that subject and object do not exist [as such]?

40

Mind is but a name. It is nothing apart from [its] name. Consciousness must be regarded as but a name. The name too has no own-being.

41

The Jinas have never found mind to exist, either internally, externally, or else between the two. Therefore mind has an illusory nature.

42

Mind has no fixed forms such as various colors and shapes, subject and object, or male, female, and neuter.

43

In brief: Buddhas do not see [what cannot] be seen. How could they see what has lack of own-being as its own-being?

44

A 'thing' is a construct. Śūnyatā is absence of constructs. Where constructs have appeared, how can there be śūnyatā?

45

I rtogs bya rtogs byed rnam pa'i sems I I de bzhin gshegs rnams kyis ma gzigs I I gang na rtogs bya rtogs byed yod I I der ni byang chub yod ma yin I

46

I mtshan nyid med cing skye ba med I I yod gyur ma yin ngag lam bral I I mkha' dang byang chub sems dang ni I I byang chub gnyis med mtshan nyid can I

47

I byang chub snying po la bzhugs pa'i I I bdag nyid chen po'i sangs rgyas dang I I brtse ldan kun gyis dus kun tu I I stong pa mkha' dang mtshungs par mkhyen I

48

I de phyir chos rnams kun gyi gzhi I I zhi zhing sgyu ma dang mtshungs par I I gzhi med srid par 'jig byed pa'i I I stong po nyid 'di rtag tu bsgom I

49

I skye med dang ni stong nyid dang I I bdag med ces byar stong pa nyid I I bdag nyid dman pa gang sgom pa I I de de sgom par byed pa min I

50

I dge dang mi dge'i rnam rtog ni I I rgyun chad pa yi mtshan nyid can I I stong nyid sangs rgyas kyis gsungs gzhan I I de dag stong pa nyid mi bzhed I

45

The Tathāgatas do not regard mind under the form of knowable and knower. Where knower and knowable prevail there is no enlightenment.

46

Space, bodhicitta, and enlightenment are without marks; without generation. They have no structure; they are beyond the path of words. Their 'mark' is non-duality.

47

The magnanimous Buddhas who reside in the heart of enlightenment and all the compassionate [Bodhisattvas] always know śūnyatā to be like space.

48

Therefore [Bodhisattvas] perpetually develop this śūnyatā, which is the basis of all phenomena; calm, illusory, baseless; the destroyer of existence.

49

Śūnyatā expresses non-origination, voidness, and lack of self. Those who practice it should not practice what is cultivated by the inferior.

50

Notions about positive and negative have the mark of disintegration. The Buddhas have spoken [of them in terms of] śūnyatā, [but] the others do not accept śūnyatā.

51

| sems la dmigs pa med pa ni | | gnas pa nam mkha'i mtshan nyid yin | | de dag stong nyid sgom pa ni | | nam mkha' sgom par bzhed pa yin |

52

| stong nyid seng ge'i sgra yis ni | | smra ba thams cad skrag par mdzad | | gang dang gang du de dag bzhugs | | de dang der ni stong nyid 'gyur |

53

| gang gi rnam shes skad cig ma | | de yi de ni rtag ma yin | | sems ni mi rtag nyid yin na | | stong pa nyid du ji ltar 'gal |

54

| mdor na sangs rgyas rnams kyis ni | | sems ni mi rtag nyid bzhed na | | de dag sems ni stong nyid du | | ci'i phyir na bzhed mi 'gyur |

55

| thog ma nyid nas sems kyi ni | | rang bzhin rtag tu med par 'gyur | | dngos po rang bzhin gyis grub pa | | rang bzhin med nyid brjod pa min |

56

| de skad brjod na sems kyi ni | | bdag gi gnas pa spangs pa yin | | rang gi rang bzhin las 'das pa | | de ni chos rnams chos ma yin |

51

The abode of a mind that has no support has the mark of [empty] space. These [Bodhisattvas] maintain that development of śūnyatā is development of space.

52

All the dogmatists have been terrified by the lion's roar of śūnyatā. Wherever they may reside, śūnyatā lies in wait!

53

Whoever regards consciousness as momentary cannot accept it as permanent. If mind is impermanent, how does this contradict śūnyatā?

54

In brief: When the Buddhas accept mind as impermanent, why should they not accept mind as empty?

55

From the very beginning mind has no own-being. If things could be proved through own-being, [we would] not declare them to be without substance.

56

This statement results in abandoning mind as having substantial foundation. It is not the nature of things to transcend [their] own own-being!

57

| ji ltar bu ram mngar ba dang | | me yi rang bzhin tsha ba bzhin | | de bzhin chos rnams thams cad kyi | | rang bzhin stong pa nyid du 'dod |

58

| stong nyid rang bzhin du brjod pas | | gang zhig chad par smra ba min | | des ni rtag pa nyid du yang | | 'ga' zhig smras pa ma yin no |

59

| ma rig nas brtsams rga ba yi | | mthar thug yan lag bcu gnyis kyi | | brten nas byung ba'i bya ba ni | | kho bo rmi lam sgyu 'drar 'dod |

60

| yan lag bcu gnyis 'khor lo 'di | | srid pa'i lam du 'khor ba ste | | de las gzhan du sems can gang | | las 'bras spyod par 'dod pa med |

61

| ji ltar me long la brten nas | | bzhin gyi dkyil 'khor snang gyur pa | | de ni der 'pho ma yin zhing | | de med par yang de yod min |

62

| de bzhin phung po nying mtshams sbyor | | srid pa gzhan du skye ba dang | | 'pho ba med par mkhas rnams kyis | | rtag tu nges par bya ba yin |

57

As sweetness is the nature of sugar and hotness that of fire, so [we] maintain the nature of all things to be śūnyatā.

58

When one declares śūnyatā to be the nature [of all phenomena] one in no sense asserts that anything is destroyed or that something is eternal.

59

The activity of dependent co-origination with its twelve spokes starting with ignorance and ending with decay [we] maintain to be like a dream and an illusion.

60

This wheel with twelve spokes rolls along the road of life. Apart from this, no sentient being that partakes of the fruit of its deeds can be found.

61

Depending on a mirror the outline of a face appears: It has not moved into it but also does not exist without it.

62

Just so, the wise must always be convinced that the skandhas appear in a new existence [due to] recomposition, but do not migrate [as identical or different].

63

| mdor na stong pa'i chos rnams las | | chos rnams stong pa skye bar 'gyur | | byed po las 'bras longs spyod pa | | kun rdzob tu ni rgyal bas bstan |

64

| ji ltar rnga yi sgra dang ni | | de bzhin myu gu tshogs pas bskyed | | phyi yi rten cing 'brel 'byung ba | | rmi lam sgyu ma dang mtshungs 'dod |

65

| chos rnams rgyu las skyes pa ni | | rnam yang 'gal bar mi 'gyur te | | rgyu ni rgyu nyid kyis stong pas | | de ni skye ba med par rtogs |

66

| chos rnams kyi ni skye ba med | | stong nyid yin par rab tu bshad | | mdor na phung po lnga rnams ni | | chos kun zhes ni bshad pa yin |

67

| de nyid ji bzhin bshad pas na | | kun rdzob rgyun ni 'chad mi 'gyur | | kun rdzob las ni tha dad par | | de nyid dmigs pa ma yin te |

68

| kun rdzob stong pa nyid du bshad | | stong pa kho na kun rdzob yin | | med na mi 'byung nges pa'i phyir | | byas dang mi rtag ji bzhin no |

63

To sum up: Empty things are born from empty things. The Jina has taught that agent and deed, result and enjoyer are [all only] conventional.

64

Just as the totality [of their causes and conditions] create the sound of a drum or a sprout, [so we] maintain that external dependent co-origination is like a dream and an illusion.

65

It is not at all inconsistent that phenomena are born from causes. Since a cause is empty of cause, [we] understand it to be unoriginated.

66

That phenomena [are said] not to arise indicates that they are empty. Briefly, 'all phenomena' denotes the five skandhas.

67

When truth is [accepted] as has been explained, convention is not disrupted. The true is not an object separate from the conventional.

68

Convention is explained as śūnyatā; convention is simply śūnyatā. For [these two] do not occur without one another, just as created and impermanent [invariably concur].

69

| kun rdzob nyon mongs las las byung | | las ni sems las byung ba yin | | sems ni bag chags rnams kyis bsags | | bag chags bral na bde ba ste |

70

| bde ba'i sems ni zhi ba nyid | | sems zhi ba ni rmongs mi 'gyur | | rmongs med de nyid rtogs pa ste | | de nyid rtogs pas grol thob 'gyur |

71

| de bzhin nyid dang yang dag mtha' | | mtshan ma med dang don dam nyid | | byang chub sems mchog de nyid dang | | stong nyid du yang bshad pa yin |

72

| gang dag stong nyid mi shes pa | | de dag thar pa'i rten ma yin | | 'gro drug srid pa'i btson rar ni | | rmongs pa de dag 'khor bar 'gyur |

73

| de ltar stong pa nyid 'di ni | | rnal 'byor pa yis bsgom byas na | | gzhan gyi don la chags pa'i blo | | 'byung bar 'gyur ba the tshom med |

74

| gang dag pha dang ma dang ni | | gnyen bshes gyur pas bdag la sngon | | phan pa byas par gyur pa yi | | sems can de dag rnams la ni | | byas pa bzo bar gyur par bya |

69

Convention is born from karma [due to the various] kleśas, and karma is created by mind. Mind is accumulated by the vāsanās. Happiness consists in being free from the vāsanās.

70

A happy mind is tranquil. A tranquil mind is not confused. To be unperplexed is to understand the truth. By understanding truth one obtains liberation.

71

It is also defined as reality, real limit, signless, ultimate meaning, the highest bodhicitta, and śūnyatā.

72

Those who do not know śūnyatā will have no share in liberation. Such deluded beings wander [among] the six destinies, imprisoned within existence.

73

When ascetics (yogācārin) have thus developed this śūnyatā, their minds will without doubt become devoted to the welfare of others, [as they think]:

74

"I should be grateful to those beings who in the past bestowed benefits upon me by being my parents or friends.

75

| srid pa'i btson rar sems can ni | | nyon mongs me yis gdungs rnams la | | bdag gis sdug bsngal byin pa ltar | | de bzhin bde ba sbyin bar rigs |

76

| 'jig rten bde 'gro ngan 'gro yis | | 'dod dang mi 'dod 'bras bu de | | sems can rnams la phan pa dang | | gnod pa las ni 'byung bar 'gyur |

77

| sems can brten pas sangs rgyas kyis | | go 'phang bla med nyid 'gyur na | | lha dang mi yi longs spyod gang | | tshangs dang dbang po drag po dang |

78

| 'jig rten skyong bas brten de dag | | sems can phan pa tsam zhig gis | | ma drangs pa ni 'gro gsum 'dir | | 'ga' yang med la mtshar ci yod |

79

| sems dmyal dud 'gro yi dwags su | | sdug bsngal rnam pa du ma'i dngos | | sems can rnams kyis myong ba gang | | de ni sems can gnod las byung |

80

| bkres skom phan tshun bdeg pa dang | | gzir ba yi ni sdug bsngal nyid | | bzlog par dka' zhing zad med de | | sems can gnod pa'i 'bras bu yin |

75

"As I have brought suffering to beings living in the prison of existence, who are scorched by the fire of the kleśas, it is fitting that I [now] afford them happiness."

76

The sweet and bitter fruit [that beings in] the world [obtain] in the form of a good or bad rebirth is the outcome of whether they hurt or benefit living beings.

77–78

If Buddhas attain the unsurpassed stage by [giving] living beings support, what is so strange if [those] not guided by the slightest concern for others receive none of the pleasures of gods and men that support the guardians of the world, Brahmā, Indra, and Rudra?

79

The different kinds of suffering that beings experience in the hell realms, as beasts, and as ghosts result from causing beings pain.

80

The inevitable and unceasing suffering of hunger, thirst, mutual slaughter, and torments result from causing pain.

81

| sangs rgyas byang chub sems nyid dang | | bde 'gro dang ni ngan 'gro gang | | sems can gang gi rnam smin kyang | | ngo bo gnyis su shes par bya |

82

| dngos po kun gyis rten bya zhing | | rang gi lus bzhin bsrung bar bya | | sems can rnams la chags bral ba | | dug bzhin 'bad pas spang bar bya |

83

| nyan thos rnams ni chags bral bas | | byang chub dman pa thob min nam | | sems can yongs su ma dor bas | | rdzogs sangs rgyas kyi byang chub thob |

84

| de ltar phan dang mi phan pa'i | | 'bras bu 'byung bar dpyad pa na | | de dag skad cig gcig kyang ni | | rang don gnas zhin ji ltar gnas |

85

| snying rjes brtan pa'i rtsa ba can | | byang sems myu gu las byung ba | | gzhan don gcig 'bras byang chub ni | | rgyal ba'i sras rnams sgom par byed |

86

| gang zhig bsgom pas brtan pa ni | | gzhan gyi sdug bsngal gyis bred nas | | bsam gtan bde ba dor nas kyang | | mnar med pa yang 'jug par byed |

81

Know that beings are subject to two kinds of maturation: [that of] Buddhas [and] Bodhisattvas and that of good and bad rebirth.

82

Support [living beings] with your whole nature and protect them like your own body. Indifference toward beings must be avoided like poison!

83

Though the Śrāvakas obtain a lesser enlightenment thanks to indifference, the bodhi of the Perfect Buddhas is obtained by not abandoning living beings.

84

How can those who consider how the fruit of helpful and harmful deeds ripens persist in their selfishness for even a single moment?

85

The sons of the Buddha are active in developing enlightenment, which has steadfast compassion as its root, grows from the sprout of bodhicitta, and has the benefit of others as its sole fruit.

86

Those who are strengthened by meditational development find the suffering of others frightening. [In order to support others] they forsake even the pleasures of dhyāna; they even enter the Avīci hell!

87

| 'di ni ngo mtshar 'di bsngags 'os | | 'di ni dam pa'i tshul lugs mchog | | de dag rnams kyi rang lus dang | | nor rnams byin pa ngo mtshar min |

88

| chos rnams stong pa 'di shes nas | | las dang 'bras bu sten pa gang | | de ni ngo mtshar bas ngo mtshar | | rmad du 'byung bas rmad du 'byung |

89

| sems can bskyab pa'i bsam pa can | | de dag srid pa'i 'dam skyes kyang | | de byung nyid pas ma gos pa | | chu yi padma'i 'dab ma bzhin |

90

| kun bzang la sogs rgyal ba'i sras | | stong nyid ye shes me yis ni | | nyon mongs bud shing bsregs mod kyi | | de lta'ang snying rjes brlan 'gyur cing |

91

| snying rje'i dbang du gyur pa rnams | | gshegs dang bltam dang rol pa dang | | khab nas 'byung dang dka' ba spyod | | byang chub che dang bdud sde 'joms |

92

| chos kyi 'khor lo skor ba dang | | lha rnams kun gyis zhus pa dang | | de bzhin du ni mya ngan las | | 'das pa ston par mdzad pa yin |

87

They are wonderful; they are admirable; they are most extraordinarily excellent! Nothing is more amazing than those who sacrifice their person and riches!

88

Those who understand the śūnyatā of phenomena [but also] believe in [the law of] karma and its results are more wonderful than wonderful, more astonishing than astonishing!

89

Wishing to protect living beings, they take rebirth in the mud of existence. Unsullied by its events, they are like a lotus [rooted] in the mire.

90

Though sons of the Buddha such as Samantabhadra have consumed the fuel of the kleśas through the cognitive fire of śūnyatā, the waters of compassion still flow within them!

91–92

Having come under the guiding power of compassion they display the descent [from Tuṣita], birth, merriments, renunciation, ascetic practices, great enlightenment, victory over the hosts of Māra, turning of the Dharmacakra, the request of all the gods, and [the entry into] nirvana.

93

| tshangs dang dbang po khyab 'jug dang | | drag sogs gzugs su sprul mdzad nas | | 'gro ba 'dul ba'i sbyor ba yis | | thugs rje'i rang bzhin can gar mdzad |

94

| srid pa'i lam la skyo rnams la | | ngal so'i don du theg pa che | | 'byung ba'i ye shes gnyis po yang | | gsungs pa yin te don dam min |

95

| ji srid sangs rgyas kyis ma bskul | | de srid ye shes lus dngos can | | ting 'dzin myos pas rgyal 'gyur ba | | nyan thos de dag gnas par 'gyur |

96

| bskul na sna tshogs gzugs kyis ni | | sems can don la chags gyur cing | | bsod nams ye shes tshogs bsags nas | | sangs rgyas byang chub thob par 'gyur |

97

| gnyis kyi bag chags yod pa'i phyir | | bag chags sa bon brjod pa yin | | sa bon de dngos tshogs pa ni | | srid pa'i myu gu skyed par byed |

98

| 'jig rten mgon rnams kyi bstan pa | | sems can bsam dbang rjes 'gro ba | | 'jig rten du ni thabs mang po | | rnam pa mang po tha dad 'gyur |

93

Having emanated such forms as Brahmā, Indra, Viṣṇu, and Rudra, they present through their compassionate natures a performance suitable to beings in need of guidance.

94

Two [kinds] of knowledge arise [from] the Mahāyāna to give comfort and ease to those who journey in sorrow along life's path — so it is said. But [this] is not the ultimate meaning.

95

As long as they have not been admonished by the Buddhas, Śrāvakas [who are] in a bodily state of cognition remain in a swoon, intoxicated by samādhi.

96

But once admonished, they devote themselves to living beings in varied ways. Accumulating stores of merit and knowledge, they obtain the enlightenment of Buddhas.

97

As the potentiality of both [accumulations], the vāsanās are said to be the seed [of enlightenment]. That seed, [which is] the accumulation of things, produces the sprout of life.

98

The teachings of the protectors of the world accord with the [varying] resolve of living beings. The Buddhas employ a wealth of skillful means, which take many worldly forms.

99

I zab cing rgya che'i dbye ba dang I I la lar gnyis ka'i mtshan nyid can I I tha dad bstan pa yin yang ni I I stong dang gnyis med tha dad min I

100

I gzungs rnams dang ni sa rnams dang I I sangs rgyas pha rol phyin gang dag I I de dag byang chub sems kyi char I I kun mkhyen rnams kyis gsungs pa yin I

101

I lus ngag yid kyis rtag par ni I I de ltar sems can don byed pa I I stong nyid rtsod par smra rnams la I I chad pa'i rtsod pa nyid yod min I

102

I 'khor ba mya ngan 'das pa la I I bdag nyid che de mi gnas pa I I de phyir sangs rgyas rnams kyis ni I I mi gnas mya ngan 'das 'dir bshad I

103

I snying rje ro gcig bsod nams gyur I I stong nyid ro ni mchog gyur pa I I bdag dang gzhan don sgrub don du I I gang 'thung de dag rgyal sras yin I

104

I dngos po kun gyis de la 'dud I I srid pa gsum na rtag mchod 'os I I sangs rgyas gdung ni 'tshob don du I I 'jig rten 'dren pa de dag bzhugs I

99

[Teachings may differ] in being either profound or vast; at times they are both. Though they sometimes may differ, they are invariably characterized by śūnyatā and non-duality.

100

Whatever the dhāraṇīs, stages, and pāramitās of the Buddhas, the omniscient [Tathāgatas] have stated that they form a part of bodhicitta.

101

Those who thus always benefit living beings through body, words, and mind advocate the claims of śūnyatā, not the contentions of annihilation.

102

The magnanimous [Bodhisattvas] do not abide in nirvana or samsara. Therefore the Buddhas have spoken of this as "the non-abiding nirvana."

103

The unique elixir of compassion functions as merit, [but] the elixir of śūnyatā functions as the highest. Those who drink it for the sake of themselves and others are sons of the Buddha.

104

Salute these Bodhisattvas with your entire being! Always worthy of honor in the three worlds, guides of the world, they strive to represent the lineage of the Buddhas.

105

| byang chub sems 'di theg chen po | | mchog ni yin par bshad pa ste | | mnyam par gzhag pa'i 'bad pa yis | | byang chub sems ni bskyed par gyis |

106

| rang dang gzhan don bsgrub don du | | srid na thabs gzhan yod ma yin | | byang chub sems ni ma gtogs pas | | sangs rgyas kyis sngar thabs ma gzigs |

107

| byang chub sems bskyed tsam gyis ni | | bsod nams phung po gang thob pa | | gal te gzugs can yin na ni | | nam mkha' gang ba las ni lhag |

108

| skyes bu gang zhig skad cig tsam | | byang chub sems ni sgom byed pa | | de yi bsod nams phung po ni | | rgyal ba yis kyang bgrang mi spyod |

109

| nyon mongs med pa'i rin chen sems | | 'di ni nor mchog gcig pu ste | | nyon mongs bdud sogs chom rkun gyis | | gnod min phrogs par bya ba min |

110

| ji ltar 'khor bar sangs rgyas dang | | byang chub sems dpa'i smon lam ni | | mi g·yo de ltar blo nyid ni | | byang chub sems gzhol rnams kyis bya |

105

[In] Mahāyāna this bodhicitta is said to be the very best. So produce bodhicitta through firm and balanced efforts.

106

[In this] existence there is no other means for the realization of one's own and others' benefit. The Buddhas have until now seen no means apart from bodhicitta.

107

Simply by generating bodhicitta a mass of merit is collected. If it took form, it would more than fill the expanse of space!

108

If a person developed bodhicitta only for a moment, not even the Jinas could calculate the mass of his merit!

109

The one finest jewel is a precious mind free of kleśas. Robbers like the kleśas or Māra cannot steal or damage it.

110

Just as the high aspirations of Buddhas and Bodhisattvas in samsara are unswerving, those who set their course on bodhicitta must make [firm their] resolve.

111

| ngo mtshar gyis kyang khyed cag gis | | ji ltar bshad pa la 'bad kyis | | de rjes kun bzang spyod pa ni | | rang nyid kyis ni rtogs par 'gyur |

112

| rgyal mchog rnams kyis bstod pa'i byang chub sems ni bstod byas pa'i | | bsod nams mtshungs med deng du bdag gis thob pa gang yin pa | | de yis srid pa'i rgya mtsho dba' klong nang du nub pa yi | | sems can rkang gnyis dbang pos bsten pa'i lam du 'gro bar shog |

111

No matter how amazing [all this seems], you must make efforts as explained. Thereafter you yourself will understand the course of Samantabhadra!

112

Through the incomparable merit I have now collected by praising the excellent bodhicitta praised by the excellent Jinas, may living beings submerged in the waves of life's ocean gain a foothold on the path followed by the leader of those who walk on two legs.

Yuktiṣaṣṭikā

Rigs pa drug cu pa ||

| gang gis skye dang 'jig pa dag | | tshul 'di yis ni spangs gyur pa | | rten cing 'byung ba gsungs pa yi | | thub dbang de la phyag 'tshal lo |

1

| gang dag gi blo yod med las | | rnam par 'das shing mi gnas pa | | de dag gis ni rkyen gyi don | | zab mo dmigs med rnam par rtogs |

2

| re zhig nyes kun 'byung ba'i gnas | | med nyid rnam par bzlog zin gyis | | rigs pa gang gis yod nyid dang | | bzlog par 'gyur ba mnyan par gyis |

3

| ji ltar byis pas rnam brtags bzhin | | dngos po gal te bden gyur na | | de dngos med pas rnam thar du | | gang gis mi 'dod rgyu ci zhig |

4

| yod pas rnam par mi grol te | | med pas srid pa 'di las min | | dngos dang dngos med yongs shes pas | | bdag nyid chen po rnam par grol |

Sixty Verses of Arguments

Obeisance to the Buddha, the Munīndra, who has proclaimed dependent co-arising, the principle by which origination and destruction are eliminated!

1

Those whose intelligence has transcended being and non-being and is unsupported have discovered the profound and non-objective meaning of 'condition'.

2

First you must reject non-being, the source of all faults. But now hear the argument by which being also is rejected!

3

If things were 'true' as fools imagine, why not accept liberation as tantamount to non-being?

4

One is not liberated by being; one does not [transcend] present existence by non-being. [But] by thorough knowledge of being and non-being the magnanimous are liberated.

5

| de nyid ma mthong 'jig rten dang | | mya ngan 'das par rlom sems te | | de nyid gzigs rnams 'jig rten dang | | mya ngan 'das par rlom sems med |

6

| srid pa dang ni mya ngan 'das | | gnyis po 'di ni yod ma yin | | srid pa yongs su shes pa nyid | | mya ngan 'das zhes bya bar brjod |

7

| dngos po byung ba zhig pa la | | ji ltar 'gog par brtags pa bzhin | | de bzhin dam pa rnams kyis kyang | | sgyu ma byas pa'i 'gog pa bzhed |

8

| rnam par 'jig pas 'gog 'gyur gyi | | 'dus byas yongs su shes pas min | | de ni su la mngon sum 'gyur | | zhig ces pa der ji ltar 'gyur |

9

| gal te phung po ma 'gags na | | nyon mongs zad kyang 'das mi 'gyur | | gang tshe 'dir ni 'gags gyur pa | | de yi tshe na grol bar 'gyur |

10

| ma rig rkyen gyis byung ba la | | yang dag ye shes kyis gzigs na | | skye ba dang ni 'gags pa'ang rung | | 'ga' yang dmigs par mi 'gyur ro | |

5

Those who do not see reality believe in samsara and nirvana, [but] those who see reality believe in neither.

6

Existence and nirvana: These two are not [really] to be found. [Instead,] nirvana [may be] defined as the thorough knowledge of existence.

7

While [the ignorant] imagine that annihilation pertains to a created thing that is dissolved, the wise are convinced that annihilation of [something] created is an illusion.

8

Though [something apparently] is annihilated by being destroyed, it is not [destroyed] when one thoroughly understands it to be compound. To whom will it be evident? How could one speak of it as dissolved?

9

Opponent: If the skandhas are not annihilated [an Arhat] does not enter nirvana, though his kleśas are exhausted. [Only] when the skandhas have been annihilated is [he] liberated.

10

Reply: When one sees with correct knowledge that which arises conditioned by ignorance, no origination or destruction whatsoever is perceived.

11

| de nyid mthong chos mya ngan las | | 'das shing bya ba byas pa'ang yin | | gal te chos shes mjug thogs su | | 'di la bye brag yod na ni |

12

| dngos po shin tu phra ba la'ang | | gang gis skye bar rnam brtags pa | | rnam par mi mkhas de yis ni | | rkyen las byung ba'i don ma mthong |

13

| nyon mongs zad pa'i dge slong gi | | gal te 'khor ba rnam ldog na | | ci phyir rdzogs sangs rgyas rnams kyis | | de yi rtsom pa rnam mi bshad |

14

| rtsom pa yod na nges par yang | | lta bar gyur pa yongs su 'dzin | | rten cing 'brel bar 'byung ba gang | | de la sngon dang tha ma ci |

15

| sngon skyes pa ni ji ltar na | | phyi nas slar yang bzlog par 'gyur | | sngon dang phyi ma'i mtha' bral ba | | 'gro ba sgyu ma bzhin du snang |

16

| gang tshe sgyu ma 'byung zhe'am | | gang tshe 'jig par 'gyur snyam du | | sgyu ma shes pa der mi rmongs | | sgyu ma mi shes yongs su sred |

11

This is nirvana in this very life — one's task is accomplished. [But] if a distinction is made here, just before knowledge of the Dharma —

12

One who imagines that even the most subtle thing arises: Such an ignorant man does not see what it means to be dependently born!

13

Opponent: If samsara has stopped for a monk whose kleśas are exhausted, then why would the Perfect Buddhas deny that it has a beginning?

14

Reply: [To say] there was a beginning would clearly be holding on to a dogma. How can that which is dependently co-arisen have a first and a last?

15

How could what has previously been generated later be negated again? [No, actually] the world, devoid of an initial and a final limit, appears like an illusion.

16

When one thinks [something] illusory arises or is destroyed, one who recognizes the illusion is not bewildered by it, but one who does not recognize it longs for it.

17

| srid pa smig rgyu sgyu 'dra bar | | blo yis mthong bar gyur pa ni | | sngon gyi mtha' 'am phyi ma'i mtha' | | lta bas yongs su slad mi 'gyur |

18

| gang dag gis ni 'dus byas la | | skye dang 'jig pa rnam brtags pa | | de dag rten 'byung 'khor lo yi | | 'gro ba rnam par mi shes so |

19

| de dang de brten gang byung de | | rang gi dngos por skyes ma yin | | rang gi dngos por gang ma skyes | | de ni skyes zhes ji ltar bya |

20

| rgyu zad nyid las zhi ba ni | | zad ces bya bar rtogs pa ste | | rang bzhin gyis ni gang ma zad | | de la zad ces ji ltar brjod |

21

| de ltar ci yang skye ba med | | ci yang 'gag par mi 'gyur ro | | skye ba dang ni 'jig pa'i lam | | dgos pa'i don du bstan pa'o |

22

| skye ba shes pas 'jig pa shes | | 'jig pa shes pas mi rtag shes | | mi rtag nyid la 'jug shes pas | | dam pa'i chos kyang rtogs par 'gyur |

17

One who comes to see by means of his undertanding that existence is like a mirage [and] an illusion is not corrupted by dogmas [based on] an initial or a final limit.

18

Those who imagine that something compounded possesses origination or destruction do not understand the movement of the wheel of dependent origination.

19

Whatever arises depending on this and that has not arisen substantially. That which has not arisen substantially: How can it literally be called 'arisen'?

20

A [compound thing] quieted due to a spent cause is understood to be spent. [But] how can what is not spent by nature be spoken of as spent?

21

So to conclude: There is no origination; there is no destruction. The path of origination and destruction has [however] been expounded [by the Buddhas] for a practical purpose:

22

By knowing origination destruction is known; by knowing destruction impermanence is known; by knowing impermanence the Holy Dharma is understood.

23

| gang dag rten cing 'brel 'byung ba | | skye dang 'jig pa rnam spangs par | | shes par gyur pa de dag ni | | ltar gyur srid pa'i rgya mtsho brgal |

24

| so so skye bo dngos bdag can | | yod dang med par phyin ci log | | nyes pas nyon mongs dbang gyur rnams | | rang gi sems kyis bslus par 'gyur |

25

| dngos la mkhas pa rnams kyis mi | | dngos po mi rtag bslu ba'i chos | | gsog dang stong pa bdag med pa | | rnam par dben zhes bya bar mthong |

26

| gnas med dmigs pa yod ma yin | | rtsa ba med cing gnas pa med | | ma rig rgyu las shin tu byung | | thog ma dbus mtha' rnam par spangs |

27

| chu shing bzhin du snying po med | | dri za'i grong khyer 'dra ba ste | | rmongs pa'i grong khyer mi bzad pa'i | | 'gro ba sgyu ma bzhin du snang |

28

| tshangs sogs 'jig rten 'di la ni | | bden par rab tu gang snang ba | | de ni 'phags la rdzun zhes gsungs | | 'di las gzhan lta ci zhig lus |

23

Those who have come to understand that dependent co-origination is devoid of origination and destruction have crossed the ocean of existence, consisting of dogmas.

24

Common people who hold a positivistic attitude are dominated by kleśas, due to the fault of being mistaken about being and non-being. They are deceived by their own minds!

25

Those who understand things see that things are impermanent, fraudulent, vain, empty, selfless, and void.

26

Homeless, non-objective, rootless, unfixed, arising wholly through ignorance, without a beginning, middle or end;

27

Without a core (like a plantain), or like the city of gandharvas: [Thus] the dreadful world — a city of confusion — appears like an illusion!

28

It is said that Brahmā and the others, who appear to this world to be most true, are, to the noble, false. What of the rest, apart from that?

29

| 'jig rten ma rig ldongs gyur pa | | sred pa rgyun gyi rjes 'brangs dang | | mkhas pa sred pa dang bral ba | | dge ba rnams lta ga la mnyam |

30

| de nyid tshol la thog mar ni | | thams cad yod ces brjod par bya | | don rnams rtogs shing chags med la | | phyis ni rnam par dben pa'o |

31

| rnam par dben don mi shes la | | thos pa tsam la 'jug byed cing | | gang dag bsod nams mi byed pa | | skyes bu tha shal de dag brlag |

32

| las rnams 'bras bu bcas nyid dang | | 'gro ba dag kyang yang dag bshad | | de yi rang bzhin yongs shes dang | | skye ba med pa dag kyang bstan |

33

| dgos pa'i dbang gis rgyal ba rnams | | nga dang nga'i zhes gsungs pa ltar | | phung po khams dang skye mched rnams | | de bzhin dgos pa'i dbang gis gsungs |

34

| 'byung ba che la sogs bshad pa | | rnam par shes su yang dag 'du | | de shes pas ni 'bral 'gyur na | | log pas rnam brtags ma yin nam |

29

The world, blinded by ignorance, following the current of craving, and the wise, who are free from craving: How can their view of the good be similar?

30

To begin with, [a teacher] should say to his truth-seeking [student] that everything exists. Later, to [the student] who understands the meaning and is free from attachment, [he should say] "All things are void."

31

Those who do not understand the meaning of separation but merely keep on learning without enacting merit: Such base people are lost!

32

Karma [in all its variety], together with its results and the places of rebirth have also been fully explained [by the Buddhas]. [They] have taught as well full knowledge of its nature and its non-origination.

33

Just as the Buddhas have spoken of 'my' and 'I' for pragmatic reasons, so they have also spoken of the skandhas, the sense-fields, and the elements for pragmatic reasons.

34

Things spoken of, such as the great elements, are made to cohere in consciousness; they are dissolved by understanding them. Certainly they are falsely imagined!

35

| mya ngan 'das pa bden gcig pur | | rgyal ba rnams kyis gang gsungs pa | | de tshe lhag ma log min zhes | | mkhas pa su zhig rtog par byed |

36

| ji srid yid kyi rnam g·yo ba | | de srid bdud kyi spyod yul te | | de lta yin na 'di la ni | | nyes pa med par cis mi 'thad |

37

| 'jig rten ma rig rkyen can du | | gang phyir sangs rgyas rnams gsungs pa | | 'di yi phyir na 'jig rten 'di | | rnam rtog yin zhes cis mi 'thad |

38

| ma rig 'gags par gyur pa na | | gang zhig 'gog par 'gyur ba de | | mi shes pa las kun brtags par | | ji lta bu na gsal mi 'gyur |

39

| gang zhig rgyu dang bcas 'byung zhing | | rkyen med par ni gnas pa med | | rkyen med phyir yang 'jig 'gyur ba | | de ni yod ces ji ltar rtogs |

40

| gal te yod par smra ba rnams | | dngos mchog zhen nas gnas pa ni | | lam de nyid la gnas pa ste | | de la ngo mtshar cung zad med |

35

When the Jinas have stated that nirvana alone is true, what learned person will then imagine that the rest is not false?

36

As long as mind is unstable it is [under] Māra's dominion. If it is as [has been explained], there is surely no mistake [in maintaining non-origination].

37

Since the Buddhas have stated that the world is conditioned by ignorance, does it not stand to reason that this world is a [result of] discrimination?

38

When ignorance ceases, how can it not be clear that what ceases was imagined by ignorance?

39

That which originates due to a cause and does not abide without [certain] conditions, but disappears when the conditions are absent: How can it be understood to 'exist'?

40

If the advocates of being, who continue clinging to being, go on in the same way, there is nothing strange about that;

41

| sangs rgyas lam la brten nas ni | | kun la mi rtag smra ba rnams | | rtsod pas dngos rnams mchog gzung bas | | gnas pa gang yin de rmad do |

42

| 'di 'am de'o zhes gang du | | rnam par dpyad nas mi dmigs na | | rtsod pas 'di 'am de bden zhes | | mkhas pa su zhig smra bar 'gyur |

43

| gang dag gis ni ma brten par | | bdag.gam 'jig rten mngon zhen pa | | de dag kye ma rtag mi rtag | | la sogs lta bas phrogs pa yin |

44

| gang dag brten nas dngos po rnams | | de nyid du ni grub 'dod pa | | de dag la yang rtag sogs skyon | | de dag ji ltar 'byung mi 'gyur |

45

| gang dag brten nas dngos po rnams | | chu yi zla ba lta bur ni | | yang dag ma yin log min par | | 'dod pa de dag bltas mi 'phrog |

46

| dngos por khas len yod na ni | | 'dod chags zhe sdang 'byung ba yi | | lta ba mi bzad ma rungs 'dzin | | de las byung ba'i rtsod par 'gyur |

41

But it is strange indeed that the proponents of the impermanence of everything, [who] rely on the Buddha's method, contentiously cling to things.

42

When "this" and "that," said about something, are not perceived through analysis, what wise man will contentiously maintain that "this" or "that" is true?

43

Those who adhere to a self or to the world as unconditioned, Alas! They are captivated by dogmas about 'permanent', 'impermanent', and so forth.

44

Those who postulate that conditioned things are established in reality are overtaken by faults related to permanence and the rest.

45

But those who are convinced that conditioned things are like the moon in the water, neither true nor false, are not carried away by dogmas.

46

When one affirms 'being' there is a seizing of awful and vicious dogmas that arise from desire and hatred. From that contentions arise.

47

| de ni lta ba kun gyi rgyu | | de med nyon mongs mi skye ste | | de phyir de ni yongs shes na | | lta dang nyon mongs yongs su 'byang |

48

| gang gis de shes 'gyur snyam na | | brten nas 'byung ba mthong ba de | | brten nas skye ba ma skyes par | | de nyid mkhyen pa mchog gis gsungs |

49

| log pa'i shes pas zil gnon pa | | bden pa min la bden 'dzin pa'i | | yongs su 'dzin dang rtsod sogs kyi | | rim pas chags las 'byung bar 'gyur |

50

| che ba'i bdag nyid can de dag | | rnams la phyogs med rtsod pa med | | gang rnams la ni phyogs med pa | | de la gzhan phyogs ga la yod |

51

| gang yang rung ba'i gnas rnyed nas | | nyon mongs sbrul gdug g·yo can gyis | | zin par gyur te gang gi sems | | gnas med de dag zin mi 'gyur |

52

| gnas bcas sems dang ldan rnams la | | nyon mongs dug chen cis mi 'byung | | gang tshe tha mal 'dug pa yang | | nyon mongs sbrul gyis zin par 'gyur |

47

That is the cause of all dogmas. Without it the kleśas do not arise. When this is thoroughly understood, dogmas and kleśas disappear.

48

But how is it thoroughly known? By seeing dependent origination! The [Buddha], best among knowers of reality, also said that what is dependently born is unborn.

49

For those who—oppressed by false knowledge—take the untrue as true, the sequence of seizing, contending, and so forth will arise.

50

The magnanimous have neither thesis nor contention. How can there be an opposing thesis to those who have no thesis?

51

By taking any standpoint whatsoever one is attacked by the twisting snakes of the kleśas. But those whose minds have no standpoint are not caught.

52

How can those whose mind takes a stand avoid the strong poison of the kleśas? Even if they live an ordinary [life], they are consumed by the snakes of the kleśas.

53

| byis pa bden par 'du shes pas | | gzugs brnyan la ni chags pa bzhin | | de ltar 'jig rten rmongs pa'i phyir | | yul gyi gzeb la thogs par 'gyur |

54

| bdag nyid che rnams dngos po dag | | gzugs brnyan lta bur ye shes kyi | | mig gis mthong nas yul zhes ni | | bya ba'i 'dam la mi thogs so |

55

| byis pa rnams ni gzugs la chags | | bar ma dag ni chags bral 'gyur | | gzugs kyi rang bzhin shes pa yi | | blo mchog ldan pa rnam par grol |

56

| sdug snyam pa las chags par 'gyur | | de las bzlog pas 'dod chags bral | | sgyu ma'i skyes bu ltar dben par | | mthong nas mya ngan 'da' bar 'gyur |

57

| log pa'i shes pas mngon gdung ba'i | | nyon mongs skyon rnams gang yin te | | dngos dang dngos med rnam rtog pa | | don shes 'gyur la mi 'byung ngo |

58

| gnas yod na ni 'dod chags dang | | 'dod chags bral bar 'gyur zhig na | | gnas med bdag nyid chen po rnams | | chags pa med cing chags bral min |

53

Just as a fool is attached to a reflection through conceiving it to be true, so the world is trapped in the cage of objects through stupidity.

54

When the magnanimous see with their eye of knowledge that things are like a reflection, they are not trapped in the swamp of so-called 'objects'.

55

The simple-minded are attached to material form, those of middling level attain absence of the kleśas, but those of supreme understanding are liberated by knowing the nature of form.

56

One awakens desires through thinking of a pleasant [thing]; one becomes free from desires through turning away from it; but one obtains nirvana by seeing it to be void like a phantom.

57

The faults of the kleśas that torment due to false knowledge do not arise for those who understand the meaning of judgments concerning being and non-being.

58

If there were a standpoint, there would be passion and dispassion. But the great souls without standpoint have neither passion nor dispassion.

59

| gang dag rnam par dben snyam du | | g·yo ba'i yid kyang mi g·yo ba | | nyon mongs sbrul gyis dkrugs gyur pa | | mi bzad srid pa'i rgya mtsho brgal |

60

| dge ba 'di yis skye bo kun | | bsod nams ye shes tshogs bsags te | | bsod nams ye shes las byung ba'i | | dam pa gnyis ni thob par shog |

59

Those for whom the wavering mind does not waver, not even at the thought of the void, have crossed the awful ocean of existence that is agitated by the monsters of the kleśas.

60

May all people by this merit accumulate merit and insight and obtain the two goods that arise from merit and insight.

Śūnyatāsaptati

sTong pa nyid bdun cu pa ||

1

| gnas pa'am skye 'jig yod med dam | | dman pa'am mnyam dang khyad par can | | sangs rgyas 'jig rten snyad dbang gis | | gsung gi yang dag dbang gis min |

2

| bdag med bdag med min bdag dang | | bdag med min pas brjod 'ga'ang med | | brjod bya mya ngan 'das dang mtshungs | | dgnos po kun gyi rang bzhin stong |

3

| gang phyir dngos rnams thams cad kyi | | rang bzhin rgyu rkyen tshogs pa'am | | so so'i dngos po thams cad la | | yod min de phyir stong pa yin |

4

| yod phyir yod pa skye min te | | med phyir med pa skye ma yin | | chos mi mthun phyir yod med min | | skye ba med pas gnas 'gag med |

5

| gang zhig skyes de bskyed bya min | | ma skyes pa yang bskyed bya min | | skyes pa dang ni ma skyes pa'i | | skye bzhin pa yang bskyed bya min |

Seventy Verses on Śūnyatā

1

Though the Buddhas have spoken of duration, origination, destruction, being, non-being, low, moderate, and excellent by force of worldly convention, [they] have not done [so] in an absolute sense.

2

Designations are without significance, for self, non-self, and self–non-self do not exist. [For] like nirvana, all expressible things are empty (śūnya) of own-being.

3

Since all things altogether lack substance—either in causes or conditions, [in their] totality, or separately—they are empty.

4

Being does not arise, since it exists. Non-being does not arise, since it does not exist. Being and non-being [together] do not arise, due to [their] heterogeneity. Consequently they do not endure or vanish.

5

That which has been born cannot be born, nor can that which is unborn be born. What is being born now, being [partly] born, [partly] unborn, cannot be born either.

6

। 'bras bu yod par 'bras ldan rgyu । । med de la 'ang rgyu min mtshungs । । yod min med pa'ang min na 'gal । । dus gsum rnams su 'thad ma yin ।

7

। gcig med par ni mang po dang । । mang po med par gcig mi 'jug । । de phyir rten cing 'brel 'byung ba'i । । dngos po mtshan ma med pa yin ।

8

। rten 'byung yan lag bcu gnyis gang । । sdug bsngal 'bras can de ma skyes । । sems gcig la yang mi 'thad cing । । du ma la yang 'thad ma yin ।

9

। rtag min mi rtag min bdag dang । । bdag min gtsang min mi gtsang min । । bde min sdug bsngal ma yin te । । de phyir phyin ci log rnams med ।

10

। de med phyin ci log bzhi las । । skyes pa'i ma rig mi srid la । । de med 'du byed mi 'byung zhing । । lhag ma rnams kyang de bzhin no ।

11

। ma rig 'du byed med mi 'byung । । de med 'du byed mi 'byung zhing । । phan tshun rgyu phyir de gnyis ni । । rang bzhin gyis ni ma grub yin ।

6

A cause has an effect when there is an effect, but when there is no [effect] the [cause] amounts to no cause. It is inconsistent that [the effect] neither exists nor does not exist. It is illogical that [the cause is active] in the three times.

7

Without one, there are not many. Without many, one is not possible. Whatever arises dependently is indeterminable.

8

The twelve dependently arising members, which result in suffering, are unborn. They are possible neither in one mind nor in many.

9

Permanent is not, impermanent is not, not-self is not, self is not, impure is not, pure is not, pleasure is not, and suffering is not. Therefore the perverted views do not exist.

10

Without these, ignorance based on the perverted views is not possible. Without this [ignorance], the formative forces do not arise. The same [is true] for the [ten] remaining [dependently arising members].

11

Ignorance does not occur without the formative forces [and] without it the formative forces do not arise. Caused by one another, they are not established by own-being.

12

| gang zhig bdag nyid rang bzhin gyis | | ma grub de gzhan ji ltar bskyed | | de phyir gzhan las grub pa yi | | rkyen gzhan dag ni skyed byed min |

13

| pha ni bu min bu pha min | | de gnyis phan tshun med min la | | de gnyis cig car yang min ltar | | yan lag bcu gnyis de bzhin no |

14

| ji ltar rmi lam yul brten pa'i | | bde sdug de yi yul med pa | | de bzhin gang zhig la brten nas | | gang zhig rten 'byung dang 'di med |

15

| gal te dngos rnams rang bzhin gyis | | med na dman mnyam khyad 'phags dang | | sna tshogs nyid ni mi 'grub cing | | rgyu las kyang ni mngon 'grub min |

16

| rang bzhin grub na rten 'byung gi | | dngos po med 'gyur ma brten na | | rang bzhin med par ga la 'gyur | | dngos po yod dang dngos med kyang |

17

| med la rang dngos gzhan dngos sam | | dngos med 'gyur ba ga la zhig | | des na rang dngos gzhan dngos dang | | dngos med phyin ci log pa yin |

12

How can that which is not established by own-being create others? Conditions established by others cannot create others.

13

A father is not a son, a son is not a father. Neither exists except in correlation with the other. Nor are they simultaneous. Likewise for the twelve members.

14

Just as pleasure and pain depending on an object in a dream do not have [a real] object, so neither that which arises dependently nor that which it arises in dependence on exists.

15

Opponent: If things do not exist by own-being, then low, moderate, and excellent and the manifold world are not established and cannot be established, even through a cause.

16

Reply: If own-being were established, dependently arising things would not occur. If [they were] unconditioned, how could own-being be lacking? True being also does not vanish.

17

How can the non-existing have own-being, other-being, or non-being? Consequently, own-being, other-being, and non-being [result from] perverted views.

18

| gal te dngos po stong yin na | | 'gag pa med cing skye mi 'gyur | | ngo bo nyid kyis stong pa la | | gang la 'gag cing gang la skye |

19

| dngos dang dngos med cig car min | | dngos med med na dngos po med | | rtag tu dngos po'ang dngos med 'gyur | | dngos med med par dngos mi srid |

20

| dngos po med par dngos med min | | rang las min zhing gzhan las min | | de lta bas na de med na | | dngos po med cing dngos med med |

21

| yod pa nyid na rtag nyid dang | | med na nges par chad nyid yin | | dngos po yod na de gnyis 'gyur | | de phyir dngos po khas blangs min |

22

| rgyun gyi phyir na 'di med de | | rgyu byin nas ni dngos po 'gag | | sngar bzhin 'di yang ma grub cing | | rgyun chad par yang thal bar 'gyur |

23

| skye 'jig bstan phyir sangs rgyas kyi | | lam bstan ma yin stong nyid phyir | | 'di dag phan tshun bzlog pa ru | | mthong ba phyin ci log las yin |

18

Opponent: If things were empty, origination and cessation would not occur. That which is empty of own-being: How does it arise and how does it cease?

19

Reply: Being and non-being are not simultaneous. Without non-being, no being. Being and non-being would always be. There is no being independent of non-being.

20

Without being there is no non-being. [Being] neither arises from itself nor from [something] else. This being so, this [being] does not exist: So there is no being, and [therefore] no non-being.

21

If there is being there is permanence; if there is non-being there is necessarily annihilation. When there is being, these two [dogmas] occur. Therefore [one should] not accept being.

22

Opponent: These [dogmas] do not occur due to continuity: Things cease after having caused [an effect]. *Reply:* As before [see v. 19], this [continuity] is unestablished. It also follows that the continuity would be interrupted.

23

Opponent: [No!] The Buddha's teaching of the path aims at showing origination and cessation, not śūnyatā! *Reply:* To experience the two as mutually exclusive is a mistake.

24

| gal te skye 'gag med yin na | | ci zhig 'gags pas mya ngan 'das | | rang bzhin gyis ni skye med cing | | 'gag med gang de thar min nam |

25

| gal te 'gags las myang 'das chad | | gal te cig shos ltar na rtag | | de phyir dngos dang dngos med dag | | mya ngan 'das par rung ma yin |

26

| gal te 'gog pa 'ga' gnas na | | dngos po las gzhan de yod 'gyur | | dngos po med phyir 'di med la | | dngos po med phyir de yang med |

27

| mtshan gzhi las gzhan mtshan nyid las | | mtshan gzhi grub par rang ma grub | | phan tshun las kyang ma grub ste | | ma grub ma grub sgrub byed min |

28

| 'dis ni rgyu dang 'bras du dang | | tshor dang tshor ba po sogs dang | | lta po lta bya sogs ci'ang rung | | de kun ma lus bshad pa yin |

29

| gnas med phan tshun las grub dang | | 'chol phyir rang nyid ma grub phyir | | dngos po med phyir dus gsum ni | | yod pa ma yin rtog pa tsam |

24

Opponent: If there is no origination and cessation, then to the cessation of what is nirvana due? *Reply:* Is not liberation this: that by nature nothing arises and ceases?

25

If nirvana [resulted] from cessation, [then there would be] destruction. If the contrary, [there would be] permanence. Therefore it is not logical that nirvana is being or non-being.

26

If a definite cessation did abide, it would be independent of being. It does not exist without being, nor does it exist without non-being.

27

The marked is established through a mark different from the marked; it is not established by itself. Nor are the [two] established by each other, [since what is] not established cannot establish the not-established.

28

In this [way], cause, effect, feeling, feeler, and so forth, the seer, the visible, and so forth — whatever may be — all are explained, without exception.

29

The three times do not exist (substantially) since they are unfixed and are mutually established, since they change [and] are not self-established, [and] since there is no being. They are merely discriminations.

30

| gang phyir skye dang gnas dang 'jig | | 'dus byas mtshan nyid 'di gsum med | | de phyir 'dus byas nyid ma yin | | 'dus ma byas la'ang cung zad med |

31

| ma zhig mi 'jig zhig pa'ang min | | gnas pa gnas pa ma yin te | | mi gnas pa la'ang gnas ma yin | | skyes pa mi skye ma skyes min |

32

| 'dus byas dang ni 'dus ma byas | | du ma ma yin gcig ma yin | | yod min med min yod med min | | mtshams 'dir sna tshogs thams cad 'dus |

33

| bcom ldan bla mas las gnas dang | | las bdag las kyi 'bras bu dang | | sems can rang gi las dang ni | | las rnams chud mi za bar gsungs |

34

| las rnams rang bzhin med gsungs te | | ma skyes gang de chud mi za | | de las kyang ni bdag 'dzin skye | | de bskyed 'dzin de'ang rnam rtog las |

35

| gal te las la rang bzhin yod | | de bskyed lus ni rtag par 'gyur | | las kyang sdug bsngal rnam smin can | | mi 'gyur de phyir bdag tu 'gyur |

30

Since the three marks of the conditioned — origination, duration, and cessation — do not exist, there is not the slightest conditioned or unconditioned [phenomenon].

31

The non-destroyed does not cease, nor does the destroyed. The abiding does not abide, nor does the non-abiding. The born is not born, nor is the unborn.

32

Composite and non-composite are not many [and] not one; are not being [and] are not non-being; are not being–non-being. All [possibilities] are comprised within these limits.

33

Opponent: The Bhagavat, the Teacher, has spoken of karma's duration, of karma's nature, and of karma's result, and also of the personal karma of living beings and of the non-destruction of karma.

34

Reply: Karma is said to lack own-being. [Karma] that is not born is not destroyed. From that again I-making is born. But the belief that creates it is due to discrimination.

35

If karma had own-being the body created by it would be permanent. So karma would not result in suffering and would therefore be substantial.

36

| las ni rkyen skyes yod min zhing | | rkyen min las skyes cung zad med | | 'du byed rnams ni sgyu ma dang | | dri za'i grong khyer smig rgyu mtshungs |

37

| las ni nyon mongs rgyu mtshan can | | nyon mongs 'du byed las bdag nyid | | lus ni las kyi rgyu mtshan can | | gsum ka'ang ngo bo nyid kyis stong |

38

| las med na ni byed po med | | de gnyis med pas 'bras bu med | | de med nye bar spyod po med | | de bas dngos po dben pa yin |

39

| las ni stong par yang dag par | | shes na de nyid mthong ba'i phyir | | las mi 'byung ste de med na | | las las 'byung gang mi 'byung ngo |

40

| ji ltar bcom ldan de bzhin gshegs | | rdzu 'phrul gyis ni sprul pa sprul | | sprul pa de yis slar yang ni | | sprul pa gzhan zhig sprul gyur pa |

41

| de la de bzhin gshegs sprul stong | | sprul pas sprul pa smos ci dgos | | gnyis po ming tsam yod pa yang | | ci yang rung ste rtog pa tsam |

36

Karma is not born from conditions and by no means from non-conditions, for karma-formations are like an illusion, a city of gandharvas, and a mirage.

37

Karma has kleśas as its cause. [Being] kleśas, the karma-formations are of impassioned nature (kleśātmaka). A body has karma as its cause. So [all] three are empty of own-being.

38

Without karma, no agent. Without these two, no result. Without these, no enjoyer. Therefore things are void.

39

When—because the truth is seen—one correctly understands that karma is empty, karma does not arise. When [karma] is no more, what arises from karma arises no more.

40

Just as when the Lord Tathāgata magically projects an apparition and this apparition again projects another apparition—

41

In that case the Tathāgata's apparition is empty (not to mention the apparition [created] by the apparition!). Both of them are but names, merely insignificant discriminations.

42

| de bzhin byed po sprul dang mtshungs | | las ni sprul pas sprul dang mtshungs | | rang bzhin gyis ni gang cung zad | | yod pa de dag rtog pa tsam |

43

| gal te las kyi rang bzhin yod | | myang 'das byed po las kyang med | | gal te med na las bskyed pa'i | | 'bras bu sdug dang mi sdug med |

44

| yod ces pa dang yod med ces | | yod dang med ces de yang yod | | sangs rgyas rnams kyis dgongs pa yis | | gsungs pa rtogs par sla ma yin |

45

| gal te gzugs ni rang 'byung bzhin | | gzugs de 'byung las 'byung ma yin | | rang las 'byung min ma yin nam | | gzhan las kyang min de med phyir |

46

| gcig la bzhi nyid yod min cing | | bzhi la'ang gcig nyid yod min pas | | gzugs ni 'byung ba chen po bzhi | | rgyur byas nas grub ji ltar yod |

47

| shin tu mi 'dzin phyir de med | | rtags las zhe na rtags de'ang med | | rgyu dang rkyen las skyes pa'i phyir | | rtags med par yang mi rigs so |

42

Just so, the agent is like the apparition, and karma is like the apparition [created] by the apparition. By nature [they are] without significance: mere discriminations.

43

If karma possessed own-being, there would be no nirvana nor deeds [of an] agent. If [karma] does not exist, the pleasant or unpleasant result created by karma does not exist.

44

'Is' and 'is not' and also 'is – is not' have been stated by the Buddhas for a purpose. It is not easy to understand!

45

If form is material (bhautika) in itself, it does not arise from the elements (bhūta). It is not derived from itself — It does not exist, does it? — nor from anything else. Therefore it does not exist [at all].

46

The four [great elements] are not [found] in one [element], nor is one of them [found] in [any of] the four. How can form be established with the four great elements as [its] cause?

47

Since it is not conceived directly, [it seems form does] not exist. But if [you maintain it to be conceived] through a mark, that mark, born from causes and conditions, does not exist. And it would be illogical [if form could exist] without a mark.

48

I gal te blo des gzugs 'dzin na I I rang gi rang bzhin la 'dzin 'gyur I I rkyen las skyes pas yod min pas I I yang dag gzugs med ji ltar 'dzin I

49

I ji skad bshad gzugs skyes pa'i blo'i I I skad cig skad cig gis mi 'dzin I I 'das dang ma 'ongs pa gzugs kyang I I de yis ji ltar rtogs par 'gyur I

50

I gang tshe nam yang kha dog dang I I dbyibs dag tha dad nyid med pas I I de dag tha dad 'dzin yod min I I gzugs de gcig tu'ang grags pa min I

51

I mig blo mig la yod min te I I gzugs la yod min bar na med I I gzugs dang mig la brten nas de I I yongs su rtog pa log pa yin I

52

I gal te mig bdag mi mthong na I I des gzugs mthong bar ji ltar 'gyur I I de phyir mig dang gzugs bdag med I I skye mched lhag ma'ang de bzhin no I

53

I mig ni rang bdag nyid kyis stong I I de ni gzhan bdag gis kyang stong I I gzugs kyang de bzhin stong pa ste I I skye mched lhag ma'ang de bzhin no I

48

If mind could grasp form, it would grasp its own own-being. How could a [mind] that does not exist (since it is born from conditions) really conceive absence of form?

49

Since one moment of mind cannot within [the very same] moment grasp a form born (as explained), how could it understand a past and a future form?

50

Since color and shape never exist apart, they cannot be conceived apart. Is form not acknowledged to be one?

51

The sense of sight is not inside the eye, not inside form, and not in between. [Therefore] an image depending upon form and eye is false.

52

If the eye does not see itself, how can it see form? Therefore eye and form are without self. The same [is true for the] remaining sense-fields.

53

Eye is empty of its own self [and] of another's self. Form is also empty. Likewise [for the] remaining sense-fields.

54

I gang tshe gcig reg lhan cig 'gyur I I de tshe gzhan rnams stong pa nyid I I stong pa'am mi stong mi bsten la I mi stong pa yang stong mi brten I

55

I ngo bo mi gnas yod min pas I I gsum 'dus pa yod ma yin no I I de bdag nyid kyi reg med pas I I de tshe tshor ba yod ma yin I

56

I nang dang phyi yi skye mched la I I brten nas rnam par shes pa 'byung I I de lta bas na rnam shes med I I smig rgyu sgyu ma bzhin du stong I

57

I rnam shes shes bya la brten nas I I 'byung la shes bya yod ma yin I I shes bya shes pa med pa'i phyir I I de phyir shes pa po nyid med I

58

I thams cad mi rtag yang na ni I I mi rtag pa yang rtag pa med I I dngos po rtag dang mi rtag nyid I I 'gyur na de lta ga la yod I

59

I sdug dang mi sdug phyin ci log I I rkyen las chags sdang gti mug dngos I I 'byung phyir chags sdang gti mug dang I I rang bzhin gyis ni yod ma yin I

54

When one [sense-field] occurs simultaneously with contact, the others are empty. Empty does not depend upon non-empty, nor does non-empty depend upon empty.

55

Having no [independent] fixed nature, the three [namely, indriya, viṣaya, and vijñāna] cannot come into contact. Since there is no contact having this nature, feeling does not exist.

56

Consciousness occurs in dependence on the internal and external sense-fields. Therefore consciousness is empty, like mirages and illusions.

57

Since consciousness arises in dependence on a discernible object, the discernible does not exist [in itself]. Since [the conscious subject] does not exist without the discernible and consciousness, the conscious subject does not exist [by itself].

58

[In a relative sense] everything is impermanent, but [in the absolute sense] nothing is permanent or impermanent. [If there] were things, they would be either permanent or impermanent. But how is that [possible]?

59

Since the entities 'desire', 'hatred', and 'delusion' arise through perverted views about pleasant and unpleasant, desire, hatred, and delusion do not exist by own-being.

60

| gang phyir de nyid la chags shing | | de la zhe sdang de la rmongs | | de phyir rnam par rtog pas bskyed | | rtog de'ang yang dag nyid du med |

61

| brtag bya gang de yod ma yin | | brtag bya med rtog ga la yod | | de phyir brtag bya rtog pa dag | | rkyen las skyes phyir stong pa nyid |

62

| de nyid rtogs pas phyin ci log | | bzhi las byung ba'i ma rig med | | de med na ni 'du byed rnams | | mi 'byung lhag ma'ang de bzhin no |

63

| gang gang la brten skye ba'i dngos | | de de med pas de mi skye | | dngos dang dngos med 'dus byas dang | | 'dus ma byas zhi mya ngan 'das |

64

| rgyu rkyen las skyes dngos po rnams | | yang dag nyid du rtog pa gang | | de ni ston pas ma rig gsungs | | de las yan lag bcu gnyis 'byung |

65

| dngos po stong par de rtogs na | | yang dag mthong phyir rmongs mi 'gyur | | de ni ma rig 'gog pa yin | | de las yan lag bcu gnyis 'gag |

60

Since one [may] desire, hate, and be deluded regarding the very same [thing], [the passions] are created by discrimination. And that discrimination is nothing real.

61

That which is imagined does not exist. Without an imagined object, how can there be imagination? Since the imagined and the imagination are born from conditions, [they are] śūnyatā.

62

Through understanding the truth, ignorance, which arises from the four perverted views, does not exist. When this is no more, the karma-formations do not arise. The remaining [ten members vanish] likewise.

63

The thing that arises in dependence upon this or that does not arise when that is absent. Being and non-being, composite and non-composite are at peace — this is nirvana.

64

To imagine that things born through causes and conditions are real the Teacher calls ignorance. From that the twelve members arise.

65

But when one has understood by seeing fully that things are empty, one is no longer deluded. Ignorance ceases, and the twelve spokes [of the wheel] come to a halt.

66

| 'du byed dri za'i grong khyer dang | | sgyu ma smig rgyu skra shad dang | | dbu ba chu bur sprul pa dang | | rmi lam mgal me'i 'khor lo mtshungs |

67

| rang bzhin gyis ni 'ga' yang med | | 'di la dngos po med pa'ang med | | rgyu dang rkyen las skyes pa yi | | dngos dang dngos med stong pa yin |

68

| dngos kun rang bzhin stong pas na | | de bzhin gshegs pa mtshungs med pas | | rten cing 'brel par 'byung ba 'di | | dngos po rnams su nye bar bstan |

69

| dam pa'i don ni der zad de | | 'jig rten ngor byas tha snyad dag | | sna tshogs thams cad rdzogs sangs rgyas | | bcom ldan 'das kyis bden brtags mdzad |

70

| 'jig rten pa yi chos bstan mi 'jig cing | | yang dag nyid du nam yang chos bstan med | | de bzhin gshegs pas gsungs pa ma rig pas | | de las dri med brjod pa 'di las skrag |

71

| 'di la brten nas 'di 'byung zhes | | 'jig rten tshul 'di mi 'gog cing | | gang brten rang bzhin med pas de | | ji ltar yod 'gyur de nyid nges |

66

Karma-formations are like the city of gandharvas, illusions, mirages, nets of hair, foam, bubbles, phantoms, dreams, and wheels made with a firebrand.

67

Nothing exists by virtue of own-being, nor is there any non-being here. Being and non-being, born through causes and conditions, are empty.

68

Since all things are empty of own-being, the incomparable Tathāgata teaches dependent co-origination regarding things.

69

The ultimate meaning consists in that! The perfect Buddhas, the Bhagavats, have [only] conceived the entire multiplicity in reliance upon worldly convention.

70

The worldly norms [dharmas] are not violated. In reality [the Tathāgata] has not taught the Dharma. Not understanding the Tathāgata's words, [fools] fear this spotless discourse.

71

The worldly principle, "This arises depending on that," is not violated. But since what is dependent lacks own-being, how can it exist? That is certain!

72

| dad ldan de nyid tshol la brtson | | tshul 'di rigs pas rjes dpog gang | | rten med chos 'ga' brten pa yi | | srid dang srid min spangs nas zhi |

73

| 'di dag rkyen 'di las rig nas | | lta ngan dra ba kun ldog des | | chags rmongs khong khro spangs pa'i phyir | | ma gos mya ngan 'das pa thob |

72

One with faith who tries to seek the truth, one who considers this principle logically [and] relies [upon] the Dharma that is lacking all supports leaves behind existence and non-existence [and abides in] peace.

73

When one understands that "This is a result of that," the nets of bad views all vanish. Undefiled, one abandons desire, delusion, and hatred and gains nirvana.

*Vyavahārasiddhi

Tha snyad grub pa ||

(1)

| yi ge gcig sngags gang yang med | | yi ge mang po gzhan yang med | | yi ge 'gags pa rnams min la | | rten nas de ni med pa'ang min |

(2)

| de bzhin rang gi yan lag las | | sman ni gud nas mi snang ngo | | sgyu ma'i glang po snang ba de | | de dag las min gzhan yang min |

(3)

| rten cing 'brel par 'byung ba de | | yod dam med par su zhig 'dod | | de la dmigs par byed pa yi | | mig gi rnam shes byung ba ltar |

(4)

| las dang nyon mongs dbang 'phangs pa | | len bcas srid las 'byung ba dang | | de bzhin du ni gzugs 'byung ba | | yod dam med par su zhig 'dod |

(5)

| de ltar srid pa'i yan lag kun | | tha snyad kyis ni gdags pa ste | | de ltar 'gog la sogs pa yi | | chos kun dgongs te gsungs pa yin |

Establishment of Convention: Six Verses from a Lost Text

(1)

One syllable is not a mantra; many syllables are not a mantra either. Dependent upon syllables that are [thus] insubstantial, this [mantra is neither existent] nor non-existent.

(2)

Likewise, no medicine appears apart from its specific ingredients. It appears [like] an illusory elephant: It is not [identical with them] nor is it [absolutely] different from them.

(3)

It arises in dependent co-origination! Who would maintain that it is existent or non-existent? [Similarly,] visual consciousness arises based on [eye and form].

(4)

Projected by the power of karma and passions, the appropriator arises out of existence. Form arises likewise. Who would maintain its existence or non-existence?

(5)

Similarly, all the [twelve] members of existence are [simply] conventional designations. All the dharmas, such as extinction, have [only] been advocated [by the Buddhas] for a specific purpose.

(6)

| ji ltar sngags te sngags min dang | | ji ltar sman yang sman min pa | | de ltar rten nas gsungs pa de | | gnyis ka 'grub par 'gyur ma yin |

(6)

Just as a mantra is not a mantra and medicine is not medicine, so [all phenomena] are stated to be dependent. Neither of the two [i.e., cause or effect] can be established [as existing independently].

Bodhisaṁbhāra[ka]

The Accumulations for Enlightenment

1

Now, in the presence of the Buddhas, I fold my hands and bow my head. I intend to explain according to tradition a Buddha's accumulations for enlightenment.

2

How is it possible to explain without omission the accumulations for enlightenment? [For] the Buddhas are the only ones who individually obtain infinite enlightenment!

3

The body of a Buddha has infinite qualities. The [two] accumulations for enlightenment constitute the basis. Therefore the accumulations for enlightenment have no final limit either.

4

I can only explain a small part of these [two accumulations]. I praise the Buddhas and the Bodhisattvas. All the Bodhisattvas and the rest I revere successively to the Buddhas.

5

Since [Prajñāpāramitā] is the mother of Bodhisattvas it is also the mother of Buddhas. Prajñāpāramitā is the foremost collection for enlightenment.

6

Prajñāpāramitā is the mother of Bodhisattvas, skill in means is their father, and compassion is their daughter.

7

Generosity, morality, patience, energy, dhyāna and the [other pāramitās] beyond these five are all due to prajñā—Prajñāpāramitā comprises them all.

8

Great compassion penetrates into the marrow of the bone. It is the support of all living beings. Like [the love of a] father for his only son, the tenderness [of a Buddha] is all-pervasive.

9

If one thinks of the Buddha's virtues and listens to [accounts of] the miracles of the Buddha, [this creates] love, joy, a feeling [of happiness], and purity. This is called great joy.

10

A Bodhisattva must not desert or abandon living beings. He should always care for them to the best of his ability.

11

From the very beginning [of the path], in accord with the strength available, a Bodhisattva ought to be skilled in ways of converting people so that they may enter the Mahāyāna.

12

One may convert beings [as numerous as] the grains of sand in the Ganges so that they obtain sainthood, but to convert one [single person] to Mahāyāna — that creates greater merit!

13

Some are instructed according to the Śrāvakayāna and the Pratyekabuddhayāna. Because of their limited powers they are not suitable for conversion [to the Mahāyāna].

14

Those who are not fit for conversion to the Śrāvakayāna, the Pratyekabuddhayāna, or the Mahāyāna must be assigned meritorious tasks.

15

If people are [utterly] unfit to receive conversion [conducive to] heaven and liberation, then [a Bodhisattva] must attract them through advantages in this world, in accordance with the power available.

16

Toward people who cannot possibly be induced to conversion a Bodhisattva should generate great compassion. He must never discard them!

17

Attracting with gifts, teaching the Dharma, listening to the teaching of the Dharma, and also practicing acts of benefit to others — these are skillful means for attracting [others].

18

While benefitting living beings without tiring and without carelessness, [a Bodhisattva] expresses his aspiration for enlightenment: To benefit others is to benefit oneself!

19

By entering the profound foundation of dharmas, exempt and separate from conceptual constructs, entirely without effort, all matters are spontaneously abandoned.

20

Profit, reputation, honors, and pleasure are four things one should not be attached to. Nor should one become embroiled in their opposites. This is called [worldly] renunciation.

21

As long as he has not obtained the Irreversible [Stage], a Bodhisattva should perform these actions for the sake of enlightenment as zealously as if his headdress were on fire.

22

All the Bodhisattvas who seek enlightenment display energy without rest, for they shoulder a heavy burden.

23

If he has not yet produced great compassion and patience, although he may have attained the Irreversible [Stage], a Bodhisattva can become like a mortal by being careless.

24

If he enters the Śrāvaka and Pratyekabuddha levels, he becomes a mortal, because the roots of the knowledge of deliverance of the Bodhisattvas are cut off.

25

Even if he fell into hell a Bodhisattva would not be afraid, but the level of the Śrāvakas and Pratyekabuddhas horrifies him.

26

While falling into hell creates no absolute barrier to enlightenment, it is an absolute barrier to fall into the lands of the Śrāvakas and Pratyekabuddhas.

27

It is said that people who love life are afraid to have their head cut off. In just the same way, the lands of the Śrāvakas and Pratyekabuddhas ought to evoke similar fear.

28

[To accept all reality as non-arising means seeing everything as] unborn, undestroyed, neither unborn nor undestroyed, neither both nor neither, neither empty nor non-empty.

29

When one does not swerve from the Middle View with regard to any phenomenon whatsoever, there is acceptance [of] non-arising, because all ideas are eliminated.

30

As soon as you have obtained this conviction, at that very moment you receive the prediction [that you will become a Buddha]. You certainly will become a Buddha once you have attained the Irreversible [Stage].

31

Until a Bodhisattva attains the stage of Presence, he should strengthen his samādhi and ought not to become careless.

32

The [sixth stage], the Stage of Presence of a [future] Buddha, is steadfast concentration. This is the father of a Bodhisattva [and] great compassion is his mother.

33

Prajñāpāramitā is his mother and [skill in] means is his father. The term 'parents of the Bodhisattva' is employed because the latter generates and the former sustains.

34

A small quantity of merit cannot bring about enlightenment. One brings it about by collecting a quantity of merit the size of a hundred Sumerus.

35

Though [a Bodhisattva's] merit be slight, it must be skillful. He must produce a support for all living beings, [thinking:]

36

"All the actions I perform shall always be for the benefit of living beings!" Who can measure the merit of an intention such as this?

37

Not to cherish one's own family or one's body, life, or riches, not to covet pleasures and power or the world of Brahmā and the other gods;

38

Not to covet nirvana, but to act to benefit living beings—just this is to care for living beings. Who can measure such merit?

39

To save and protect a world lacking support and protection from suffering and pain—who can measure the merit of forming such intentions?

40

To possess the Prajñāpāramitā for one or several months, as when briefly milking a cow—who can measure the merit?

41

To recite to oneself and to teach others the profound scriptures praised by the Buddha, and to explain the various meanings: This is called a mass of merit.

42

By causing innumerable beings to turn their minds to enlightenment the store of merit will wax ever greater, so that one will obtain the Immovable Stage.

43

To follow [the Buddha], to turn the victorious Dharmacakra turned by the Buddha, and to calm and quench bad impulse: This is a Bodhisattva's store of merit.

44

Bearing the great suffering of hell (and a little extra suffering as well), so as to benefit and bring pleasure to living beings—this will place enlightenment close at hand.

45

Initiating action not for oneself but only to benefit and please living beings, motivated by compassion—this will place enlightenment close at hand.

46

Wisdom without conceptualization, zeal without sloth, unstinting generosity—this places enlightenment close at hand.

47

Being independent, by thoughts not obsessed, having perfect morality, complete and unstained, accepting [that things] are unborn—this places enlightenment close at hand.

48

In front of the fully enlightened Buddhas who are present in the ten regions, I entirely confess my sins.

49

If the Buddhas who have attained enlightenment in the universe of the ten directions are reluctant to expound their teaching, I entreat them to turn the Dharmacakra!

50

If the fully enlightened Buddhas present in the universe of the ten directions desire to give up life [in samsara], I bow my head and request them to remain.

51

The merit of generosity and good morals, of [good] thoughts and actions produced by living beings by means of body, speech, and mind—

52

We all rejoice in [such] merit, accumulated by holy men and common people of the past, present, and future.

53

If only I could gather all the merit I have and pass it on to living beings so that they might obtain full enlightenment!

54

In this way I repent, exhort [the Buddha to preach], request [the Buddha to remain], and dedicate [my merit] to enlightenment. One must know: [Thus will I be] like the Buddhas.

55

Express remorse for unwholesome acts, request the Buddhas [to abide in samsara], rejoice in merit, and transfer it to enlightenment, as the Jinas have stated.

56

Do so every third hour, day and night, joining palms, with the right kneecap touching the ground and the upper garment arranged on one shoulder.

57

If the merit [thus] created in one hour had outward form, [realms amounting to] many thousands [of times the] number of grains of sand in the Ganges still could not contain it.

58

Once [a Bodhisattva] has first produced the thought [of enlightenment: bodhicitta], he ought to show respect and kindness towards all the minor Bodhisattvas as if they were his teacher or parents.

59

Even if a Bodhisattva has committed a wrong he should not talk about it, much less tell an untruth. Speak only the truth.

60

If a man expresses the vow to become a Buddha, wish that he not fall back, show [him the merit of the Buddha], fire his zeal, and awaken joy.

61

If he has not yet unravelled the very profound Sūtras, he must not say that they are not the Buddha's words. If he makes such statements, he will reap great suffering in return.

62

If all wrongs, including the five ānantarya, were to be added together and compared with these two wrongs, they would not amount to a fraction [of them].

63

Develop carefully the three doors to liberation: śūnyatā, the markless, and the wishless.

64

Since dharmas lack own-being, they are empty (śūnya). Being empty, how can they have marks? All marks being extinguished, how can the wise wish [for anything]?

65

While [the Bodhisattva] is cultivating and contemplating these [three and] traversing the path to nirvana, he must not think that the Buddhakāya does not exist. Do not relax your efforts on this score!

66

As for nirvana, he will not realize it at once, but must produce this thought: We must ripen the Prajñāpāramitā.

67

A master archer releases his arrows so that each of them is aimed one at the other; each supporting the one before it, they do not fall. The great Bodhisattva is like that.

68

Carefully he aims the arrow of the mind at the door to liberation called 'empty'. The arrows of [skill in means] act together to support it, so that [his prajña] is not allowed to fall into nirvana.

69

Let us not desert living beings! In order to benefit living beings, first generate this attitude and then come to possess the practice of the doors to liberation.

70

There are living beings whose attachments persist a long time, and who cultivate misconceptions and [wrong] notions. All this is due to delusion.

71

Those who are addicted to [wrong] notions [and] misconceptions can abandon them by proclaiming the Dharma. First one focuses the mind on reality, and then one comes to possess the practice of the doors to liberation.

72

Bodhisattvas benefit living beings, yet they see no living beings! A difficult point indeed; an exquisite point! One cannot grasp it.

73

Even if a Bodhisattva is predestined, he must practice the doors to liberation. Since the original vow is not yet fulfilled, [the Bodhisattva] does not realize nirvana.

74

If he has not yet attained his predestination, being [only] concerned with skillful means, the original vow is not yet fulfilled. So again he does not realize nirvana.

75

[A Bodhisattva has] extreme distaste for samsara but still turns toward samsara. He has faith and joy in nirvana, yet turns his back on nirvana.

76

Fear the kleśas but do not be exhausted by the kleśas; accumulate good karma in order to suppress the suppressing kleśas.

77

A Bodhisattva has a passionate nature; he does not yet have a nirvana nature. [So only when] the kleśas are not yet burned away [can he] produce the seed of enlightenment.

78

A Bodhisattva predicts [the destiny of] other beings. This prediction has as necessary condition a Tathāgata's merit and skill, enabling them to reach the farther shore.

79

A [Bodhisattva should] propagate and establish all the śāstras, techniques, sciences, and arts for the use and benefit of all humanity.

80

According to the stages of transmigration and caste in the world of potential converts, a Bodhisattva proceeds there as he wishes; by virtue of his vows he accepts rebirth.

81

When faced with various evil matters and people's flattery or deception, put on strong armor. Do not be disgusted [by samsara] and do not be afraid [of seeking enlightenment].

82

Bodhisattvas with a completely pure mind do not flatter or deceive. They reveal all [their] sins and evils, but conceal and store [their] good deeds [without boasting].

83

Pure [in] the karma of body and speech and also [in] the karma of mind, [a Bodhisattva] cultivates all the moral rules, allowing no shortcoming or diminution.

84

[A Bodhisattva must] peacefully dwell in mindfulness. He selects an object and contemplates in solitude, employing mindfulness to safeguard himself, [so that his] mind becomes a mind without attachment.

85

If discursive thoughts arise, he must determine whether they are wholesome or unwholesome, abandoning the unwholesome and increasing the wholesome.

86

If his mind is disturbed by objects, he should concentrate his mindfulness, lead his mind back to the object, and (if it wavers) cause it to remain still.

87

Do not relax or fall into clinging, but cultivate strenuousness. If a Bodhisattva cannot uphold his samādhi, he must constantly strive [to do so].

88

[Those who are about to] ascend the Śrāvakayāna or the Pratyekabuddhayāna, merely acting for [their, or its] own benefit, must not abandon firm energy—

89

Then what of the great Bodhisattva! As his own savior and the savior of others, should he not put forth ten thousand million times the zeal?

90

For half an hour one may practice various [meditations] and for another follow different procedures, but this is not the way to practice samādhi! Let the mind be fixed on one object!

91

There should be no affection for the body and no regret for one's life. Even if one wants to protect this body, still in the end it will prove subject to decay and misery by nature.

92

Be altogether unattached to gain, honors, and fame. Act vigorously to fulfill the vow [to liberate oneself and others], as if your head [or] clothes were on fire.

93

Determined to produce the highest good, a Bodhisattva cannot wait till tomorrow. Tomorrow is far away. How can one preserve a transient existence?

94

[A Bodhisattva must] peacefully dwell in mindfulness [with utter equanimity]. If he [had] to eat the flesh of his favorite son, he would eat without being either attracted or repelled.

95

The purpose of renouncing worldly life, and how to determine whether what we have done or left undone must be done or not — this is explained in the Daśadharmakasūtra.

96

See that compound things are impermanent, and that there is no I or mine. Aware of all the deeds of Māra, abandon them!

97

Produce zeal and cultivate the [five] powers, the [five] strengths, the [seven] branches of enlightenment, the [four] bases of miraculous power, the [four] restraints, the [eight-fold] path, and the four applications of mindfulness.

98

A mind can be a place for the continuous birth of good things, happiness, and merit, but it can also be a root of evil. Reflect on this carefully!

99

Regarding positive dharmas, watch daily how they increase and how they diminish.

100

If one sees others gain in profit, support, respect, and fame, one's mind should not react with even the slightest bit of envy or jealousy.

101

Live without desiring the objects [of the senses], as if dull-witted, blind, dumb, and deaf. At the right moment the lion's roar frightens the tīrthika deer.

102

In welcoming and taking leave, honor those to be respected. In all matters of Dharma, be kind and helpful.

103

By saving and liberating those who suffer annihilation, one prospers and is not destroyed. [By] cultivating the sciences and crafts well, one trains oneself and instructs others.

104

Regarding particularly good dharmas, keep to them strenuously. Practice the four foundations of propitiation and make donations of clothing, drink, and food.

105

Do not rebuff those who beg for alms. Reconcile all your kindred. Do not turn against your followers. Make donations of dwellings and property.

106

Give parents, relatives, and friends their due; accord them the treatment due the supreme Lord.

107

Speak kindly even to a slave and care for him. Show him great respect, make medicine available, and heal all diseases.

108

[Those whose] head is [adorned with an uṣṇīṣa due to] the good karma of prior actions, [whose] voice is fine, smooth, beautiful,and wonderful, [whose] voice [i.e., brahmasvara, is due to] good karma and the right way of mind, will [never] fail to be respected, in the future as in the past.

109

Do not harm the followers of others. Look at living beings with a compassionate eye and without a jealous spirit, as if they were relatives and friends.

110

One must always do as one has promised. Acting according to one's words wins the confidence of others.

111

Support the Dharma and be wary of the idle. Make precious nets of gold and cast them over the caityas.

112

If one wants to seek out a fair maid, one should give her ornaments. But in addition to giving her jewels, one must also discourse [to her] on the qualities of the Buddha.

113

Cast statues of the Buddha sitting upright on exquisite lotus blossoms. Practice the six dharmas [with] joy and pleasure.

114

Those who are honorable are not to be dishonored. Do not criticize the Dharma spoken by the Buddha or by those who discourse on the Dharma, even to [save your] life.

115

Distribute gold and jewels to the teachers and to the caityas of the teachers. If you [find that you] forget what you learn, concentrate so as not to be confused.

116

When one has not yet fully thought out one's actions, one must neither panic nor just imitate [the actions] of others. Do not believe in the gods, nāgas, or yakṣas of the tīrthikas.

117

One's mind should be like a vajra, capable of penetrating all dharmas, or like a mountain, unperturbed in all situations.

118

Enjoy expressions transcending the world. Take no pleasure in transactions of the world. Keep all the virtues in yourself and help others to keep them too.

119

Develop the five spheres of liberation, contemplate the ten notions of impurity, and reflect upon the eight thoughts of a great Being.

120

Clearly develop the five superknowledges: the eye of the gods, the hearing of the gods, the ability to perform miraculous transformations, the ability to read the minds of others, and remembrance of past lives.

121

The four bases of power form the root: will, mind, energy, and deliberation. The four infinite foundations are love, compassion, joy, and equanimity.

122

Look upon the four elements as a poisonous snake, the six bases as an empty village, the five skandhas as a murderer.

123

Revere the Dharma and the teachers of the Dharma, and put aside any animosity toward the Dharma. The teacher must not clench his hand; those who listen must not be annoyed.

124

Preach the Dharma to others without rudeness and without expectations, with only a compassionate heart and a devoted and respectful mind.

125

Be insatiable for learning and commit to memory what you have learned. Do not be deceitful toward respected holy personages, but give pleasure to the teacher.

126

[When] investigating other teachings, do not let your heart cherish reverence. Do not study or recite worldly texts on account of the difficulty of the [Buddhist] treatises.

127

Do not, on account of anger, slander any of the Bodhisattvas. When one has not yet grasped and learned the Dharma one must not cause calumny.

128

Abandon pride and abide by the four noble principles. Do not despise others; do not be self-important either.

129

Whether an offense is real or fictitious, do not inform others of it. Take no notice of the faults of others; just be aware of your own faults.

130

The Buddha and the Buddhadharma should not be objects of speculation or doubt. Although the Dharma is very difficult to believe in, one must have faith in it.

131

Even if [a Bodhisattva] dies by stating the truth, or is deprived of [his exalted status as] cakravartin king or Indra, he must state the truth and nothing else.

132

[Even if you are] hit, insulted, threatened, flogged, or tied up by someone, bear him no resentment. Future and present [evils] are all due to one's own bad karma.

133

Respect, love, and support your parents greatly; serve your instructor and revere the teacher.

134

It is an error for the Bodhisattva to discourse on the very profound Dharma [i.e., the Mahāyāna] to those who believe in the Śrāvakayāna and the Pratyekabuddhayāna.

135

If people believe in the profound Mahāyāna and one still advocates the Śravakayāna and Pratyekabuddhayāna, this also is an error for the Bodhisattva.

136

Many people come [to the monastery] out of interest in the Dharma. If they are careless, one should not offer them discourses, but should care for evildoers and establish non-believers in the Mahāyāna.

137

[A Bodhisattva] must abandon these four errors. The virtues of a purified man should be recited and learned, practiced and cultivated.

138

[The four Bodhisattvamārgas are] equanimity, balanced discourse [on the Dharma], being well-established in impartiality, and being the same toward all living beings.

139

[The four kinds of Bodhisattvas] act for the Dharma, not for profit; for merit, not for reputation. [They] wish to save living beings from suffering, wanting no pleasure for themselves.

140

[If a Bodhisattva] sincerely seeks to have his actions mature, he must make the [three] meritorious practices arise. He must also mature living beings and reject his own affairs.

141

[The Bodhisattva] should approach four kinds of good friends: the teacher, the Buddha, those who offer encouragement to ascetics, and monks.

142

Those who rely on worldly knowledge, who especially crave worldly goods, who believe in the Pratyekabuddhayāna, or [believe in] the Śrāvakayāna:

143

A Bodhisattva must be aware of these four bad friends. Seek instead what are known as the four great treasuries:

144

The superworldly Buddha, study of the [six] pāramitās, a mind that looks upon the teacher without impediments, [and] being happy to dwell in empty places.

145

Like earth, water, fire, wind, and space, entirely and everywhere, [Bodhisattvas] benefit living beings equally.

146

Consider the very meaning of the Buddha's words and unremittingly produce the dhāraṇīs. Do not hinder in any way those who are studying the Dharma.

147

Those who are to be disciplined in the nine bases of quarreling [must] put aside the [twenty] minor matters without exception. The eight kinds of sloth must also be extinguished.

148

Harbor no improper affection, [for] unreasonable desire is not in accord with one's [true] wishes. Those who are disunited should be united, without asking whether they are friends.

149

A sage does not base his actions on śūnyatā by apprehending śūnyatā. If one [absolutely] must apprehend śūnyatā, this error amounts to the fault of belief in a personal substance.

150

Sweep the dust, smear [cow dung], make decorations, and perform worship of the caityas with many kinds of drum music and offerings such as incense, dressing the hair in a knot, and so forth.

151

Make various lamp-wheels, worship the caityas, and donate parasols, leather sandals, riding horses, carriages, chariots, and so forth.

152

[A Bodhisattva] should take special delight in the Dharma and enjoy an intellectual belief in the Buddha's attainments. He should gladly supply and serve the Sangha and take pleasure in listening to the Holy Dharma.

153

Unborn in the past, not remaining in the present, and not arrived in the future — look upon all dharmas thus.

154

Be gracious to living beings without seeking a reward from them. Bear [their] troubles alone, without grasping after pleasure for yourself.

155

Even if one is worthy of [rebirth in heaven as] the result of great merit, one's heart should not be uplifted or elated. Even if one is in great need like a hungry ghost, one should be neither downcast nor sad.

156

Those who are fully disciplined must be paid full respect. Those who are not yet disciplined should enter the discipline, and must not be objects of contempt.

157

Those whose good conduct is perfect should be respected. If [they] violate good conduct, they should return to its practice. Those whose wisdom is perfect [should be] approached as friends. Those who are dull should be established in wisdom.

158

The suffering of samsara is manifold: birth, old age, death, and bad rebirth. But do not fear such perils! Conquer Māra and bad understanding.

159

Gather all the virtues in all the Buddha fields. Make lofty vows, so that all may attain them.

160

Never appropriate dharmas, but always give them up. To do this is to accept the burden, taking on responsibility for the sake of all living beings.

161

One who correctly examines all dharmas sees that there is no I and no mine. Still he does not abandon great compassion and great kindness.

162

One must surpass all worship in order to worship the Buddha Bhagavat. Of what nature is this worship? It is known as Dharma worship.

163

If one grasps the Bodhisattvapiṭaka and obtains the various dhāraṇīs while penetrating the profound foundation of [all] dharmas, that is Dharma worship.

164

Hold to the main thing, without preferring this or that articulation. Enter the profound path of the Dharma with joy, not showing heedlessness.

165

When ascetics and householders have collected these accumulations for great aeons numerous as the sands of the Ganges, they shall attain perfect enlightenment!

1/29/2012

Sources and Variants

Lokātītastava

Sources

N Narthang (sNar thang) edition of the Lokātītastava by Kṛṣṇapaṇḍita and Tshul khrims rgyal ba (Narthang ed. 12, Ka, fol. 75b–77a).

P Peking edition of the Lokātītastava by the same translators, Pek. ed. 2012, Ka, fol. 79a–80b.

Variants

1d yun ring N : yul ring P **5a** gzung : gzugs NP
6c tshor bya : tshor ba NP **9c** gang : kyang NP
10a bya : pa NP **11a** na : ni NP
18d MV, p. 97 : zhig dang ma zhig pa dag gis | | rgyu las 'bras bu 'byung ba dag | | sgyu ma 'byung ba bzhin du 'byung | | kun kyang de bzhin khyod kyis bsrungs || NP
26c NP *corrup. sed v. Q* (ŚV, f. 315a): 'phags pa brten pa'i 'di lta bu | | dngos por rtogs pa ma yin zhing | | rgyu mtshan med pa rnam shes ni | | nam yang 'byung bar mi 'gyur to || (*sic*)
27c la : rnams NP **28b** gis : gi NP

Acintyastava

Sources

N Narthang (sNar thang) edition of the Acintyastava by Tilaka and Nyi ma grags. (Narthang ed. 19, Ka, fol. 84b–87a).

P Peking edition of the Acintyastava by the same translators, Pek. ed. 2019, Ka, fol. 88b–91a.

Variants

4b brag ca N : brag cha P **6b** kun rdzob : de ltar NP
7b 'brid : bgyid NP **8 b** ci : yi NP **9d** gang zhig : gzhan zhig NP
10b ci phyir : de phyir NP **14a** du : sogs NP
14c rnam byang : rnams kyang NP **16c** dbang : dngos NP
16d gdon : don NP **17a** de tshe : gang tshe NP **22a** rtag N : ltag P
23d NP † **29a** la : las NP **29d** gzod : bzod NP
32b rang las *pro* myang 'das ? NP **33a** sgyu N : sgyur P
33d gsungs : gsung NP **35b** gsung P : bsung N **38c** gzhi : bzhi NP
41a dam : dang NP **46a** brtags : btags NP **47a** bzhed : bshad NP
53d *omm.* NP **55a** dang *pro* kyi NP **55c** sgra N : dgra P

Bodhicittavivaraṇa

Sources

A Bodhicittavivaraṇa, tr. by Rab zhi chos kyi bshes gnyen et. al. Pek. ed. 5470, Gi, fol. 221a–226b; Narthang ed. 3461, Gi, fol. 210b–215b.

B Bodhicittavivaraṇa, tr. by Guṇākara and Rab zhi [chos kyi] bshes gnyen, revised by Kanakavarman and Nyi ma grags. Pek. ed. 2665, Gi, fol. 42b–48a; Narthang ed. 664, Gi, fol. 41b–46b.

C Bodhicittavivaraṇaṭīkā, tr. by Smṛtijñānakīrti (the author). Pek. ed. 2694, Gi, fol. 454b–484b; Narthang ed. 693, Gi, fol. 449b–476b.

Variants

1a dngos B : sku AC **1b** rnams B: 'chang A
6d spyod BC : dpyod A (cf. Derge ed. 3868, Ya, fol. 344a4: dpyad)
8a ci de B : ci phyir A **10a** 'di B : ni A
10cd A *pro* : gzung 'dzin blo yis 'joms par 'gyur B
12b dang 'dra A : 'dra snang B **14b** bshad BA : gsal C
14d med na mi 'byung . . . B : the tshom med par . . . A
16 AC, *sed om.* B **17d** tshogs pa de yang B : 'dus par yang ni A
19a ni rnam gcig la B : rnams gcig la yang A : . . . rnam pa gcig dang | yang C
21b gnod pa bzhin min nam B : na ni rmis pa bzhin A : gnod sbyin don byed pa C (cf. Viṁśatikā 4) **23c** snang ba 'di B : snang ba ni A : snang ba'i C
25b khams sogs BS: la sogs A **26c** da B : 'dir A
28c gcig pu yi B : tshul gcig gi A **29c** sems ni B : rang sems AC (*recte?*)
32b min AC : yin B **33d** bzhin AC : zhing B **34c** 'gro AC : sgra B

35 A *valde differt* **38a** de bzhin B : nges bzhin A **40b** 'ga' A : dga' B
41c kyis A : kyi B **42a** kyi A : kyis B
46b yod gyur ma yin B : gnas pa med cing ACS **50a** ni AC : gi B
51a dmigs pa BA : mtshan bya C; ni C(A) : yi B **51c** ni B : 'di A
52b smra ba BC: rgol ba A **57a** bu ram A : bur ram B
59a rga ba yi : rga shi'i (mtha') A : dga' ba yin B **63a** las A : la B
68d byas : byas pa B **70d** rtogs pas : rtogs pa B : rig pas A
74c yi : yis B (A *quattuor* pāda) **77a** brten A : bsten B
80c zad med B : mi bzod AC **81a** sems nyid B : sems dpa' A
83d kyi : kyis B : pa'i A **86a** gang zhig BA : gang gis C
89c de byung nyid pas B : srid pa'i skyon gyis A(d) **90b** A, *sed om.* B
94c ye shes (*jñāna-) B : theg pa (*yāna-) A(a)C
97c de dngos tshogs pa ni B : rjes mthar tshogs pa yis A(C)
98a kyi S : kyis B **101a** rtag par : brtags par B : rtag tu A(b)C
102b de (cf. Tattvasārasaṁgraha 97a) : ste B : *om.* A
110b 'khor bar (*saṁsāra-) B : sdom pa (*saṁvara-) AC

Yuktiṣaṣṭikā-kārikā

Sources

K Yuktiṣaṣṭikākārikā, tr. by Muditaśrī and Nyi ma grags. Pek. ed. 5225, Tsa, fol. 22b–25a; Narthang ed. 3216, Tsa, fol. 20b–22b.

V Yuktiṣaṣṭikāvṛtti, tr. by Jinamitra, Dānaśīla, Śilendrabodhi, and Ye shes sde. Pek. ed. 5265, Ya, fol. 1–33b; Narthang ed. 3256, Ya, fol. 1–34b.

C Chinese translation by *Dānapāla. Taishō 1575, 254b–256a.

Variants

2d bzlog P : bzlag N **7b** brtags N : brtag P **8d** ces : shes NP
11c mjug : 'jug NP **14a** rtsom : rtson NP **16d** sred N : srid P
18c yi : yis NP **19d** skyes : skye NP **21c** lam : las NP
22d dam pa'i chos NP : de ni chos V
27c rmongs : smongs NP, bzad : zad NP
28b snang ba NP : brjod pa C *et* V **30d** phyis : 'phyis NP
41c rtsod N : brtsod P **41d** rmad : smad NP
42c pas : pa NP, 'di 'am N : 'am P **43a** gang dag V : de dag NP
43d phrogs : 'phrogs NP **46b** yi : yin NP
46c bzad : zad NP; 'dzin V : 'byung NP **49a** pas : pa NP
53c *omm.* NP, *sed* v. V **59d** bzad : zad NP

Śūnyatāsaptati-kārikā

Sources

K Śūnyatāsaptati, tr. by gZhon nu mchog, gNyan Dharma grags, and Khu lo. Pek. ed. 5227, Tsa, fol. 27a–30b; Narthang ed. 3218, Tsa, fol. 24a–26a.

C Śūnyatāsaptativṛtti of Candrakīrti, tr. by Abhayākara and Dharma grags. Pek. ed. 5268, Ya, fol. 305–381b; Narthang ed. 3259, Ya, fol. 295a–375b.

P Śūnyatāsaptativivṛtti of Parahita, tr. by Parahita and gZhon nu mchog. Pek. ed. 5269, Ya, fol. 381b–425a; Narthang ed. 3260, Ya, fol. 357a–420b.

See also the edition of the Śūnyatāsaptativṛtti in Part II, which contains the root verses; cf. the sources and variants cited for that text.

Variants

4b med pa : med pas NP **5c** skyes pa : skyed pa NP
8b 'bras can N : 'bral can P **9a** rtag min P : brtag min N
11c gnyis : nyid NP **12c** yi : yis NP **22b** 'gag : 'ga' NP
26d yang : las NP **29b** 'chol : 'tshol NP **32c** mtshams : mtshan NP
44c kyis : kyi NP **44d** rtogs par sla : rtog par bla NP
47b zhe na rtags : zhen na rtag NP **47d** rtags : rtag NP **48b** gi : gis NP
49d yis : yi NP **52a** mi : mig NP **53b** bdag : dag NP
53d skye mched : skye med NP **54c** pa'ang : pa'am NP
54d stong mi : brten mi NP **55c** bdag : dag NP **56c** med : ni NP
57a nas : na NP **59b** gti mug P : gti mus N **61b** yod P : lod N
62a pas : pa'i NP **63d** zhi (cf. C) : 'di NP **65d** yan lag : yan yag NP
66b smig : mig NP **72b** dpog : dpogs NP **72c** 'ga' brten : 'gal bstan NP

EDITIONS

Lokātītastava

1

lokātīta namas tubhyaṁ viviktajñānavedine ǀ
yas tvaṁ jagaddhitāyaiva khinnaḥ karuṇayā ciram ǁ

2

skandhamātravinirmukto na sattvo 'stīti te matam ǀ
sattvārthaṁ ca paraṁ khedam agamas tvaṁ mahāmune ǁ

3

te 'pi skandhās tvayā dhīman dhīmadbhyaḥ saṁprakāśitāḥ ǀ
māyāmarīcigandharvanagarasvapnasaṁnibhāḥ ǁ

4

hetutaḥ saṁbhavo yeṣāṁ tadabhāvān na santi ye ǀ
kathaṁ nāma na te spaṣṭaṁ pratibimbasamā matāḥ ǁ

5

bhūtāny acakṣurgrāhyāṇi tanmayaṁ cākṣuṣaṁ katham ǀ
rūpaṁ tvayaivaṁ bruvatā rūpagrāho nivāritaḥ ǁ

6

vedanīyaṁ vinā nāsti vedanāto nirātmikā ǀ
tac ca vedyaṁ svabhāvena nāstīty abhimataṁ tava ǁ

7

saṁjñārthayor ananyatve mukhaṁ dahyeta vahninā ı
anyatve 'dhigamābhāvas tvayoktaṁ bhūtavādinā ıı

8

kartā svatantraḥ karmāpi tvayoktaṁ vyavahārataḥ ı
parasparāpekṣikī tu siddhis te 'bhimatānayoḥ ıı

9

na kartāsti na bhoktāsti puṇyāpuṇyaṁ pratītyajam ı
yat pratītya na taj jātaṁ proktaṁ vācaspate tvayā ıı

10

ajñāyamānaṁ na jñeyaṁ vijñānaṁ tad vinā na ca ı
tasmāt svabhāvato na sto jñānajñeye tvam ūcivān ıı

11

lakṣyāl lakṣaṇam anyac cet syāt tal lakṣyam alakṣaṇam ı
tayor abhāvo 'nanyatve vispaṣṭaṁ kathitaṁ tvayā ıı

12

lakṣyalakṣaṇanirmuktaṁ vāgudāhāravarjitam ı
śāntaṁ jagad idaṁ dṛṣṭaṁ bhavatā jñānacakṣuṣā ıı

13

na sann utpadyate bhāvo nāpy asan sadasan na ca ı
na svato nāpi parato na dvābhyāṁ jāyate katham ıı

14

na sataḥ sthitiyuktasya vināśa upapadyate |
nāsato 'śvaviṣāṇena samasya śamatā katham ||

15

bhāvān nārthāntaraṁ nāśo nāpy anarthāntaraṁ matam |
arthāntare bhaven nityo nāpy anarthāntare bhavet ||

16

ekatve na hi bhāvasya vināśa upapadyate |
pṛthaktve na hi bhāvasya vināśa upapadyate ||

17

vinaṣṭāt kāraṇāt tāvat kāryotpattir na yujyate |
na cāvinaṣṭāt svapnena tulyotpattir matā tava ||

18

na niruddhān nāniruddhād bījād aṅkurasaṁbhavaḥ |
māyotpādavad utpādaḥ sarva eva tvayocyate ||

19

atas tvayā jagad idaṁ parikalpasamudbhavam |
parijñātam asadbhūtam anutpannam na naśyati ||

20

nityasya saṁsṛtir nāsti naivānityasya saṁsṛtiḥ |
svapnavat saṁsṛtiḥ proktā tvayā tattvavidāṁ vara ||

21

svayaṁkṛtaṁ parakṛtaṁ dvābhyāṁ kṛtam ahetukam I
tārkikair iṣyate duḥkhaṁ tvayā tūktaṁ pratītyajam II

22

yaḥ pratītyasamutpādaḥ śūnyatā saiva te matā I
bhāvaḥ svatantro nāstīti siṁhanādas tavātulaḥ II

23

sarvasaṁkalpanāśāya śūnyatāmṛtadeśanā I
yasya tasyām api grāhas tvayāsāv avasāditaḥ II

24

nirīhā vaśikāḥ śūnyā māyāvat pratyayodbhavāḥ I
sarvadharmās tvayā nātha niḥsvabhāvāḥ prakāśitāḥ II

25

na tvayotpāditaṁ kiṁ cin na ca kiṁ cin nirodhitam I
yathā pūrvaṁ tathā paścāt tathatāṁ buddhavān asi II

26

āryair nisevitām enām anāgamya hi bhāvanām I
nānimittam hi vijñānaṁ bhavatīha kathaṁ cana II

27

animittam anāgamya mokṣo nāsti tvam uktavān I
atas tvayā mahāyāne tat sākalyena deśitam II

28

yad avāptaṁ mayā puṇyaṁ stutvā tvāṁ stutibhājanam I
nimittabandhanāpetaṁ bhūyāt tenākhilaṁ jagat II

II iti lokātītastavaḥ samāptaḥ II

Acintyastava

1

pratītyajānāṁ bhāvānāṁ naiḥsvābhāvyaṁ jagāda yaḥ ।
taṁ namāmy asamajñānam acintyam anidarśanam ॥

2

yathā tvayā mahāyāne dharmanairātmyam ātmanā ।
viditaṁ deśitaṁ tadvad dhīmadbhyaḥ karuṇāvaśāt ॥

3

pratyayebhyaḥ samutpannam anutpannaṁ tvayoditam ।
svabhāvena na taj jātam iti śūnyaṁ prakāśitam ॥

4

yadvac chabdaṁ pratītyeha pratiśabdasamudbhavaḥ ।
māyāmarīcivac cāpi tathā bhavasamudbhavaḥ ॥

5

māyāmarīcigandharvanagarapratibimbakāḥ ।
yady ajātāḥ saha svapnair na syāt taddarśanādikam ॥

6

hetupratyayasaṁbhūtā yathaite kṛtakāḥ smṛtāḥ ।
tadvat pratyayajaṁ viśvaṁ tvayoktaṁ nātha sāṁvṛtam ॥

7

asty etat kṛtakaṁ sarvaṁ yat kiṁcid bālalāpanam I
riktamuṣṭipratīkāśam ayathārthaprakāśitam II

8

kṛtakaṁ vastu no jātaṁ tadā kiṁ vārtamānikam I
kasya nāśād atītaṁ syād utpitsuḥ kim apekṣate II

9

svasmān na jāyate bhāvaḥ parasmān nobhayād api I
na san nāsan na sadasan kutaḥ kasyodayas tadā II

10

ajāte na svabhāvo 'sti kutaḥ svasmāt samudbhavaḥ I
svabhāvābhāvasiddhyaiva parasmād apy asaṁbhavaḥ II

11

svatve sati paratvaṁ syāt paratve svatvam iṣyate I
āpekṣikī tayoḥ siddhiḥ pārāvāram ivoditā II

12

yadā nāpekṣate kiṁ cit kutaḥ kiṁ cit tadā bhavet I
yadā nāpekṣate dīrghaṁ kuto hrasvādikaṁ tadā II

13

astitve sati nāstitvaṁ dīrghe hrasvaṁ tathā sati I
nāstitve sati cāstitvaṁ yat tasmād ubhayaṁ na sat II

14

ekatvaṁ ca tathānekam atītānāgatādi ca |
saṁkleśo vyavadānaṁ ca samyaṅmithyā svataḥ kutaḥ ||

15

svata eva hi yo nāsti bhāvaḥ sarvo 'sti kas tadā |
para ity ucyate yo 'yaṁ na vinā svasvabhāvataḥ ||

16

na svabhāvo 'sti bhāvānāṁ parabhāvo 'sti no yadā |
bhāvagrahagrahāveśaḥ paratantro 'sti kas tadā ||

17

ādāv eva samaṁ jātāḥ svabhāvena ca nirvṛtāḥ |
anutpannāś ca tattvena tasmād dharmās tvayoditāḥ ||

18

niḥsvabhāvās tvayā dhīman rūpādyāḥ saṁprakāśitāḥ |
phenabudbudamāyābhramarīcikadalīsamāḥ ||

19

indriyair upalabdhaṁ yat tat tattvena bhaved yadi |
jātās tattvavido bālās tattvajñānena kiṁ tadā |

20

jaḍatvam apramāṇatvam athāvyākṛtatām api |
viparītaparijñānam indriyāṇāṁ tvam ūcivān ||

21

ajñānenāvṛto yena yathāvan na prapadyate I
lokas tena yathābhūtam iti matvā tvayoditam II

22

astīti śāśvatī dṛṣṭir nāstīty ucchedadarśanam I
tenāntadvayanirmukto dharmo 'yaṁ deśitas tvayā II

23

catuṣkoṭivinirmuktās tena dharmās tvayoditāḥ I
vijñānasyāpy avijñeyā vācāṁ kim uta gocarāḥ II

24

svapnendrajālikodbhūtaṁ dvicandrodvīkṣaṇaṁ yathā I
bhūtaṁ tadvastu no bhūtaṁ tathā dṛṣṭaṁ jagat tvayā II

25

utpannaś ca sthito naṣṭaḥ svapne yadvat sutas tathā I
na cotpannaḥ sthito naṣṭa ukto loko 'rthatas tvayā II

26

kāraṇāt saṁbhavo dṛṣṭo yathā svapne tathetaraḥ I
saṁbhavaḥ sarvabhāvānāṁ vibhavo 'pi matas tathā II

27

rāgādijaṁ yathā duḥkhaṁ saṁkleśasaṁsṛtī tathā I
saṁbhārapūraṇān muktiḥ svapnavad bhāṣitā tvayā II

28

jātaṁ tathaiva no jātam āgataṁ gatam ity api ।
baddho muktas tathā jñānī dvayam icchen na tattvavit ॥

29

utpattir yasya naivāsti tasya kā nirvṛtir bhavet ।
māyāgajaprakāśatvād ādiśāntatvam arthataḥ ॥

30

utpanno 'pi na cotpanno yadvan māyāgajo mataḥ ।
utpannaṁ ca tathā viśvam anutpannaṁ ca tattvataḥ ।

31

ameyair aprameyānāṁ pratyekaṁ nirvṛtiḥ kṛtā ।
lokanāthair hi sattvānāṁ na kaś cin mocitaś ca taiḥ ॥

32

te ca sattvāś ca no jātā ye nirvānti na te sphuṭam ।
na kaś cin mocitaḥ kaiś cid iti proktaṁ mahāmune ॥

33

māyākārakṛtaṁ yadvad vastuśūnyaṁ tathetarat ।
vastuśūnyaṁ jagat sarvaṁ tvayoktaṁ kārakas tathā ॥

34

kārako 'pi kṛto 'nyena kṛtatvaṁ nātivartate ।
atha vā tatkriyākartṛ kārakasya prasajyate ॥

35

nāmamātraṁ jagat sarvam ity uccair bhāṣitaṁ tvayā I
abhidhānāt pṛthagbhūtam abhidheyaṁ na vidyate II

36

kalpanāmātram ity asmāt sarvadharmāḥ prakāśitāḥ I
kalpanāpy asatī proktā yayā śūnyaṁ vikalpyate II

37

bhāvābhāvadvayātītam anatītaṁ ca kutra cit I
na ca jñānaṁ na ca jñeyaṁ na cāsti na ca nāsti yat II

38

yan na caikaṁ na cānekaṁ nobhayaṁ na ca nobhayam I
anālayam athāvyaktam acintyam anidarśanam II

39

yan nodeti na ca vyeti nocchedi na ca śāśvatam I
tad ākāśapratīkāśaṁ nākṣarajñānagocaram II

40

yaḥ pratītyasamutpādaḥ śūnyatā saiva te matā I
tathāvidhaś ca saddharmas tatsamaś ca tathāgataḥ II

41

tat tattvaṁ paramārtho 'pi tathatā dravyam iṣyate I
bhūtaṁ tad avisaṁvādi tadbodhād buddha ucyate II

42

buddhānāṁ sattvadhātoś ca tenābhinnatvam arthataḥ I
ātmanaś ca pareṣāṁ ca samatā tena te matā II

43

bhāvebhyaḥ śūnyatā nānyā na ca bhāvo 'sti tāṁ vinā I
tasmāt pratītyajā bhāvās tvayā śūnyāḥ prakāśitāḥ II

44

hetupratyayasaṁbhūtā paratantrā ca saṁvṛtiḥ I
paratantra iti proktaḥ paramārthas tv akṛtrimaḥ II

45

svabhāvaḥ prakṛtis tattvaṁ dravyaṁ vastu sad ity api I
nāsti vai kalpito bhāvo paratantras tu vidyate II

46

astīti kalpite bhāve samāropas tvayoditah I
nāstīti kṛtakocchedād ucchedaś ca prakāśitaḥ II

47

tattvajñānena nocchedo na ca śāśvatatā matā I
vastuśūnyaṁ jagat sarvaṁ marīcipratimaṁ matam II

48

mṛgatṛṣṇājalaṁ yadvan nocchedi na ca śāśvatam I
tadvat sarvaṁ jagat proktaṁ nocchedi na ca śāśvatam II

49

dravyam utpadyate yasya tasyocchedādikaṁ bhavet ı
antavān nāntavāṁś cāpi lokas tasya prasajyate ıı

50

jñāne sati yathā jñeyaṁ jñeye jñānaṁ tathā sati ı
yatrobhayam anutpannam iti buddhaṁ tadāsti kim ıı

51

iti māyādidṛṣṭāntaiḥ sphuṭam uktvā bhiṣagvaraḥ ı
deśayām āsa saddharmaṁ sarvadṛṣṭicikitsakam ıı

52

etat tat paramaṁ tattvaṁ niḥsvabhāvārthadeśanā ı
bhāvagrahagṛhītānāṁ cikitseyam anuttarā ıı

53

dharmayājñika tenaiva dharmayajño niruttaraḥ ı
abhīkṣṇam iṣṭas trailokye niṣkapāṭo nirargalaḥ ıı

54

vastugrāhabhayocchedī kutīrthyamṛgabhīkaraḥ ı
nairātmyasiṁhanādo 'yam adbhuto naditas tvayā ıı

55

śūnyatādharmagambhīrā dharmabherī parāhatā ı
naiḥsvābhāvyamahānādo dharmaśaṅkhaḥ prapūritaḥ ıı

56

dharmayautukam ākhyātaṁ buddhānāṁ śāsanāmṛtam I
nītārtham iti nirdiṣṭaṁ dharmāṇāṁ śūnyataiva hi II

57

yā tūtpādanirodhādisattvajīvādideśanā I
neyārthā ca tvayā nātha bhāṣitā saṁvṛtiś ca sā II

58

prajñāpāramitāmbhodher yo 'tyantam pāram āgataḥ I
sa puṇyaguṇaratnāḍhyas tvadguṇārṇavapāragaḥ II

59

iti stutvā jagannātham acintyam anidarśanam I
yad avāptaṁ mayā puṇyaṁ tenāstu tvatsamaṁ jagat II

II ity acintyastavaḥ samāptaḥ II

Bodhicittavivaraṇa (Fragments)

12

phenapiṇḍopamaṁ rūpaṁ vedanā budbudopamā I
marīcisadṛśī saṁjñā saṁskārāḥ kadalīnibhāḥ II

13

māyopamaṁ ca vijñānaṁ . . .

20

parivrāṭkāmukaśunām ekasyāṁ pramadātanau I
kuṇapaḥ kāminī bhakṣya iti tisro vikalpanāh II

25

ātmagrahanivṛttyarthaṁ skandhadhātvādideśenā I
sāpi dhvastā mahābhāgaiś cittamātravyavasthayā II

27

cittamātram idaṁ sarvam iti yā deśanā muneḥ I
uttrāsaparihārārthaṁ bālānāṁ sā na' tattvataḥ II

45

na bodhyabodhakākāraṁ cittaṁ dṛṣṭaṁ tathāgataiḥ I
yatra boddhā ca bodhyaṁ ca tatra bodhir na vidyate II

46

alakṣaṇam anutpādam asaṁsthitam avāṅmayam ǀ
ākāśaṁ bodhicittaṁ ca bodhir advayalakṣaṇā ǁ

52

śūnyatāsiṁhanādena trasitāḥ sarvavādinaḥ ǀ

57

guḍe madhuratā cāgner uṣṇatvaṁ prakṛtir yathā ǀ
śūnyatā sarvadharmāṇāṁ tathā prakṛtir iṣyate ǁ

98

deśanā lokanāthānāṁ sattvāśayavaśānugāḥ ǀ
bhidyante bahudhā loka upāyair bahubhiḥ punaḥ ǁ

99

gambhīrottānabhedena kva cid vobhayalakṣaṇā ǁ
bhinnāpi deśanābhinnā śūnyatādvayalakṣaṇā ǁ

Yuktiṣaṣṭikā-kārikā [Fragments]

1

astināstivyatikrāntā buddhir yeṣāṁ nirāśrayā I
gambhīras tair nirālambaḥ pratyayārtho vibhāvyate I

5

saṁsāraṁ caiva nirvāṇaṁ manyante 'tattvadarśinaḥ I
na saṁsāraṁ na nirvāṇaṁ manyante tattvadarśinaḥ II

6

nirvāṇaṁ ca bhavaś caiva dvayam etan na vidyate I
parajñānaṁ bhavasyaiva nirvāṇam iti kathyate II

19

tat tat prāpya yad utpannaṁ notpannaṁ tat svabhāvataḥ I
svabhāvena yan notpannam utpannaṁ nāma tat katham II

30

sarvam astīti vaktavyam ādau tattvagaveṣiṇaḥ I
paścād avagatārthasya niḥsaṅgasya viviktatā II

33

mamety aham iti proktaṁ yathā kāryavaśāj jinaiḥ I
tathā kāryavaśāt proktāḥ skandhāyatanadhātavaḥ II

34

mahābhūtādi vijñāne proktaṁ samavarudhyate I
tajjñāne vagamaṁ yāti nanu mithyā vikalpitam II

39

hetutaḥ saṁbhavo yasya sthitir na pratyayair vinā I
vigamaḥ pratyayābhāvāt so 'stīty avagataḥ katham II

46

rāgadveṣodbhavas tīvraduṣṭadṛṣṭiparigrahaḥ I
vivādās tatsamutthāś ca bhāvābhyupagame sati II

47

sa hetuḥ sarvadṛṣṭīnāṁ kleśotpattir na taṁ vinā I
tasmāt tasmin parijñāte dṛṣṭikleśaparikṣayaḥ II

48

parijñā tasya keneti pratītyotpādadarśanāt I
pratītya jātaṁ cājātam āha tattvavidāṁ varaḥ II

55

bālāḥ sajjanti rūpeṣu vairāgyaṁ yānti madhyamāḥ I
svabhāvajñā vimucyante rūpasyottamabuddhayaḥ II

Śūnyatāsaptativṛtti

sTong pa nyid bdun cu pa'i 'grel pa ||

1

| gnas pa'am skye 'jig yod med dam |
| dman pa'am mnyam pa'am khyad par can |
| sangs rgyas 'jig rten bsnyad dbang gis |
| gsung gis yang dag dbang gi min |

| gnas pa'am skye ba'am jig pa'am | | yod pa'am med pa'am dman pa'am | | mnyam pa'am khyad par can yang rung ste | de thams cad ni 'jig rten gyi tha snyad kyi dbang gis sangs rgyas gsungs kyi de kho na'i dbang gis ni ma yin no | | 'dir smras pa | bdag ces bya ba de lta bu la sogs pa'i mngon par brjod pa gang yin pa 'di ci nas med pa zhig yin nam bdag med do snyam pa'i blo dag kyang 'jug pas bdag ni gdon mi za ba kho nar yod do | | 'dir bshad pa |

2

| bdag med bdag med min bdag dang |
| bdag med min pas brjod 'ga'ang med |

| ci'i phyir zhe na |

| brjod par bya ba'i chos rnams kun |
| mya ngan 'das mtshungs rang bzhin stong |

| 'dir smras pa | dngos po thams cad kyang rang bzhin gyis stong | | zhes bya ba 'di ci rgyal po'i bka'i tshig gam | 'on te gang gis dngos po thams cad rang bzhin gyis stong ngo zhes bya ba de ltar khong du chud par bya ba'i rigs pa 'ga' zhig yod | 'dir bshad pa |

3

| gang phyir dngos po thams cad kyi |
| rang bzhin rgyu rkyen tshogs pa 'am |
| so so rnams la'am thams cad la |
| yod min de'i phyir stong pa yin |

| gang gi phyir dngos po thams cad kyi rang bzhin rgyu'am rkyen rnams sam | rgyu rkyen tshogs pa'am | so so'i dngos po thams cad la'am rung ste | thams cad la yod pa ma yin pa de'i phyir dngos po thams cad rang bzhin gyis stong ngo zhe smra'o | | gzhan yang |

4

| yod pa yod phyir skye ma yin |
| med pa med pa'i phyir ma yin |
| chos mi mthun phyir yod med min |
| skye ba med phyir gnas 'gog med |

| dngos po yod pa'i phyir rgyu las skyes bar mi 'gyur te | yod pa ni yod bzhin pa zhes bshad pas so | | med pa ni med pa'i phyir rgyu las skye ba med do | | yod med ni mi 'dra ba'i phyir skye ba ma yin te phan tshun 'gal lo | | 'di ltar yod pa dang med pa dag ni phan tshun 'gal ba'i chos can yin pas chos mi mthun pa'i phyir yod pa yang ma yin med pa yang ma yin pa ga la skye | skye ba med pa'i phyir gnas pa dang 'gag pa yang med do | | 'dir smras pa | 'dus byas ni mtshan nyid gsum po skye ba dang | gnas pa dang | 'jig pa dang ldan par gsungs la | skye ba'i tshe skye ba yang ston te | de lta bas na 'ga' zhig las 'dus byas skye ba yod do | | 'dir bshad pa |

5

| skyes pa bskyed par bya ba min |
| ma skyes pa yang bskyed bya min |
| skye ba'i tshe yang bskyed bya min |
| skyes dang ma skyes pa yi phyir |

| re zhig skyes pa ni bskyed par bya ba ma yin no | | ci'i phyir zhe na | skyes zin pa'i phyir ro | | skyes zin pa ni bskyed par bya ba ma yin no | | ma skyes pa yang bskyed par bya ba ma yin te | ci'i phyir zhe na ma skyes pa'i phyir ro | | gang ma skyes pa de ni bskyed par bya ba ma yin te | bya ba dang bral ba dang | mthu med pa dang | yod pa ma yin pa de'i phyir bskyed par bya ba ma yin no | | skye ba'i tshe yang bskyed par bya ba ma yin te | ci'i phyir zhe na | de ni skyes pa dang ma skyes par zad la | | skyes pa dang ma skyes pa gang yin pa de yang sngar bshad pa'i rim pa | kho nas bskyed par bya ba ma yin te | de la re zhig skyes pa ni skyes zin pa'i phyir bskyed par bya ba ma yin no | | ma skyes pa gang yin pa de yang ma skyes pa'i phyir dang | skye ba'i bya ba dang bral ba'i phyir dang | mthu med pa'i phyir dang | med pa'i phyir bskyed par bya ba ma yin no | | de lta bas na gang gi phyir skyes pa dang ma skyes pa las ma gtogs pa gzhan gsum pa skye ba'i tshe de ni ci yang med pa de'i phyir skye ba'i tshe yang bskyed par bya ba ma yin no | | gzhan yang | rgyu mi 'thad pa'i phyir yang skye ba med pa yin no | | ci'i phyir zhe na |

6

| 'bras yod 'bras dang ldan pa'i rgyu |
| de med na ni rgyu min mtshungs |
| yod min med pa min na 'gal |
| dus gsum rnams su'ang 'thad ma yin |

| 'bras bu yod na 'bras bu dang ldan pa de rgyu yin no | | 'bras bu de med na ni rgyu ma yin pa dang mtshungs par 'gyur ro | | 'bras bu yod pa yang ma yin med pa yang ma yin pa ni 'gal te | | med pa dang yod pa dus gcig kho na yod pa ni ma yin no | | gzhan yang | dus gsum du yang rgyur 'thad pa ma yin no | | ji ltar zhe na | re zhig gal te rgyu snga bar brtag na ni gang gi rgyu yin | 'on te 'phyi bar brtag na ni grub zin pa la rgyu ci dgos | 'on te rgyu dang 'bras bu gcig car yin par brtag na ni rgyu dang 'bras bu cig car

skyes pa gnyis gang gi rgyu gang yin | gang gi 'bras bu ni gang yin | de ltar dus gsum char du'ang rgyur mi 'thad do | | 'dir smras pa | grangs 'thad pa'i phyir dngos po thams cad stong pa ma yin te | gcig dang gnyis dang mang po zhes bya ba'i grangs gang dag yin pa 'di ni yod do | | grangs kyang dngos po rnams yod na 'thad pas de'i phyir dngos po thams cad stong pa ma yin no | | 'dir bshad pa |

7

| gcig med par ni mang po dang |
| mang po med par gcig mi 'jug |
| de phyir brten nas dngos po rnams |
| byung ba mtshan ma med pa yin |

| gang gi phyir gcig med na mang po mi 'jug la mang po med na yang gcig mi 'jug pa de'i phyir dngos po rnams brten nas 'byung ba yin la | de nyid kyi phyir mtshan ma med pa yin no | | 'dir smras pa | mdo sde las | rten cing 'brel par 'byung ba sdug bsngal gyi 'bras bu can yang rgyas par bstan zhing lung 'bogs par byed pa'i slob dpon rnams kyis sems gcig dang sems tha dad pa la bstan te | de lta bas na dngos po thams cad stong pa ma yin no | | 'dir bshad pa |

8

| rten 'byung yan la bcu gnyis gang |
| sdug bsngal 'bras can de ma skyes |
| sems gcig la yang mi 'thad la |
| du ma la yang mi 'thad do |

| rten cing 'brel par 'byung ba'i yan lag bcu gnyis la sdug bsngal 'bras bu can gang yin pa de ma skyes pa'o | | de ni sems gcig la yang mi 'thad la | mang po la yang mi 'thad de | gang gi ltar na sems gcig yin pa de'i ltar na 'bras bu rgyu dang lhan cig skyes par 'gyur ro | | gang gi ltar na sems tha dad pa yin pa de'i ltar na yang yan lag snga ma snga ma zhig pa phyi ma phyi ma'i rgyu ma yin no | | de lta bas

na gnyi ga ltar yang mi 'thad pa de'i phyir rten cing 'brel par 'byung ba ni ma skyes pa yin no | | ci'i phyir mi skye zhe na | 'di la rten cing 'brel par 'byung ba ni ma rig pa'i rgyu las byung bar brtags la | ma rig pa de'i yang rkyen phyin ci log yin par ston te | phyin ci log de dag kyang rang bzhin gyis stong pa yin pa'i phyir ro | | ci'i phyir zhe na |

9

| mi rtag rtag min bdag med pa |
| bdag min mi gtsang gtsang ma yin |
| sdug bsngal bde ba ma yin te |
| de phyir phyin ci log rnams med |

| mi rtag pa ni rtag pa med pa'o | | rtag pa med na de'i gnyen por gyur pa mi rtag pa yang med do | | de bzhin du lhag ma rnams la yang sbyar ro | | de lta bas na phyin ci log rnams med do |

10

| de med na ni phyin ci log |
| bzhi las skyes pa'i ma rig med |
| de med na ni 'du byed rnams |
| mi 'byung lhag ma'ang de bzhin no |

| phyin ci log de dag med na de las skyes pa'i rig pa med la | ma rig pa med na 'du byed rnams mi 'byung ste | lhag ma yang de dang 'dra'o | | gzhan yang |

11

| ma rig 'du byed med mi 'byung |
| de med 'du byed mi 'byung bas |
| de gnyis phan tshun rgyu phyir yang |
| rang bzhin gyis ni ma grub yin |

12

| gang zhig bdag nyid rang bzhin gyis |
| ma grub de gzhan ji ltar bskyed |
| de lta bas na pha rol po |
| ma grub rkyen gzhan bskyed byed min |

| re zhig ma rig pa ni 'du byed med na mi 'byung ngo | | ma rig pa de med par yang 'du byed rnams mi 'byung ste | de gnyis ni phan tshun rgyu las byung ba yin pa'i phyir yang rang bzhin gyis ma grub pa yin no | | gang zhig bdag nyid rang bzhin gyis ma grub pa des gzhan ji ltar bskyed | de lta bas na pha rol ma grub pa'i rkyen rnams ni gzhan skyed par byed pa dag ma yin no | | gzhan yang |

13

| pha bu ma yin bu pha min |
| de gnyis phan tshun med min la |
| de gnyis cig car yang min ltar |
| yan lag bcu gnyis de bzhin no |

| re zhig pha yang bu ma yin la bu yang pha ma yin no | | de gnyis ni phan tshun med par yang med la | de gnyis cig car yang ma yin no | | ji ltar rim pa 'dis pha dang bu dag ma grub pa ltar rten cing 'brel par 'byung ba yan lag bcu gnyis kyang de dang 'dra'o | | gzhan yang |

14

| rmi lam yul brten bde sdug dang |
| yul de'ang med ltar brten nas gang |
| byung ba de yang de bzhin med |
| brten nas gang yin de yang med |

| dper na rmi lam na yul la brten pa'i bde ba dang sdug bsngal med pa dang | ji ltar yul yang yod pa ma yin pa de ltar brten nas 'byung ba gang yin pa de dang | brten nas gang yin pa de yang de bzhin du med do | | 'dir smras pa |

15

| gal te dngos rnams rang bzhin gyis |
| med na dman mnyam khyad 'phags nyid |
| yod min sna tshogs nyid mi 'grub |
| rgyu las mngon par grub pa'ang med |

| de lta bas na dngos po rnams rang bzhin gyis med do | | zhes bya ba de ni mi rung ngo | | 'dir bshad pa |

16

| rang bzhin grub rten dngos mi 'gyur |
| ma brten par yang ga la yod |
| rang bzhin med nyid mi 'gyur zhing |
| rang bzhin yod pa mi 'jig go |

| gal te dngos po rnams rang bzhin gyis yod par gyur na brten nas dngos por mi 'gyur ro | | de la 'di snyam du ma brten par yang dngos po yin du zad mod snyam du sems na | 'dir bshad pa | ma brten par yang ga la yod | | ma brten par yang dngos por mi 'gyur ro | | gal te ma brten par yang dngos zhig tu 'gyur na rang bzhin med pa nyid du 'mi 'gyur zhing | rang bzhin yod par ni 'jig par yang mi 'gyur te | med par yang mi 'gyur ro | | zhes bshad pa yin no | | 'dir smras pa | rang gi dngos po dang | gzhan gyi dngos po dang | dngos po dang dngos po med pa zhes bya ba'i blo 'di brten med pa ma yin te | de lta bas na dngos po rnams stong pa ma yin no | | 'dir bshad pa |

17

| med la rang gi dngos po'am |
| gzhan dngos 'jig par ga la 'gyur |
| de phyir gzhan dngos dngos med dang |
| dngos dang rang dngos log pa yin |

| med pa la zhes bya ba ni yod pa ma yin pa la zhes bshad pa yin te | med pa de la rang gi dngos po zhes bya ba'am |

gzhan gyi dngos po zhes bya ba'am | 'jig pa zhes bya bar lta ga la 'gyur | | de phyir gzhan gyi dngos po dang | dngos po med pa dang | dngos po dang rang gi dngos po ni log pa yin no | | 'dir smras pa |

18

| gal te dngos po stong yin na |
| 'gag par mi 'gyur skye mi 'gyur |
| ngo bo nyid kyis stong pa la |
| gang la 'gag cing gang la skye |

| gal te dngos po rang bzhin gyis stong pa yin du zin na 'gag par mi 'gyur zhing | skye bar yang mi 'gyur ro | | ci ste rang bzhin gyis stong pa la skye ba dang 'gag par 'dod na | 'dir ngo bo nyid kyis stong pa la gang la 'gag cing gang la skye zhes smra'o | | 'dir bshad pa | chos thams cad stong pa kho na yin no | | ci'i phyir zhe na |

19

| dngos dang dngos med cig car med |
| dngos med med par dngos po med |
| rtag tu dngos dang dngos med 'gyur |
| dngos dang dngos po med mi 'gyur |

| dngos po dang dngos po med pa dag cig car ba yang med do | | ji skad du bshad pa yin zhe na | dngos po dang dngos po med pa gnyis dus gcig na mi srid do zhes bshad pa yin no | | de la 'di snyam du dngos po gcig pu yin du zad mod snyam du sems na | 'dir bshad pa | dngos med med par dngos po med | gang gi phyir dngos po med pa med par dngos po mi 'thad do | | mi rtag pa nyid med par de med do | | gzhan yang | rtag tu dngos dang dngos med 'gyur | | rtag tu dngos po dang mi rtag pa nyid du 'gyur ro | | de la 'di snyam du de 'di ltar yin te | rtag tu dngos po mi rtag pa ni rtag tu dngos po'i rjes su 'brel la |

skye ba'i tshe'am gnas pa'i tshe ni las mi byed kyi dngos po 'jig pa'i tshe dngos po 'jig par byed do snyam du sems na 'dir bshad pa dngos med dngos po med mi 'byung | dngos po med par dngos po med pa yod pa ma yin no | | gang gi phyir 'jig pa med na 'jig pa'i mtshan nyid mi rtag pa nyid mi rung ste | mi 'jig na mi rtag pa nyid ces bya ba mi 'thad pa nyid kyi phyir rtag tu dngos po dang dngos po med pa kho nar 'gyur ro | | 'dir smras pa | dngos po med pa gcig pu yin du zad mod | 'dir bshad pa |

20

| dngos po med par dngos med med |
| bdag las ma yin gzhan las min |
| de lta bas na dngos po med |
| de med na ni dngos med med |

| dngos po med par ni dngos po med pa med la | dngos po de yang bdag las ma yin gzhan las ma yin no | | de lta bas na gang gi phyir rigs pa 'dis yod pa ma yin pa de'i phyir dngos po med pa ni ma skyes pa yin no | | zhes bshad pa yin no | | de med na ni dngos po med | dngos po de med na dngos po de med pa yang med do | | dngos po de'i dngos po med pa'ang mi srid do zhes bshad pa yin no | | gzhan yang |

21

| dngos po yod pa nyid na rtag |
| med na nges par chad pa yin |
| dngos po yod na de gnyis yin |
| de'i phyir dngos po khas blangs min |

| gang gi phyir dngos po yod pa nyid yin na ni rtag par thal bar 'gyur la | med pa nyid na ni nges par chad par thal bar 'gyur te | dngos po yod na de gnyis su thal bar 'gyur bas

de'i phyir dngos po khas blang bar mi bya'o | | 'dir smras pa |

22

| rgyun gyi phyir na de med de |
| rgyu byin nas ni dngos po 'gag |

| skye ba dang 'jig pa'i rgyun gyi phyir rtag pa dang chad pa 'di gnyi gar mi 'gyur te | rgyu byin nas dngos po 'gag par 'gyur ro | | 'dir bshad pa |

| snga ma bzhin du 'di ma grub |
| rgyun chad pa yi nyes pa'ang yod |

| kho bo cag ni sngar dngos po dang dngos po med pa gnyis cig car du mi srid do | | zhes brtags zin te | de'i phyir rgyun zhes khas len pa gang yin pa de yang snga ma kho na bzhin du ma grub pa yin no | | gzhan yang | rgyun chad pa'i nyes pa'ang yod par thal bar 'gyur ro | | 'dir smras pa |

23

| skye 'jig gzigs pas mya ngan 'das |
| lam bstan stong nyid phyir ma yin |

skye ba dang 'jig pa gzigs nas | mya ngan las 'das pa'i lam bstan gyi | stong pa nyid kyi phyir ni ma yin no | | 'dir bshad pa |

| 'di dag phan tshun bzlog phyir dang |
| log pa'i phyir na mthong ba yin |

| re zhig bshad pa 'di ni gang ma skyes pa shes pa de'i ma yin gyi | gang skye ba dang 'jig pa mthong gi skye ba de yang 'jig pa las bzlog par mthong | 'jig pa yang skye ba las bzlog par mthong ba de'i skye ba dang | 'jig pa 'di gnyis phan

tshun bzlog pa yin pa'i phyir dang | shes pa yang log pa yin pa'i phyir skye ba dang 'jig par mthong ba yin no | | gang gi phyir skye ba la brten nas 'jig pa dang | 'jig pa la brten nas skye ba yin pa de'i phyir yang stong nyid kho na yin no | | 'dir smras pa |

24

| gal te skye dang 'gag med na |
| gang zhig 'gag phyir mya ngan 'das |

| gal te skye ba yang med 'gag pa yang med na gang zhig 'gag pa'i phyir mya ngan las 'das par 'gyur | 'dir bshad pa |

| gang zhig rang bzhin skye med cing |
| 'gag med de thar ma yin nam |

| gang rang bzhin gyis skye ba med pa dang 'gag pa med pa de thar pa ma yin nam | gzhan yang |

25

| gal te mya ngan 'das 'gog chad |
| gal te cig shos ltar na rtag |
| de phyir dngos dang dngos med min |
| skye med 'gag pa'ang med pa yin |

| gal te mya 'ngan las 'das pa 'gog pa yin na chad par thal bar 'gyur ro | | ji ltar 'gog pa ma yin na ni rtag par thal bar 'gyur ro | | de lta bas na mya ngan las 'das pa ni dngos po dang dngos po med pa ma yin gyi | skye ba med cing 'gag pa med pa de lta bu ni mya ngan las 'das pa yin no | | 'dir smras pa | 'gog pa ni yod de de yang rtag tu gnas pa yin no zhe na | 'dir bshad pa |

26

| gal te 'gog pa 'ga' gnas yod |
| dngos med par yang der 'gyur ro |

| gal te 'gog pa 'ga' zhig gnas par 'gyur na de'i tshe dngos po med par yang 'gyur te | ma brten par yang 'gyur ro zhes bshad pa yin no | | de yang rigs pa ma yin te |

| dngos med par yang de med de |
| dngos med med par yang de med |

| dngos po dang dngos po med pa gnyi ga ltar yang 'gog pa de med do | | ji skad bshad pa yin zhe na | dngos po med par yang dngos po med pa med par yang dngos po la ma brten par yang dngos po med pa la ma brten par yang zhes bshad pa yin no | | 'dir smras pa | mtshan gzhi dang mtshan nyid 'brel pa'i phyir dngos po rnams ni yod do | | 'dir bshad pa |

27

| mtshan gzhi las mtshan grub mtshan las |
| mtshan gzhi grub ste rang ma grub |
| gcig las gcig kyang ma grub ste |
| ma grub ma grub sgrub byed min |

| mtshan nyid kyang mtshan gzhi las grub la | mtshan gzhi yang mtshan nyid las grub pa las rang gis grub pa ma yin no | | gcig las gcig kyang ma grub ste phan tshun du yang ma grub bo | | zhes bshad pa yin no | | gang gi phyir rim pa 'dis mtshan gzhi dang mtshan nyid gnyis grub pa med pa de'i phyir mtshan gzhi dang mtshan nyid ma grub ste | dngos po 'di dag grub par byed pa ma yin no |

28

| 'dis ni rgyu dang 'bras du dang |
| tshor bcas tshor ba po sogs dang |
| lta po blta bya sogs ci'ang rung |
| de kun ma lus bshad pa yin |

| 'dir smras pa | dus rig pa dag dus rnam pa du mar sems te | de lta bas na dus ni yod do | | 'dir bshad pa |

29

| mi gnas phan tshun grub phyir dang |
| 'chol phyir bdag nyid ma grub phyir |
| dngos po med phyir dus gsum ni |
| yod pa ma yin rtog pa tsam |

| dus ni ma grub bo | | ci'i phyir zhe na | mi gnas pa'i phyir te | dus ni mi gnas pa yin par bsam pa'o | | gang mi gnas pa de ni gzung bar mi nus so | | gang gzung du med pa de ji ltar gdags par 'gyur | de lta bas na ma grub bo | | gzhan yang | phan tshun grub phyir phan tshun las grub par brtags pa ste | 'das pa la brten nas da ltar dang ma 'ongs pa sgrub par byed | da ltar la brten nas 'das pa dang ma 'ongs pa sgrub par byed | ma 'ongs pa la brten nas da ltar dang 'das pa sgrub par byed pas gang gi phyir brten nas grub pa yin par brtags pa yin pa de'i phyir dus ma grub bo | | de nyid da ltar la brtags nas da ltar zhes bya | de nyid ma 'ongs pa la brtags nas 'das pa yin la | de nyid 'das pa la brtags nas ma 'ongs pa yin te | gang gi phyir de ltar 'chol ba yin pa de'i phyir ma grub bo | | gzhan yang | bdag nyid ma grub phyir dus 'di ni bdag nyid kyis ma grub pas de lta bas na ma grub yin no | | gzhan yang | dngos po med phyir yod pa yang ma yin no | | dngos po grub na ni dus kyang grub par 'gyur ba zhig na | dngos po de ni btsal na rang gi ngo bor grub pa med do | | de'i phyir dus ni ngo bo nyid kyis grub pa med pa kho na ste | rnam par rtog pa tsam 'ba' zhig tu zad do | | 'dir smras pa | 'dus byas thams cad ni mtshan nyid gsum po skye ba dang | gnas pa dang | 'jig pa dang ldan pa yin la | de las bzlog pa ni 'dus ma byas yin par gsungs te | de lta bas na 'dus byas dang 'dus ma byas ni yod do | | 'dir bshad pa |

30

| gang phyir skye dang gnas dang 'jig |
| 'dus byas mtshan nyid 'di gsum med |
| de phyir 'dus byas 'dus ma byas |
| ci yang yod pa ma yin no |

| skye ba dang gnas pa dan 'jig pa gang dag 'dus byas kyi mtshan nyid du gsungs pa de dag dpyad na mi 'thad pa'i phyir med do | | gang gi phyir de med pa de'i phyir 'dus byas sam | 'dus ma byas ci yang yod pa ma yin no | | gzhan yang | 'dus byas khas blangs su zin yang gang gi phyir dpyad na mi 'thad pa de'i phyir med do | | zhes smra'o | | ci'i phyir zhe na |

31

| ma zhig mi 'jig zhig pa'ang min |
| gnas pa gnas pa ma yin te |
| mi gnas pa yang gnas ma yin |
| skyes pa mi skye ma skyes min |

| 'di la skyes pa zhig skye bar 'gyur ram | ma skyes pa zhig skye bar 'gyur grang na | de la re zhig skyes pa ni skye ba ma yin no | | ci'i phyir zhe na | skyes zin pa'i phyir ro | | ma skyes pa'ang skye ba ma yin te | ci'i phyir zhe na | ma skyes pa'i phyir ro | skyes pa de nyid gnas pa zhig gnas pa'am | mi gnas pa zhig gnas par 'gyur grang na | 'di la yang gnas pa ni gnas pa ma yin te | gnas zin pa'i phyir ro | | mi gnas pa yang gnas pa ma yin te | | ci'i phyir zhe na | gnas par ma gyur pa'i phyir ro | | da ni zhig pa zhig 'jig par 'gyur ba'am | ma zhig 'jig par 'gyur grang na | gnyi ga ltar yang mi 'thad do | | gang gi phyir 'dus byas khas blangs su zin yang rim pa 'di gsum gyis btsal na mi 'thad pa de'i phyir 'dus byas med do | | 'dus byas med pa'i phyir 'dus ma byas kyang mi srid do | | gzhan yang |

32

| 'dus byas dang ni 'dus ma byas |
| du ma ma yin gcig ma yin |
| yod min med min yod med min |
| mtshams 'dir rnam pa 'di kun 'dus |

| dpyad na 'dus byas dang 'dus ma byas 'di ni du ma yang ma yin | gcig kyang yin | yod pa yang ma yin | med pa yang ma yin | yod med kyang ma yin no | | mtshams 'dir te nges par gzung ba 'dir ni 'di kun 'dus te ma lus pa thams cad 'ub ces bshad pa yin no | | thams cad ni mtha' dag go | | 'di gnyis kyi rnam pa rnams bsdus par rig par bya'o | | 'dir smras pa |

33

| las gnas pa ni bcom ldan gsungs |
| bla ma las bdag 'bras bu dang |
| sems can las bdag bya ba dang |
| las rnams chud za min par gsungs |

| bcom ldan 'das kyis mdo sde dag las | las dang las kyi 'bras bu yang rnam pa du mar yongs su bstan | las rnams 'bras bu med pa ma yin par yang gsungs | las rnams chud mi za ba dang | | sems can rnams ni las bdag gir bya ba yin no | | zhes kyang gsungs te | de lta bas na las dang las kyi 'bras bu yod do | | 'dir bshad pa |

34

| gang phyir rang bzhin med bstan pa |
| de phyir de ma skyes pa las |
| mi 'jig bdag 'dzin de las skye |
| de skyed 'dzin de'ang rnam rtog las |

| gang gi phyir las rang bzhin med par bstan zin pa de'i phyir | ma skyes pas ni de 'jig pa med do | | gzhan yang bdag 'dzin de las skyes | de'i phyir las ni bdag tu 'dzin pas

bskyed la | de yang rnam par rtog pa las byung ngo | | gzhan yang |

35

| gal te las ni rang bzhin 'gyur |
| de las skyes lus rtag par 'gyur |
| sdug bsngal rnam smin can mi 'gyur |
| de phyir las kyang bdag tu 'gyur |

| gal te las rang bzhin can du 'gyur na | de lta yin na ni las de las skyes pa'i lus gang yin pa de yang rtag par 'gyur te ther zug gi rang bzhin du 'gyur ro zhes bshad pa yin no | | gzhan yang | sdug bsngal rnam smin can mi 'gyur | las de sdug bsngal gyi rnam par smin pa can du yang mi 'gyur ro | | gzhan yang de phyir las kyang bdag tu 'gyur | gang gi phyir las de rtag pa de'i phyir bdag tu 'gyur te | gang mi rtag pa de sdug bsngal ba gang sdug bsngal ba de ni bdag med pa'i phyir ro | | de lta bas na las rang bzhin med pa'i phyir skyes ba med do | | ma skye ba'i phyir chud mi za'o | | gzhan yang |

36

| las ni rkyen skyes ci yang med |
| rkyen min skyes pa'ang yod min te |

| las ni rkyen las skyes pa'ang med la | | rkyen ma yin pa las skyes pa ci yang med do | | ci'i phyir zhe na |

| 'du byed rnams ni sgyu ma dang |
| dri za'i grong khyer smig rgyu 'dra |

| gang gi phyir 'du byed rnams ni dri za'i grong khyer dang | sgyu ma dang | smig rgyu dag dang 'dra ba de'i phyir las rang bzhin gyis med do | | gzhan yang |

37

| las ni nyon mongs rgyu mtshan can |
| 'du byed nyon mongs las bdag nyid |
| lus ni las kyi rgyu mtshan can |
| gsum ka'ang ngo bo nyid kyis stong |

gang gi phyir las ni nyon mongs pa'i rgyu las byung ba yin pa dang | gang gi phyir 'du byed rnams las dang nyon mongs pa'i rgyu las byung ba yin pa dang | gang gi phyir lus las kyi rgyu las byung ba de'i phyir de gsum char yang rang bzhin gyis stong ngo | | de ltar yin na |

38

| las med na ni byed pa med |
| de gnyis med par 'bras bu med |
| de med phyir na za ba po |
| med pa yin par dben pa yin |

| de ltar rigs pas kyang dpyad na 'bras bu rang bzhin med na las med pa yin no | | las med na byed pa po med pa yin no | | las dang byed pa po med na 'bras bu med do | | de med na za ba po med pa yin te | de'i phyir dben pa yin no | | gzhan yang |

39

| yang dag mthong phyir las stong par |
| legs par rnam par shes na ni |
| las mi 'byung ste las med na |
| las las gang byung mi 'byung ngo |

| de kho na mthong ba'i rgyu las rang bzhin gyis stong par legs par rnam par shes na las mi 'byung ngo | | las de med na las de las byung ba gang yin pa de yang mi 'byung ngo | | 'dir smras pa | da ci med kho na yin nam | 'on te 'ga' zhig yod | 'dir bshad pa yod do | | gal te ji ltar zhe na |

40

| ji ltar bcom ldan de bzhig gshegs |
| de ni rdzu 'phrul gyis sprul pa |
| sprul pa mdzad la sprul des kyang |
| sprul pa gzhan zhig sprul par byed |

41

| de la de bzhin gshegs sprul stong |
| sprul pas sprul pa smos ci dgos |
| rtog pa tsam gang ci yang rung |
| de dag gnyi ga yod pa yin |

42

| de bzhin byed po sprul par mtshungs |
| las ni sprul pas sprul dang mtshungs |
| rang bzhin gyis ni stong pa yin |
| rtog tsam gang ci'ang rung bar yod |

| ji ltar bcom ldan 'das de bzhin gshegs pa de rdzu 'phrul gyis sprul pa mdzad la | sprul pa des kyang sprul pa gzhan zhig sprul par byed pa de bzhin du las kyang khong du chud par bya'o | | de la re zhig de bzhin gshegs pas sprul pa yang rang bzhin gyis stong na | sprul pas sprul pa lta smos kyang ci dgos | ji ltar rtog pa tsam gang ci yang rung ba gnyi ga la yang yod pa ltar las kyang de dang 'dra'o | | gzhan yang |

43

| gal te rang bzhin gyis las yod |
| mya ngan 'das las byed po med |
| gal te med na las bskyed pa'i |
| 'bras bu sdug dang mi sdug med |

| gal te las rang bzhin yod na las rang bzhin gyis grub pa phan chad mya ngan las 'das pa thob pa med do | | gzhan

yang | las kyi byed pa po yang med do | | ci'i phyir zhe na | byed pa po med par yang las rab tu 'grub pa'i phyir ro | | gal te las rang bzhin gyis med na ni las kyis bskyed pa'i 'bras bu sdug dang mi sdug pa gang yin pa de yang med do | | 'dir smras pa | mdo sde las las yod do zhes rgya cher gsungs na de ji ltar med do zhes bya bar 'gyur | 'dir bshad pa |

44

| yod ces pa yod med ces pa'ang |
| yod de yod med ces de'ang yod |
| sangs rgyas rnams kyis dgongs nas ni |
| gsungs pa rtogs par sla ma yin |

| yod do zhes gsungs pa gang yin pa de yang brtags par yod do | | med do zhes gsungs pa gang yin pa de yang brtags par yod do | | yod med ces bya ba gang yin pa de yang brtags pa kho nar zad do | | sangs rgyas rnams kyis dgongs te gsungs pa rnams ni | rnam pa thams cad du rtogs par sla ba ma yin no | | 'dir smras pa | 'di la gzugs ni 'byung ba las gyur pa yin par 'dod de yod la | lhag ma gzugs can ma yin pa'i chos rnams kyang ci rigs par yod do | | 'dir bshad pa |

45

| gal te gzugs 'byung las byung na |
| yang dag min las gzugs 'byung 'gyur |
| rang gi ngo bo las ma yin |
| de med phyir nas gzhan las min |

| gal te gzugs 'byung ba las byung ba yin par 'dod na | de lta yin na ni gzugs yang dag pa ma yin pa las byung ba yin te | yang dag pa ma yin pa las zhe bya ba ni bdag ma yin pa las bshad pa yin no | | de ltar gzugs ni rang gi ngo bo las ma yin pa'o | | 'dir smras pa | de de bzhin te rang gi ngo bo las ni ma yin te | gzhan las yin te 'byung ba rnams ni de'i

gzhan no | | 'dir bshad pa de med phyir na gzhan las min | gzugs de gzhan las ma yin no | | ci'i phyir zhe na | de med pa'i phyir gzhan de med pa'i phyir ro | | ji ltar zhe na | 'di ltar rang gi ngo bo nyid ma grub pa'i phyir gzhan las zhes bya ba mi 'thad de | med pa ni de'i gzhan las zhes bya ba mi 'thad | med pa de'i gzhan zhes bya ba ma yin no | | gzhan yang | 'byung ba bzhi po de dag nyid med pa'i phyir te | 'di la mtshan nyid las 'byung ba | | rnams 'grub par 'dod na mtshan nyid de yang 'byung ba rnams kyi sngon rol du 'grub pa mi 'thad do | | de ma grub pa'i phyir mtshan gzhi 'byung ba rnams kyang ma grub bo |

46

| gcig la'ang bzhi ni yod min zhing |
| bzhi la'ang gcig ni yod min na |
| 'byung ba che bzhi med brten nas |
| gzugs ni ji ltar 'grub par 'gyur |

| de lta bas na | bzhi la'ang gcig nyid med la | | gcig la'ang bzhi nyid med pa'i phyir | | 'byung ba chen po bzhi med pa la brten nas gzugs ji ltar 'grub par 'gyur | med pa zhes bya ba ni yod pa ma yin pa zhes bshad pa yin no | | gzhan yang |

47

| shin tu mi 'dzin phyir gal te |
| rtags las she na rtags de med |
| rgyu dang rkyen las skyes phyir ro |
| yod na'ang rtags med rigs ma yin |

| shin tu mi 'dzin pa'i phyir gzugs ni yod pa ma yin pa nyid do | | ci'i phyir zhe na | shin tu mi 'dzin phyir gzugs ni shin tu mi 'dzin pa nyid de | gang la 'dzin pa mi srid pa de ji ltar yod do | | zhes bya bar 'gyur | 'di la 'di snyam du rtags las te | gal te 'di'i rtags gzugs so snyam pa'i blo gzugs can gyi blo yod na gzugs zhes bya ba 'grub par 'gyur te |

gang gi phyir don med pa la blo mi 'jug pa de'i phyir rtags blo la gzugs yod do snyam du sems na | 'dir bshad pa | gal te | rtags las she na rtags de med | rtags de ni med de yod pa ma yin no | ci'i phyir zhe na | rgyu dang rkyen las skyes phyir ro | | gang gi rtags blo de ni rgyu dang rkyen rnams las skyes pa de'i phyir de med do | | gzhan yang | yod na'ang rtags med rigs ma yin | | gal te gzugs de yod du zin na | yang de lta na yang | gzugs yod pa'i rtags med pa rigs ma yin te | rtags yod pa ma yin pa ni mi rigs so | | gzhan yang |

48

| gal te gzugs ni 'dzin 'gyur na |
| bdag gi rang bzhin nyid 'dzin 'gyur |
| med pa rkyen las skyes pa'i blos |
| gzugs med ji ltar 'dzin par 'gyur |

| gal te gzugs 'dzin par 'gyur na | de lta yin na ni bdag gi rang bzhin nyid ji lta bar 'gyur te | rang gi bdag nyid la 'dzin par 'gyur ro | | zhes bshad pa yin no | | de yang ma mthong ste de nyid kyis de la 'dzin pa ni ma yin no | | gang gi phyir blo de rang bzhin gyis stong pa de'i phyir med pa rkyen las skyes pa'i blo des gzugs med pa ji ltar 'dzin par 'gyur | 'dir smras pa | mdo sde las gzugs 'das pa dang ma 'ongs pa'i gzugs 'dzin pa mang du gsungs te | de lta bas na gzugs 'dzin pa ni yod do | | 'dir bshad pa |

49

| gang tshe blo 'byung skad cig pas |
| gzugs skyes skad cig mi 'dzin na |
| de yis 'das dang ma 'ongs pa'i |
| gzugs ni ji ltar rtogs par 'gyur |

| 'di la gzugs dang blo 'di gnyi ga yang skad cig yin par bsams te | gang gi tshe blo byung ba skad cig pa yin pas gzugs skyes pa skad cig pa mi 'dzin na 'das pa dang ma 'ongs

pa'i gzugs ji ltar rtogs par 'gyur te I mi srid pa'i phyir rtogs par mi 'gyur ro I I ji ltar zhes bya ba ni gsal ba'i don yin pa'i phyir ro I I rigs pa 'dis ni gzugs shin tu mi 'dzin no I I gzhan yang kha dog dang dbyibs su khas blangs su zin yang gzugs 'dzin par mi 'thad pa nyid do I I ci'i phyir zhe na I

50

I gang tshe nam yang kha dog dbyibs I
I tha dad nyid ni yod ma yin I
I tha dad gcig tu 'dzin pa med I
I de gnyis gzugs su grags phyir ro I

I gal te kha dog dang dbyibs tha dad pa nyid du gyur na ni I de'i phyir de gnyis tha dad du 'dzin pa 'thad par 'gyur na I gang gi tshe kha dog dang dbyibs de dag gzugs yin par 'dod pa de'i tshe 'thad par mi 'gyur ro I I gzhan yang I

51

I mig blo mig la yod min te I
I gzugs la yod min bar na'ang med I
I mig dang gzugs la brten nas de I
I yongs su rtog pa log pa yin I

I de ni brtags na mig gi blo ni mig la yang med I gzugs la yang med I de gnyi ga'i bar na yang med na I de ni mig dang gzugs la brten nas skyes bar yongs su rtog pa de ni log pa yin no I I 'dir smras pa I mig la sogs pa'i skye mched rnams ni yod de I de dag gi spyod yul blta bar bya ba la sogs pa yod pa yin no I I de la mig ni gzugs la lta la I rna ba la sogs pa yang ci rigs par de dang 'dra'o I I 'dir bshad pa I

52

I gal te mig bdag mi mthong na I
I de gzugs mthong bar ji ltar 'gyur I

| de phyir mig dang gzugs bdag med |
| skye mched lhag ma'ang de dang 'dra |

| gal te mig gis bdag nyid mi mthong na des gzugs mthong bar ji ltar 'gyur | gang gi phyir bdag nyid kyang mi mthong na gzugs kyang mi mthong ba de'i phyir mig ni bdag med de rang bzhin med do | | zhes bshad pa yin no | | gzhan yang | gzugs ni bdag med do | | mi snang ba ni gzugs ma yin pa ltar skye mched lhag ma de dang 'dra | rim pa de nyid kyis skye mched lhag ma rnams bdag nyid med de rang bzhin med pa yin no | | 'dir smras pa | mig ni bdag nyid mthong gi | blo ni ma yin no | | ci'i phyir zhe na | blo ni 'dzin par byed pa yin pa'i phyir te | gang gi phyir blo ni don phra mo la sogs pa 'dzin par byed pa de'i phyir blo ma yin la mig gis ni bdag nyid mthong ngo | 'di lta ste | mig ni 'byung ba dang ba'i bdag nyid yin te | de ni mig gi rang bzhin yin no | | de 'dzin par byed pa'i blo kho na yin no | | de bzhin du kha dog dang dbyibs kyi khyad par gzugs rnams 'dzin par byed pa yang blo kho na yin te | de lta bas na | gal te mig bdag mi mthong na | de gzugs mthong bar ji ltar 'gyur | zhes khyod kyis gang smras pa de ni mi 'thad do | | 'dir shad pa | de ni de lta ma yin te | ci'i phyir zhe na |

53

| mig de rang bdag nyid kyis stong |
| de ni gzhan bdag nyid kyis stong |
| gzugs kyang de bzhin stong pa ste |
| skye mched lhag ma'ang de bzhin stong |

| 'di la mig ni rang gi bdag nyid kyis stong ngo | | rang gi bdag nyid ces bya ba ni rang nyid yin no | | stong zhes bya ba ni mi dmigs pa zhes bya ba'i tha tshig go | | mig ni brten nas byung ba'i phyir stong ste | mig nyid ni brten nas grub pa'i phyir ro | | gang brten nas grub pa de ni rang gi bdag nyid du ma grub pa'i phyir de lta bas na mig ni rang gi bdag nyid kyis stong ngo | | ci ste gzhan gyi bdag nyid du yod

par 'dod na de yang mi rung ste | ci'i phyir zhe na | gang la rang gi bdag nyid med pa de la gzhan gyi dngos po ga la yod | de gzhan gyi dngos po yang med do | | de lta bas na gzhan gyi bdag nyid kyis stong ngo | | rnam pa gcig tu na gzhan gyi bdag nyid kyis kyang stong zhes bya ba ni de yang de'i gzhan ni blo yin te | mig ni blos kynag stong zhes bya ba'i tha tshig go | | ci'i phyir zhe na | mig ni shes pa yod pa ma yin pa'i phyir te | gang gi phyir shes pa med pa ni shes pa yod pa'i bdag nyid du 'gyur bar 'os pa ma yin pa de'i phyir gzhan gyi bdag nyid kyis kyang stong ngo | | gzhan yang blo nyid stong pa yin no | | gang las she na blo nyid gang las brten nas byung ba'i phyir te | ji ltar brten grub pa yin zhe na | blo nyid ni rtogs par bya ba nyid la sogs pa la brten nas grub pa yin no | | gang brten nas grub pa de ni rang gi bdag nyid kyis ma grub ste de lta bas na blo de ni rang gi bdag nyid med do | | de'i phyir blo ni don phra mo la sogs pa 'dzin par byed pa yin no zhes bya ba de mi rung ngo | | gzugs kyang de bzhin zhes bya ba ni de dang mtshungs pa ste | ji ltar mig rang gi bdag nyid dang gzhan gyi bdag nyid kyis stong pa de bzhin du gzugs kyang rang gi bdag nyid dang gzhan gyi bdag nyid kyis stong ngo | | gzugs ji ltar rang gi bdag nyid dang gzhan bdag nyid kyis stong ngo zhe na | | gang phyir dngos po thams cad kyi | rang bzhin kun la yod ma yin zhes brtag pa bshad par sngar byas zin to | | brtags na dngos po thams cad yod pa ma yin te | dngos po thams cad kyi rang bzhin nyid med do zhes bya ba'i tha tshig go | | gzhan yang | brten nas byung ba'i phyir yang stong pa yin te | 'di la gzugs nyid kyi 'byung ba rnams rgyur byas nas grub pa de ni brten nas grub pa yin la | gang la brten nas grub pa de ni rang gi ngo bos ma grub ste | de lta bas na gzugs ni rang gi ngo bos stong pa yin no | | gzhan gyi bdag nyid kyis kyang stong pa yin te | de'i gzhan ni mig dang blo yin no | | blo dang bcas pa'i mig de ni yul can yin la gzugs ni yul ste | yul gang yin pa de ni yul can ma yin no | | de lta bas na gzhan gyi bdag nyid kyis kyang stong ngo | | rnam pa gcig tu na blo ni nang yin la | gzugs ni spyad par bya ba dang phyi rol yin te | nang gi ma yin pa de'i phyir gzhan bdag nyid kyis kyang stong ngo I I de bzhin zhes bya ba ni ji ltar gzugs rang gi bdag nyid dang gzhan gyi bdag nyid kyis stong pa de bzhin du skye mched lhag ma yang rang gi bdag nyid dang gzhan gyi bdag nyid kyis stong ngo I I zhes mthun par bstan te I de lta bas na gzugs ni rang gi bdag nyid dang gzhan gyi bdag nyid kyis stong pa yin no I I gzhan yang I

54

I gang tshe gcig reg lhan cig 'gyur I
I de tshe gzhan rnams stong pa yin I
I stong pa'ang mi stong mi sten te I
I mi stong pa 'ang stong pa min I

I gang gi tshe skye mched gcig reg pa dang lhan cig tu gyur pa'i tshe gzhan rnams stong pa yin te I stong pa yin pa'ang mi stong pa mi brten la I mi stong pa nyid kyang stong pa nyid mi brten to I I gzhan yang I

55

I gsum po yod min mi gnas pa'i I
I rang bzhin 'du ba yod min pas I
I de bdag nyid kyi reg pa med I
I de phyir tshor ba yod ma yin I

I gsum po yod pa ma yin pa de med pa mi gnas pa'i rang bzhin rnams la 'du ba med do I I 'du ba med pa'i phyir de'i bdag nyid kyi reg pa med de de las byung ba'i reg pa med do zhes bshad pa yin no I I reg pa med pa'i phyir tshor ba med do I I gzhan yang I

56

I nang dang phyi yi skye mched la I
I brten nas rnam par shes pa 'byung I
I de lta bas na rnam shes med I
I smig rgyu sgyu ma bzhin du stong I

| gang gi phyir phyi dang nang gi skye mched la brten nas rnam par shes pa skye ba de'i phyir rnam par shes pa de yang med de | smig rgyu sgyu ma bzhin du stong ngo | | de la 'di snyam du rnam par shes par byed pa yod do snyam du sems na de yang mi 'thad do | | 'ci'i phyir zhe na |

57

| rnam shes rnam shes bya brten nas |
| 'byung bas yod min shes pa dang |
| rnam shes bya med phyir de'i phyir |
| rnam shes byed pa med pa nyid |

| gang gi phyir rnam par shes pa ni rnam par shes par bya ba la brten nas 'byung ba de'i phyir med de | rnam par shes par bya ba dang rnam par shes pa med pa'i phyir | rnam par shes par byed pa yang med pa nyid do | | 'dir smras pa | thams cad mi rtag go zhes gsungs ste thams cad mi rtag par bstan pas mi stong pa nyid kyang bstan pa mdzad pa yin no | | 'dir bshad pa |

58

| thams cad mi rtag mi rtag pa'am |
| yang na rtag pa ci yang med |
| dngos yod rtag dang mi rtag nyid |
| yin na de ltar ga la yod |

| thams cad mi rtag ces gsungs pa ni 'dir brjod par bzhed pa shes par bya ste | gang gi phyir mi rtag pa'am rtag pa ni ci yang med do | | dngos po yod na rtag pa'am mi rtag pa nyid yin na | dngos po de dag ga la yod de med do zhes bshad pa yin no | | 'dir smras pa | 'di ltar mdo sde las rgyas par bstan pas 'dod chags dang zhe sdang dang gti mug rnams ni yod do | | 'dir bshad pa |

59

| sdug dang mi sdug phyin ci log |
| rkyen skyes chags sdang gti mug rnams |
| 'byung ste de phyir rang bzhin gyis |
| 'dod chags zhe sdang gti mug med |

| gang gi phyir sdug pa'i rkyen dang | mi sdug pa'i rkyen dang | phyin ci log gi rkyen las 'dod chags dang zhe sdang dang gti mug rnams 'byung ba de'i phyir rang bzhin gyis 'dod chags dang zhe sdang dang gti mug rnams med do | | gzhan yang |

60

| gang phyir der chags der sdang der |
| rmongs pa de phyir de dag ni |
| rnam rtog gis bskyed rnam rtog kyang |
| yang dag nyid du yod ma yin |

| gang gi phyir gcig po de nyid la chags | de nyid la sdang | de nyid la rmongs pa de'i phyir 'dod chags dang zhe sdang dang gti mug rnams ni rnam par rtog pas bskyed pa yin no | | gzhan yang | rnam par rtog pa dag kyang yang dag pa ma yin te | rnam par rtog pa gang dag gis 'dod chags dang zhe sdang dang gti mug rnam par bskyed par byed pa de dag kyang yang dag par med do | | ji ltar med ce na | de bshad pa |

61

| rnam brtag bya gang de yod min |
| brtag bya med rtog ga la yod |
| de phyir rkyen las skyes pa'i phyir |
| brtag bya rnam par rtog pa stong |

| rnam par brtag par bya ba gang yin pa de ni med do | | rnam par brtag par bya ba med na rnam par rtog pa yod

par ga la 'gyur te | rkyen las skyes pa'i phyir rnam par brtag par bya ba yang rang bzhin gyis stong la | rnam par rtog pa yang rang bzhin gyis stong ngo | | gzhan yang |

62

| yang dag mthong phyir phyin ci log |
| bzhi las skyes pa'i ma rig med |
| de med phyir na 'du byed rnams |
| mi 'byung lhag ma'ang de bzhin no |

| de ltar yang dag par rtogs pas phyin ci log bzhi las skyes pa'i ma rig pa mi 'byung ngo | | de med pa'i phyir na ma rig pa de med pas 'du byed rnams mi 'byung ste | | de bzhin du lhag ma mi 'byung ngo | | gzhan yang |

63

| gang brten gang skyes de de las |
| skyes de de med mi 'byung ngo |
| dngos dang dngos med 'dus byas dang |
| 'dus ma byas zhi mya ngan 'das |

| gang la brten nas gang skyes pa de ni de las skyes pa yin te de med na mi 'byung | dngos dang dngos po med pa zhi ba dang | 'dus byas dang 'dus ma byas zhi ba dang | mya ngan las 'das pa yin no | | gzhan yang |

64

| rgyu dang rkyen las skyes dngos rnams |
| yang dag par ni rtog pa gang |

| brten pa'i dngos por mngon par zhen pa dang lta ba dang rtog pa dang 'dzin pa |

| de ni ston pas ma rig gsungs |
| de las yan lag bcu gnyis 'byung |

| gzhan yang |

65

| yang dag mthong phyir dngos stong par |
| legs shes ma rig mi 'byung ba |
| de ni ma rig 'gog pa yin |
| de phyir yan lag bcu gnyis 'gag |

| dngos po de dag rang bzhin gyis stong par yang dag pa ji lta ba bzhin du legs par she nas ma rig pa mi 'byung ba de ni ma rig pa 'gog pa yin no | | de'i phyir yan lag bcu gnyis 'gog go | | ci'i phyir zhe na |

66

| 'du byed dri za'i grong khyer dang |
| sgyu ma smig rgyu chu bur dang |
| chu yi dbu ba mtshungs pa ste |
| rmi lam mgal me'i 'khor lo 'dra |

| gang gi phyir yongs su brtags nas 'du byed rnams sgyu ma dang | smig rgyu dang | dri za'i grong khyer dang 'dra ba de'i phyir rang bzhin gyis stong par de dag legs par rnam par shes na ma rig pa mi 'byung ba de nyid ma rig pa 'gog pa yin te | de'i phyir yan lag bcu gnyis 'gag par 'gyur ro |

67

| rang bzhin gyis ni dngos 'ga' med |
| 'di la dngos po med pa'ang med |
| rgyu dang rkyen las skyes pa yi |
| dngos dang dngos med stong pa yin |

| btsal na don dam par rang bzhin gyis dngos po 'ga' yang med la | 'di la dngos po med pa 'ga' yang med de | rgyu dang rkyen las skyes pa'i dngos po dang dngos po med pa ni stong pa yin no |

68

। dngos po thams cad rang bzhin gyis ।
। stong pa yin pas dngos rnams kyi ।
। rten 'byung de ni de bzhin gshegs ।
। mtshungs pa med pas nye bar bstan ।

। dngos po thams cad rang bzhin gyis stong pa yin pas । dngos po rnams kyi rten nas 'byung ba 'di de bzhin gshegs pas nye bar bstan to ।

69

। dam pa'i don ni der zad do ।
। sangs rgyas bcom ldan 'das kyis ni ।
। 'jig rten tha snyad brten nas su ।
। sna tshogs thams cad yang dag brtags ।

। don dam pa ni rten cing 'brel par 'byung ba'i dngos po thams cad rang bzhin gyis stong ngo । । zhes bya ba der zad do । । sangs rgyas bcom ldan 'das kyis ni 'jig rten pa'i tha snyad la brten nas । । sna tshogs ma lus pa thams cad yang dag pa de bzhin nyid du brtags par mdzad do ।

70

। 'jig rten pa yi bstan mi 'jig ।
। yang dag chos bstan ci yang med ।
। de bzhin gshegs bshad ma rtogs nas ।
। de phyir sgrub rtogs med 'dir skrag ।

। 'jig rten pa'i chos bshad pa gang yin pa de yang mi 'jig la । yang dag par na nam yang chos bstan par mdzad pa ma yin no de ltar brten pa'i don rnam par ma shes te । de bzhin gshegs pas bshad pa ma rtogs nas de'i phyir rmongs pa rnams sgrub pa rtogs pa med pa । mtshan nyid med pa 'di la skrag par 'gyur ro ।

71

| 'di brten 'di 'byung zhes bya ba'i |
| 'jig rten sgrub 'di 'gog mi mdzad |
| rten 'byung gang de rang bzhin med |
| ji ltar de yod yang dag nges |

| 'di la brten nas 'di byung ngo | | zhes bya ba'i 'jig rten pa'i sgrub pa 'di ni mi 'gog go | | brten nas skyes pa gang yin pa 'di ni rang bzhin gyis med na | gang med pa de ni ji ltar yod ces bya ba 'di ni de'i nges pa yin no |

72

| dad ldan yang dag tshol lhur len |
| chos bstan gang la'ang mi brten gang |
| sgrub 'di rigs pas rjes gnyer te |
| dngos dang dngos med spangs nas zhi |

| dad pa dang ldan pa yang dag tshol ba lhur len pa | chos bstan pa gang la yang mi brten pa gang zhig bsgrub pa 'di rigs pas rjes su gnyer zhin | rjes su 'dod pa ni dngos po dang dngos po med pa spangs nas zhi bar 'gyur ro |

73

| rkyen nyid 'di pa 'di shes nas |
| lta ngan dra ba'i rtog pa ldog |
| chags rmongs khong khro spangs phyir te |
| ma gos mya ngan 'das nyer 'gro |

| sTong pa nyid bdun cu pa'i bshad pa || slob dpon 'phags pa klu sgrub kyis mdzad pa rdzogs so ||

Vigrahavyāvartanī

Vigrahavyāvartanī-kārikā ||

1

sarveṣāṁ bhāvānāṁ sarvatra na vidyate svabhāvaś cet |
tvadvacanam asvabhāvaṁ na nivartayituṁ svabhāvam alam ||

2

atha savabhāvam etad vākyaṁ pūrvā hatā pratijñā te |
vaiṣamikatvaṁ tasmin viśeṣahetuś ca vaktavyaḥ ||

3

mā śabdavad ity etat syāt te buddhir na caitad upapannam |
śabdena hy atra satā bhaviṣyato vāraṇaṁ tasya ||

4

pratiṣedhapratiṣedho 'py evam iti mataṁ bhavet tad asad eva |
evaṁ tava pratijñā lakṣaṅato dūṣyate na mama ||

5

pratyakṣeṇa hi tāvad yady upalabhya vinivartayasi bhāvān |
tan nāsti pratyakṣaṁ bhāvā yenopalabhyante ||

6

anumānaṁ pratyuktaṁ pratyakṣeṇāgamopamāne ca |
anumānāgamasādhyā ye 'rthā dṛṣṭāntasādhyāś ca ||

7

kuśalānāṁ dharmāvasthāvidaś ca manyante I
kuśalaṁ janāḥ svabhāvaṁ śeṣeṣv apy eṣa viniyogah II

8

nairyāṇikasvabhāvo dharmā nairyāṇikāś ca ye teṣām I
dharmāvasthoktānām evaṁ anairyāṇikādīnām II

9

yadi ca na bhavet svabhāvo dharmāṇāṁ niḥsvabhāva ity
evam II nāmāpi bhaven naivaṁ nāma hi nirvastukaṁ nāsti II

10

atha vidyate svabhāvaḥ sa ca dharmāṇāṁ na vidyate tasmāt I
dharmair vinā svabhāvaḥ sa yasya tad yuktam upadeṣṭum II

11

sata eva pratiṣedho nāsti ghaṭo geha ity ayaṁ yasmāt I
dṛṣṭaḥ pratiṣedho 'yaṁ sataḥ svabhāvasya te tasmāt II

12

atha nāsti sa svabhāvaḥ kiṁ nu pratiṣidhyate tvayānena I
vacanenarte vacanāt pratiṣedhaḥ sidhyate hy asataḥ II

13

bālānām iva mithyā mṛgatṛṣṇāyāṁ yathājalagrāhaḥ I
evaṁ mithyāgrāhaḥ syāt te pratiṣedhyato hy asataḥ II

14

nanv evaṁ saty asti grāho grāhyaṁ ca tadgrahītā ca ǀ
pratiṣedhaḥ pratiṣedhyaṁ pratiṣeddhā ceti ṣaṭkaṁ tat ǁ

15

atha naivāsti grāho naiva grāhyaṁ na ca grahītāraḥ ǀ
pratiṣedhaḥ pratiṣedhyaṁ pratiṣeddhāro nanu sa santi ǁ

16

pratiṣedhaḥ pratiṣedhyaṁ pratiṣeddhāraś ca yady uta na santi ǀ siddhā hi sarvabhāvās teṣam eva svabhāvaś ca ǁ

17

hetoś ca te na siddhir naiḥsvābhāvyāt kuto hi te hetuḥ ǀ
nirhetukasya siddhir na copapannāsya te 'rthasya ǁ

18

yadi cāhetoḥ siddhiḥ svabhāvavinivartanasya te bhavati ǀ
svābhāvyasyāstitvaṁ mamāpi nirhetukaṁ siddham ǁ

19

atha hetor astitvaṁ bhāvāsvābhāvyam ity anupapannam ǀ
lokeṣu niḥsvabhāvo na hi kaś cana vidyate bhāvaḥ ǀ

20

pūrvaṁ cet pratiṣedhaḥ paścāt pratiṣedhyam ity anupapannam ǀ
paścāc cānupapanno yugapac ca yataḥ svabhāvaḥ san ǁ

21

hetupratyayasāmagryāṁ ca pṛthak cāpi madvaco na yadi |
manu śūnyatvaṁ siddhaṁ bhāvānām asvabhāvatvāt ||

22

yaś ca pratītyabhāvo bhāvānāṁ śūnyateti sā proktā |
yaś pratītyabhāvo bhavati hi tasyāsvabhāvatvam ||

23

nirmitako nirmitakaṁ māyāpuruṣaḥ svamāyayā sṛṣṭam |
pratiṣedhayeta yadvat pratiṣedho 'yaṁ tathaiva syāt ||

24

na svābhāvikam etad vākyaṁ tasmān na vādahānir me |
nāsti ca vaiṣamikatvaṁ viśeṣahetuś ca na nigadyaḥ ||

25

mā śabdavad iti nāyaṁ dṛṣṭānto yas tvayā samārabdhaḥ |
śabdena hi tac chabdasya vāraṇaṁ naivam etac ca ||

26

naiḥsvābhāvyānāṁ cen naiḥsvābhāvyena vāraṇaṁ yadi hi |
naiḥsvābhāvyanivṛttau svābhāvyaṁ hi prasiddhaṁ syāt ||

27

atha vā nirmitakāyāṁ yathā striyāṁ strīyam ity asadgrāham |
nirmitakaḥ pratihanyāt kasya cid evaṁ bhaved etat ||

28

atha vā sādhyasamo 'yaṁ hetur na hi vidyate dhvaneḥ sattā |
saṁvyavahāraṁ ca vayaṁ nānabhyupagamya kathayāmaḥ ||

29

yadi kā cana pratijñā syān me tata eṣa me bhaved doṣaḥ |
nāsti ca mama pratijñā tasmān naivāsti me doṣaḥ ||

30

yadi kiṁ cid upalabheyaṁ pravartayeyaṁ nivartayeyaṁ vā |
pratyakṣādibhir arthais tadabhāvān me 'nupālambhaḥ ||

31

yadi ca pramāṇatas te teṣāṁ teṣāṁ prasiddhir arthānām |
teṣāṁ punaḥ prasiddhiṁ brūhi kathaṁ te pramāṇānām ||

32

anyair yadi pramāṇaiḥ pramāṇasiddhir bhavet tad anavasthā |
nādeḥ siddhis tatrāsti naiva madhyasya nāntasya ||

33

teṣām atha pramāṇair vinā prasiddhir vihīyate vādaḥ |
vaiṣamikatvaṁ tasmin viśeṣahetuś ca vaktavyaḥ ||

34

viṣamopanyāso 'yaṁ na hy ātmānaṁ prakāśayaty agniḥ |
na hi tasyānupalabdhir dṛṣṭā tamasīva kumbhasya ||

35

yadi ca svātmānam ayaṁ tvadvacanena prakāśayaty agniḥ I
param iva nanv ātmānaṁ svaṁ paridhakṣyaty api hutāśaḥ II

36

yadi ca svaparātmānau tvadvacanena prakāśayaty agniḥ I
pracchādayiṣyati tamaḥ svaparātmānau hutāśa iva II

37

nāsti tamaś ca jvalane yatra ca tiṣṭhati parātmani jvalanaḥ I
kurute kathaṁ prakāśaṁ sa hi prakāśo 'ndhakāravadhaḥ II

38

utpadyamāna eva prakāśayaty agnir ity asadvādaḥ I
utpadyamāna eva prāpnoti tamo na hi hutāśaḥ II

39

aprāpto 'pi jvalano yadi vā punar andhakāram upahanyāt I
sarveṣu lokadhātuṣu tamo 'yam iha saṁsthito hanyāt II

40

yadi svataś ca pramāṇasiddhir anapekṣya tava prameyāṇi I
bhavati pramāṇasiddhir na parāpekṣā svataḥsiddhiḥ II

41

anapekṣya hi prameyān arthān yadi te pramāṇasiddhir iti I
na bhavanti kasya cid evam imāni tāni pramāṇāni II

42

atha matam apekṣya siddhis teṣām ity atra bhavati ko doṣaḥ I
siddhasya sādhanaṁ syān nāsiddho 'pekṣate hy anyat II

43

sidhyanti hi prameyāṇy apekṣya yadi sarvathā pramāṇāni I
bhavati prameyasiddhir nāpekṣyaiva pramāṇāni II

44

yadi ca prameyasiddhir nāpekṣyaiva bhavati pramāṇāni I
kiṁ te pramāṇasiddhyā tāni yadarthaṁ prasiddhaṁ tat II

45

atha tu pramāṇasiddhir bhavaty apekṣyaiva te prameyāṇi I
vyatyaya evaṁ sati te dhruvaṁ pramāṇaprameyāṇām II

46

atha te pramāṇasiddhyā prameyasiddhiḥ prameyasiddhyā ca I
bhavati pramāṇasiddhir nāsty ubhayasyāpi te siddhiḥ II

47

sidhyanti hi pramāṇair yadi prameyāṇi tāni tair eva I
sādhyāni ca prameyais tāni kathaṁ sādhayiṣyanti II

48

sidhyanti ca prameyair yadi pramāṇāni tāni tair eva I
sādhyāni ca pramāṇais tāni kathaṁ sādhayiṣyanti II

49

pitrā yady utpādyaḥ putro yadi tena caiva putreṇa I
utpādyaḥ sa yadi pitā vada tatrotpādayati kaḥ kam II

50

kaś ca pitā kaḥ putras tatra tvaṁ brūhi tāv ubhāv api ca I
pitṛputralakṣaṇadharau yato bhavati no 'tra saṁdehaḥ II

51

naiva svataḥ prasiddhir na parasparataḥ parapramāṇair vā I
na bhavati na ca prameyair na cāpy akasmāt pramāṇānām II

52

kuśalānāṁ dharmāṇāṁ dharmāvasthāvido bruvīran yat I
kuśalaṁ svabhāvam evaṁ pravibhāgenābhidheyaḥ syāt II

53

yadi ca pratīya kuśalaḥ svabhāva utpadyate sa kuśalānām I
dharmāṇāṁ parabhāvaḥ svabhāva evaṁ kathaṁ bhavati II

54

atha na pratītya kiṁ cit svabhāva uppadyate sa kuśalānām I
dharmāṇam evaṁ syād vāso na brahmacaryasya II

55

nādharmo dharmo vā saṁvyavahārāś ca laukikā na syuḥ I
nityāś ca sasvabhāvāḥ syur nityatvād ahetumataḥ II

56

evam akuśaleṣv avyākṛteṣu nairyāṇikādiṣu ca doṣaḥ I
tasmāt sarvaṁ saṁskṛtam asaṁskṛtaṁ te bhavaty eva II

57

yaḥ sadbhūtaṁ nāmātra brūyāt sasvabhāva ity evam I
bhavatā prativaktavyo nāma brūmaś ca na vayaṁ sat II

58

nāmāsad iti ca yad idaṁ tat kiṁ nu sato bhavaty utāpy asataḥ I
yadi hi sato yady asato dvidhāpi te hīyate vādaḥ II

59

sarveṣāṁ bhāvānāṁ śūnyatvaṁ copapāditaṁ pūrvam I
sa upālambhas tasmād bhavaty ayaṁ cāpratijñāyāḥ II

60

atha vidyate svabhāvaḥ sa ca dharmāṇāṁ na vidyata itīdam I
āśaṅkitaṁ yad uktaṁ bhavaty anāśaṅkitaṁ tac ca II

61

sata eva pratiṣedho yadi śūnyatvaṁ nanu prasiddham idam I
pratiṣedhayate hi bhavān bhāvānāṁ niḥsvabhāvatvam II

62

pratiṣedhayase 'tha tvaṁ śūnyatvaṁ tac ca nāsti śūnyatvam I
pratiṣedhaḥ sata iti te nanv eṣa vihīyate vādaḥ II

63

pratiṣedhayāmi nāhaṁ kiṁ cit pratiṣedhyam asti na ca kiṁ cit |
tasmāt pratiṣedhayasīty adhilaya eṣa tvayā kriyate ||

64

yac cāharte vacanād asataḥ pratiṣedhavacanasiddhir iti |
atra jñāpayate vāg asad iti tan na pratinihanti ||

65

mṛgatṛṣṇādṛṣṭānte yaḥ punar uktas tvayā mahāṁś carcaḥ |
tatrāpi nirṇayaṁ śṛṇu yathā sa dṛṣṭānta upapannaḥ ||

66

sa yadi svabhāvataḥ syād grāho na syāt pratītya saṁbhūtaḥ |
yaś ca pratītya bhavati grāho nanu śūnyatā saiva ||

67

yadi ca svabhāvataḥ syād grāhaḥ kas taṁ nivartayed grāham |
śeṣeṣv apy eṣa vidhis tasmād eṣo 'nupālambhaḥ ||

68

etena hetvabhāvaḥ pratyuktaḥ pūrvam eva sa samatvāt |
mṛgatṛṣṇādṛṣṭāntavyāvṛttividhau ya uktaḥ prāk ||

69

yas traikālye hetuḥ pratyuktaḥ pūrvam eva sa samatvāt |
traikālyapratihetuś ca śūnyatāvādināṁ prāptaḥ ||

70

prabhavati ca śūnyateyaṁ yasya prabhavanti tasya sarvārthāḥ I
prabhavati na tasya kiṁ cin na prabhavati śūnyatā yasya II

71

yaḥ śūnyatāṁ pratītyasamutpādaṁ madhyamāṁ pratipadaṁ ca I ekārthāṁ nijagāda praṇamāmi tam apratimabuddham II

Vigrahavyāvartanī

rTsod pa bzlog pa ||

1

| gal te dngos po thams cad kyi | | rang bzhin kun la yod min na | | khyod kyi tshig kyang rang bzhin med | | rang bzhin bzlog par mi nus so |

2

| 'on te tshig de rang bzhin bcas | | khyod kyi dam bca' snga ma nyams | mi 'dra nyid de de yin na | | khyad par gtan tshigs brjod par gyis |

3

| de sgra ma 'byin lta bu'o zhes | | khyod blo sems na de mi 'thad | | 'di la sgra ni yod pa yis | | 'byung bar 'gyur ba de bzlog yin |

4

| 'gog pa'i 'gog pa'ang de lta zhes | | 'dod na de yang bzang min te | | khyod kyi dam bca'i mtshan nyid las | | de ltar skyon yod nged la med |

5

| re zhig gal te mngon sum gyis | | dngos rnams dmigs nas bzlog byed pa | | gang gis dngos rnams dmigs 'gyur ba | | mngon sum de ni med pa yin |

6

| rjes dpag lung dang nyer 'jal dang | | rjes dpag lung gis bsgrub bya dang | | dpes bsgrub bya ba'i don gang yin | | mngon sum gyis ni lan btab po |

7

| skye bo chos kyi gnas skabs mkhas | | dge ba dag gi chos rnams la | | dge ba'i rang bzhin yin par ni | | sems shing lhag ma rnams la yang |

8

| gang dag nges par 'byin pa'i chos | | chos kyi gnas skabs gsungs de rnams | | nges par 'byin pa'i rang bzhin nyid | | de bzhin nges 'byin min la sogs |

9

| gal te chos rnams rang bzhin med | | rang bzhin med ces bya ba yi | | ming yang de bzhin med 'gyur te | | gzhi med ming ni med phyir ro |

10

| 'on te rang bzhin yid mod kyi | | de ni chos rnams la med na | | de phyir chos rnams spangs pa yi | | rang bzhin gang de bstan par rigs |

11

| gang phyir khyim na bum pa med | | ces bya'i 'gog pa yod nyid la | | mthong ba de phyir khyod kyi yang | | 'gog 'di yod la rang bzhin yin |

12

| ci ste rang bzhin de med na | | khyod kyis tshig 'dis ci zhig dgag | | tshig med par yang med pa yi | | 'gog pa rab tu grub pa yin |

13

| byis pa rnams kyis smig rgyu la | | ji ltar chu zhes log 'dzin ltar | | de bzhin khyod kyi yod min la | | log par 'dzin pa 'gog byed na |

14

| de lta na ni 'dzin pa dang | | gzung dang de yi 'dzin po dang | | 'gog dang dgag bya 'gog pa po | | de drug yod pa ma yin nam |

15

| ci ste 'dzin pa yod min zhing | | gzung med 'dzin pa po med na | | 'o na 'gog dang dgag bya dang | | 'gog pa po yang yod ma yin |

16

| gal te 'gog dang dgag bya dang | | 'gog pa po yang yod min na | | dngos po kun dang de rnams kyi | | rang bzhin nyid kyang grub pa yin |

17

| khyed la gtan tshigs mi 'grub ste | | rang bzhin med phyir khyod kyi rtags | | ga la yod de khyod don de | | gtan tshigs med phyir 'grub mi 'thad |

18

| khyod la gtan tshigs med par yang | | rang bzhin bzlog pa grub yin na | | nga la'ang gtan tshigs med par ni | | rang bzhin yod pa nyid du 'grub |

19

| ci ste gtan tshigs yod na dngos | | rang bzhin med ces bya mi 'thad | | srid na rang bzhin med pa yi | | dngos 'ga' yod pa ma yin no |

20

| gang las rang bzhin yod min pa'i | | 'gog pa gal te snga 'gyur zhing | | dgag bya 'phyi zhes 'thad min la | | phyis dang cig car yang mi 'thad |

21

| nga yi tshig ni rgyu rkyen dang | | tshogs dang so so la yang med | | 'o na dngos rnams stong grub ste | | rang bzhin med pa nyid phyir ro |

22

| rten nas 'byung ba'i dngos rnams gang | | de ni stong nyid ces brjod de | | gang zhig brten nas 'byung ba de | | rang bzhin med pa nyid yin no |

23

| sprul pa yis ni sprul pa dang | | sgyu ma yi ni skyes bu yis | | sgyu mas phyung la 'gog byed ltar | | 'gog pa 'di yang de bzhin 'gyur |

24

| nga yi tshig 'di rang bzhin med | | de phyir nga phyogs ma nyams la | | mi 'dra nyid kyang med pas na | | gtan tshigs khyad par brjod mi bya |

25

| sgra mi 'byin bya bzhin zhe na | | khyod kyis gang brtsams dpe 'di min | | de ni sgra yis sgra bzlog la | | 'dir ni de lta ma yin no |

26

| gal te rang bzhin med nyid kyis | | ce ste rang bzhin med pa bzlog | | rang bzhin med pa nyid log na | | rang bzhin nyid du rab grub 'gyur |

27

| yang na kha cig sprul pa yi | | bud med la ni bud med snyam | | log 'dzin 'byung la sprul pa yis | | 'gog byed de ni de lta yin |

28

| yang na rtags 'di bsgrub bya dang | | mtshungs te gang phyir sgra yod min | | tha snyad khas ni ma blangs par | | nged cag 'chad par mi byed do |

29

| gal te ngas dam bca' 'ga' yod | | des na nga la skyon de yod | | nga la dam bca' med pas na | | nga la skyon med kho na yin |

30

| gal te mngon sum la sogs pa'i | | don gyis 'ga' zhig dmigs na ni | | bsgrub pa'am bzlog par bya na de | | med phyir nga la klan ka med |

31

| gal te khyod kyi don de rnams | | tshad ma nyid kyis rab bsgrub na | | khyod kyi tshad ma de rnams kyang | | ji ltar rab tu 'grub pa smros |

32

| gal te tshad ma gzhan rnams kyis | | grub bo snyam na thug pa med | | de yang dang po 'grub min la | | bar ma yin zhing tha ma'ang min |

33

| 'on te tshad ma med par yang | | de rnams sgrub na smra ba nyams | | mi 'dra nyid de de yi na | | gtan tshigs khyad par smra bar gyis |

34

| smras pa de ni mi mthun te | | mun khung nang gi bum pa bzhin | | de la mi dmigs ma mthong bas | | me ni rang nyid gsal byed min |

35

| gal te khyod kyi tshig gis ni | | me yis rang bdag gsal byed na | | 'o na me yis gzhan bzhin du | | rang nyid sreg pa'ang byed par 'gyur |

36

| gal te khyod kyi tshig gis ni | | me yis rang gzhan gsal byed na | | me bzhin du ni mun pa yang | | rang gzhan bdag nyid sgrib par 'gyur |

37

| 'bar byed dang ni gang gzhan na | | me 'dug pa na mun pa med | | gsal byed de ni mun sel na | | ji ltar gsal bar byed pa yin |

38

| me 'byung nyid na gsal byed pa | | yang dag min par smra ba ste | | me 'byung nyid na mun pa dang | | phrad pa med pa kho na yin |

39

| yang na me dang ma phrad kyang | | mun pa sel bar byed na ni | | 'di na yod pa gang yin pas | | 'jig rten kun gyi mun sel 'gyur |

40

| gal te rang las tshad ma grub | | gzhal bya rnams la ma bltos par | | khyod kyi tshad ma grub 'gyur 'di | | rang grub gzhan la bltos ma yin |

41

| gal te gzhal bya'i don rnams la | | ma bltos khyod kyi tshad ma grub | | de ltar tshad ma 'di rnams ni | | gang gi'ang yin par mi 'gyur ro |

42

I 'on te bltos nas de rnams 'grub I I 'dod na de la skyon cir 'gyur I I ma grub gzhan la mi bltos pas I I grub pa sgrub par byed pa yin I

43

I gal te yongs ye gzhal bya la I I bltos nas tshad ma grub yin na I I tshad ma rnams la ma bltos par I I gzhal byar bya ba 'grub par 'gyur I

44

I gal te tshad ma rnams la ni I I ma bltos par yang gzhal bya 'grub I I gang phyir de dag de 'grub na I I khyod kyi tshad ma grub pas ci I

45

I ci ste khyod kyi tshad ma rnams I I gzhal bya rnams la bltos nas 'grub I I de ltar khyod kyi tshad ma dang I I gzhal bya nges par ldog par 'gyur I

46

I 'on te khyod kyi tshad grub pas I I gzhal bar bya ba 'grub 'gyur la I I gzhal bya grub pas tshad sgrub na I I khyod kyi gnyis ka'ang 'grub mi 'gyur I

47

I gal te tshad ma gzhal bya 'grub I I gzhal bya de dag rnams kyis kyang I I de dag bsgrub par bya yin na I I de dag ji ltar sgrub par 'gyur I

48

| gal te gzhal byas tshad ma 'grub | | tshad ma de rnams sgrub kyis kyang | | de dag sgrub par bya yin na | | de dag ji ltar sgrub par 'gyur |

49

| gal te pha yis bu bskyed bya | | gal te bu de nyid kyis kyang | | ci ste pha de bskyed bya na | | des na gang gis gang bskyed smros |

50

| de dag gnyis ka'ang pha dang bu'i | | mtshan nyid 'dzin pas de'i phyir | | de la kho bo the tshom 'gyur | | de la pha gang bu gang smros |

51

| tshad ma rnams kyi rang nyid kyis | | 'grub min phan tshun gyis min pa'am | | tshad ma gzhan gyis ma yin la | | gzhal byas ma yin rgyu med min |

52

| chos kyi gnas skabs rab mkhas pa | | dge ba yi ni chos rnams kyi | | dge ba'i rang bzhin smra ba gang | | de ltar rab phye brjod bya yin |

53

| gal te dge ba'i chos rnams kyi | | rang bzhin 'ga' zhig brten skye ba | | de ni gzhan lta de lta na | | rang gi ngo bor ji ltar 'gyur |

54

| 'on te dge ba'i chos rnams kyi | | rang gi ngo bo de 'ga' la'ang | | ma brten skye na de lta na'ang | | tshangs par spyod pa gnas mi 'gyur |

55

| rgyu mi ldan pa rtag pa'i phyir | | rang bzhin bcas pa rtag par 'gyur | chos dang chos ma yin med cing | | 'jig rten pa yi tha snyad med |

56

| mi dge ba dang lung ma bstan | | nges 'byin sog la'ang skyon de bzhin | | de bas khyod kyi 'dus byas kun | | 'dus ma byas pa nyid du 'gyur |

57

| gang zhig rang bzhin bcas pa zhes | | ming 'dir yod par smra ba la | de ltar khyod kyis lan btab kyis | | nga yis ming yod mi smra'o |

58

| ming med ces bya gang yin 'di | | ci de yod pa'am med pa yin | | gal te yod dam med kyang rung | | khyod kyis smras pa'ang gnyis ka'ang nyams |

59

| dngos po dag ni thams cad kyi | | stong pa nyid ni sngar bstan pas | | de phyir dam bcas med par yang | | klan ka gang yin de tshol byed |

60

| 'on te rang bzhin zhig yod la | | de ni chos la med do zhes | | dogs 'di rigs pa ma yin mod | | dogs pa de ni khyod kyis byas |

61

| gal te yod nyid 'gog yin na | | 'o na stong nyid rab 'grub ste | | dngos rnams rang bzhin med nyid la | | khyod ni 'gog par byed pas so |

62

| stong nyid gang la khyod 'gog pa'i | | stong nyid de yang med yin na | | 'o na yod pa 'gog yin zhes | | smras pa de nyams ma yin nam |

63

| dgag bya ci yang med pas na | | nga ni ci yang mi 'gog go | | de phyir 'gog pa byed do zhes | | yang dag min te khyod kyis smras |

64

| tshig med par yang med pa yi | | 'gog tshig mi 'grub min zhe na | | de la tshig ni med ces par | | go bar byed kyi skyes sel min |

65

| smig rgyu dpe la khyod kyis kyang | | rtsod pa chen po smras pa gang | | der yang ci nas dpe de 'thad | | gtan la dbab pa mnyam par gyis |

66

| gal te 'dzin de rang bzhin yod | | rten nas 'byung bar mi 'gyur ro | | 'dzin pa gang zhig brten 'byung ba | | de nyid stong nyid ma yin nam |

67

| gal te 'dzin pa rang bzhin yod | | 'dzin pa de la su yis bzlog | | lhag ma rnams la'ang tshul de bzhin | | de phyir klan ka de med do |

68

| smig rgyu'i dpes bzlog bsgrub pa'i tshe | | sngar smras gang yin de dang ni | | snga mas gtan tshigs med pa yi | | lan btab gyur te mtshungs phyir ro |

69

| dus gsum gtan tshigs gang yin sngar | | lan btab nyid de mtshungs phyir ro | | dus gsum med kyi gtan tshigs ni | | stong nyid smra ba rnams la rung |

70

| gang la stong pa nyid srid pa | | de la don rnams thams cad srid | | gang la stong nyid mi srid pa | | de la ci yang mi srid do |

71

| gang zhig stong dang rten 'byung dag | | dbu ma'i lam du don gcig par | | gsung mchog mtshungs pa med pa yi | | sangs rgyas de la phyag 'tshal lo |

Sources and Variants

Lokātītastava

Sources

T Sanskrit manuscript of the Catuḥstava (accompanied by A) kept in the Tokyo University Library. 36 numbered pages. Material: paper. Size: 23.5 × 7 cm. Number of lines: 9. An occasional *secunda manus* in the upper or lower margin. Date: uncertain, but hardly more than a few centuries. Quality: on the whole, very good.

M A copy (microfilm in my posession) of the late Prof. M. Tubiansky's transcript or recension (cf. Obermiller [1960], p. 3) of a Sanskrit manuscript of the Catuḥstava from Mongolia. No information available concerning the date, condition, etc. of this manuscript.

G Photocopy (in my possession) of a handcopy of the Catuḥstava prepared by Dr. V.V. Gokhale (Poona): "In 1949 I was permitted to take a hand copy of the original paper manuscript [of the Catuḥstava and other texts] by the abbot of the Kundeling monastery. It was a manuscript written in the Bengal script of about the thirteenth or fourteenth century, I suppose . . ." Quoted from a letter dated October 7, 1976.

A The Akāriṭīkā, subjoined to the text of the Catuḥstava in T, described above. Merely provides simple synonyms and analyzes the syntax in a most elementary manner. It lacks the slightest philosophical import, but remains valuable for substantiating the readings of the root text.

W Microfiche of a Sanskrit manuscript in the possession of Manavajra Vajracharya, Kathmandu. Written in Nevārī script on fairly recent Nepali paper. 6 lines to a page. Size: 8 × 20 cm. Lokātītastava 1–5 and 15–25 are missing (at least on the microfiche edition kindly put at my disposal by the Institute for the Advanced Study of World Religions). Quality: on the whole not as good as T, M, or G.

S A variant reading in the Sanskrit manuscript(s), now presumably lost, but inferable from a recension of the Tibetan translation, based on N and P (as cited in Part I).

Variants

1d karuṇayā ci : T *mutil.* **2a** skandhamātravini : T *mutil.*
2b na sattvo 'stīti T : sattvo nāstīti GM **3a** 'pi skandhās tvayā dhī : T *mutil.*
5c vam : T *mutil.*, bruvatā TG : vādinā M **6d** nāstīty abhima : T *mutil.*
7b dahyeta va : T *mutil.*
8c parasparāpekṣikī tu TMGA : parasparāpremaṣikīndrā W
10a tvam ūcivān TG : te sūcitam M **11c** abhāvo TM : abhāve G
14c nāsato 'śvaviṣāṇena TG : nāsataś ca viṣāṇena M
14d śamatā T : samatā GM : samata W **15c** nityo TG : nityam M
17c svapnena TM : svapne 'pi G **19c** parijñeyaṁ ca saṁbhūtaṁ ? S
19d na naśyati TG : anaśvaram M **22d** tavātulaḥ AGMQW : tavātula TS
23c yasya TMS : tasya G **24d** prakāśitāḥ TGM : prabhāvitāḥ ? S
26c nānimittaṁ hi TMGA : nimittaṁ na W

Acintyastava

Sources

See the sources cited for the Lokātītastava

Variants

1b naiḥsvābhāvyaṁ AGMQ : naiḥsvabhāvyaṁ T
2c deśitaṁ TG : karuṇāvaśāt M **2d** karuṇāvaśāt TG : deśitam M
4b pratītyeha AGMQT : pratītyajam W **6b** smṛtāḥ TG : matāḥ M
6d sāṁvṛtam TG : saṁvṛtam M **7a** asty etat AGTW : asti tat MTW
7b bālalāpanam T : bālalāpitam GM
7d ayathārthaprakāśitam TG : yathārtham aprakāśitam M
9d kutaḥ TGS : kṛtaḥ M **10b** svasmāt TMS : kasmāt G
11d pārāvāram TM : pārāvāra G **13b** tathā AGMQT : yathā W
14a ekatvaṁ ca AGMQT : ekatvādi W **15c** yo 'yaṁ M : yo yaṁ TG
15d svasvabhāvataḥ : GMS : sa svabhāvataḥ T
16b 'sti no yadā AGMQT : yadāsti na W
16c bhāvagrāha° M (cf. note to. v. 16 in Part III)
20d ūcivān TG : uktavān M (cf. CS I, 10)
21b prapadyate TG : pratipannaḥ M **22a** śāśvatī TG : śāśvata° M

23d vācāṁ TG : vācaḥ M : vātā W
24b dvicandrodvīkṣaṇaṁ AGMQT : divicandrādikṣaṇa W
24c tadvastu no bhūtam TM (nodbhūtam G) : tadvastunābhūtam ? S
25b sutas TM : svatas G **26d** matas tathā TG : tathā mataḥ MW
27a rāgādijaṁ AGMQT : rāgādikaṁ WS; yathā TGM : tathā WS
27b saṁkleśasaṁsṛtī (°saṁsṛtir M) tathā TM : tathā . . . saṁsṛtī G
27c °pūraṇān TGM : °pūraṇaṁ ? S
28c baddho muktas AGMQT : mukto baddhas W
28d icchen TG : icchan M : icche W
29a yasya naivāsti T : naiva yasyāsti GM
32b sphuṭam TMS : 'sphuṭam G **34b** kṛtatvaṁ TGMS : kartṛtvaṁ AW
34c °kartṛ T (= S?) : °kartrā ? G: °kartrī (!) M : °kartā W
36d yayā TMS : yathā G **37c** jñātaṁ T (= S?) : jñānaṁ GM
40a °samutpādaḥ TGQS : °samudbhavaḥ M
42a sattvadhātos TGMQ : dharmadhātoś S
44c paratantra iti proktaḥ AGMQT : paratantram iti proktaṁ W
45b dravyaṁ vastu TM : dravyavastu G (= S?)
45c vai kalpito MG (= S?): vaikalpito TA
45d tu vidyate TG : na vidyate S (cf. note to v. 45 in Part III) : vidyetāpi (!) M
46c kṛtakocchedād TMS : kṛtakoccheda G
47a °jñānena no° TGS : °jñāne na co° M
48c sarvam TG (= S?) : sarva° M
50c yatrobhayam TG : yadobhayam MSW
50d buddham GM (= S?) : buddha T
52a etat tat P : etad eva (!) G : etat tu M; tattvaṁ TMS : satyaṁ G
53a tenaiva TG (= S?) : tvayaiva M **53c** iṣṭas PG (= S?) : hutas M
53d nirargalaḥ AGMQT : niramtalam W
55a °gambhīrā TG (= S?) : °gambhīra° M
55c °nādo PG (= S?) : °nada° (!) M **56a** °yautukam TG : °yautakam M
57c ca T : sā MQW : yā G **57d** sā AGMQT : tu W
58b pāram AGM : param T : svayam ? S (rang NP), *aut* gtan ('tyantam ?)
58d tvadgu° TG : tvaṁ gu° M (= S?)

Śūnyatāsaptativṛtti

Sources

V Śūnyatāsaptativṛtti, tr. by Jinamitra and Ye shes sde. Pek. ed. 5231, Tsa, fol. 126a–138a; Narthang ed. 3222, Tsa, fol. 116b–128b.

See also Sources and Variants for Śūnyatāsaptati in Part I

Variants

Variants are given for the root verses only.

6c min : yin NP **10b** bzhi : gzhi NP **11d** yin : min NP
12b gzhan : bzhin NP **15d** grub P : 'grub N
17b 'jig N : 'jog P; V *om.* c **18c** kyis : kyi NP **21c** yin : min NP
28c ci'ang : ci yang NP **35b** rtag : brtag NP **38d** yin : ni NP
39d las : la NP **41a** de la : de las NP **42d** ci'ang : ci yang NP
47d ma : pa NP **48d** par N : pa N **49c** yis : yi NP
49d rtogs : rtog NP **55c** kyi : kyis NP **57a** nas : na NP
61a rnam P : nam N **63d** shing NP **66d** mgal : 'gal NP
67a 'ga' : 'gags NP **68b** kyi : kyis NP
70c bshad ma rtogs : pa bshad rtogs P (rtog N)
70d rtogs : rtog NP **71a** brten : rten NP

Vigrahavyāvartanī

Sources

K Vigrahavyāvartanīkārikā, tr. by Jñānagarbha and dPal brtsegs, revised by Jayānanda and mDo sde dpal. Pek. ed. 5228, Tsa, fol. 30b–34a; Narthang ed. 3219, Tsa, fol. 26b–29b.

V Vigrahavyāvartanīvṛtti, tr. by Jñānagarbha and Devendrarakṣita. Pek. ed. 5232, Tsa, fol. 138a–156a; Narthang ed. 3223, Tsa, fol. 128b–146b.

S A Sanskrit recension by E.H. Johnston & A. Kunst (see n. 106).

C Chinese trans. by Gautama Prajñāruci. Taishō 1631, 13b–23a.

Variants: Sanskrit

9b evam (cf. 57) : eva S : *omm.* NP
20d svabhāvaḥ san CS : *svabhāvo 'san NP
24a me tad *pro* etad S? (see Tib.) **25c** hi tat *melius quam* tac ca S
25d etac ca : evaitat S
35c svaṁ paridhakṣyaty : saṁparidhakṣyaty S (p. 3)
39d hanyāt : hānyat S **44d** tāni : tani S **57d** sat : tat S

Variants: Tibetan

5a gyis : gyi NP **6d** po P : pa N **8d** de bzhin : rang bzhin NP
12a ci ste : ci de NP **12b** kyis : kyi NP **13a** kyis : kyi NP
23b ma yi . . . bu yis : ma yis . . . bu yi NP
24a 'di rang bzhin : ni de bzhin NP **27b** bud med la N : bu med la P
27c yis : yi NP **28a** yang na : gang na NP **31b** kyis : kyi NP
34c ma mthong bas V : mthong bas na NP **36a** kyi : kyis NP
38a me N : mi P **40b** la : las NP **40d** la : las NP **43a** la : las NP
46bc gzhal P : bzhal N **46d** kyi V : kyis NP **49c** ci ste V : ci de NP
50d la : las NP **52b** yi . . . kyi : yis . . . kyis NP
52c smra ba V : chos rnams (*ante* rang bzhin) NP
53c lta NP (*pro* dngos ?) **54b** ngo bo N : ngo 'o P
55b rang bzhin bcas pa rtag V : chos rnams thams cad brtag NP
57b 'dir : ni NP **57d** yis : yi NP **61a** 'gog P : dgog N
62c zhes P : zhe N **63c** do P : de N **66b** rten P : brten N
68b sngar smras gang yin N : smras gang yin pa P
69a sngar || : sngar N : pa P **69c** med kyi P : ched kyi N

STUDIES

Catuḥstava

Though the question which of the numerous hymns ascribed to Nāgārjuna[32] belong to "the *four* hymns"[33] has given rise to some controversy,[34] such hesitation is unwarranted for at least three reasons.

First, the Sanskrit text of the Catuḥstava is available in four manuscripts.[35] The titles and order of the hymns given here are invariably: Lokātītastava, Niraupamyastava, Acintyastava and Paramārthastava. This coincides with the testimony found in the Catuḥstavasamāsārtha, composed by a certain Amṛtākara.[36] Finally, precisely these four hymns are in fact those that are quoted by the commentators, not only Bhavya, Candrakīrti and Śāntarakṣita, but also several lesser-known Indian authors.[37]

Since the doctrine and, to a certain extent, the style of the hymns—especially the Lokātītastava and Acintyastava[38]—matches well with that of the Mūlamadhyamakakārikā and other works of Nāgārjuna, I see no reason to dispute the authenticity of the Catuḥstava.[39]

I have presented an *editio princeps* of the Sanskrit text of the first and third hymns in Part II.[40] The Tibetan texts with an English translation for these same two works appear in Part I. These two works are philosophically the most significant of all the hymns ascribed to Nāgārjuna, and even of all ancient Buddhist hymns in general.[41] Their content is too reflective and abstract to render it credible that they were composed with some ritual objective in mind.[42] Nor should we attach too much importance to the motive of obtaining merit.[43] No, these hymns are outbursts of a sincere and enthusiastic appraisal of the Buddha as the teacher who out of sheer compassion took pains to propagate his conviction of the emptiness of all phenomena. This accounts for the curious composition of the two hymns compared with the other genuine works: An abundance of quotations from or allusions to Mahāyāna Sūtras are intertwined with the author's own comments, either rationalizing or approving, all *in majorem Buddhae gloriam*.[44]

I give below a *conspectus testium* for all four hymns, as well as notes on the verses for those hymns presented in Parts I and II.

Conspectus Testium

Abbreviations

AĀ	Abhisamayālaṁkārāloka, by Haribhadra (ed. P.L. Vaidya)
AS	Advayavajrasaṁgraha, by Advayavajra (collected and edited by H.P. Śastrī)
BT	Bhavasaṁkrāntiṭīkā, by Maitreyanātha (II?) (ed. N.A. Śāstrī)
BC	Bodhi[sattva]caryāvatārapañjikā, by Prajñākaramati (ed. La Vallée Poussin)
BD	Bodhimārgadīpapañjikā, by Atiśa (Pek. ed. 5344)
BP	Bodhisattvacaryāvatārapañjikā, by Vairocanarakṣita (Pek. ed. 5277)
BV	Bodhicaryāvatāratatparyapañjikāviśeṣadyotanī, by Vibhūticandra (Pek. ed. 5282)
CG	Caryāgītikośavṛtti, by Munidatta (ed. P. Kværne)
CP	Caryāmelāyanapradīpa, by Āryadeva (II) (Pek. ed. 2668)
CS	Catuḥstavasamāsārtha, by Amṛtākara (ed. G. Tucci)
MP	Madhyamakaratnapradīpa, by Bhavya (Pek. ed. 5254)
MV	Madhyamakāvatārabhāṣya, by Candrakīrti (ed. La Vallée Poussin)
PK	Pañcakrama, by Nāgārjuna (II) (ed. La Vallée Poussin)
PP	Prasannapadā, by Candrakīrti (ed. La Vallée Poussin)
PS	Pañcaskandhaprakaraṇa, by Candrakīrti (ed. C. Lindtner)
PU	Pradīpoddyotanābhisaṁdhiprakāśikā, by Āryadeva (II) (Pek. ed. 2658)
SP	Sekacatuḥprakaraṇa, by Nāgārjuna (II) (Pek. ed. 2664)
SŚ	Sākārasiddhiśāstra, by Jñānaśrīmitra (ed. A. Thakur)
SS	Subhāṣitasaṁgraha, by an unknown author (ed. C. Bendall)
ŚV	Śūnyatāsaptativṛtti, by Candrakīrti (Pek. ed. 5259)
TA	Tattvāvatārākhyasakalasugatavāksaṁkṣiptavyākhyāprakaraṇa, by Jñānakīrti (Pek. ed. 4532)

TS Tattvasiddhi, by Śāntarakṣita (Pek. ed. 4531)
TV Tattvasārasaṁgraha, by Dharmendra (Pek. ed. 4534)
YV Yuktiṣaṣṭikāvṛtti, by Candrakīrti (Pek. ed. 5265)

Verses Quoted

Lokātītastava (CS I)

4 PP, p. 413; BC, p. 583; TV, f. 95a; BP, f. 183b
5 MV, p. 200; TV, f. 95a
8 BC, p. 476
9 BC, p. 476
11 PP, p. 64
12 AĀ, p. 299; AS, p. 28
13 BC, p. 587
18 BC, p. 533; MV, p. 97
19 BC, p. 533
20 BC, p. 533
21 PP, pp. 55, 234
22 AĀ, pp. 348, 381, 405, 441, 482, 490, 536; SŚ, p. 481 ; BC, p. 417; PS, p. 26
23 BC, pp. 359, 415; TV, f. 98b; MV, p. 310
24 BC, p. 489; TV, f. 98b
26 ŚV, f. 315a
27 MV, p. 23

Niraupamyastava (CS II)

1 CS, p. 239
7 BC, p. 420; AS, p. 22; BP, f. 169a
9 BC, p. 489; BP, f. 174b
13 PP, p. 215; ŚV, f. 335b
15 TS, f. 30b
18 PK, p. 36; CP, f. 104a; PU, f. 212a; SP, f. 33a
19 PK, p. 36; CP, f. 104a; PU, f. 212a; SP, f. 33a
21 SS, p. 388; AS, p. 22; BD, f. 298b; TV, f. 92b; TA, f. 46a
24 AS, p. 22; MP, f. 361a

Acintyastava (CS III)

1 CS, p. 242
4 BV, f. 310a
9 TS, f. 40a
19 BC, p. 375; BT, p. 82; MP, f. 372; TV, f. 105a; BV, f. 308b
25 BC, p. 573 (a/d)
29 BC, p. 573

36 BC, p. 573
38 TV, f. 102a
39 TV, f. 102a
40 TV, f. 102a; BC, p. 528
41 TV, f. 102a; BC, p. 528
43 AS, p. 24 (a/b); CG, p. 209 (a/b)
48 TV, f. 97a
49 TV, f. 97a
57 TS, f. 39b

Paramārthastava (CS IV)

1 CS, p. 245 (a/b)
3 CS, p. 245 (a)
4 SŚ, p. 489 (d)
5 SŚ, p. 489 (a); CG, p. 190 (a/b)
8 CS, p. 245 (d)
9 CS, p. 245 (a); BD, f. 284a (c/d)
10 CS, p. 245 (a); BD, f. 284a

Notes on the Verses

Lokatitastava (CS I)

1 Cf. Niraupamyastava 1: niraupamya namas tubhyaṁ niḥsvabhāva-arthavedine I yas tvaṁ dṛṣṭivipannasya lokasyāsya hitodyataḥ II; Prajñāpāramitāstotra 1 for pādas a and c. For vivikta, etc. (śūnya), see references in Conze (1973), pp. 363–364; YṢ 30–31, 56; ŚS 38; also Bodhicaryāvatāra VIII, 2 (kāyacittaviveka). For khinnaḥ karuṇayā ciram cf. Śatapañcāśatka 58: tvaṁ jagatkleśamokṣārthaṁ baddhaḥ karuṇayā ciram; RĀ III, 26 (cited in the Madhyamakāvatāra, p. 29): de ni snying rjes 'jig rten sdug II de nyid kyis ni yun ring gnas II). Similarly Rāhulastava 9: ciraṁ kliṣṭo 'si saṁsāre kārunyād eva kevalam II; Bodhicaryāvatāra VIII, 104–105; Praṇidhānasaptati 17.

2 For a similar paradox (na sattvo 'stīti . . . sattvārthaṁ ca), see BS 72; CS II, 9. For skandhamātra, see Abhidharmakośa III, p. 57.

3 This verse states that Bodhisattvas (= dhīmat; cf. Pañjikā, p. 23, n. 2) not only accept pudgalanairātmya but also dharmanairātmya. Compare CS III, 2; *MCB* II, p. 17; Vimalakīrtinirdeśa, pp. 407–408; Traité, pp. 1995–2151. For the various māyādṛṣṭāntas, see Traité, pp. 357–387; May (1959), pp. 507–509 (references).

4 This stanza (of which pāda a may be compared with YṢ 39) refutes the skandhas in general whereas the following stanzas refute them separately: rūpa (5), vedanā (6), saṁjñā (7), saṁskāra (8–9), and vijñāna (10).

5 According to the Abhidharma, rūpa (= saṁsthāna and varṇa; see ŚS 50) is made up of catvāri mahābhūtāni serving as rūpakāraṇa; cf. MK IV, 1 ff. The notion of rūpa (rūpabuddhi) is refuted at length in ŚS 45–54; BV 16–24. See also RĀ I, 99 (cited in Prasannapadā, p. 413); VI, 58; YṢ 34. The argument is: no bhūta, no bhautika. See also the Bhavasaṁkrāntisūtra, quoted in the Prasannapadā, p. 120 (na cakṣuḥ prekṣate rūpam . . .)

6 This skandha is also refuted in ŚS 55.

7 A celebrated argument: Traité, p. 1617; Laṅkāvatārasūtra, p. 87; Nyāyasūtra II, 1, 51. Similarly VP 51. See also Prajñāpāramitāpiṇḍārthasaṁgraha 48 ff.

8 kartā svatantraḥ = Pāṇini I, 4, 54. It is clear from the context that kartṛ here signifies a pudgala who "punarbhavāya saṁskārān avidyānivṛtas tridhā abhisaṁskurute . . ." (MK XXVI, 1) and not, as usual, and as the ṭīkā supposes, īśvarādi (cf. CS III, 33–34 and notes). On the use of √iṣ, √man, etc. (ṭīkā glosses abhimata with svīkṛta) to indicate philosophical persuasion, compare the use of Latin *placet* (translating Greek *areskhei*) and Spinoza's remark: "Voluntas et intellectus unum et idem sunt" (*Corr. ad Ethicam* 2, 49). Nyāyabhāṣya (KSS XLIII, p. 194) attempts to refute the notion of parasparāpekṣikī siddhi thus: ". . . yasmād ekābhāve 'nyatarābhāvād ubhayābhāvaḥ": yady ekasyānyatarāpekṣā siddhir anyatarasyedānīṁ apekṣā? yady anyatarasyaikāpekṣā siddhir ekasyedānīṁ kim apekṣā? evam ekasyābhave anyataran na sidhyatīty ubhayābhavaḥ prasajyate. Cf. BV 63; MK XVII, YṢ, 32; ŚS 33–44.

9 Probably (like YṢ 48: pratītya jātaṁ cājātam āha tattvavidāṁ varaḥ) an allusion to the Anavataptahradāpasaṁkramaṇasūtra (see Vimalakīrtinirdeśa, p. 26). See also Varṇārhavarṇastotra V, 23–28; MK VIII, 12.

10 A refutation of vijñānaskandha; see also BV 26–56. Regarding jñāna/vijñāna, etc., see references in May (1959), p. 104, n. 252. For Nāgārjuna (as for Vasubandhu and others) manas, vijñāna and citta are synonyms, as are buddhi, mati and (tattva-)jñāna. Here jñāna and jñeya are of course used, *metri causa*, for vijñāna and vijñeya. For the form svabhāvena, see Mahāyānaviṁśikā 1–2; YṢ 19; CS III, 3.

11 For other refutations of lakṣaṇalakṣya see *Dvādaśadvāraka VI, 1; ŚS 27; MK V.

12 The first pāda is equivalent to Laṅkāvatārasūtra X, 255. In pāda b CS II, 14 has lakṣyalakṣaṇavarjitam; cf. MK V, 5. Its use is not confined to saṁskṛtalakṣaṇa, but to any dharmalakṣaṇa, and thus it alludes polemically to Abhidharma. There are pañca cakṣūṁṣi; cf. Traité, pp. 2260 ff., 439; Vimalakīrtinirdeśa, p. 168, n. 57. This verse refers to the prajñācakṣus; cf. CS II, 16.

13 This is, to use later terminology, the catuṣkoṭyutpādapratiṣedhamahāhetu (cf. Atiśa, Bodhipathapradīpa 193–196), for which see MK I, 1; *Dvādaśadvāraka II, 1; ŚS 3; CS III, 9; *Madhyamaka-Śālistambasūtra (BST XII, p. 115), quoting MK I, 1 and Jñānasārasamuccaya 28. See also MK I, 7 (compare Nyāyasūtra IV, I, 44 and Laṅkāvatārasūtra II, 22).

14 Here sthitiyukta = sat. The verse corresponds to MK VII, 27 (cf. ibid., 20). In pādas c and d the translators had: nāsato 'sthitiyuktasya vināśa upapadyate ||.

15 This and the following verse (which both lack Tibetan versions) should be compared with MK VII, 30–31. For matam in pāda c (not mataḥ), see e.g. 11, 22.

17 A kāraṇa (= hetu) neither exists previously nor subsequently to a kārya (= phala), let alone simultaneously with its effect. This is demonstrated in MK XX, 7–14. See also RĀ I, 47; ŚS 6.

18 This verse is inspired by the Śālistambasūtra, cited in the Madhyamakāvatāra, p. 97; Pañjikā, p. 579.

19 For parikalpa see the Laṅkāvatārasūtra, *passim* (Suzuki's *Index*, p. 104) and May (1959), p. 65, n. 64. While sadbhūta taken saṁvṛtitaḥ amounts to kriyāyukta (cf. May, op. cit., p. 144, n. 414), paramārthataḥ it indicates anapekṣyasiddha, sasvabhāva, etc. (cf. Akutobhayā *ad* MK II, 24; VV 57; MK XXIV, 38).

20 This verse corresponds to MK XVII.

21 Again this verse is closely related to MK XII, 1 (= *Dvādaśadvāraka X, 1); cf. Saṁyutta II, p. 19. tārkikaiḥ = vaiṣṇavādibhiḥ.

22 For this celebrated stanza see the references given by May (1959), p. 237, n. 840. It is also discussed by La Vallée Poussin, *MCB* III, pp. 380. For siṁhanāda see the note to BS 101.

23 Like MK XIII, 8 (see Kāśyapaparivarta §§ 63–65) and XVII, 30, this verse leaves no doubt about śūnyatāprayojana as presented by Nāgārjuna. See also Candrakīrti's commentary to Catuḥśataka XVI, 7; Madhyamakāvatāra, p. 310. For grāha, see May (1959), p. 190, n. 618.

24 See Pañjikā, p. 488 for this verse, which may be inspired by Lalitavistara XIII, 97–98 (cited ibid., p. 532).

25 According to the ṭīkā, kiṁ cit = dharmādikam. The phrase yathā pūrvaṁ tathā paścāt also occurs in Dharmadhātustava 31; Ratnagotravibhāga I, 51; Samādhirāja XXIV, 5; Aṅguttara I, p. 236. For the thought, see ŚS 70; CS II, 4; and for the conception of sarvadharmasamatā see *Hōbōgirin*, under byōdō. See Siddhi, pp. 757–761 for tathatā according to the Mādhyamikas.

26 Ānimitta (or animitta) is the second vimokṣamukha. Cf. BS 63 ff.; Mahābhārata XII, 190, 11; XII, 191, 7; CPD; Laṅkāvatāra, p. 200; BHSD. For bhāvanā, see especially Madhyamakaratnapradīpa VII (Bhāvanākramādhikāra); *MCB* II, pp. 102–104.

27 The Pañjikā, p. 154 glosses sākalyena with vistarataḥ.

28 This verse forms a dedication of merit, as do the final verses in the other hymns. Cf. also the verse ascribed to Nāgārjuna by Jñānaśrīmitra (Sākārasiddhiśāstra, p. 405): bādhe (for bandhe?) nāmanimittānām ākārasya ca na kṣatiḥ . . .

Acintyastava (CS III)

1 For the form naiḥsvābhāvya, see VV 17 with editorial note. The epithet acintya is confined to five things; see Traité, pp. 1639, 1983. Pāda d also occurs at v. 59, which equals Śatapañcāśatka 151.

2 The Buddha's motivation for delivering his dharmadeśanā (= pudgaladharmanairātmya) to Bodhisattvas (dhīmat) is karuṇā. See CS I, 1–3 and the accompanying notes, as well as the initial stanza of the Mahāyānaviṁśikā: avācyo vācakair dharmaḥ kṛpayā yena deśitaḥ | namo 'cintyaprabhavāya buddhāyāsaṅgabuddhaye ||.

3 Perhaps the same canonical allusion as in CS I, 9; cf. YṢ 18–19; Stutyatītastava 5: gang zhig rkyen las de ma mchis || dngos rnams rkyen las ji ltar skye || de skad mkhas pa khyod gsungs pas | spros pa rnams ni bcad pa lags ||.

4 As is often true, bhava here refers to the five skandhas. See MK XXVI, 8. For the various examples see the references at the note to CS I, 3, above.

5 The commentary takes tad° (in pāda d) as referring to māyādi, but surely the context requires that it refers to skandha. Cf. BV 24.

6 For kṛtaka, see MK XV, 1-2. On sāṁvṛta, see May (1959), p. 226, n. 777.

7 Sarvam, like viśvam in v. 6, refers to sarve dharmāḥ; i.e., the skandhas, the āyatanas, and the dhātus. See YṢ 30; BV 66; Traité, p. 1748; also Tattvasaṁgrahapañjikā, p. 14; May, op. cit., p. 206, n. 689 (references); Schayer, *Contributions . . .*, p. 41, note. Nāgārjuna's point is that one cannot say 'asti' about something which is pratītyasamutpanna; cf. YṢ 37; ŚS 71. For yat kiṁcit, see May, op. cit., p. 62, n. 51 (references). The form bālalāpana is probably a metrical substitute for the common bālollāpana (see references at Traité, p. 1195, n. 2) but bālapralāpa (Prasannapadā, p. 12), bālopalāpana (Ālokamālā 177), and bālālāpana (Daśabhūmika, p. 43) also occur. For riktamuṣṭi, see Traité, loc. cit.; Upāliparipṛcchā, p. 131, n. 12; Suvikrāntavikrāmiparipṛcchā, p. 110; most recently see CPD II, p. 476, under upalāpanā. Bālalāpana is also found in Majjhima II, p. 261 (not in PED).

8 Other refutations of kālatraya (the three times) found in MK XIX; ŚS 29; BV 31; Traité, pp. 1691-1996. Utpitsu = anāgata (as in the Madhyamakahṛdayakārikā III, 161).

9 In other words: nothing whatsoever (cf. the catuṣkoṭyutpādapratiṣedhamahāhetu, referred to above in the note on CS I, 13) arises from anything whatsoever (for the vajrakaṇamahāhetu, see ibid. and Pañjikā to Bodhipathapradīpa 197-200). For pāda c see also the note to CS I, 13 and Madhyamakahṛdayakārikā III, 241-242.

10 The commentary reads ajātena (. . . kena? ajātena, anutpannena . . .), which is most unlikely. See the Tibetan, as well as the verse quoted by Haribhadra (in the Āloka, p. 39): ajātasya svabhāvena śāśvatocchedatā kutaḥ . . . . Svabhāvābhāvasiddhyaiva . . . corresponds to kutaḥ svabhāvasyābhāve . . . , MK XV, 3.

11 For pārāvāra in this sense, see Prasannapadā, pp. 101, 264, 458; Mahāyānaviṁśikā 2: pārāvāram ivotpannāḥ svabhāvena pratītyajāḥ (against Tucci's reading . . . na cotpannāḥ . . .). Svatva in pādas a and b ~ rang gi bdag nyid (ŚS 53).

12 For this and the next verse see RĀ I, 48-49 (cf. Prasannapadā, p. 10, n. 4; Madhyamakāvatāra, p. 227). This standpoint is related to the Viśeṣāvaśyakabhāṣya, p. 337-338: . . . bhavato 'bhiprāyo yathā na svataḥ, na parataḥ, nobhayataḥ, na cānyataḥ siddhiḥ sambhāvyate bhāvānām, hrasvadīrghādivyapadeśavat; iha na

hrasvaṁ svataḥ sidhyati dīrghāpekṣatvāt; na parataḥ, parasiddhyabhāvāt; nobhayataḥ, tabudhayābhāvat; na cānyato 'napekṣatvāt . . .

14 Eka/aneka, etc. are pratītyasamutpanna. Cf. ŚS 7. On saṁkleśa-vyavadāna, see Siddhi, pp. 214–220.

15 See MK XV, 3 for the interpretation: svabhāvaḥ parabhāvasya parabhāvo hi kathyate I.

16 The compound bhāvagrahagrahāveśa also occurs in a verse quoted in the Subhāṣitasaṁgraha (ed. Bendall), p. 388. The form bhāvagrāha° would be more correct (cf. May, op. cit., p. 190, n. 618) but it is poorly supported textually. However, cf. Gauḍapādīyakārikā II, 29; III, 32, 38; IV, 82, 84 (graha for grāha). Here paratantra, like sarva in 15b, signifies a relative entity, something dependent conceived as a whole.

·17 An allusion to an often cited verse from the Ratnameghasūtra; see Prasannapadā, p. 225; May, op. cit., p. 177, n. 572. See also Mahāyānaviṁśikā 1: svabhāvena na cotpannā nirvṛtāś ca na tattvataḥ I yathākāśaṁ tathā buddhāḥ sattvāś caivaikalakṣaṇāḥ II.

18 See CS I, 3; ŚS 6; Catuḥśataka XIII, 25. The author above all has Saṁyutta III, p. 142 in mind; see Traité, p. 358; BV 12–13.

19 This is an echo of Laṅkāvatāra III, 36; X, 136. Cf. also YṢ 3.

20 I have not traced the source of this important verse. For jaḍa, see SS 231b.

21 Perhaps the same canonical allusion as MK XVII, 28 avidyānivṛto jantus tṛṣṇāsaṁyojanaś ca saḥ . . . It is quoted *in extenso* in Jñānaprasthāna I, 5, 9.

22 Similarly MK XV, 10; YṢ 1. Dharmo 'yam, or saddharmo 'yam refers to the Buddha's dharmadeśanā; i.e. pratītyasamutpāda or śūnyatā. See RĀ I, 25 ff.; II, 16–18; MK XXIV, 12; XXV, 24; XXVI, 30.

23 Cf. Prasannapadā, p. 374: . . . paramārthasatyaṁ katamat? yatra jñānasyāpy apracāraḥ kaḥ punar vādo 'kṣarāṇām . . . . Quoted in Prajñāpradīpa (234a7) from Akṣayamatinirdeśasūtra; also in the Prajñāpradīpaṭīkā, (Za, 101a4) and the Satyadvaya-vibhaṅgavṛtti (Sa, 5a). The notion of catuṣkoṭi (or catuṣprakāra; cf. RĀ II, 15) has been widely discussed. See recently D.S. Ruegg, "The Uses of the Four Positions of the Catuṣkoṭi and the Problem of the Description of Reality in Mahāyāna Buddhism," *JIP* V, pp. 1–71.

24 Cf. the references listed in the note to CS I, 3.

25 This verse, which does not occur in the Tibetan, is quoted in the Pañjikā, p. 573 (pādas c and d). It is inspired by Samādhirāja IX, 17 (cited in the Prasannapadā, p. 178; Caryāgīti, p. 217; Tattvasārasaṁgraha 89b7, etc.)

26 MK XX is devoted to a critique of saṁbhava-vibhava. See in particular v. 11: dṛśyate saṁbhavaś caiva mohād vibhava eva ca, which is clearly modeled on Laṅkāvatāra X, 37: saṁbhavaṁ vibhavaṁ caiva mohāt paśyanti bāliśāḥ I na saṁbhavaṁ na vibhavaṁ prajñāyukto vipaśyati II.

27 This and the following verse would seem to allude to some such passage as that from the Aṣṭasāhasrikā cited in Prasannapadā, pp. 449–450. Regarding advaya in Mahāyāna in general, see the Vimalakīrtinirdeśasūtra, pp. 301–318.

29 For the māyāgaja, see RĀ II, 10–13; VS '2'; *MCB* II, p. 48.

31 For this see Traité, pp. 1260–1261 and the Vajracchedikā § 3: . . . na kaś cit sattvaḥ parinirvāpito bhavati. tat kasya hetoḥ? sacet . . . bodhisattvasya sattvasaṁjñā pravarteta, na sa bodhisattva iti vaktavyaḥ. Cf. CS II, 9, etc.

33 For the māyākāra, see Saṁdhinirmocanasūtra, p. 170; Mahāyānaviṁśikā 17–18.

34 For a refutation of kāraka, see BV 6–9; *Dvādaśadvāraka X; *WZKSO* XII–XIII, pp. 85–100; MK VIII; Bhāvanākrama I, pp. 200–201.

35 This and the following allude to the Bhavasaṁkrāntisūtra (ed. N.A. Śāstrī), pp. 5–6. See also Āloka, pp. 44, 685. For pādas c and d cf. Laṅkāvatāra III, 78: abhidhānavinirmuktam abhidheyaṁ na lakṣyate II.

36 Laṅkāvatāra X, 10: asārakā ime dharmā manyanāyāḥ samutthitāḥ I sāpy atra manyanā śūnyā yayā śūnyeti manyate II. Cf. MK XXII, 11; Stutyatītastava 9: lta ba thams cad spang ba'i phyir I I mgon po khyod kyis stong pa gsungs I I de yang yongs su brtags pa ste I I dngos su mgon po khyod mi bzhed II.

37 This and the following verses treat paramārtha (tattva) and its paryāyas: advaya, anālaya, avyakta, etc.

38 pāda d also in v. 1, above. For anālaya, see YṢ 1; CS IV, 1.

39 On ākāśa, see BV 46. CS IV, 1: vākpathātītagocaram; see also v. 23.

40 See CS I, 22. On saddharma, see note to v. 22, above. On tathāgata see MK XXII, 16: tathāgato niḥsvabhāvo . . . .

41 On tattva, etc. see Ramanan (1966), pp. 251–275; Traité, pp. 2181–2201. Pāda d also occurs in Madhyamakahṛdayakārikā III, 267; Sākārasiddhiśāstra, p. 433. The distinction between prajñaptisat and dravyasat already occurs in Laṅkāvatāra III, 27. See also May, op. cit., p. 159, n. 489.

42 On the relationship between dharma- and sattvadhātu see D.S. Ruegg (1971), pp. 459–461, with references; also MK XXII, 16. For samatā, see Vimalakīrtinirdeśa, p. 474 (references).

43 On sarvadharmaśūnyatā, see Traité, pp. 2015 ff.; BV 57–58.

44 This and the following three verses show the relationship between svabhāvatraya (as expounded in the Laṅkāvatāra [see this term in Suzuki's *Index*]) and satyadvaya according to Nāgārjuna. Paramārthataḥ they are śūnya (see BV 28) but saṁvṛtitaḥ, paramārtha (that is, pariniṣpannasvabhāva = prakṛti, tattva, etc.) is akṛtrima, etc. (cf. MK XV, 2) and paratantra; that is, saṁvṛti exists, whereas parikalpita does not.

45 See above, vv. 37–42, and Laṅkāvatāra II, 189: nāsti vai kalpito bhāvaḥ paratantraś ca vidyate . . . . The interpretation of this verse was to become the starting-point of a long controversy between Mādhyamikas, who held that paratantrasvabhāva exists only saṁvṛtitaḥ, not paramārthataḥ, and Yogācāras, who held that paratantra exists (as the Laṅkāvatāra itself states). See Prajñāpradīpa 305b1; Dharmapāla, Taishō 1571, 247b; Pañcaskandhaprakaraṇa, p. 22; Śūnyatāsaptativṛtti 320b4. Also discussed by Avalokitavrata, Jñānagarbha, Śāntarakṣita, and Kamalaśīla.

46 Here the term uccheda found in pāda d corresponds to apavāda (see the Laṅkāvatāra, loc. cit., pāda c). Negation is understood similarly saṁvṛtitaḥ, RĀ I, 72: vināśāt pratipakṣād vā syād astitvasya nāstitā . . . .

47 This is paramārthataḥ. Cf. MK XV, 10; XVII, 11, etc. For marīci, see RĀ I, 52–56; Traité, p. 363.

48 The mṛgatṛṣṇā is very common in the Laṅkāvatāra. See e.g. III, 151 for an explanation.

49 That is, the acceptance (abhyupagama, abhiniveśa) of dravya, (i.e. bhāva; cf. ŚS 21; YṢ 46–47; MK XXI, 14) invariably entails śāśvatocchedagrāha (references in May, op. cit., p. 213, n. 720), which again ramifies itself in various ātmalokadṛṣṭi (ibid., p. 276, n. 1015). See also supra, v. 22.

50 See BV 39, 45; YṢ 1; RĀ I, 93–97; vv. 37 ff. above.

51 Cf. CS I, 23 and v. 22 above.

52 For bhāvagraha, see vv. 16, 49 above. This verse leaves no doubt regarding Nāgārjuna's conception of tattva and the purpose of teaching it. Cf. ŚS 68–69, 73; VV 22; YṢ 1; BV 48–49.

53 For dharmayajña, see Vimalakīrtinirdeśasūtra, pp. 212–216. For niṣkapāṭa, see BHSD, p. 167 (under kapāṭa); Bodhicaryāvatāra VI, 101 (Tibetan sgo 'phar). For nirargala (or nirargaḍa), often said about yajña (the Tibetan is usually srungs ma med pa'i mchod sbyin), see BHSD, p. 299; CPD, under aggaḷa.

54 For the terrifying siṁhanāda, see BS 101; CS I, 22; BV 52.

55 For dharmabherī and śaṅkha, also clichés, see Suvarṇabhāsottamasūtra V, 22–23; Saddharmapuṇḍarīka VII, 42; Aṣṭasāhasrikā, p. 327.

56 See RĀ I, 62 for dharmayautuka (or -yautaka?). Cf. Prasannapadā, p. 275 (read khud pa in n. 7 for khyud pa; cf. Madhyamakāvatāra, p. 184). Pāda b also occurs in RĀ I, 62; II, 9; MK XVIII, 11. For nītārtha, see Prasannapadā, pp. 43–44; cf. ibid., p. 276.

57 This verse also seems to refer to the Samādhirāja and to the Akṣayamatinirdeśa, v. 56. See also Madhyamakāvatāra, p. 200; Wayman (1978), pp. 178–180; May, op. cit., p. 298, n. 1089 (references).

58 An allusion to the usual 'etymology' of pāramitā (pāram ita); cf. Traité, p. 1058 (references); final verse of the Mahāyānaviṁśikā; Har Dayal, op. cit., p. 165. As in the Mūlamadhyamakakārikā, the main abhidheya of this hymn has been prajñā, the foremost pāramitā. See BS 5–7.

59 A puṇyapariṇāmanā (dedication of merit).

Bodhicittavivaraṇa

This regrettably neglected text comprises 112 stanzas (anuṣṭubh) introduced by a brief prologue in prose. It has sometimes been grouped as a tantric work,[45] but a glance at its contents shows how unwarranted such a classification is.

The Bodhicittavivaraṇa is never mentioned or cited by Buddhapālita or Candrakīrti. On the other hand it forms one of the basic authorities for Bhavya in his most mature work, the Ratnapradīpa.[46] It is never quoted in his earlier works, the Tarkajvālā, Prajñāpradīpa, and [*Kara-]talaratna. Among other 'good' authors citing the Bodhicittavivaraṇa are especially Asvabhāva and Śāntarakṣita.[47] I have also come across scores of quotations by other commentators; fortunately several of these are in Sanskrit.[48] It is my general impression that the Yuktiṣaṣṭikā, Catuḥstava, and Bodhicittavivaraṇa are the most frequently quoted among all works ascribed to Nāgārjuna in later Indian literature.

The style of the Bodhicittavivaraṇa is similar to that of the Yuktiṣaṣṭikā, Ratnāvalī, and Catuḥstava. From a historical point of view the most significant feature of this text is its extensive critique of Vijñānavāda; i.e. Buddhist idealism as testified in the Laṅkāvatārasūtra.[49] Having seen how vehemently Nāgārjuna attacks any kind of acceptance of svabhāva, one would also expect him to have criticized those who might have thought themselves justified in maintaining the absolute existence of vijñāna, or citta. But in the texts dealt with hitherto this happens only incidentally.[50] The Bodhicittavivaraṇa provides us with the missing link.

None of Nāgārjuna's other works exhibit such a well-balanced and coherent structure as the Bodhicittavivaraṇa. This is to some extent a natural consequence of the fact that the theme is at once simple and comprehensive: bodhicitta. It has a relative aspect consisting in the desire (prārthanā) for the bodhi of all living beings,[51] and an absolute consisting in the unlimited cognition of śūnyatā, or bodhi.[52] The Bodhicittavivaraṇa thus provides us with a compendium of the practice and theory of

Mahāyāna addressed to Bodhisattvas, gṛhasthas as well as pravrajitas. It may indeed be said to be nothing but a vivaraṇa of the celebrated formula of RĀ IV, 96: śūnyatākaruṇāgarbham ekeṣāṁ bodhisādhanam.

Sanskrit fragments apart, only two Tibetan versions of the Bodhicittavivaraṇa are at our disposal.[53] I have identified these in the section on sources and variants in Part I, using the abbreviations A, B, and C. B, as we would expect from the names of the revisors, is an excellent piece of work, and it forms the basis of my edition. Throughout I have carefully compared A and C. In a few cases A has proved invaluable, (for example, for verse 16, left out in B due to haplography (homoearcton).[54] C is a commentary of high standard. It quotes pratīkas from all the 112 stanzas and explains all debatable points exhaustively. In a few cases, like A, it permits us to emend corruptions in B. I have, however, only registered variants in A and C when they affect the sense in such a way that it may possibly be more authentic than the one transmitted by B.[55]

I present here a synopsis of the text, followed by notes on the individual verses.

Synopsis

Prologue

The theme of this treatise is bodhicitta. Saṁvṛtitaḥ it is a yearning for the bodhi of all living beings; paramārthataḥ it is the realization of śūnyatā; i.e., bodhi.[56]

Content

The significance of developing bodhicitta. (1–3)

Refutation of the belief in an ātman, a permanent soul and a creator, as held by tīrthikas. (4–9)

Refutation of the existence of the skandhas, as held by the Śrāvakas. (10–25)

Refutation of the fundamentals of the Vijñānavāda: trisvabhāva, svasaṁvedanā, āśrayaparivṛtti, and ālayavijñāna. In reality, vijñāna is dependent, momentary, illusory, and empty. (26–56)

All internal and external dharmas are pratītyasamutpanna, or śūnya. To understand this is to realize the absolute bodhicitta, or liberation from the bonds of karma due to the kleśas. (57–72)

A Bodhisattva who has thus become a Buddha is motivated by karuṇā (that is, by the power of his previous praṇidhānas) to apply all possible means (= upāyakauśalya) in order to rescue all beings from samsara. (73–104)

Conclusion

The reader is encouraged to produce bodhicitta. (105–111)

A final dedication of merit. (112)

Notes on the Verses

1 I take bdag nyid dngos (or bdag nyid sku in A and C) as translating ātmabhāva, for which cf. May, op. cit., p. 278, n. 1017. In pāda b, A reads Śrī Vajradhara (dpal ldan rdo rje 'chang), whereas C speaks of rdo rje sems dpa'i sku (which it identifies with mahāmudrā, hence the epithet śrī, which may also be explained lha'i rigs phun sum tshogs pa dang ldan pa'i phyir . . . etc. in accord with the Tantra [see 461a5–8]) without showing any sign of the plural. If B transmits the authentic reading I take this to indicate Bodhisattvas such as Samantabhadra, mentioned in BV 90, 111. For bhava see C 461b2: de la srid pa ni nye bar len gyi phung po lnga'i rang bzhin 'dod pa dang | gzugs dang gzugs med pa'i srid pa ste | 'byung zhing 'gyur ba'i phyir ro ||. Cf. MK XXVI, 8.

2 The genitive kyi (which C 462a2 also has) should be retained and construed with bzhed. It reflects *buddhānām . . . mata or iṣṭa.

3 C 462a3 ff. lists the eight arthākāra of mahākaruṇā, explained in the Traité, p. 1707.

4–5 One cannot conceive ātman (skandhas) as eka or anya. MK XVIII; Schayer (1931) , p. 90, n. 60.

6 A kāraka who is nitya is impossible, not only because there is no ātman (see above) but also because as a dharmin related to dharmas he would have to be anitya like them. See vv. 7–9. See also CS III, 34 with references in the note.

7–8 A creation all at once is against experience; a gradual one is incompatible with the notion of a creator's omnipotence (śakti/sāmarthya). Cf. Siddhi, p. 30; Pramāṇavārttika I, 9 ff. This may be the earliest occurrence of this celebrated argument.

9 Being included among 'all things' a creator (C 463b7: dbang phyug la sogs pa) must also be anitya.

10 This refers to the Śrāvakas (BS 25–26 etc.). As in its canonical usage the term loko 'yam or ayaṁ loka occasionally has a somewhat pejorative tone.

11~ The Śrāvakas only endorse pudgalanairātmya, but by quoting a celebrated passage from their āgama (Saṁyutta III, p. 142; Sanskrit version in Prasannapadā, p. 41; cf. also Traité, p. 370) Nāgārjuna shows that even here we find evidence of the Buddha's teaching of dharmanairātmya. (Cf. CS I, 3 with references in the note.) See the discussion of Mahāyāna Buddhism in the Concluding Essay, below.

14 The following (vv. 14–24) constitutes a refutation of rūpa (i.e., upādāyarūpa [cf. Traité, p. 782] or bhautika), for which see CS I, 5 with references in the notes.

15 Cf. e.g. MK III–V.

16~ A refutation of anu/paramāṇu; Traité, p. 725; Bhāvanākrama I, pp. 20–22; May (1959), p. 54, n. 15 (references). This is sūkṣmarūpa.

19~ A refutation of sthūlarūpa. Cf. Traité, p. 733, which also cites the Sanskrit verse from the Sarvadarśanasaṁgraha. For further references consult Mimaki (1976), p. 309, n. 432. Similarly ŚS 60; Catuḥśataka VIII, 2; Saundarananda XIII, 52.

21 Though things can be efficacious, they are nevertheless śūnya. See the svavṛtti *ad* VV 22. For svapnopaghāta, see Viṁśatikā 4.

22 The following concludes that there is no bāhyārtha. Compare Mahāyānaviṁśikā 19: utpādo hi vikalpo 'yam artho bāhyo na vidyate ||. See also Laṅkāvatāra X, 154–155. But as we shall see the author takes great pains to show that the cittamātratā of the Laṅkāvatāra (see Suzuki's *Index*, p. 69) should be taken neyārtha; i.e. nairātmyāvatārataḥ.

24 Note that "dans les textes des Śrāvakas, on ne recontre jamais l'exemple de la ville de Gandharva" (Traité, p. 370) ; cf. also CS III, 5; RĀ II, 12–13 (cittamohana).

25 For the Sanskrit, see the Jñānaśrīmitranibandhāvalī, p. 488 (with the variant reading citra°).

26 The following (vv. 26–45) is a refutation of those who interpret cittamātratā, especially as presented in the Laṅkāvatāra, as nītārtha.

27 The Sanskrit can be found in the Subhāṣitasaṁgraha (ed. Bendall), p. 20; Jñānaśrīmitra, loc. cit. (with tattrāsa° for uttrāsa°). Cf. Śikṣāsamuccaya, p. 263; Prasannapadā, p. 264, n. 2.

28 C 476b7: de la kun brtags ni gzung 'dzin te I phyi nang brtags pa tsam ni yin la rang bzhin med pa'i phyir ro I I gzhan dbang ni rtog pa'i rang bzhin te I rgyu rkyen gzhan dbang byas pa'i phyir ro I I yongs su grub pa ni gzung 'dzin gyi rnam par rtogs pa med pas so I I mi 'gyur bar yongs su gnas pa'i phyir ro II. For svabhāvatraya, see Laṅkāvatāra, pp. 127–133; CS III, 44; Siddhi, pp. 514–561. Nāgārjuna's position is that of Laṅkāvatāra II, 198.

29 This seems to allude to the verse quoted above as being from the 'Guhyasamāja'; now, however, it is a question of Bodhisattvas devoted to Mahāyāna! On the samatā of all dharmas, see e.g. Prasannapadā, p. 374.

30 For āśrayaparāvṛtti (presented as here in the Laṅkāvatārasūtra) or āśrayaparivṛtti, see L. Schmithausen (1969), pp. 90–104. For the term svapratyātmagatigocara, see Suzuki's *Index*, p. 193.

31 Thus the author refutes this notion ekaprahāreṇa!

32 C 468b7: tshogs drug gi rnam par shes pa dang I nyon mongs pa can gyi yid ji ltar rnam pa dang dmigs pa dang snang ba de ltar kun gzhi ma yin te phyi rol gyi spyod yul la yongs su spyod mi nus pa'i phyir ro I I des na ngo bo nyid bdag med rnam shes te don dam par rang bzhin med pa'i phyir ro II.

33 For this comparison, see Laṅkāvatāra X, 14.

35 Ibid., X, 57–59.

37 One should not speak of that which cannot be spoken of. But here the author is not being quite fair; cf. MK XXII, 11.

38 Recalls Dhammapada XII, 2.

39 Cf. CS III, 50. Though B and A have rig bya / rig byed this surely refers to vedanāskandha (as v. 40 refers to saṁjñāskandha). Thus C469b7 is correct in having tshor bya / tshor ba. Cf. CS I, 6; ŚS 55.

40 Ibid., I, 7; III, 35 (with references in the notes).

41 Cf. ŚS 51.

42 citta (= manas = vijñāna) is — saṁvṛtitaḥ — arūpin. Thus it cannot be established by means of rūpa.

43 For the buddhacakṣus see CS II, 2: na ca nāma tvayā kiṁ cid dṛṣṭaṁ bauddhena cakṣuṣā I.

44 Cf. e.g. MK V, 7; XV, 4; May, op. cit., p. 92, n. 204. (śūnyatā = niḥsvabhāvatā = tattva = nirvikalpa, etc.)

45 Sanskrit in the Pañjikā, p. 406. Cf. CS II, 2: na boddhā na ca boddhavyam astīha paramārthataḥ I.

46 Sanskrit ibid., p. 421, with asaṁskṛtam in b (thus also C 471a8), which I have corrected to asaṁsthitam in accord with A (gnas pa med) and B (yod gyur ma yin). In pāda b, the Sanskrit may have read avākpatham (cf. CS IV, 1, etc.).

48 That is, śūnyatā destroys those dṛṣṭis which give rise to kleśa, karma, and punarbhava. Cf. MK XVIII, 5; YṢ 46–48; CS I, 23.

49 C 472a3 refers to MK XIII, 8. For bdag nyid dman pa, cf. alpabuddhi (MK V, 8), mandamedhas (MK XXIV, 11); avipaścit (RĀ II, 19). The bdag nyid chen po is to the contrary: YṢ 50, 54.

50 All vikalpas are kṣaṇika; i.e., śūnya. Cf. v. 53. This is of course only saṁvṛtitaḥ; cf. RĀ I, 66–70.

52 The Sanskrit is found in the Caryāgīti (ed. Kværne), p. 246 with °śatravaḥ, which I have emended in accord with A's rgol ba, B's smra ba and C's (dngos por) smra ba (472b5). For śūnyatāsiṁhanāda, see CS I, 22 and BS 101 with the accompanying note.

56 For this axiom see MK XV, 7–8.

57 Sanskrit in the Advayavajrasaṁgraha (ed. Śāstrī), p. 42.

58 The madhyamā pratipad avoids the extremes of uccheda and śāśvata. MK XV, 10; XVII, 21; CS III, 49.

59~ As I have shown in *WZKS* XXVI (1982), these verses are quite closely related to the Pratītyasamutpādahṛdayakārikā. See also the Daśabhūmika (ed. Rahder), p. 50, which reduces avidyā, tṛṣṇā, and upādāna to kleśavartman, saṁskāra and bhava to karmavartman, and the remaining seven aṅgas to duḥkhavartman. As C observes (473b7), avidyā, saṁskāra, tṛṣṇā, upādāna, and bhava may also be regarded as hetu, whereas the remaining aṅgas are phala. Similarly in the small treatise Dharmadhātugarbhavivaraṇa ascribed to Nāgārjuna (see *IHQ* XXXIII, pp. 246–249); cf. PK 4. See also Traité, pp. 349–351. For the final pādas of 63, see CS I, 8; Saṁyutta II, pp. 75–76; Daśabhūmika, p. 49.

64 As the previous verses treated ādhyātmikapratītyasamutpāda—saṁvṛtitaḥ, of course—this verse refers to bāhyapratītyasamutpāda, presumably as treated in the Śālistambasūtra (quoted in the Pañjikā, pp. 577–579), though the bherīśabda (cf. Prasannapadā, p. 72) does not figure here.

65 In the saṁsāramaṇḍala any 'hetu' is also 'phala' and vice versa. Thus it is hetusvabhāvaśūnya. Cf. RĀ I, 36, 47.

66 Cf. RĀ IV, 86: anutpādo mahāyāne pareṣām śūnyatā kṣayaḥ |. For sarve dharmāḥ (= sarvam), see references in May, op. cit., p. 206, n. 689; see also YṢ 30.

67 Cf. MK XXIV, 8–10.

68 Here I understand saṁvṛti as sarve dharmāḥ (cf. Madhyamakahṛdayakārikā III, 13; also CS III, 44, with which compare Laṅkāvatāra II, 187). I take śūnyatā to equal pratītyasamutpāda (cf. MK XXIV, 18); i.e. pratītyasamutpanna (CS III, 44).

69 For the interpretation of this verse, see MK XVII, 26: karma kleśātmakam, and ibid., XVIII, 5: karmakleśā vikalpataḥ. For citta (= vikalpa), cf. Laṅkāvatāra III, 38: cittena cīyate karma. Again, citta itself is the outcome of previous karma (vāsanā) due to kleśa born from vikalpa (citta), etc. from time without beginning.

70 By thus destroying vikalpa (= citta, avidyā, etc.) by means of śūnyatā, the result is karmakleśakṣayān mokṣaḥ (MK XVIII, 5).

71 For other synonyms of the absolute, see CS I, 27; III, 37–41, 52; MK XVIII, 9; XXV, 3; ŚS 24.

72 Cf. YṢ 31.

73 What follows (vv. 74–104) is mainly devoted to an exposition of the tathyasaṁvṛtibodhicitta (C 476a8) and only calls for a few notes. In general we find here the same ideal of karuṇā as in the Ratnāvalī, *Bodhisaṁbhāra[ka], and Śūnyatāsaptati.

77 On these gods, see RĀ I, 24; SL 69; Traité, pp. 137 ff.

81 C 477b8: sangs rgyas dang byang chub sems dpa' zag pa med pa'i dge ba'i rtsa ba'i las kyi rnam par smin pa'i sems can no ||. The vipāka specific to Buddhas and Bodhisattvas is the kāyadvaya. Cf. BS 3 and references in the notes.

83 The Śrāvakas' pratisaṁkhyānirodha is inferior to the anuttarā samyaksaṁbodhi of the Buddhas. Cf. Vimalakīrtinirdeśa, p. 422.

86 See BS 164 and references in the notes.

91 For pāda a cf. CS I, 1 with accompanying note. On the Twelve Acts of a Buddha see e.g. CS II, 23; Dvādaśakāranayastotra (Pek. ed. 2026); Bu ston I, p. 133 (the verse cited by Bu ston as being from the Ratnāvalī is actually BV 91–92).

96 On puṇyajñānasaṁbhāra see RĀ III and the Bodhisaṁbhāra[ka].

97 See v. 81 above.

98~ The Sanskrit is quoted in Sarvadarśanasaṁgraha (ed. Abhyankar), p. 45 with cobha° in 99b and bhinnā hi in 99c. Also in Bhāmatī (ed. Sastri), p. 414 with kila in 98d. For the idea see MK XVIII, 8; RĀ II, 35.

100 For dhāraṇī, see Traité, pp. 1854 ff. I have not traced the Sūtra.

101 See v. 58 above.

102 Cf. BS 75 and references in the accompanying note, and G.M. Nagao in L.S. Kawamura (ed.), *The Bodhisattva Doctrine in Buddhism*, Waterloo, Ontario, 1981, pp. 61–79.

105~ For similar bodhicittānuśaṁsā, see BS 57 and Bodhicaryāvatāra I.

110 In pāda a, A and C apparently read *saṁvaro (sdom pa) against B's *saṁsāre ('khor bar).

111 This refers to Samantabhadra's celebrated praṇidhānas. For the Bhadracaryāpraṇidhāna (or Bhadracarīpraṇidhānarāja), see *Encyclopedia of Buddhism* II, pp. 632–638. I do not think that the commentary ascribed to Nāgārjuna (Pek. ed. 5512) is authentic. For a modern edition of the verses see J.P. Asmussen, *The Khotanese Bhadracaryādeśanā*, Copenhagen, 1961. See also SS 247b.

112 The final verse forms a pariṇāmanā. Cf. YṢ 60; CS III, 59; BS 165, etc. for other such dedications of merit.

Mūlamadhyamakakārikā

As indicated by its very title, ("The fundamental verses on the Middle [Way], called 'Wisdom'"),[57] by the large number of important commentaries by renowned teachers, and by its very thorough and radical treatment of the cardinal concepts (dharmas) of Buddhist systematic soteriology (Abhidharma), the Mūlamadhyamakakārikā may suitably be labelled the chief among Nāgārjuna's dialectical works.[58]

For a correct understanding of the Mūlamadhyamakakārikā three main issues require clarification: the subject-matter and composition of the work, its aim, and the method employed for achieving that aim.

The chart given on the next page reviews the twenty-seven chapters (448 verses) of the Sanskrit text as it has been handed down to us,[59] compared with the recensions now only available within the body of four Indian commentaries transmitted in Tibetan versions.[60] Each prakaraṇa forms a critical examination (parīkṣā) of a specific subject.

Though it remains uncertain whether these titles are authentic, they are in any case both ancient and appropriate.[61] As to the wording of the 448 verses, it is, if not identical, at least very close to the text as it left the hand of its author (or his scribe).[62]

Each chapter is mainly concerned with (but by no means strictly confined to) one of these basic topics:[63]

Specific Buddhist concepts as found in the Canon or the Abhidharma: I, III–V, VII, XVII, XXIII–XXVII.

Various aspects of the belief in the existence of ātman: VIII–X, XII, XVI, XVIII, XXII.

Common-sense notions underlying all realistic ('positivistic') views concerning dharmas and ātman: II, VI, XI, XIII–XV, XIX–XXI.

The scope of Nāgārjuna's criticism is not to disavow the practical value of traditional Buddhist concepts but to demonstrate that the right attitude toward them is one of pragmatic relativism rather than stubborn

Chapters of the Mūlamadhyamakakārikā

Chapter	*Topic*		*Verses*
I	pratyaya	conditions	16
II	gatāgatagamyamāna	change or movement	25
III	āyatana	the sense-fields	9
IV	skandha	the aggregates	9
V	dhātu	the elements	8
VI	rāgarakta	affection and the [person] affected	10
VII	utpādasthitibhaṅga	origination, duration, and decay	34
VIII	karmakāraka	action and agent	13
IX	upādātrupādāna	grasper and grasping	12
X	agnīndhana	fire and fuel	16
XI	saṁsāra	samsara	8
XII	duḥkha	suffering	10
XIII	tattva	the real	8
XIV	saṁsarga	combination	8
XV	bhāvābhāva	being and non-being	11
XVI	bandhanamokṣa	bondage and release	10
XVII	karmaphala	action and its results	33
XVIII	ātmadharma	the self and phenomena	12
XIX	kāla	time	6
XX	hetuphala	cause and effect	24
XXI	saṁbhavavibhava	coming to be and passing away	21
XXII	Tathāgata	the Buddha	16
XXIII	viparyāsa	the perverted views	20
XXIV	āryasatya	the noble truths	40
XXV	nirvāṇa	nirvana	24
XXVI	dvādaśāṅga	the twelve spokes	12
XXVII	dṛṣṭi	dogmas	30

dogmatic absolutism.[64] He wants to reform, not to reject Buddhist traditions.[65]

The procedure adopted for this purpose—as Nāgārjuna informs us from time to time in the text itself[66]—takes as its starting point the relentless demand for own-being (svabhāva).[67] To be real (sat) implies being permanent (nitya), independent (nirapekṣa), numerically one (eka), and self-created (svayaṁkṛta). However, neither experience nor logic warrants our assumption of the existence of real entities (bhāva). Hence Nāgārjuna can readily show the absurdities implicit (prasaṅga) in all the claims put forward by a 'realistic' point of view. Moreover, since positive existence is unfounded, non-existence (abhāva)—the negation or the destruction of existence (bhāva)[68]—is also unfounded. Thus Nāgārjuna proceeds along the middle way (madhyamā pratipad) empty of extremes towards his intangible goal: the non-origination of all phenomena.[69]

Yuktiṣaṣṭikā

The Yuktiṣaṣṭikā, in 61 verses, is one of the most frequently quoted of the texts ascribed to Nāgārjuna, not only by Bhavya,[70] Candrakīrti,[71] and Śāntarakṣita,[72] but especially in the later commentarial literature.[73] Owing to such citations the Tibetan and Chinese translations of this text,[74] now lost in its original language, may be augmented by no less than 12 verses (as far as I have identified them) in Sanskrit.[75]

The style of the Yuktiṣaṣṭikā from time to time recalls that of the Mūlamadhyamakakārikā, Ratnāvalī, and especially the Catuḥstava and Bodhicittavivaraṇa.[76] It is, on the whole, a collection of aphorisms loosely tied together by a subject-matter in common: pratītyasamutpāda.[77] The author sets himself to demonstrate this principle (naya) by means of arguments (yukti) that are occasionally supported by references to āgama (scriptural authority).

The argument is as follows: Reality (tattva) is beyond all ontological and epistemological dualities (dvaya), while the empirical world of origination, destruction, and so forth is illusory — due merely to ignorance (avidyā). This ignorance subjects mankind to the tyranny of passions (kleśa) and endless evil. Buddhism is a practical system solely intended to overcome such kleśas.[78]

Notes on the Verses

I have left the initial stanza of YṢ unnumbered, as is also the case with the first eight pādas of the Mūlamadhyamakakārikā and the final verse of the Vigrahavyāvartanī. All are noteworthy for stressing the fact that to Nāgārjuna the Buddha above all deserves credit for preaching the law of pratītyasamutpāda; i.e. śūnyatā (cf. MK XXIV, 18; RĀ II, 18; CS III, 1).

1 The Sanskrit is cited in the Sekoddeśaṭīkā (ed. Carelli), p. 48. For the thought, see RĀ I, 62. Vibhū-, etc. is very common in the

Laṅkāvatārasūtra; see Suzuki's *Index*, p. 159 (cf. v. 3 of the YṢ and MK XV, 8).

2 Cf. RĀ I, 38, 57; MK XV, 10. Here the word *yukti (rigs pa; compare the title of the text) is used in the sense of 'argument'; i.e., in contrast to āgama. This accords with its use in the Laṅkāvatāra. See Suzuki's *Index*, p. 143.

3 Closely related to Laṅkāvatāra X, 466. If things are real, then nirvana, their annulment, must imply abhāva. But this is untenable; cf. RĀ I, 42; MK XXV, 8.

4 For other definitions of nirvana, see RĀ I, 42; MK XVIII, 7–11; XXV, 9; SL 105, 123; SS 221a (cf. ŚS 73).

5 The Sanskrit has been incorporated in 'Āryadeva's' Cittaviśuddhiprakaraṇa (ed. Patel) 24. For the thought see MK XXV, 19–20. On manyante see Conze (1975), p. 10 ('fancy', etc.)

6 The Sanskrit is found in the Ratnakīrtinibandhāvalī (ed. Thakur), p. 132 (with eva for etan in b). See also Advayavajrasaṁgraha (ed. Śāstrī), p. 42; Caryāgīti (ed. Kværne), p. 102; Śuklavidarśanā (ref. in May, op. cit., p. 237, n. 840); Jñānaśrīmitranibandhāvali (ed. Thakur), pp. 389, 464 (with etan in b), 555.

7 For sat (= Bodhisattva), see RĀ I, 45; also CS I, 2. That which is kṛtaka (saṁskṛta, kṛtima) cannot really be destroyed; cf. CS III, 6 ff.

8 See references to v. 7.

9 Allusion to the two kinds of nirvana: nirupadhiśeṣa°, where kleśa and skandha are abandoned, and sopadhiśeṣa°, where the skandhas still remain. See MK XXV, 1 with commentaries; La Vallée Poussin in *IHQ* IV, pp. 39–45.

10~ In other words: samyagjñāna (i.e. tattvajñāna; cf. CS III, 47) destroys avidyā (cf. MK XXVI, 11). This is true Arhatship (cf. kṛtakṛtya, etc. in PED, p. 77), here and now (PED, p. 320), and there is no difference between nirvana and samsara (see above, v. 5; MK XXV, 20; PK '6').

13~ MK XI, 1: saṁsāro 'navarāgro hi . . . (see references in CPD, under anamatagga). Therefore one can only speak of a bhavacakra (see PK 1–5; RĀ I, 36; II, 7–15) under the law of pratītyasamutpāda, māyāvat.

19 Sanskrit quoted (from Subhāṣitasaṁgraha) in the notes to the Vimalakīrtinirdeśasūtra, p. 41, n. 7. Here the reading svabhāve na yad utpannam has been emended to svabhāvena yan notpannam

(cf. Madhyamakāvatāra, p. 228) in accord with the Tibetan and with a quotation in the Advayavajrasaṁgraha (ed. Śāstrī), p. 25.

20 See vv. 7–8 above.

21 Cf. ŚS 1. Inspired by Laṅkāvatāra II, 138 (often cited with variant readings).

22 The reading *saddharma (for the significance of which see SS 227b and the note to CS III, 22, above) is supported by a quotation of this verse in Kamalaśīla's Madhyamakāloka (Pek. ed. 5287, Sa, fol. 230a: dam pa'i chos).

23 On dṛṣṭi, see vv. 14, 46–53; May, op. cit., p. 277, n. 1015.

24~ On māyā, see references in note to CS I, 3.

28 The same canonical allusion as in v. 35. Cf. Laṅkāvatāra III, 122.

29 Cf. MK XVII, 28 (Saṁyutta II, p. 178 ff., which is also the source of SL 66 ff.).

30 The Sanskrit cited in the Subhāṣitasaṁgraha, p. 385 (with tattve gaveṣiṇā in b, which I have emended in accord with the Tibetan) and in Nyāyaviniścayavivaraṇa (ed. M.K. Jain) II, p. 17–18 (with gaveṣiṇā in b and bhāvagrāho nivartate in d). On sarvam asti (i.e. skandha, āyatana and dhātu), see references in *MCB* V, p. 88, n. 1.

31 A similar verse appears in the Subhāṣitasaṁgraha, p. 46.

32 See MK XVII; ŚS 33–44; and SL, SS, RĀ, *passim*.

33 Cited and identified by La Vallée Poussin in his edition of the Pañjikā, p. 376.

34 Cited in Jñānaśrīmitranibandhāvalī (ed. Thakur), p. 545 and 405 (with variant readings °vijñāne and yānti). The āgama is Dīgha I, p. 223 (cf. RĀ I, 94); also Laṅkāvatāra III, 9. See also CPD, under uparujjhati.

35 The canonical passage is given in the Prasannapadā, p. 41, 237: . . . etad dhi bhikṣavaḥ paramaṁ satyaṁ yad uta amoṣadharma nirvāṇam, sarvasaṁskārāś ca mṛṣā moṣadharmāṇaḥ. See Majjhima III, 245 and Akutobhayā *ad* MK XIII, 1.

36 On Mārakarman, see SS 190b ff.; BS 96 with accompanying note.

37 Cf. v. 29; ŚS 64 (on kalpanā/vikalpa/avidyā); CS III, 21. Candrakīrti glosses loka with nye bar len pa'i phung po rnams (25b). References in CPD II, p. 490.

38 Similarly RĀ I, 98 (cited in Prasannapadā, p. 188; Āloka, p. 66).

39 The Sanskrit is found in the Pañjikā, p. 500. Compare vv. 7–8 and the references in the accompanying notes.

40~ This and the following verses indicate that the Sarvāstivādins lack true analytical insight (prajñā). One must resort to vicāra (cf. parīkṣā in the titles of the chapters of the Mūlamadhyamakakārikā) to see śūnyatā. Otherwise one is captivated by viparyāsa (MK XXIII), giving rise to kleśa, etc. See also ŚS 59–62.

45 Cf. RĀ II, 4: na satyaṁ na mṛṣoditam. (Vajracchedikā § 5)

46~ The Sanskrit of these oft-quoted stanzas can be found in the Āloka, pp. 343–344 (with parijñātasya in 48a for parijñā tasya; compare the Tibetan). For 48 cd see the references to v. 19, and cf. ŚS 21. For 46 in particular, see Dīgha II, p. 58.

49~ This and following verses show some affinity to the Suttanipāta, especially the Aṭṭhakavagga. See L.O. Gómez: "Proto-Mādhyamika in the Pāli Canon," *PEW* XXVI, pp. 137–165.

50 Cf. Suttanipāta 919: ajjhattaṁ upasantassa n' atthi attā, kuto nirattaṁ vā. On vivāda, ibid., 863, 877, 912, 832, etc. See also Madhyamakāvatāra, p. 233.

51~ Ibid.

55 The Sanskrit is incorporated in Cittaviśuddhiprakaraṇa 20 (cf. v. 5 above) with the variant reading rajyanti in a. It also occurs in the Śuklavidarśanā (see *MCB* I, p. 395), with matsamāḥ in b for madhyamāḥ; compare the Tibetan.

58 Cf. Suttanipāta 795: na rāgarāgī na virāgaratto . . .

59 Cf. MK XXII, 11: śūnyam iti na vaktavyam . . .

60 An allusion to Rūpa- and Dharmakāya, respectively the result of puṇya- and jñānasaṁbhāra (the two accumulations of merit and wisdom). See RĀ III, 12–13 (cf. Madhyamakāvatāra, p. 62). The verse forms a pariṇāmanā; see RĀ IV, 90.

Śūnyatāsaptati

This text is in 73 verses (originally composed in the āryā meter like the Vigrahavyāvartanī and the Pratītyasamutpādahṛdayakārikā), accompanied by a commentary from the author's own hand (svavṛtti). It is ascribed to Nāgārjuna by Bhavya,[79] Candrakīrti,[80] and Śāntarakṣita.[81] Testimonies anterior to these are found in the Akutobhayā[82] and the *Dvādaśadvāraka.[83] Later on it is also referred to by Atiśa.[84] I have seen no references or allusions to the svavṛtti, but as its prose style (in Tibetan, to be sure) is quite similar to the style of the commentaries on the Vigrahavyāvartanī and Vaidalyaprakaraṇa, there is no good reason to impeach its authenticity.[85]

The doctrine and scope of the Śūnyatāsaptati do not differ from those of the Mūlamadhyamakakārikā, to which it may be said to form an appendix,[86] as it partly summarizes its verses, partly introduces new topics and elaborates old ones.[87] Like the Mūlamadhyamakakārikā, it reveals no strict underlying structure of composition, but it may, as I have ventured, be divided into at least seven paragraphs.

For the study of the Śūnyatāsaptati I have had available several texts preserved in Tibetan, all of which are cited in the section on sources and variants in Part I.[88] The translations of the kārikās included in the commentaries by Candrakīrti and Parahita sometimes differ considerably — at times unhappily — from that given in Nāgārjuna's svavṛtti, and more often agree with the root text as it is found in the Tibetan Canon.[89]

As editions and translations of all the commentaries are expected, I have confined myself to an edition and translation of the root text. However, my translation of the kārikās strictly follows the svavṛtti, with only one or two exceptions, and should therfore be read in conjunction with the edition of the svavṛtti given in Part II. Though I have consulted the commentaries of other authors, Nāgārjuna's own remarks must of course remain the final authority in questions of interpretation.[90]

I present here the briefest possible summary of the text (based on the analysis given in the introduction to my Danish rendering of the verses with the svavṛtti), followed by notes on the specific verses.

Summary

The dharmas exist only vyavahāravaśāt (i.e. saṁvṛtitaḥ), as yukti shows that paramārthataḥ everything is anutpanna. (1–6)

All entities (bhāva) are pratītyasamutpanna, or śūnya. So nirvana is simply anutpāda. (7–26)

Various aspects of bhāva are shown to be relative. (27–32)

Karma is also śūnya according to orthodox Buddhism. (33–44)

Refutation of the five skandhas, above all rūpa. (45–57)

Avidyā vanishes when it is understood, as shown, that there is really no bhāva or the like whatsoever. (58–66)

Paramārtha is simply śūnyatā, anutpāda, and so forth. Since this is not generally realized, one must resort to saṁvṛti with śraddhā in order to comprehend it oneself.[91] (67–73)

Notes on the Verses

1 In the words of MK XXIV, 8: dve satye samupāśritya buddhānāṁ dharmadeśanā; cf. VV 28; YṢ 30–33. For vyavahāra in general, see May (1959), p. 221, n. 760. Here *lokavyavahāravaśāt equals the kāryavaśāt of YṢ 33.

2 This verse about tattva (i.e., paramārtha, etc.) summarizes MK XVIII, 1–7.

3 For a similar reason for anutpāda, see VV 1, 21; MK I; XX. Due to the fact that things lack svabhāva they are termed śūnya. VV, *passim*.

4 This refutes the three hypothetically possible subjects of origination: sat, etc. Really there are four koṭis; see e.g. CS III, 23. Similar refutations in MK VII, 20; CS I, 13, and elsewhere.

5 Refutation of utpāda as the first of the three saṁskṛtalakṣaṇa; cf. MK VII, 1–2. While this verse corresponds to *Dvādaśadvāraka 26 (Taishō 1568, 167a23–24), the latter may have read *jātājātavinirmukta (cf. MK II, 1) in pāda c.

6 Again, utpāda is absurd because the notion of hetu (i.e. to utpāda) is untenable. See MK XX; RĀ I, 47: prāgjātaḥ sahajātaś ca hetur ahetuko 'rthataḥ | prajñapter apratītatvād utpatteś caiva tattvataḥ ||

7 Things (bhāva) are also empty because they cannot be indicated (animitta) in terms of numbers (saṁkhyā), since numbers also are pratītyasamutpanna. Here the concept of eka/aneka seems quite concrete, so that eka = kṣaṇa or paramāṇu. Cf. RĀ I, 67–71.

8 Nor can citta (sems) be called eka or bhinna (i.e. aneka) because, as we shall see, its 'content' (i.e., duḥkha due to avidyādi) is in fact ajāta. This verse is 'quoted' at *Dvādaśadvāraka 2 (160a22–23).

9~ The four viparyāsas (see MK XXIII) do not exist in themselves. Hence avidyādi, which is based on them, does not exist either.

11~ Again, avidyādi are anutpanna (i.e. śūnya) because they are pratītyasamutpanna (in the sense of MK XXVI, 1–12 and/or PK 1–5), pitāputravat (cf. VV 49–50). Thus sukha and duḥkha (compare v. 8) are no more real than experiences in a dream (cf. CS I, 17; III, 5).

15~ In fact, all the laukika–saṁvyavahāra (see MK XIV, 6–40; VV 70; v. 1 above) are only possible because they are pratītyasamutpanna.

17~ The various forms of bhāva (svabhāva, parabhāva, abhāva and bhāva as such) are only conceivable in mutual dependence. They do not occur independently. Compare MK XV. For v. 18 in particular cf. MK XXIV, 1; XXV, 1–2. The Akutobhayā *ad* MK XXI, 6 quotes 19–21 as being from the Śūnyatāsaptati. *Dvādaśadvāraka 20 (164b27–28) seems to be identical with ŚS 19.

21 Acceptance of bhāva would also imply śāśvatocchedagrāha. Cf. May, op. cit., p. 213, n. 720; *IIJ* XXIII, p. 179, n. 58 (cf. ibid., p. 178, n. 9); MK XXI, 14. The verse is quoted in Madhyamakālaṁkāravṛtti, Pek. ed. 5285, Sa, fol. 75a (with Catuḥśataka X, 25 and RĀ I, 60 to the same effect).

22 The notion of saṁtāna does not prevent śāśvatocchedagrāha. Cf. v. 19; MK XVII; XXI, 15–21. This, of course, is the case only paramārthataḥ. Cf. MK XXVII, 22; Catuḥśataka X, 25.

23~ Since there is no bhāva, etc., nirvana cannot be defined as (bhāva)nirodha, or abhāva. In fact, utpāda and nirodha are sheer illusions (cf. MK XXI, 11 and Laṅkāvatāra X, 37; MK XXV; RĀ I, 42; SL 105, 123). Thus Nāgārjuna's notion of nirvana does not incur śāśvatocchedagrāha.

27~ Again, bhāva in its various forms cannot be established by means of lakṣyalakṣaṇa because they are asiddha (see MK II, 21). Cf. MK IV, 7; V; CS I, 12; *Dvādaśadvāraka 18–19 (163c16–17; 164a10–11).

29 This refutation of kāla is a summary of MK XIX. See also *Dvādaśadvāraka 25 (166c21–22); Catuḥśataka XI.

30~ Saṁskṛta and asaṁskṛta cannot be established because their three lakṣaṇas (utpāda, sthiti, bhaṅga) cannot be established as either eka or aneka, etc. See MK VII and *Dvādaśadvāraka IV (162c–163c13).

33~ What follows is a rather lengthy treatment of karma according to Madhyamaka. 33 summarizes MK XVII, 1–10. The remaining verses explain why, paramārthataḥ, karma is śūnya and how it is pratītyasamutpanna: Vikalpa (cf. v. 64) in the form of ahaṁkāra (cf. RĀ I, 27–35) generates kleśa (cf. MK XXIII, 1; XVIII 5), which again gives rise to karma, which finally conditions one's deha (MK XVII, 27) or rebirth (janma; see RĀ I, 35; II, 24). This cyclic process (cf. PK 1–5) can only cease through cognition (jñāna, darśana, etc.) of tattva; that is, of śūnyatā. ŚS 40–42 rec. by La Vallée Poussin, Prasannapadā, p. 330, n. 1. The Buddha's deśanā (v. 44) varies, as it depends upon sattvāśaya. See MK XVIII, 6; BV 98–99; RĀ IV, 94–96; YṢ 33.

41 Is this verse a later interpolation?

44 An allusion to satyadvaya, the two truths.

45 In vv. 45–54 the author refutes the existence of rūpa, which, saṁvṛtitaḥ, is varṇa and saṁsthāna (see v. 50). First, rūpa is unreal because it is neither one with the mahābhūta nor different from them. Similarly MK IV, 1–5.

46 Again, the mahābhūta cannot be established as eka or aneka (RĀ I, 83–89). So rūpa cannot be bhautika. Cf. RĀ I, 99; CS I, 5.

47 One cannot infer the existence of rūpa from its liṅga. This means, I assume, that bhautika cannot e.g. be subtle, as it is derived from bhūta that must be gross. See RĀ I, 90; Pañcaskandhaprakaraṇa, p. 2. If, on the other hand, rūpa really did exist (as the Ābhidhārmika contends), it could not be without liṅga (i.e. it could not change its liṅga under the influence of the mahābhūta).

48 Here I take buddhi in the sense of cakṣurvijñāna (cf. the use of ghaṭabuddhi at VP 16–19). Since cakṣūrūpe pratītyaivam ukto vijñānasaṁbhavaḥ (RĀ IV, 55), such a buddhi is med pa; i.e., śūnya. So it cannot perceive rūpa, to which a similar argument applies. Moreover, buddhi would have to perceive itself (which is absurd) in order to perceive other things (i.e. rūpa). Cf. MK III, 2 (which must be understood in the sense of Catuḥśataka XIII, 16); RĀ IV, 64.

49 Again, buddhi cannot perceive rūpa/viṣaya, for being kṣaṇika, objects are never sāṁprata. A buddhi which has atīta or anāgata as its object is vyartha. See RĀ IV, 56–57.

50 That rūpaṁ dvidhā varṇaḥ saṁsthānaṁ ca is well-known; cf. e.g. Amṛtarasa, p. 115; Pañcaskandhaprakaraṇa, p. 4. See also Catuḥśataka XIII, 7.

51 Similarly Catuḥśataka XIII, 17.

52~ As each of the twelve āyatanas cannot fulfill its respective function in itself it lacks svabhāva and is śūnya, for akṛtrimaḥ svabhāvo hi nirapekṣaḥ paratra ca (MK XV, 2). Cf. MK III.

54 The commentaries to this verse are far from exhaustive. But see RĀ IV, 52–54. Since each of the six sparśāyatana (= indriya, for which see the references in CPD II, p. 129) can have only one object (artha/viṣaya) at a time (RĀ IV, 52; Catuḥśataka XI, 18), the senses and their respective objects, taken pratyekam, must be vyartha (RĀ IV, 54).

55 There can be no saṁnipāta (i.e., sparśa: MK XXVI, 5) between indriya, viṣaya, and vijñāna, since as shown (see also MK XIV) none of the three exist by themselves. Hence they cannot come together. Thus it is only saṁvṛtitaḥ that one can say sparśāc ca vedanā saṁpravartate (MK XXVI, 5).

56~ A refutation of the fifth skandha, its objects, and its agent. Similarly CS I, 10; BV 26–56; Catuḥśataka XIII, 23. Cf. CS III, 50.

58 Verses 58–61 argue that the four perverted views, the source of avidyā (see vv. 10, 62), do not exist paramārthataḥ. Since the concept of bhāva is untenable (as shown in vv. 7, 17 ff.), nothing can really be either nitya or anitya, etc. The verse is quoted in Madhyamakālaṁkāravṛtti, loc. cit., 72b: thams cad rtag min mi rtag pa'ang | | ci yang med de rtag de bzhin | | dngos yod rtag dang mi rtag par | | 'gyur na de ni ga la yod ||.

59~ The kleśas are — saṁvṛtitaḥ — born from the perverted views (MK XXIII, 1). But as experience shows (cf. BV 19–20; Catuḥśataka VIII, 2–3), the perverted views must be sheer vikalpas. This implies that a vikalpa really has no definite object before it. Thus, paramārthataḥ, without an object a vikalpa is simply nothing.

62 Now that avidyā has been deprived of its basis, the eleven aṅgas based upon avidyā also vanish, QED. Cf. the identification of avidyā with piṇḍasaṁjñā, etc. (= viparyāsa) in the Śālistambasūtra, quoted in the Prasannapadā, p. 562.

63~ So avidyā is simply lack of awareness of the universal law of pratītyasamutpāda. See MK XVIII, 9–11. It is, as the svavṛtti to v. 64 says, brten pa'i dngos por mngon par zhen pa dang lta ba dang rtog pa dang 'dzin pa. We may add bhāvābhāvaparāmarśa, RĀ I, 42; bhāvābhyupagama, YṢ 46. See the Dhammasaṅgaṇi, p. 213 for these equivalents (. . . gāha, paṭiggāha, abhinivesa, parāmāsa, vipariyāsaggāha . . .)

65~ When one realizes that bhāva, etc. are śūnya; that they lack svabhāva and are like illusions, etc., avidyā and the rest vanish. This amounts to paramārtha. Cf. MK XXVI, 11; CS III, 36 ff.

69~ However, as long as one has not yet realized paramārtha, one must have śraddhā (cf. RĀ I 5–6) and rely on vyavahāra (cf. MK XXIV, 8–10; BV 67). In this way is nirvana; i.e. rāgadveṣamohaprahāṇa (°kṣaya) (see SS 221a4, quoting Saṁyuktāgama; cf. Saṁyutta IV, p. 251 ff.), approached and attained (cf. MK XXIV, 10).

Vigrahavyāvartanī

This text is ascribed to Nāgārjuna by Bhavya,[92] Candrakīrti,[93] and Śāntarakṣita,[94] and later testimonies are also known.[95] It is written in the āryā meter and provided with a svavṛtti in a simple and clear prose, but not without some tiresome pedantry.[96] The Vigrahavyāvartanī is extant in Sanskrit,[97] Tibetan, and Chinese, and has often been translated into modern languages.[98]

Like the Śūnyatāsaptati, the text was probably composed later than the Mūlamadhyamakakārikā.[99] I follow Candrakīrti in holding that it, together with the Śūnyatāsaptati, forms an appendix to the *opus magnum*.[100] Its scope — in accord with the prevailing rules of debate[101] — is to defend Nāgārjuna's thesis that all things are empty, because they lack own-being: like, for instance, a phantom. This is done on a relative (saṁvṛtitaḥ) and absolute (paramārthataḥ) level.[102]

The available sources, cited in Part II, are from the Tibetan, Chinese, and Sanskrit. The Sanskrit recension is an excellent piece of work, perhaps "the possibly nearest approximation of Nāgārjuna's original text." Still, the other versions, and particularly the commentary found in the Tibetan, provide variants that cannot be objectively eliminated. I have regarded it as being of some use to offer a critical edition of the Tibetan translation of the root verses — which is the best such translation, ancient or modern — as well as a slightly revised edition of the verses given in the Sanskrit edition of Johnston and Kunst, which is based in turn upon the *editio princeps* of Rāhula Sāṅkṛtyāyana.

I present here a brief review of the closely-knit and partly implicit arguments of the text, since they have not been clearly articulated in the existing translations.[103] The basis for the analysis is a consideration of the objections offered against Nāgārjuna, followed by his replies.

Objections

Nāgārjuna's initial thesis is that all things are empty. The opponent (real or imagined) takes this to mean that Nāgārjuna denies everything, and thus attempts to point out various contradictions in this attitude:

1 If everything is empty as Nāgārjuna claims, his statements must either be empty — but then they cannot negate own-being (v. 1) — or (atha) non-empty (sasvabhāva) — but this would imply an inconsistency (vaiṣamikatvam) and Nāgārjuna would have to abandon his initial thesis (that all things are empty) (v. 2).

2 Again, Nāgārjuna cannot support this thesis with an example, śabdavat, because that would imply the acceptance of something real; that is, non-empty (v. 3).

3 Besides, Nāgārjuna cannot refute the opponent's refutation of Nāgārjuna's thesis, because, according to Nāgārjuna himself, everything, including Nāgārjuna's thesis, can be negated (v. 4).

4 Before Nāgārjuna can deny things, he must accept (some of) the pramāṇas thanks to which he obtains his neganda, and this implies a self-contradiction (vv. 5–6).

5 Nāgārjuna's standpoint is also antagonistic towards authoritative teachers of Abhidharma. Thus he is in conflict with āgama (vv. 7–8).

6 If there is an absolute lack of own-being, what could be said to lack own-being? Of course the term 'lacking own-being' must refer to something manifest. Otherwise (atha) own-being must be totally transcendental! (vv. 9–10).

7 Any negation implies that a real negandum is accepted. Otherwise (i.e., if an unreal negandum could be negated), negation would establish itself endlessly without words, which is absurd (vv. 11–12). Even if the possibility of negation of an unreal negandum be granted, however, this would have to imply the reality of the misconception of the negandum as real (vv. 13–14), for otherwise (i.e., if there is no misconception, etc.), there is also no negandum, etc.! In other words: own-being exists (vv. 15–16).

8 Again, Nāgārjuna's thesis that all things are empty cannot be proved by the reason he advances; namely, that it is due to their lack of own-being. For, as Nāgārjuna himself maintains, there is no own-being to be negated. And of course a reason for one's statements must be advanced, otherwise the opposite standpoint might just as well be maintained (vv. 17–18). On the other hand, if Nāgārjuna feels inclined to accept the reason (hetu, gtan tshigs); namely, existence of own-being, he once again encounters a self-contradiction (v. 19).

9 Finally, Nāgārjuna's arguments have boomeranged—there is no period of time in which Nāgārjuna can negate. Hence own-being is a fact.[104]

Replies

Before replying to the objections, Nāgārjuna restates his position: All things are empty (v. 21), because they only exist in mutual dependence (v. 22): like, for instance, a phantom (v. 23). Note that Nāgārjuna argues saṁvṛtitaḥ in vv. 21–26. Now come the replies.

1 Since his statements, like everything else, are empty, he is not at all guilty of inconsistency or anything like it (v. 24).

2 The example alleged is not acceptable to Nāgārjuna. Hence he commits no dṛṣṭāntavirodha (vv. 25–26). A good example would be one which shows how one phantom eliminates another (v. 27). But in another sense (atha vā = paramārthataḥ) the sound adduced in the example does not exist. (It is, of course, empty like everything else.) (v. 28).

3 Nāgārjuna has no thesis (i.e., paramārthataḥ). So he cannot possibly contradict his own thesis (v. 29).

4 No, Nāgārjuna accepts no pramāṇa (i.e., paramārthataḥ) (v. 30), because pramāṇas cannot be established (v. 31), either by other pramāṇas (v. 32), without pramāṇas (v. 33), or by themselves. This is so partly because the example (one of Nāgārjuna's favorites) to support this thesis is unwarranted (vv. 34–39), and partly because it would imply that they were independent of their respective objects (prameya) (vv. 40–41). On the other hand pramāṇas cannot be established by prameyas (vv. 42–45), nor are they mutually establishing, like a father and his son (vv. 46–50). So pramāṇas cannot be established at all, QED (v. 51).

5 All the concepts of Buddhism are also empty, but they are efficacious, which could not be if own-being existed (vv. 52–56).

6 To Nāgārjuna not only the object referred to but also the term referring to it lack own-being (v. 57). Besides it is absurd, on the opponent's own premises, to speak of an nonexistent name (v. 58). Again, names like everything else are empty, as shown (v. 59). And of course Nāgārjuna does not acknowledge a transcendental form of own-being (v. 60).

7 If the opponent thinks that negation must always have something real as its negandum, he obviously accepts emptiness (v. 61) or else

he must give up this thesis (v. 62). As far as Nāgārjuna is concerned he does not negate anything (as this would presuppose the acceptance of neganda) (v. 63). He merely tries to suggest or indicate (jñāpayate) the absence of own-being (vv. 64–67) .[105]

8 Similarly there is no own-being lacking as a logical reason to be negated in support of Nāgārjuna's thesis (v. 68).

9 On the contrary! Since there is never any own-being, Nāgārjuna's 'negations' are valid at all times! (v.69).

Thus it has been shown that 'emptiness' is consistent not only with the demands of logic but also with the practice of Buddhism (v. 70). The text concludes with a final salutation to the Buddha.[106]

Vaidalyaprakaraṇa

This work, which is in 73 sūtras with a svavṛtti, is extant only in Tibetan.[107] References to it are found in Bhavya[108] and Candrakīrti,[109] but I have never found it quoted. The Vaidalyaprakaraṇa has not received the attention its historical importance and enjoyable style entitle it to.[110]

Judging solely from the text itself, the style and tenets would indicate the same author as for the Vigrahavyāvartanī, the work with the closest parallels of all those ascribed to Nāgārjuna. The introductory stanza indicates its scope: "In order to put an end to the arrogance of those logicians (tārika) who out of conceit regarding their knowledge are keen to debate, I shall grind them to little pieces."[111]

Who these sophists are and in what their conceit consists is made clear when Nāgārjuna begins by quoting the following well-known verse, Nyāya-sūtra (NS) I.1.1: "pramāṇa – prameya – saṁśaya – prayojana – dṛṣṭānta – siddhānta – avayava – tarka – nirṇaya – vāda – jalpa – vitaṇḍā – hetvābhāsa – cchala – jāti – nigrahasthānānām . . . ."

In the following seventy-three sūtras and in their commentary Nāgārjuna proposes to split and crush these sixteen basic concepts (padārtha) one by one.[112]

Analysis

padārtha 1 and 2: pramāṇa-prameya (sūtras 1–19)

Nāgārjuna's initial pratijñā is that pramāṇa and prameya are inseparably joined (miśra) (s. 1) and therefore they cannot be established (siddha) per se (svataḥ) (s. 2). The opponent allows that they are correlates, but thinks all the same that they can establish each other. Therefore Nāgārjuna must refute the three ways in which this could hypothetically come about: Neither sat, asat, nor sadasat can enter into relation. This is of general application, including, of course, pramāṇa-prameya (s. 3). If the opponent insists that everything is established by pramāṇas, then this must either include the pramāṇas as well—but this leads to anavasthā—or else exclude the pramāṇas—but this leads to pratijñāhāni (s. 4) (cf. VV 2).

But the opponent persists in maintaining that pramāṇas are self-established because they "illuminate" themselves, pradīpavat (s. 5) (cf. NS II.1.19). Nāgārjuna rejoins that the dṛṣṭānta is unhappily chosen, since a lamp cannot possibly illuminate itself or anything else, whether it is in contact (prāpta) with its object or not (ss. 6–10).[113] Besides, pramāṇa-prameya are traikālyāsiddha (s. 11).[114] The opponent's reply—so is Nāgārjuna's pratiṣedha (s. 12, equivalent to NS II.1.12)—makes Nāgārjuna triumph: If the opponent thinks that Nāgārjuna then instead maintains his pratiṣedha, and if the opponent accepts this, then he *eo ipso* accepts that pramāṇa-prameya are pratiṣedhya ("deserve to be negated"). But then all disputes (vivāda) are settled in a flash (s. 14)! (cf. ss. 1–2). But actually Nāgārjuna accepts neither a pratiṣeda nor a pratiṣedya—he merely tries to indicate the absence of own-being (cf. VV 64).

The opponent still insists that the pramāṇas exist because they provide correct understanding (s. 16). When Nāgārjuna asks how one can be sure that prameya exists independently of buddhi (i.e., how one can avoid the position that is associated in Western philosophy with Bishop Berkeley: "To be is to be perceived") the opponent claims that the ghaṭabuddhi is pramāṇa, whereas the jar as such (ghaṭa eva) is prameya (s. 17). But, replies Nāgārjuna, the opponent recognizes that buddhi arises indriya-artha-saṁnikarṣāt (= NS I.1.11 and I.1.15). And since the ghaṭa must be a specific pratyaya beforehand, buddhi cannot be pramāṇa, and the ghaṭa is not prameya (s. 18). Besides, the opponent himself (= NS I.1.9, but cf. ibid., II.1.16) categorizes buddhi as pramāṇa, not as prameya (s. 19).

padārtha 3 and 4: saṁśaya and prayojana (sūtras 20–23)

Could Nāgārjuna's treatment of pramāṇa-prameya not give rise to some doubt (saṁśaya)? No, there is nothing to be in doubt about: neither that which is comprehended, which is a fact (sat), nor that which is not comprehended, which is null and void (asat) (s. 20). Even if the opponent finds lack of decisive characteristics (viśeṣa) (*in dubitandum*) to be the cause of doubt (s. 21) (cf. NS I.1.23), the same argument also applies here (s. 22). But may one not be uncertain about a prayojana? No, for the opponent himself maintains that "yam artham adhikṛtya pravartate tat prayojanam" (= NS I.1.24), and the object can only be sat or asat, hence not an object of doubt.

padārtha 5: dṛṣṭānta (sūtras 24–30)

If the opponent objects that there are examples of things that serve a purpose (prayojana), such as sand, Nāgārjuna's refutation remains the same as before (ss. 24–25). Besides, there is no (dṛṣṭa-)anta because there is no ādi or madhyama (s. 26). Still the opponent (cf. NS I.1.25) maintains the possibility of a dṛṣṭānta that may be either sādharmya or vaidharmya. But Nāgārjuna rejoins that neither that which is sādharmya to what it is supposed to exemplify (e.g., fire of fire) nor that which is vaidharmya — whether it be totally or only to some extent — can serve as dṛṣṭānta (ss. 27–30).

padārtha 6: siddhānta (sūtra 31)

When Nāgārjuna claims that everything is asiddha he must himself accept siddha-anta. But the answer is no: Without a siddha-ādi how can he accept a siddha-anta?

padārtha 7: avayava (sūtras 32–48)

First (ss. 32–39) the five members of the syllogism are refuted in general: Since they are not subject to a whole (avayavī) (s. 32) or parts of an independent group (samūha) (s. 33), and since if they were one with the avayavī they would be identical (for if they were different there would be six) (s. 34), and also because they are traikālyāsiddha (s. 35) (cf. NS II.1.8), the avayava are not established. But the opponent finds that the five avayava can operate together, like cotton threads: A single one accomplishes nothing, but many combined into one can tether an elephant (s. 36). No, comes the reply: the individual threads are sādhyasama. What cannot be achieved by a single vandhyā or jātyandha cannot be achieved by any number of them (s. 37) (cf. Mahābhāṣya I, p. 31). And even if it be granted that they might do so by working simultaneously, the five avayava never occur simultaneously as a single avayavī (s. 38). Besides, before the avayava can prove anything they themselves must be proved; namely, by other avayava, and so on *ad infinitum* (anavasthā) (s. 39).

Next (ss. 40–48) the five avayava are refuted one by one. A pratijñā is impossible since it is neither identical with nor different from its hetu (s. 40). A hetu is impossible since either it must have another hetu and so forth *ad infinitum*, or else a hetu is present without a hetu. But that is absurd and would lead to total confusion (s. 41) (cf. VV 17–18). Since there is no pratijñā, hetu, or dṛṣṭānta, the other two avayava, upanayana and nigamana, lapse as well (s. 42). Even if a pratijñā could be established without a hetu, that would mean that the other three members were established without a hetu (s. 43). Again, if proof were due to a hetu, then a dṛṣṭānta would be superfluous (s. 44), and if not, then the hetu would be futile. But in that case dṛṣṭānta, etc. would be superfluous all over again (s. 45).

The opponent's specific pratijñā, that ātman is nitya, amūrtatvād ākāśavat, is refuted (s. 46). Further, since pratijñā and hetu can only be denominated successively, a pratijñā cannot be a pratijñā to its (co-existing) hetu, and vice versa (s. 47).

But when Nāgārjuna denies all avayava, does he not implicitly accept a pratijñā, and accordingly the four remaining avayava? No, since there is no pratijñā, for prati and jñā must be enunciated separately one after the other (s. 48).

padārtha 8: tarka (sūtra 49)

This cannot be sanctioned either. Neither the artha that is jñāta nor the artha that is ajñāta can be its object.

padārtha 9: nirṇaya (sūtra 50)

This is also impossible. Dravya, sat, eka, etc., which would serve to fix something definitely, are neither identical, nor different, nor both.

padārtha 10: vāda (sūtras 51–55)

Surely Nāgārjuna must accept the concept of debate (vāda)! No, because abhidhāna and abhidheya ("the issue under debate") cannot be established—they are neither eka nor aneka (s. 51). Nor can they alternatively be connected by a definite nāma-artha-saṁketa (which would, incidentally—devānāṁpriya—imply that the artha of the opponent's 16 padārthas [cf. NS I.1.1] should not be taken more seriously than the significance of names such as Devadatta or Indragupta), because the very fact that any word can function as a synonym or homonym of virtually anything[115] excludes any definite relationship (nges pa, niyama) between nāma and artha (ss. 52–54). Nor can they belong to one another. Thus the preconditions of vāda are absent (s. 55).

padārtha 11 and 12: jalpa and vitaṇḍā (sūtra 56)

These two concepts are refuted in the same manner as vāda.

padārtha 13: hetvābhāsa (sūtras 57–66)

Everything that Nāgārjuna says is hetvābhāsa, and thus incapable of refuting anything! No, answers Nāgārjuna, neither by being sādharmya nor by being vaidharmya with the actual hetu can hetvābhāsa come into question (s. 57). If a hetvābhāsa is qualified as a hetu that is savyabhicāra (cf. NS I.2.4), this is mistaken. Neither the hetu that is sādhyasādhaka nor the one that is not can rightly be classified as savyabhicāra (s. 58).

The opponent insists that a hetu may be savyabhicāra (i.e., in the sense of anaikāntika; cf. NS I.2.5). Thus amūrtatva can serve as hetu, now to ākāśa, now to karma (s. 59). No, comes the reply: These are two different types of amūrtatva, as it may prove the nityatva of one thing and the anityatva of another. Consequently the hetu adduced during dūṣaṇa and sādhana is not in itself savyabhicāra (s. 60). Again, there can be no hetu which is savyabhicāra in relation to the sādhya, for as things occur instantaneously, sādhana and dūṣaṇa are not concurrent with sādhya and dūṣya (s. 61).

The opponent now suggests that every hetu discarded by Nāgārjuna is, if not savyabhicāra, at least contradictory (viruddha) (s. 62) (cf. NS I.2.4). No, for how can two utterances be conflicting? It is obvious that when the first statement is being formulated, the second has not yet occurred. They can only be conflicting if they are simultaneous. And yet simultaneous statements cannot be conflicting either, since it is impossible for proponent and antagonist to put forward charge and rebuttal at the same time (s. 63).

The opponent next proposes that a hetu which is kālātīta (cf. NS I.2.4 and I.2.29) does in fact constitute a hetvā-bhāsa. Nāgārjuna disagrees, for a previous basis for something present cannot, by reason of being past, be a basis for anything present, which does not yet occur (s. 64). One had better not play fast and loose with past, present, and future, for all normal intercourse will then be suspended (s. 65)! Besides, since what is previous is past and gone, a hetu localized there cannot form the basis for anything in the present time (s. 66).

padārtha 14: chala (sūtra 67)

But all Nāgārjuna's statements are simply conscious distortions of the meaning of the opponent's words! (vacanavighāta; [cf. NS I.2.10]). Oh, no! If this is the charge, then any attempt at critical aloofness or disagreement would be distortion.

padārtha 15: jāti (sūtra 68)

The concept of jāti is impossible. Without jāta, ajāta and jāyamāna, jāti is precluded.[116]

padārtha 16: nigrahasthāna (sūtras 69–71)

Nāgārjuna is now blamed for having incriminated himself through repetition (punarvacana; [cf. NS V.2.14 and V.2.15]). But Nāgārjuna does not plead guilty, as what is supposed to have been repeated is neither identical with nor different from what it repeats (s. 69). In any case a nigrahasthāna does not exist, either when the charge has been made made or when it has not yet been made (s. 70). As for the third possibility, one is not convicted on any count as long as one is still being prosecuted, any more than one is trussed before the final knot is tied (s. 71).

Now that the 16 padārthas have been made the objects of negation (pratiṣedhya), pratiṣedha is also rendered impossible (s. 72). Hence there is no abhidhāna and no abhidheya, and therefore one cannot distinguish between nirvāṇa and apavarga (s. 73).[117]

Herewith Nāgārjuna has, as he foretold at the outset, crushed the arrogance of the heretics. The text has proceeded according to the principles that are known from Nāgārjuna's other works (that ultimately nothing can be conceived as eka or aneka), but with a wit and virtuosity not met with elsewhere.

Pratītyasamutpādahṛdayakārikā

As I have had occasion to note elsewhere, Pratītyasamutpādahṛdaya-kārikā 2–'6' is quoted and ascribed to "ācārya" (i.e. Nāgārjuna) by Bhavya. Other quotations also occur.[118] An apparent piece of counter-evidence to accepting Nāgārjuna as author is provided by the fact that one of the Chinese versions (Taishō 1651) attributes the Pratītyasamutpādahṛdayakārikā and its Vyākhyāna to a certain Bodhisattva called jìng yì, 'Clear Mind'. But if we take this as a somewhat interpretive rendering of Sanskrit *Sumati or the like (on the basis of the Tibetan blo gros bzang po, which, on the authority of Śāntarakṣita and Kamalaśīla, is known to have been another name of Nāgārjuna)—or perhaps merely an epithet, as sudhī, dhīmat, etc. are stock terms for Bodhisattvas, we may conclude that the Pratītyasamutpādahṛdayakārikā is ascribed to this author by all sources known to us.[119]

Internal evidence is provided first of all by a closely related passage: BV 59–63. RĀ I, 29 ff.; ŚS 34, 37; MK XVII, 27; XVIII, 5; XXIII, 1; and VS '6' are to the same effect. Moreover, the āgama that inspired the Pratītyasamutpādahṛdayakārikā is the same as the one behind e.g. RĀ V, 41–60; namely, the Daśabhūmikasūtra (also quoted in SS 249b7).

Though Nāgārjuna does not show any special originality in the Pratītyasamutpādahṛdayakārikā, the theory expounded here is of vital importance to him, inasmuch as it marks an exegetical attempt to reconcile the traditional dvādaśāṅgaḥ (twelve-membered) pratītyasam-utpāda with the śūnyatā doctrine.[120]

On the one hand we have the twelve sectors avidyādi. The purpose of this formula is clearly to explain the genesis of duḥkha, no matter how obscure it may seem in details. In the Abhidharma avidyā and saṁskāra are generally assigned to the past, vijñānādi to the present, and jātyādi to the future. This is also the interpretation tacitly endorsed by MK XXVI.

However, the formula should also be understood in another sense, so as to accord with Nāgārjuna's opinion that strictly speaking; i.e., paramārthataḥ, it is not rational to admit of pūrvāparasahakrama (see

MK XI, 2). In order to do so the twelve sectors are first reduced to three groups. Thus avidyā, tṛṣṇā and upādāna constitute kleśavartman, while saṁskāra and bhava make up karmavartman. The remaining seven are duḥkhavartman (in other sources, e.g. RĀ I, 35, called janman).

By adopting this scheme from the Daśabhūmikasūtra and various works of Abhidharma, Nāgārjuna has paved the way for introducing his notion of bhavacakra (or saṁsāramaṇḍala; RĀ I, 36). It has three phases preceding and succeeding one another from time to time without beginning: vikalpa (or ahaṁkāra, or simply kleśa; ŚS 34, 37), karma (RĀ I, 35), and finally janman (ibid.).[121]

Moreover, these three aspects may be reduced to two, hetu and phala (RĀ I, 38; VS '6'); i.e. (and here we have to resort to other sources for a helping hand — see references at notes to BV 59–63) avidyā, saṁskāra, tṛṣṇā and upādāna. In short, kleśa and karma are hetu, whereas the remaining aṅgas are phala. Now the author has achieved his initial purpose: Being hetu-phala, the "entire world" (i.e., the five skandhas; cf. note to BV 66) are pratītyasamutpanna; i.e., śūnya, like illusions.

Thus, in the end, the "hṛdaya" of pratītyasamutpāda amounts to the nairātmyavāda specific to Mahāyāna: Not only is there no sattva (= pudgala), but the skandhas are also empty, being neither one nor many (cf. MK II, 21).

We shall find occasion for a full discussion of this important topic.

*Vyavahārasiddhi

According to the Tibetan historian Bu-ston, Nāgārjuna wrote a work called Tha snyad grub pa, or *Vyavahārasiddhi, in order "to show that though there is no svabhāva in the ultimate sense (paramārthataḥ), still laukikavyavahāra (worldly convention) is justified saṁvṛtitaḥ . . . ."[122]

The credibility of this has been disputed.[123] I have failed to detect any references to such a title in any of Bhavya's or Candrakīrti's writings or in any other Indian śāstra written prior to these. However, in his Madhyamakālaṁkāravṛtti Śāntarakṣita quotes six verses[124] the source of which is mentioned by his pupil Kamalaśīla (who adds an exhaustive commentary): They hail from Nāgārjuna's *Vyavahārasiddhi.[125]

If we consider the content and style of this fragment, it becomes clear not only that it displays very close parallels to other passages in Nāgārjuna's authentic works, but also that one would beforehand have expected the author to express himself in more detail on this topic, clearly of paramount importance to him.[126]

Thus I do not hesitate to accept this fragment as a genuine quotation from Nāgārjuna's lost *Vyavahārasiddhi.[127]

The argument: Though all phenomena, such as mantras, etc., arise dependently and thus are neither existing nor non-existing, they are nonetheless efficacious. Likewise all internal and external phenomena arise dependently. Though they are thus mere metaphorical concepts, the Buddha has formulated his dharmas with a specific practical purpose (saṁdhāya); namely, *nairātmyāvatārataḥ.[128]

Notes on the Verses

1 Kamalaśīla introduces his commentary (Pañjikā, 123a5–124b7) by stating the purport of this text: sngags dang sman dang sgyu ma'i dpes chos thams cad rten cing 'brel par 'gyur ba nyid kyi gtan tshigs kyis don dam par yod pa dang med pa nyid las yang dag par

'das par sgrub par byed do. For pāda c see ibid., 123b2: 'gags pa zhes bya ba ni rang gi ngo bo las nyams pa zhes bya'o. In pāda d the vṛtti (69b2) reads de ni med pa yin, which I have corrected in accord with Pañjikā 123b4: de ni med pa'ang min. Though a mantra, being śūnya, neither is nor is not, it is still generally acknowledged to be efficacious (cf. vidyā, MK XXIV, 11). I have edited Kamalaśīla's commentary and discussed VS more fully in "Nāgārjuna's Vyavahārasiddhi," to appear in the *Proceedings of the Csoma de Körös Symposium, Velm/Wien, Sept. 13th–19th, 1981.*

2 Similarly RĀ II, 10–14 compares loka to a māyāgaja. They only exist vyavahārataḥ, not paramārthataḥ. See also CS III, 29.

3 The notion of pratītyasamutpāda excludes asti and nāsti; cf. e.g. YṢ 1. Consciousness (vijñāna) being ālambika/ālambanaka (dmigs par byed pa) only arises cakṣūrūpe pratītya, RĀ IV, 55; ŚS 56; MK XXVI, 4). I take de la in pāda c as vyavahārataḥ (i.e., according to Abhidharma), but Kamalaśīla does not gloss it.

4 That is, as a result of karmakleśākṣepa (cf. May, op. cit., p. 253, n. 908; MK XVII, 27; ŚS 37) one who is sopādāna (i.e. sāsrava, Pañjikā 124b2; cf. MK XXVI, 7) obtains bhava (i.e. the five skandhas, MK XXVI, 8). Similarly for all twelve bhavāṅgas; see v. 5. In pāda c I understand gzugs as catvāri mahābhūtāny upādāyarūpa (cf. MK IV; RĀ IV, 58, 60), but Kamalaśīla is silent.

5 The twelve bhavāṅgas (MK XXVI; PK, 1–5; BV, 59–63); i.e., ādhyātmikapratītyasamutpāda, like all other dharmas (including bāhyapratītyasamutpāda), only exist saṁvṛtitaḥ (vyavahārataḥ). But they are necessary for understanding paramārtha (cf. MK XXIV, 8–10; YṢ 33; ŚS 1, 69; BV 67). It is only for this reason that the Buddha has taught them. Or, as Kamalaśīla puts it (124b6): bdag med pa la 'jug pa'i phyir skye ba la sogs pa bstan to.

6 This verse (124b7): mjug bsdud do (upasaṁharati). Note that (124b7) gnyi ga zhes bya ba ni rgyu dang 'bras bu'o, which I understand in the light of PK 1–5; RĀ I, 35–38, etc. See my note to BV 59–63 for details (five aṅgas are hetu, seven are phala).

Sūtrasamuccaya

This compilation or anthology of Sūtras (mainly Mahāyānasūtras) is ascribed to Nāgārjuna by Candrakīrti[129] and Śāntadeva.[130] Some quotations are given in Kamalaśīla's Bhāvanākrama.[131] Otherwise it is only available in Tibetan and Chinese translations.[132]

Like the *Bodhisaṁbhāra[ka] and Suhṛllekha, the Sūtrasamuccaya is an exposition of Mahāyāna as a duṣkaracaryā strictly yathāgamam. It is addressed to Bodhisattvas, pravrajitas as well as gṛhasthas (as are the Ratnāvalī, *Bodhisaṁbhāra[ka], and Bodhicittavivaraṇa).

That Nāgārjuna should have felt the need to present an authoritative selection of Mahāyāna texts is only what one would expect, not only because he himself is one of the earliest and certainly the foremost exponent of that school, but also, as we gather from RĀ IV, 67–98, in his day Mahāyāna still met with severe criticism from various quarters, above all, it seems, from the 'orthodox' Śrāvakas.

On the whole the Sūtrasamuccaya is a most significant document for at least two reasons. First of all the abundance of quotations from Mahāyāna scriptures at such an early date lends it a historical value that future translators and editors of these Sūtras are bound to take into account. Secondly the outspoken religious convictions found in the Sūtrasamuccaya contribute considerably to our understanding of the author himself.

As the Sūtrasamuccaya is intended to expound Mahāyāna in the words of āgama we must not expect to discover much of a more philosophical interest. Still, at least one section — that on embracing the saddharma — has particular bearing on prajñā. Here we find some of the āgamas which most certainly inspired Nāgārjuna to his concept of śūnyatā and induced him to provide arguments (yukti) to that effect.

In its extent the Sūtrasamuccaya falls only a bit short of that of the remaining authentic writings. Thus I must abstain from translating or paraphrasing the entire text, the more so since a version of the Sūtrasamuccaya is expected from the hand of Amalia Pezzali.

Still, for our purpose this need not be deemed a serious drawback, inasmuch as the compiler himself has arranged his selections from no less than 68 (collections of) Sūtras under 13 main headings, summarizing the topics dealt with in the Sūtras cited.

I shall therefore confine myself to extracting these 'headings' from the body of the text and presenting them in their Tibetan version. In addition, I subjoin a list of the titles of Sūtras from which Nāgārjuna has drawn his selections.[133] I have reconstructed the Sanskrit titles in close agreement with the Tibetan version. Though the reconstructions offered in a few cases do not correspond exactly to the title under which the Sūtra is generally known (i.e. from other quotations, colophons, etc.) I believe they may with few exceptions easily be located in the Chinese or Tibetan Tripiṭaka (most conveniently by consulting *Hōbōgirin, Fascicule annexe: Répertoire du Canon bouddhique sino-japonais d'après l'édition Taishō Daizōkyō,* Tokyo, 1978 and e.g. the index volume to the *Tibetan Tripiṭaka,* Peking edition, Tokyo, 1962).

Major Divisions

| Sangs rgyas 'byung ba shin tu rnyed par dka' ste |

The coming of a Buddha is most rarely met with. (172b3)

| Mi 'gyur ba shin tu rnyed par dka' ste |

Birth as a human being is most rarely met with. (173b6)

| Dal ba 'byor ba rnyed par dka' ste |

The [eight and the ten] favorable circumstances are rarely met with. (174a7)

| De bzhin gshegs pa'i bstan pa la dad pa rnyed par dka' ste |

Faith in the teaching of the Tathāgata is rarely met with. (175b3)

| Gang dag byang chub tu sems bskyed pa'i sems can de dag rnyed par dka' ste |

Living beings who produce bodhicitta are rarely met with. (178a3)

| Sems can rnams la snying rje che ba ni rnyed par dka' ste |

Mahākaruṇā towards living beings is rarely met with. (182b8)

| Gang dag byang chub sems dpa' la rma 'byin pa'i las kyi sgrib pa dang | bdud kyi las dang | brnyas pa'i sems dang | dam pa'i chos spong ba la sogs pa bar du gcod pa'i chos rnams yongs su spong ba'i sems can dag ni ches rnyed par dka' ste |

Beings who renounce āntarāyikadharmas such as karmāvaraṇa, wounding a Bodhisattva, mārakarman, a contemptuous attitude (avamāna-citta) and saddharmaprahāṇa are still more rarely met with. (184b8)

| Gang dag khyim par gyur kyang chos rnams la nan tan gyis sgrub pa'i sems can rnams ni ches rnyed par dka' ste |

Beings who live as householders but still are able to accomplish the dharmas with earnestness are still more rarely met with.[134] (193a2)

| Gang dag de bzhin gshegs pa rnams kyi yongs su mya ngan las 'das pa yang dag pa ji lta ba bzhin du mos pa'i sems can de dag ni shin tu rnyed par dka'o |

Beings who are truly devoted to the parinirvāṇa of the Tathāgata are most rarely met with. (217b2)

| Theg pa gcig la mos pa'i sems can de dag ni shin tu rnyed par dka' ste |

Beings who are devoted to ekayāna are most rarely met with. (222b3)

| Byang chub sems dpa' dam pa'i chos rtag tu yongs su bzung bar bya'o |

A Bodhisattva should constantly embrace the saddharma.[135] (225b1)

| Byang chub sems dpa' thabs la mkhas pa dang bral bar chos nyid zab mo la sbyor bar mi bya ste |

A Bodhisattva must not apply himself to the gambhīradharmatā without practicing skillful means.[136] (243b7)

| Gang sangs rgyas dang byang chub sems dpa'i che ba nyid rgya chen po la 'jug pa'i sems can de dag ni shin tu rnyed par dka'o |

Beings who enter (praveśa) the lofty grandeur (māhātmya) of the Buddhas and Bodhisattvas are rarely met with.[137] (246a3)

Sources Quoted

Adhyāśayasaṁcodanasūtra
lHag pa'i bsam pa bskul ba'i mdo
210a7, 210b2, 211b8

Ajātaśatruparivarta
Ma skyes dgra'i le'u
180a7, 210a3, 211a4, 230b1, 243b5

Ākāśagarbhasūtra
Nam mkha'i snying po'i le'u
205a7

Akṣayamatinirdeśasūtra
Blo gros mi zad pas bstan pa'i mdo
182a2, 245a6

Anavataptasūtra
Ma dros pa'i mdo
212b2

Anupūrvasamudgatasūtra
Thar gyis yang dag par 'phags pa'i mdo
216b7

Arthaviniścayasūtra
Don rnam par nges pa'i mdo
200b3

Avadāna (!)
rTogs pa brjod pa
173a1

Avaivartikacakrasūtra
Phyir mi ldog pa'i 'khor lo'i mdo
224a6

Bhadrakalpikasūtra
bsKal pa bzang po'i mdo
173b2, 182a6

Bhadramāyākārasūtra
sGyu ma mkhan bzang po'i mdo
233b2

Bodhisattvapiṭaka
Byang chub sems dpa'i sde snod [kyi mdo]
173a7, 176b8, 183a3, 215a6, 215a8, 226a3, 228a6

Brahmaparipṛcchā
Tshangs pa zhus pa ['i mdo]
211b6, 221a1, 227b7, 242a4

Brahmaviśeṣacintiparipṛcchā
Tshangs pa khyad par sems kyis zhus pa'i mdo
234a5

Buddhāvataṁsakasūtra
Sangs rgyas phal po che'i mdo
233b4, 251a4, 252b6

Candragarbhaparivarta
Zla ba'i snying po'i le'u
173b1, 175a8, 175b7, 177a8, 183a1, 206a7, 228a3

Candraprabhaparivarta
Zla 'od gyi le'u
209b3

Candrapradīpa
Zla ba sgron ma'i mdo
186b4, 195a7, 211a8, 241b2

Daśabhūmikasūtra
Sa bcu'i mdo
249b7

Dhāraṇīśvararājaparipṛcchā
gZungs kyi dbang phyug gi rgyal pos zhus pa['i mdo]
184a1, 223b4

Dharmasaṁgītisūtra
Chos yang dag par sdud pa'i mdo
181b4, 227b5

Ekottarikāgama
gCig las 'phros pa'i lung
174a6

Gaṇḍavyūhasūtra
sDong po bkod pa'i mdo
173b1, 178a4, 212b4 (!), 224b7, 246b3, 248a4

Jñānavaipulyasūtra
Ye shes shin tu rgyas pa'i mdo
173a7, 221a5

Kāśyapaparivarta
'Od srungs kyi le'u
181a1

Kṣitigarbhasūtra
Sa'i snying po'i mdo
207a3, 208a5, 209a2

Laṅkāvatārasūtra
Lang kar gshegs pa'i mdo
222b2, 224b3, 240a7, 241b1

Lokottaraparivarta
'Jig rten las 'das pa'i le'u
221a1

Mahākaruṇāsūtra
sNying rje chen po'i mdo
214a5, 220b7

Mahāsaṁnipātaparivarta
'Dus pa chen po'i le'u
223b3

Maitreyasiṁhanādasūtra
Byams pa'i seng ge'i sgra'i mdo
186a7, 217a4

Mañjuśrīvikrīḍitasūtra
'Jam dpal rnam par rol pa'i mdo
186b3

Mañjuśrīvikurvitaparivarta (!)
'Jam dpal rnam par 'phrul ba'i le'u
190b6, 191b4, 234b6

Māradamanaparivarta
bDud 'dul ba'i le'u [mdo]
243a4, 244b6

Niyatāniyatāvatāramudrāsūtra
Nges pa dang ma nges pa la 'jug pa'i phyag rgya'i mdo
186b7, 188a5

Pitāputrasamāgamasūtra
Yab sras mjal ba'i mdo
181a4, 222a2, 229b3

Prajñāpāramitā (!)
Shes rab kyi pha rol tu phyin pa
182b6, 190a2, 217a7, 220b3, 223a8, 237b2, 238a5, 239b1, 242a6

Pravrajyāntarāyasūtra
Rab tu 'byung ba'i bar du gcod pa'i mdo
193a8

Praśāntaviniścayaprātihāryasūtra
Rab tu zhi ba rnam par nges pa'i cho 'phrul gyi mdo
180a4, 226b7, 227a1

Prasenajitparipṛcchā
gSal rgyal gyis zhus pa
179b4, 196b7

Puṣpakūṭasūtra
Me tog brtegs pa'i mdo
214a3

*Ratnadārikādattasūtra
Khye'u rin po ches byin pa'i mdo
241b5

Ratnameghasūtra
dKon mchog sprin gyi mdo
183b3, 209b8, 226b2

Ratnarāśisūtra
Rin po che'i phung po'i mdo
180b4, 182b4, 211a1, 213b6, 216a2, 216a4

*Ratnasamuccayadeśanāsūtra
Rin po che bsags pa bstan pa'i mdo
235b3, 235b7, 236b4

Saddharmapuṇḍarīkasūtra
Dam pa'i chos padma dkar po'i mdo
172b4, 220b4 (*bis*), 222b4

Saddharmasmṛtyupasthānasūtra
Dam pa'i chos dran pa nye bar gzhag pa'i mdo
195b4

Saptaśatikā
bDun brgya pa
234b1

Sāgaramatiparipṛcchāsūtra
Blo gros rgya mtshos zhus pa'i mdo
192b2, 193a1, 217a2, 225b7

Sāgaranāgarājaparipṛcchā
Klu'i rgyal po rgya mtshos zhus pa
177b1, 215a2

Saṁyuktāgama
Yang dag par ldan pa'i lung
173b6, 212a5, 221a3

Satyakaparivarta
bDen pa po'i le'u
203a6, 223a1

Śraddhābalādhānāvatāramudrāsūtra
Dad pa'i stobs bskyed pa la 'jug pa'i phyag rgya'i mdo
176a8, 176b4, 185a1, 187a4, 225b2

Śrīmālāsiṁhanādasūtra
dPal gyi phreng ba seng ge'i sgra'i mdo
224b2, 227b3

Sūryagarbhaparivarta
Nyi ma'i snying po'i le'u
204a4

Tathāgatabimbaparivarta
De bzhin gshegs pa'i gzugs kyi le'u
215b2

Tathāgataguhyasūtra
De bzhin gshegs pa'i gsang ba'i mdo
175b3, 175b8, 181b1, 181b2, 227b1

Tathāgataguṇajñānācintyaviṣayāvatāranirdeśasūtra
De bzhin gshegs pa'i yon tan dang ye shes bsam gyis mi khyab pa'i yul la 'jug pa bstan pa'i mdo
177b3, 250a8

Tathāgatakoṣa[garbha]sūtra
De bzhin gshegs pa'i mdzod kyi mdo
242b2

Tathāgatotpattisaṁbhavasūtra
De bzhin gshegs pa skye ba srid pa'i mdo
217b4

Udayanavatsarājaparipṛcchā
Bat sa la'i rgyal po shar pas zhus pa'i mdo
194a7

Ugraparipṛcchāsūtra
Drag shul can gyis zhus pa'i mdo
193a3

Upāyakauśalyasūtra
Thabs la mkhas pa'i mdo
192a4

Vajracchedikā
rDo rje gcod pa [*sive* sum brgya pa]
240a3 (!), 241b7

*Vimatisamudghātasūtra
Yid gnyis yang dag [legs] par 'joms pa'i mdo
174a1, 204a1

Vimalakīrtinirdeśa
Dri ma med par grags pas bstan pa'i mdo
201b7, 237a4, 237a7, 243b8, 244a7, 245a2, 246a4

*Viniścayarāja[-sūtra]
rNam par gtan la dbab pa'i rgyal po['i mdo]
172b6

Vīradattagṛhapatiparipṛcchā
Khyim bdag dpas byin gyis zhus pa
183a6, 201a6, 201b3

Ratnāvalī

This verse text, composed in five hundred anuṣṭubh with an extra verse added at the end, is not only ascribed to Nāgārjuna in the colophons of its Tibetan and Chinese versions but also by authorities such as Bhavya,[138] Candrakīrti,[139] Śāntarakṣita,[140] and many other later authors.

The Ratnāvalī is only partially extant in Sanskrit.[141] An Indian commentary composed by a certain Ajitamitra (Pek. ed. 5659) is only available in a Tibetan translation. It is particularly useful for the first two chapters, but on the whole far too brief to be of much use for the study of the remaining three paricchedas.

The philosophical tenets of the Ratnāvalī do not differ from those advanced in the Mūlamadhyamakakārikā, Śūnyatāsaptati, Yuktiṣaṣṭikā, etc., but it supplements these dialectical texts by affording a code of Mahāyāna Buddhist principles, practical as well as theoretical, with particular regard to a gṛhastha and more specifically to a king (see I, 2, 78). It thus places Nāgārjuna's philosophy within a wider framework. Taken as a whole we notice that, as with the Mūlamadhyamakakārikā, Śūnyatāsaptati, Suhṛllekha, Catuḥstava, and *Bodhisaṁbhāra[ka], no strict structural principle is adhered to. But if no unity of composition is conspicuous there is certainly, as we shall see, a unity of thought, in the light of which the Ratnāvalī may be said to be a homogeneous work.

Since the Ratnāvalī is already available in modern translations I shall confine myself to an analysis of the main themes of its five chapters.[142]

Analysis

The first pariccheda is entitled *Abhyudayanaiḥśreyasopadeśa (in Tib.: mngon par mtho ba dang nges par legs par bstan pa); the Chinese title, free though good, is ān lè jiě tuō). After a brief introduction on abhyudaya (= sukha) and naiḥśreyasa (= mokṣa) (cf. Vaiśeṣikasūtra I, 1, 2; RĀ III, 30), respectively presupposing śraddhā and prajñā, the author encourages his reader to have faith in the Dharma, which (to put it briefly) has two aspects: nivṛttir aśubhāt kṛtsnāt pravṛttis tu śubhe sadā (22). One should, in other words, not act under the influence of the kleśas but only, as we shall see, motivated by karuṇā.

Now that Nāgārjuna has spoken (1–24) of the means to true sukha here in samsara he deals with the second and the foremost mokṣasādhana, namely prajñā. This consists in realizing the pudgaladharmanairātmya specific to Mahāyāna. It amounts to nirvana, which is simply bhāvābhāvaparāmarśakṣaya (42), or freedom from rebirth in samsara. Having elaborated his doctrine about transcending being and non-being (46–75), the author finally lays down a method according to āgama for how one can argue that there is neither a pudgala nor any dharma, such as the skandhas, mahābhūtas, dhātus, and thus personally realize the nairātmyadvaya of Mahāyāna, or mokṣa (76–100).

The second chapter, *Miśraka (Tibetan: spel ma; Chinese: zá), amplifies the two mokṣasādhana discussed previously. First (1–24) some comments concerning māyāvāda, which constitutes the 'ontological' foundation of Nāgārjuna's soteriology. However, yāvad avijñāto dharmo 'haṁkāraśātanaḥ, one must (as is shown in the first part of chapter I) devote oneself to the practice of the Dharma. In the case of a king, he must be devoted to three pāramitās: dāna, śīla, and kṣānti, as well as to other virtues prescribed in Mahāyāna. In this way the other pāramitās will also gradually prosper (cf. IV, 80–83). Now some warnings against vices liable to afflict a king, and some devices for abandoning the kleśas (41–74). By following the Dharma the king will succeed in obtaining the 32 lakṣaṇas and the 80 anuvyañjanas specific to a mahāpuruṣa (76–100).

The third chapter, *Bodhisaṁbhāra (Tibetan: byang chub kyi tshogs bsdus pa; Chinese: pú tí zī liáng) resumes (1–10) the traditional doctrine of the mahāpuruṣalakṣaṇa. Now (12–13) a pair of significant verses succinctly summarize the entire purpose of Mahāyāna in theory and practice: the attainment of Buddhahood. It has two aspects: a Rūpakāya, which is the result of an immense mass of merit (puṇyasaṁbhāra), and a Dharmakāya, the fruit of an unlimited jñānasaṁbhāra. After this culmination the remaining 86 verses depict some of the endless forms a bodhisattvacaryā (cf. MK XXIV, 32) intent upon puṇyasaṁbhāra may take, motivated by karuṇā. It is a life of mental and physical happiness (sukha; cf. I, 4). In another cardinal stanza (30) the notion of saṁbhāra is linked to that of abhyudaya and naiḥśreyasa (cf. I, 3–4). With a wealth of casuistic details, often of great cultural interest, the king is advised to benefit himself as well as others by developing the pāramitās. Note that while the theme of this chapter is the same as that of the *Bodhisaṁbhāra[ka], translated in Part I, above, the treatment of this "endless subject" (cf. BS 2–4) differs so much that the author hardly ever has to repeat himself.

Again in the fourth chapter, Rājavṛttopadeśa (Tibetan: rgyal po'i tshul bstan pa; Chinese: zhéng jiāo wáng), Nāgārjuna takes up where he left off in the previous pariccheda. After a *captatio benevolentiae* (1–6) the king is admonished to practice dānapāramitā in various ways (7–17) and adhere to the principles of justice (Dharma) in matters of state and law. Punishment should only be inflicted out of compassion. These instructions, which so to speak form an arthaśāstra according to the Mahāyāna, naturally fall under the heading of puṇyasaṁbhāra. In order to enhance the king's jñānasaṁbhāra the author then (46–65) argues that vedanā (and of course the other skandhas as well) lack svabhāva, since they are pratītyasamutpanna. Indeed, it can only be ascribed to ignorance that certain individuals (i.e., Śrāvakas) mock the Mahāyāna, which is characterized by altruistic and lofty ideals of all kinds. Actually the teachings of Mahāyāna are exceedingly profound, hence easily misunderstood, and therefore the Buddha has prudently adapted his teachings to the vineyāśaya (cf. MK XVIII, 8, etc.).

So to sum up, as a gṛhastha the king should above all practice dāna, śīla, kṣānti and satya. However, lokasya vaidharmya may require him to become a pravrajita.

Accordingly, the final chapter is entitled *Bodhisattvacaryopadeśa (Tibetan: byang chub sems dpa'i spyod pa bstan pa; Chinese possibly better: chū jiā zhèng xíng, *Pravrajitacaryā). As we saw, the Dharma has a nivṛtti- and a pravṛtti-aspect (I, 22). It was thus shown how a gṛhastha should abstain from the ten akuśalakarmapatha and instead collect puṇya by engaging himself in the perfection of dāna, śīla, kṣānti, etc. Now the author focuses on the duties of a pravrajita. Disciplining himself in the (three) śikṣās (cf. SL 105) and in the code of prātimokṣa, and studying the Sūtras, etc., he should abandon the 57 doṣas.

At this point (3–33) we encounter an interesting list of upakleśas, pañcamithyājīvas, etc. Though each of these 57 items also occurs in other Abhidharma texts, the list as a whole, if I am not mistaken, occurs in no other manual of Abhidharma. Thus I am inclined to agree with my learned friend the Ven. Thrangu Rinpoche (oral communication, Nov. 1980), according to whom Nāgārjuna himself is responsible for the number and order of these doṣas. Along with the 119 kuśaladharma registered in the svavṛtti to VV 7 (see *IHQ* XIV, pp. 314–323 for a detailed discussion of these) and BS 147, this *catalogus vitiorum* proves a valuable contribution to the question of the relationship between the early Madhyamaka and traditional Abhidharma. I give below a reconstruction of the Sanskrit based on the Tibetan version — Peking and Narthang editions — occasionally compared with the Chinese version. A few emendations have tacitly been made, all obvious.

Having thus abandoned these and other doṣas, a Bodhisattva performs the six pāramitās in a spirit of karuṇā (35–39). Doing so he will gradually advance through the ten bodhisattvabhūmis (here Nāgārjuna follows the Daśabhūmikasūtra) and accomplish his task by becoming a Buddha (40–64). While still a Bodhisattva he must not forget to perform the saptavidhānuttarapūjā (cf. BS 48 ff.) regularly (65–87). The work concludes with a final exhortation to practice Buddhism so as to attain bodhi for the benefit of all living beings (88–101).

The above analysis has brought us in a position to summarize the content of the Ratnāvalī. As suggested by its title, A String of Pearls, a common theme combines the individual verses into a unity. This is puṇyajñānasaṁbhāra. While there is hardly a single verse which is not more or less directly related to that topic, many of them may to some extent be read as "ratnas" in their own right. Still their context should not be overlooked. Thus I find the title well-chosen to suggest that here a variety of instructions are unified by one basic theme, bodhisaṁbhāra.

The saptapañcāśaddoṣāḥ of ch. V, 3–33[143]

1 khro ba: krodha

2 khon du 'dzin pa: upanāha

3 'chab pa: mrakṣa

4 'tshig pa: pradāśa

5 g·yo: śāṭhya (= 6. : but m.c. 5.)

6 sgyu: māyā (= 5. : but m.c. 6.)

7 phrag dog: īrṣyā

8 ser sna: mātsarya

9 ngo tsha med pa: ahrīkatā (for āhrīkya)

10 khrel med pa: anapatrāpya

11 khengs pa: stambha

12 nyes rtsom: saṁrambha

13 rgyas pa: mada

14 bag med pa: pramāda

15 nga rgyal: māna

16 lhag pa'i nga rgyal: atimāna

17 nga rgyal las kyang nga rgyal: mānātimāna

18 nga'o snyam pa'i nga rgyal: asmimāna

19 mngon pa'i nga rgyal: abhimāna (m.c.: abhimānitā)

20 log pa'i nga rgyal: mithyāmāna

21 dman pa'i nga rgyal: adhamamāna (for ūnamāna)

22 tshul 'chos pa: kuhanā

23 kha gsag: lapanā

24 gzhogs slong: naimittikatva

25 thob kyis 'jal ba: naiṣpeṣikatva

26 rnyed pas rnyed pa rnams 'dod pa: lābhena lipsā lābhānām (m.c.)

27 skyon zlos: śiṅga? (cf. Pāli siṅga; BHS śṛṅgī)

28 spungs med pa: staimitya (cf. Pāli tintiṇa)

29 tha dad pa'i 'du shes: nānātvasaṁjñā

30 yid la mi byed pa: amanaskāra

31 bcom ldan tshul min: abhagavadvṛtti (abhāga°? cf. Pāli asabhāgavutti)

32 zhen pa: gardha (cf. Pāli gedha; BHS godha)

33 yongs su zhen pa: parigardha (cf. Pāli paligedha; BHS paligodha)

34 chags pa: lobha

35 mi rigs par chags pa: viṣamalobha

36 chos ma yin pa la 'dod pa (read thus for chags pa ma yin . . . ; cf. Chinese fēi fǎ yù): adharmarāga

37 sdig 'dod pa: pāpecchatā

38 'dod chags chen po: mahecchatā

39 thob par 'dod pa: icchepsutā (for icchasvitā?: thus Abhidharmadīpa, p. 310)

40 mi bzod pa: akṣānti

41 ma gus pa: anādara (anācāra is not definiendum in spite of the Tib.: cf. Chinese bù guì and e.g. Abhidharmadīpa, p. 311)

42 bka' blo bde ba ma yin: daurvacasya (cf. Chinese nàn yǔ)

43 nye du dang 'brel ba'i rnam par rtog pa: jñātisaṁbandhavitarka

44 yul du sred du: janapadātṛṣ? (m.c. for janapadavitarka; cf. Chinese tŭ jué and e.g. Abhidharmadīpa, p. 310)

45 mi 'chi ba'i rnam par rtog pa: amaravitarka

46 rjes rnam rigs dang ldan rtog: anavajñaptisaṁyukto vitarka (Tib. is a correct rendering of anuvijñapti° [thus Sanskrit Ms], but this must be an early corruption of anavajñapti°; cf. Chinese shùn jué jué and Pāli anavaññati° [CPD I, p. 159])

47 gzhan rjes su chags pa dang ldan pa yi rnam par rtog pa: parānudayatāpratisaṁyukto vitarka (Hahn suggests parānunayatā° against Ms, but cf. Pāli parānuddayatāpaṭisaṁyutto vitakko [see CPD ref. I, p. 190; add Vibhaṅga, p. 346])

48 mi dga' ba: arati (for this and the following see Vibhaṅga, p. 352)

49 snyoms pa: tandrī

50 'gyur ba: vijṛmbhikā (cf. Chinese pín)

51 za ma 'dod pa (read thus for zad mi 'dod pa): bhaktasaṁmada (Hahn: bhaktāsaṁmada, but cf. Pāli bhattasammada and Chinese shí zuí. Possibly also bhaktāsamatā; e.g. Abhidharmadīpa, p. 311)

52 sems zhum yin pa nyid: cetolīnatva

53 'dod dun: kāmacchanda

54 gnod sems: vyāpāda

55 rmi ba gnyid: styāna middha (cf. Chinese ruò)

56 rgod pa 'gyod pa: auddhatya kaukṛtya

57 the tshom: vicikitsā

Suhṛllekha

While not a single Sanskrit fragment seems to have survived of the 123 āryāgītis in which the Suhṛllekha was originally composed, it is available in three Chinese translations (Taishō 1672–1674), a Tibetan translation (Pek. ed. 5409; cf. 5682, which is a duplicate with a few important variants) and a very good commentary (Pek. ed.5690) corresponding to its name, Vyaktapadā Suhṛllekhaṭīkā, by a certain Mahāmati.[144]

I have only come across two quotations in Indian śāstras from the Suhṛllekha. The first occurs in Candrakīrti's Catuḥśatakaṭīkā (Pek. ed. 5266, Ya, fol. 113b), without any indication of source. It is v. 43. In addition, SL 55 and 104 are quoted in Bodhibhadra's Samādhisaṁbhāraparivarta (Derge ed. 3924, Ki, fol. 85b.)

That the Suhṛllekha is so seldom cited is perhaps not surprising when one looks at its content. It is mainly concerned with an exposition of the ethics of a layman. It was addressed to a certain king called bDe spyod (cf. ṭīkā, loc. cit., 325a) perhaps to be identified with Gautamīputra Śatakarṇī of the Śātavāhana dynasty.[145] There can be no doubt that the author is a devotee of Mahāyāna: He speaks of sugatapratimā (2), the six pāramitās (8), Avalokiteśvara (120), and Amitābha (121). On the other hand, the theory of śūnyatā is hardly mentioned (but see 40, 49) and the dialectics of prajñā known from the Mūlamadhyamakakārikā and elsewhere do not occur. But this is only what we would expect from an author who adheres to the Mahāyāna ideal of upāyakauśalya (see BS 6, 17, and elsewhere; BV 98–99). Thus the text shows great similarity to the *Bodhisaṁbhāra[ka], Sūtrasamuccaya, and certain parts of the Ratnāvalī, without, however, actually repeating the dharmadeśanā given in those texts.

The Suhṛllekha is written in a straightforward and pleasing style.[146] Though Tibetan commentators have taken great pains to detect some subtle principle of composition, there is, in my opinion, none such to be found.[147] As is often the case with Nāgārjuna a progressive composition is not to be expected. But surely there is a unity of thought: All human endeavors are subsumed under one heading; namely, the desire for release from the round of rebirth (see 104). This, as we have seen in the Ratnāvalī, is achieved by fulfilling puṇyajñānasaṁbhāra. And, to put it briefly, the Suhṛllekha deals with the puṇyasaṁbhāra of a gṛhapati (householder) according to the teachings of the ancient āgamas.

There being several modern versions of the Suhṛllekha I shall merely attempt to point out some parallels in Nāgārjuna's other works and identify some of the canonical sources upon which the Suhṛllekha proves dependent (cf. 2: ". . . ngag 'di ngan yang dam chos brjod la brten . . .") for its very rich technical inventory.[148]

Notes on the Verses

1–3 An exhortation to study the Dharma so as to aspire for punya. The Dharma comprises . . .

4 six anusmṛti (buddha°, dharma°, saṁgha°, tyāga°, śīla°, and devatānusmṛti [see references in BHSD, p. 36; CPD, under anussati, etc.])

5 and ten kuśalakarmapatha (abstention from prāṇātipāta, adattādāna, kāmamithyācāra; mṛṣāvāda, paiśunyavāda, pāruṣyavāda, saṁbinnapralāpa; abidhyā, vyāpāda, and mithyādṛṣṭi [cf. RĀ I, 7–9; MK XVII, 11; Vimalakīrtinirdeśa, p. 118, n. 73 for canonical references]). To these ten RĀ I, 8 adds amadyapāna and svājīva; cf. Traité, pp. 771, 816.

6 Cf. RĀ, ibid.: dānam ādarāt. On the nature, kṣetra, and effect of dānapāramitā in general, see Traité, pp. 650–769; Dānaparikathā (Pek. ed. 5661).

7 This verse (quoted in Guenther [1959], p. 164) describes śīlapāramitā in general (cf. Traité, pp. 770–864) whereas verse 5 specified it. See also Praṇidhānasaptati 24; Madhyamakāvatāra, pp. 32–45.

8 The six pāramitās: dāna, śīla, kṣānti, vīrya, dhyāna, and prajñā. See RĀ I, 12; II, 25; IV, 80–82; BS *passim;* Traité, pp. 650–1113; Har Dayal (1932), pp. 165–269; Guenther (1959), pp.148–231.

9 A reference to the sabrahmakāni kulāni of Aṅguttara I, p. 132, etc.

10~ For the aṣṭāṅgapoṣadha, see Traité, p. 825 ff.; Aṅguttara IV, p. 248 ff. (rep. Traité, p. 828); BHSD, under upoṣadha; CPD, under aṭṭhaṅguposatha. For kāmāvacaradeva, see Dharmasaṁgraha § 127.

12 The eight dharmas (ṭīkā, 333b) are mātsarya, śāṭhya, māyā, saṅga? (chags pa), tandrī? (snyoms las), kauśīdya (or ālasya: le lo), rāga,

and dveṣa. For similar lists of faults, see RĀ V, 3 ff.; BS 147. The five kinds of mada—kula°, rūpa°, śruta°, yauvana°, and mahābhāgamada? (dbang thang che ba)—are known from Abhidharmadīpa, p. 307, etc. Vibhaṅga, p. 350 lists 27 kinds; cf. PED, under mada.

13~ The celebrated verse on apramāda (pramāda listed as an upakleśa; cf. p. 295 above) is quoted *in extenso* by the ṭīkā (326b) with sadā (for yātha) in pāda d: Udānavarga IV, 1, etc. For Nanda, etc., see PPN.

15 Reference to Dhammapada XIV, 6 (cf. Bodhicaryāvatāra VI, 2). See also PED, under khanti, and Traité, pp. 865–926 on kṣāntipāramitā. See the Śūraṁgamasamādhi, p. 157 on avaivartikatva: the eighth or acalā bhūmi, characterized by anutpattikadharmakṣāntipratilābha. See also BS 21, 23, etc. The ṭīkā quotes a Sūtra at 335b that has not been traced.

16 Udānavarga XIV, 9, etc. (this is sattvakṣānti; cf. Traité, p. 865).

17 This verse (which all translations seem to have misunderstood, not seeing that sems = sems can) refers to Aṅguttara I, p. 283: pāsāṇalekhūpamo puggalo, paṭhavilekhūpamo puggalo, udakalekhūpamo puggalo.

18 These three persons—gūthabhāṇī, pupphabhāṇī, and madhubhāṇī—are described in Aṅguttara I, p. 128. (Kern's emendation to kūṭa° for gūtha° [cf. PED, p. 253] is not supported by the Tibetan mi gtsang).

19 Again a reference to the Aṅguttara: II, p. 85. Āryadeva also alludes to this in Catuḥśataka VII, 16.

20 The four ambūpamā puggalā occur in Aṅguttara II, p. 107.

21 The ṭīkā first refers to a Sūtra: btsun pa bud med la ji ltar bsgrub par bgyi zhes gsol ba dang | kun dga' bo mi ltas so . . . (cf. Dīgha II, p. 141) and then quotes another Sūtra (not identified) instructing householders how to look upon women (337a). Cf. RĀ II, 48 ff.

22 The ṭīkā refers to sems dul bas ni bde ba 'thob. Cf. Dhammapada III, 35 and PED, p. 267. On the dangers of kāmasukha see, e.g. the citations from the Lalitavistara in the Śikṣāsamuccaya, p. 204.

23 Possibly inspired by the Saddharmasmṛtyupasthānasūtra. See Kawamura's translation, p. 25. The form kimpaka (not, as here, kimpa) is found in Prajñādaṇḍa 204.

24 Compare, for example, Dhammapada VIII, 4.

25 See Aṅguttara IV, p. 386; Traité, p. 1154.

26 For the leper (kuṣṭhin), see Majjhima I, p. 506. Also mentioned in Catuḥśataka III, 14.

27 An important verse suggesting that only paramārthadarśana (i.e., śūnyatādarśana) can destroy the kleśas and thus karma and janma. Cf. MK XVIII, 5; XXVI, 11.

28 On śīla and jñāna (= tattvajñāna) see BS 157; Catuḥśataka XII, 11; Dhammapada XVI, 9 (here dassana = ñāṇa).

29 On the eight wordly dharmas, see BS 20 (with references in the notes); also 117.

30 For a similar warning against 'nepotism' (saṁvibhāga), see Catuḥśataka IV, 24; Narakoddharastava 4.

31 On karma, see Guenther (1959), p. 74 ff.

32 The seven dhana: śraddhā (cf. RĀ I, 5), śīla (above, 5 and 7), hrī, apatrāpya, śruta, tyāga, and prajñā. See CPD, under ariyadhana.

33 These are the cha bhogānaṁ apāyamukhāni of Dīgha III, p. 182.

34 This seems to allude to Dhammapada XV, 8: saṁtuṭṭhi paramaṁ dhanaṁ.

35 The source of this legend about the nāgarāja has not been traced.

36 The three kinds of wives to be avoided: Aṅguttara IV, p. 92.

37 The four kinds of wives to be revered: ibid., p. 92.

38 This passage on a bhikkhu bhojane mattaññū appears to be inspired by Aṅguttara I, p. 114.

39 One should be awake in five of the six watches of the day and night. See Aṅguttara I, p. 114 on a bhikkhu jāgariyam anuyutto. Cf. Dhammapada XII, 1.

40 On the four apramāṇa: maitrī, karuṇā, muditā, and upekṣā, also called the four brahmavihāra, see RĀ I, 24; Traité, pp. 1239–1273.

41 On the four dhyāna, see RĀ, ibid.; Traité, pp. 1233–1238.

42 When karma is based on rtag pa, mngon par zhen pa, gnyen po med pa and two gzhi (yon tan dang ldan pa and phan 'dogs pa), it brings a great result, kuśala or akuśala (see ṭīkā 345b).

43 For this simile, see Aṅguttara I, p. 250.

44 On the five nivaraṇa: kāmacchanda, vyāpāda, styānamiddha, auddhatyakaukṛtya, and vicikitsā, see RĀ V, 30–33; BHSD, p. 311; Dharmadhātustava 18–19; Traité, p. 1013.

45 The five bala or indriya: śraddhā, vīrya, smṛti, samādhi, and prajñā. See BS 97; Traité, pp. 1125–1127. The ṭīkā, perhaps anachronistically, relates these five to the four degrees of the prayogamārga: ūṣman, mūrdhan, kṣānti and laukikāgradharma.

46 Here rgyags (mada, see Aṅguttara III, pp. 71–75, its source) is nearly a synonym of ahaṁkāra. Cf. Catuḥśataka IV, *passim*.

47 Good karma leads to svarga but śūnyatā is conducive to mokṣa. See RĀ I, 43–45.

48 The four smṛtyupasthāna; namely, kāya°, vedanā°, citta°, and dharmasmṛtyupasthāna destroy the four viparyāsa: śuci°, sukha°, nitya° and ātmaviparyāsa. See Traité, pp. 1150 ff., with references.

49 A canonical allusion (e.g., Saṁyutta III, p. 44). For the Sanskrit, see Prasannapadā, p. 355.

50 The skandhas are created by avidyā, etc. (see MK XVII, 28; XXVI), not by any other cause such as Īśvara. See the introduction to the Akutobhayā, Pek. ed. 5229, 34a: . . .dbang phyug dang | skyes bu dang | gnyi ga dang | dus dang | rang bzhin dang | nges pa dang | 'gyur ba dang | rdul phran gyi rgyus . . . . Cf. Śvetāśvataropaniṣad I, 2: kālaḥ svabhāvo niyatir yadṛcchā bhūtāni yoniḥ puruṣa iti. . . .

51 The three saṁyojana: satkāyadṛṣṭi, vicikitsā and śīlavrataparāmarśa. See references in PED, p. 656.

52 The Four Truths must be cultivated with śruta, śīla, and dhyāna; i.e., I assume, with śīla, samādhi, and prajñā (namely, śrutamayī, cintāmayī, and bhāvanāmayī; cf. Dharmasaṁgraha § 110).

53 The three śikṣā (adhiśīla, adhicitta, and adhiprajñā; cf. BHSD, p.527) comprise all the prātimokṣa rules, 'diyaḍḍhasikkāpadasata'; see Aṅguttara I, p. 230.

54 On the four smṛtyupasthāna, see Traité, pp.1121–1123, 1150 ff.

55 An allusion to anitye nityam iti viparyāsa; cf. v. 48 above; Traité, pp. 925, 1076; MK XXIII; Catuḥśataka I.

56 Also referring to aśucau śucir iti viparyāsa; cf. ibid.

57 A reference to Aṅguttara IV, pp. 100–103.

58 Samsara (saṁsāra) without sāra; e.g. Dharmadhātustava 15. For the kadalīskandha, see RĀ II, 1; YṢ 27; PED, p. 185.

59 For the mahārṇavayugacchidrakūrmagrīvārpaṇopamā, Majjhima III, 169; Therīgāthā 500; see also Pañjikā, p. 9; Śatapañcāśatka 5; Saddharmapuṇḍarīka, p. 463.

60 The simile of the *suvarṇapātra also occurs in Catuḥśataka II, 21. See also Traité, p. 1674.

61 This refers to the four cakras; see Aṅguttara II, p. 32.

62 Seems to refer to Saṁyutta I, pp. 87–89. Cf. BS 141.

63~ The eight akṣaṇa. References at Vimalakīrtinirdeśa, p. 118, n. 71; see also RĀ III, 87.

65 According to the commentary (356a), saṁsāradoṣa is sevenfold: nges pa med pa (see 66), ngoms mi shes pa (see 67), lus yang dang yang du 'dor na (68), yang dang yang du nying mtshams sbyor ba (68), yang dang yang du mtho dman gyi ngo bor gyur pa (69 ff.), grogs med pa nyid (76), and 'gro ba drug pa (77 ff.).

66 See in general Saṁyutta II, p. 178 ff.

67 This simile occurs in Saṁyutta II, p. 180.

68 Ibid., pp. 185 and 179.

69~ An account — yathāgamam — of the repeated ascent and descent through ṣaḍgati (69–75) and an account of the sufferings of the various hells. Traité, pp. 951–968 (with references) forms a detailed commentary to this. See also Guenther (1959), pp. 55–73.

104 Reminiscent of Aṅguttara IV, p. 320. See also BS 21 and the accompanying note.

105 Śīla, samādhi, and prajñā sum up the eightfold path (see v. 52 above). For the description of nirvana see the Udāna, pp. 80–81.

106 The seven bodhyaṅga. Traité, p. 1128.

107 Here dhyāna and prajñā apparently correspond to śamatha and vipaśyanā; cf. Aṅguttara II, p. 157. The simile "gopade udaka" is also canonical; e.g. Aṅguttara III, p. 188. Dhammapada XXV, 13.

108 On caturdaśāvyākṛtavastu, see MK XXII, 12 (Prasannapadā, p. 446); Traité, p. 154; May (1959), p. 278, n. 1015; CPD.

109~ Here the author merely propounds the canonical version of the dvādaśāṅga (see PED, p. 394 for references), but in MK XXVI and in the Pratītyasamutpādahṛdayakārikā he offers two current interpretations.

112 An allusion to the Śālistambasūtra (ed. Sastri), p. 1. Cf. Majjhima I, p. 190. And see also the svavṛtti *ad* VV 54; MK XXIV, 40.

113~ The Four Noble Truths. See e.g. May (1959), pp. 206–250, with ref.

116 For the interpretation of this verse see MK XVIII, 12; CS II, 15. I have not traced the similes.

117 Like RĀ IV, 73, this refers to Dhammapada I, 1, etc.

118~ A final exhortation to practice the Dharma not only as prescribed in the āgamas but also along the lines of Mahāyāna, as is obvious from the references to puṇyānumodanā (see BS 51–52; RĀ V, 67), Avalokiteśvara (see *Encyc. of Buddhism* II, pp. 407–415), Amitābha (see RĀ III, 99), the pāramitās, and pariṇāmanā (see BS 53; RĀ IV, 90). The canonical passage for nirvana as saṁjñāmātra (cf. ṭīkā, 376a) occurs e.g. in the Prasannapadā, p. 389; Ṣaḍdarśanasamuccaya (ed. Suali), p. 46; Pañcaskandhaprakaraṇa (my ed.), p. 22.

*Bodhisaṁbhāra[ka]

The text Pú tí zī liáng lùn, *Bodhisaṁbhāraśāstra, or simply the Bodhisaṁbhāra[ka], belongs to that group of texts ascribed to Nāgārjuna that are extant only in Chinese versions. It is accompanied by a commentary composed by a certain Bǐ qiū zì zài: *Bhikṣu Īśvara, or more likely, Īśvarabhikṣu. Both texts (Taishō 1660, 517b–541b) were translated by Dharmagupta between 605 and 616 A.D. Neither the Sanskrit original nor a Tibetan version is extant, at least in the Tanjur. However, the fact that the scope of the text was known to Bu-ston (". . . rab byung gi spyod pa gtso bor ston pa byang chub kyi tshogs . . .") renders it likely that a Tibetan version may have existed, and perhaps still does.[149]

The external evidence for Nāgārjuna's authorship is provided by two quotations from Nāgārjuna's "Byang chub kyi tshogs," *Bodhisaṁbhāra (44) in Candrakīrti's Catuḥśatakaṭīkā (Pek. ed. 5266, Ya, fol. 103a).[150] I have also come across a quotation from *Bodhisaṁbhāra[ka] (v. 26) in a work by Asvabhāva, the Mahāyānasaṁgrahopanibandhana (Pek. ed. 5552, Li, fol. 329b).[151]

Moreover, an early date for the *Bodhisaṁbhāra[ka] is ensured by the fact that it is quoted in the Daśabhūmikavibhāṣā, of which a Chinese version from ca. 408 A.D. still survives, whereas an earlier one (by Dharmarakṣa) from ca. 265 A.D. is lost. In both cases Nāgārjuna was held to be the author.[152]

The subject matter of the *Bodhisaṁbhāra[ka] is the same as that of the third pariccheda of the Ratnāvalī: bodhisaṁbhāra. But the manner in which the author of the *Bodhisaṁbhāra[ka] handles his "endless" topic (v. 3) differs. Clearly these expositions are intended to be complementary to one another.

Though a Chinese version of a lost Sanskrit original is by no means an ideal starting point for a description of the author's style, one cannot fail to notice that the *Bodhisaṁbhāra[ka] bears great resemblance not only to the Ratnāvalī but also to the Suhṛllekha. The author desires to unfold his subject strictly yathāgamam, and so he does. Without in any way disavowing abstruse points such as śūnyatā, he takes pains not to deter ādikarmikas by indulging too much in such matters. Again, the style is not encumbered with philosophical arguments or abstract accounts. Here, as in the Suhṛllekha—not to mention the Sūtrasamuccaya—the author shows a fondness for numerical lists of various wholesome or unwholesome dharmas. Finally, one may observe the many dṛṣṭāntas adduced by the author. Most, if not all of them are taken out of the canonical scriptures: in the case of the Suhṛllekha mainly from the āgamas (Dīrgha, etc.); in the case of the *Bodhisaṁbhāra[ka] mainly from various Mahāyānasūtras, but also from the ancient āgamas.

The text is addressed to Bodhisattvas; that is, to pravrajitas and gṛhasthas devoted to the Mahāyāna (v. 165). The subject matter is, as indicated by the very title, the equipment or accumulations for enlightenment (bodhisaṁbhāra) (v. 1), as they have been proclaimed in various Sūtras of the Mahāyāna. Though bodhisaṁbhāra is ananta, it may conveniently be placed under two main headings (see RĀ III, 12–13) punya- and jñāna-saṁbhāra, which result respectively in the attainment of a Rūpa- and a Dharmakāya; that is (taken together) in a Buddhakāya.

Though prajñā (constituting jñānasaṁbhāra) is the most important saṁbhāra (vv. 5–7) it in fact plays only a subordinate role within the body of the *Bodhisaṁbhāra[ka] (see especially vv. 19, 28–29, 40, 63 ff., 96, 149, 153). It is reasonable to suppose that a bhājana would have to refer to the Mūlamadhyamakakārikā, also called Prajñā, though the *Bodhisaṁbhāra[ka] never refers to any of the author's other works.

The great majority of verses are devoted to an exposition of the other five pāramitās: dāna, śīla (parārtham, according to RĀ IV, 81), kṣānti, vīrya (svārtham, ibid.) and dhyāna (mokṣārtham according to ibid., together with prajñā). A Bodhisattva's fundamental attitude toward all other living beings (sattva) is one of karuṇā and upāyakauśalya. Thus all virtues (guṇa) apart from dhyāna and prajñā may be classified as various kinds of puṇyasaṁbhāra.

Obviously there is really no end to the multifarious forms a bodhisattvacaryā devoted to these ideals may take. Suffice it to mention that among the main topics treated under this broad heading in the *Bodhisaṁbhāra[ka] are saṁgrahavastu, the ten Bodhisattva stages (above all the sixth, abhimukhī, and the eighth, acalā; cf. RĀ V, 41–61 for the full list), bodhicittotpādavidhi, mahāpuruṣalakṣaṇa (extensively treated in RĀ II, 74–100), sattvaparipācana, pūjā, dharmadeśanā, and śrāvakapratyekabhūmiprahāṇa.

Rather than dilating in general upon the difficulties and uncertainties inherent in the translation that I have attempted in Part I of this book, I shall only emphasize that my main objective has been to come as close as possible to the original Sanskrit underlying the idiosyncrasies of the Chinese. Though Eric Grinstead has rendered precious support *in rebus sinicis* I expect and hope that other scholars will some day be able to improve my work in various ways.[153]

Notes on the Verses

1 With "according to tradition" Nāgārjuna here, as in the Ratnāvalī, Suhṛllekha, and other works has not only Mahāyānasūtras in mind, but also the ancient Sūtra collections. RĀ III also has the title *Bodhisaṁbhāra and treats the same subject, but it hardly ever overlaps the account given in the present work.

3 For buddhakāya see the Vimalakīrtinirdeśa, p. 138–140; Samādhirājasūtra XXII. Strictly speaking, Nāgārjuna acknowledges a Rūpakāya due to anantapuṇyasaṁbhāra and a Dharmakāya due to anantajñānasaṁbhāra. See RĀ III, 9–13; YṢ 60.

4 Vandanā and pūjanā form a part of the anuttarapūjā. Cf. note to v. 48, below.

5 Prajñāparamitā is often called the 'Mother of Buddhas'. See Murti, op. cit., p. 277; Prajñāpāramitāstotra. In RĀ I, 5 prajñā is pradhāna compared to śraddhā. This theme is elaborated in SS 175b3–178a3, following the Tathāgataguhya, *Vimatisamudghāta, and Śraddhābalādhānāvatāramudrā Sūtras, the Bodhisattvapiṭaka, Candragarbhaparivarta, Sāgaranāgarājaparipṛcchā, and the Tathāgataguṇajñānācintyaviṣayāvatāranirdeśa-sūtra. Śraddhā in buddhadeśanā is realized in pāramitācaryā, etc.

6 For a definition of upāyakauśalya, see v. 17; see also Har Dayal (1932), pp. 248 ff.; Vimalakīrtinirdeśa, p. 116; SS 243b7–246a3. Correct rén in pāda b to zíng.

7 For pāramitā see also RĀ IV, 80–82; V, 35–39; Traité, pp. 650–1111.

8 For mahākaruṇā see Traité, pp. 1705–1717. For the common image of asthimajjan, see ibid., p. 2230, n. 1; Har Dayal (1932), p. 24.

9 The buddhaguṇa are the ten bala, the four vaiśāradya, the four pratisaṁvid and the eighteen āveṇikadharma, extensively treated in Traité, pp. 1505–1707. On ṛddhi, ibid., pp. 329–330; 381–385.

Muditā is the third apramāṇa; ibid., pp. 1239–1273; mahāmuditā, ibid., p. 1709, n. See also ibid., pp. 1340–1361 on buddhānusmṛti.

14 There are three puṇyakriyāvastu (dāna, śīla, bhāvanā); Traité, pp. 2245–2260.

15 That is, these people neither perform good karma resulting in rebirth in the heaven realms, nor attain that jñāna which amounts to liberation. Cf. RĀ I, 43.

19 The word gambhīradharma (i.e., pratītyasamutpāda) is explained in Traité, pp. 337–338; 396 (the verse quoted here at 107a11–12 is surely MK XXIV, 18). Otherwise only a few stanzas in BS refer directly to śūnyatā. See especially 28–29 and 64.

20 Here the author refers to lokadharmatyāga. Cf. Vimalakīrtinirdeśa, p. 108, n. 50. For other kinds of tyāga, see also Traité, pp. 1413–1419.

21 The image śirobhūṣaṇa (or śiraścaila) is canonical. Cf. Upālipariprcchā, p. 114, n. 1; SL 104; Śūraṁgamasamādhi, p. 212, n. 217; BHSD, under ādīptaśiraścailopama. The eighth bodhisattvabhūmi (i.e. acalā) is also called avaivartika (or avivartya); see RĀ V, 55; Śūraṁgamasamādhi, p. 120, n. 5; pp. 208–210; Traité, pp. 243–245, 1502, n. 3, 1804.

26 This verse is quoted (without indication of source) in Asvabhāva's Mahāyānasaṁgrahopanibandhana, 329b1–2: dmyal bar 'gro ba byang chub la I I gtan du bgegs byed ma yin gyi I I rang sangs rgyas kyi sa dang ni I I nyan thos sa dag bgegs byed do II.

27 Sūtra quotation not traced (Saddharmasmṛtyupasthāna?).

28 For anutpāda, etc. see above all the Vimalakīṛtinirdeśa, pp. 41–43. This verse is apparently quoted (but not identified) in Traité, p. 327 (97b27–29). The lines at 12–14 are of course the maṅgalaślokau of MK; cf. Traité, p. 326). What remains of pāda d apparently occurs at 97c1 as kōng fēi kōng.

29 All this is only suggested in this text: One must turn to the Mūlamadhyamakakārikā, Śūnyatāsaptati, etc. for details.

30 For vyākaraṇa see the commentary, translated in a valuable note to the Śūraṁgamasamādhi, p. 203.

31 For the sixth bhūmi (abhimukhī) see RĀ IV, 51, which follows the Daśabhūmika; Traité, pp. 2418–2420; Har Dayal, op. cit., p. 289.

33 Compare v. 6.

44 Quoted in Candrakīrti's Catuḥśatakaṭīkā, at 103a2 (as being from "Nāgārjuna's Byang chub kyi tshogs"): sdug bsngal gzhan lta yar 'dug cig | | gang zhig sems can phan bde'i phyir | | dmyal ba'i sdug bsngal che bzod pa | | de'i lag gyas na byang chub po ||.

48 This is pāpadeśanā, followed by adhyeṣaṇā (49), yācanā (50), puṇyānumodanā (51–52), and pariṇāmanā (53). Compare RĀ V, 65–87 (śaraṇagamana, pūjanā, pāpadeśanā, adhyeṣaṇā, yācanā, bodhicittotpāda and parinām anā); Bodhicittotpādavidhi (vandanā, pāpadeśanā, puṇyānumodanā, śaraṇagamana, ātmatyāga, bodhicittotpāda and pariṇāmanā); Upālipariprcchā, p. 107, n. 4 with references; Dharmasaṁgraha XIV.

53 This recalls Aṣṭasāhasrikā, p. 70.

56 Acc. to RĀ V, 65 this rite is to be performed three times daily (nyin gcig bzhin yang dus gsum . . .). The posture is familiar; see, e.g., Suvikrāntavikrāmipariprcchā, p. 3: . . . ekāṁsam uttarāsaṅgaṁ kṛtvā dakṣiṇaṁ jānumaṇḍalaṁ pṛthivyāṁ pratiṣṭhāpya. . . .

57 The bodhicittotpādapuṇya is described similarly in RĀ V, 86. It was most likely inspired by a well known verse from the Vīradattapariprcchā, see Bodhipathapradīpa, pp. 110–111.

62 By committing one of the five ānantarya (see Vimalakīrtinirdeśa, p. 156, n. 33) one samanantaraṁ narakeṣūpapadyate. However, this is not "byang chub la gtan du bgegs" (cf. v. 26), as are the two sins mentioned in vv. 60–61.

63 The three vimokṣamukha are discussed in the Traité, pp. 321–325 (note that the verse quoted here at p. 323 [96c13–14] must be identified as MK XVIII, 7); ibid., pp. 1213–1232; Vimalakīrtinirdeśa, p. 148, n. 16.

64 This verse is cited by Tsong kha pa in the Lam rim chen mo, 414b1–2 (as being from the "Byang chub kyi tshogs"): rang bzhin med pas stong la stong pa ni | | yin dang mtshan mas ci zhig byed par 'gyur | | mtshan ma thams cad log par 'gyur ba'i phyir | | mkhas pas ci ste smon lam 'debs par 'gyur ||. His source is Catuḥśatakaṭīkā 215b2, identified by Uryūzu Ryūshin in *IBK* XVII, p. 518, to which Prof. de Jong has kindly called my attention. See also Wayman (1978), p. 252.

66 Cf. Catuḥśataka VIII, 22.

67 A celebrated image; cf. Traité, p. 1140, n. 1.

69 The correct attitude is, of course, bodhicitta; the term yoga refers to the three vimokṣamukha as the commentator notes and as shown by v. 73.

70 The first part of this verse alludes to Udānavarga I, 19, etc. (cited in Traité, p. 2296, n. 1).

72 Cf. Niraupamyastava 9: sattvasaṁjñā ca te nātha sarvathā na pravartate I duḥkhārteṣu ca sattveṣu tvam atīva kṛpātmakaḥ II. See Śūraṁgamasamādhi, p. 148.

73 Cf. RĀ I, 24; SL 40.

75 For apratiṣṭhitanirvāṇa, etc., see Vimalakīrtinirdeśa, p. 144.

79 The various śāstras are, according to the commentator: mathematics, metallurgy, medicine, exorcism, botany, mineralogy, astronomy, dream divination, and anatomy. For śilpakarmasthāna, vidyā, and kalā, see Traité, p. 1856; Śūraṁgamasamādhi, p. 145; v. 103 below; Mahāvyutpatti §§ 217–218, 76; Bu ston I, p. 44, with notes.

81 Śāṭhya and māyā often occur together; cf. the Vimalakīrtinirdeśa, p. 114, n. 61. For saṁnāha, cf. Traité, p. 1841, n. 2; Śūraṁgamasamādhi, p. 179, n. 154.

83 An allusion to daśakuśalakarmapatha, see the Vimalakīrtinirdeśa, p. 118, n. 73. See ibid., n. 72 for śikṣāpada.

84 These verses (84–87) on dhyānapāramitā may be compared with Traité, pp. 984–1057; also Arthaviniścayasūtra §§ 12–14 (the four samādhibhāvanā, smṛtyupasthāna, and samyakprahāṇa).

92 See note on v. 21. The three concepts lābhasatkārayaśas are well known as Pāli lābhasakkārasiloka; see references in PED.

93 *Summum bonum* (pradhāna- or viśiṣṭahita?) refers to naiḥśreyasa, or mokṣa. Cf. RĀ I, 4; III, 30; SL 104; also SL 55.

94 The image is canonical; see PED, under puttamaṁsa. See especially Saṁyutta II, p. 98). Adopt the variant niàn in pāda a.

95 Daśadharmakasūtra: Taishō 314 (quoted three times in all in the Śikṣāsamuccaya).

96 For Mārakarma see YṢ 36; SS 190b1 ff.; Traité, pp. 339–346. For nirmamo nirahaṁkāraḥ, see MK XVIII, 2–3.

97 The 37 bodhipākṣika are treated at length in the Traité, at pp. 1119–1207. They are also mentioned in SL 106 (bodhyaṅga),

113 (mārga), 45 (bala, indriya), 48 (smṛtyupasthāna). See v. 121 below for ṛddhipāda.

98 Cf. SL 42.

100 Cf. vv. 20, 92.

101 For siṁhanāda, Vimalakīrtinirdeśa, p. 98, n. 4; BV 52; CS III, 54.

103 Cf. v. 79.

104 These are the four saṁgrahavastu (dāna, priyavāditā, arthacaryā, and samānārtha). See the Vimalakīrtinirdeśa, p. 116, n. 67; RĀ II, 72; Akṣayamatinirdeśa, Bu, fol. 149a – 150a.

105 According to the commentator, this produces the suvarṇavarṇa-mahāpuruṣalakṣaṇa; cf. RĀ II, 86.

108 For brahmasvara (also a mahāpuruṣalakṣaṇa), see RĀ II, 91. For a complete list of the lakṣaṇa and their causes, see Traité, pp. 271 – 281; RĀ II, 74 – 100; Arthaviniścayasūtranibandhana § 26. Yathā pūrvaṁ tathā paścāt, also CS I, 25.

113 This refers to the six sārāṇīyā dhammā known from Dīgha III, p. 245. Perhaps they are also referred to at RĀ III, 35. See Traité, p. 1739, n. 4.

117 "In all situations;" i.e., according to the commentator, in regard to the eight lokadharma.

119 The pañca vimuttāyatanāni are known from Dīgha III, p. 241. For the ten aśubhasaṁjñā, see Traité, p. 1312 ff. For the list of eight mahāpuruṣavitarka, see Dīgha III, p. 287 (= aṭṭha dhammā uppādetabbā).

120 For the five abhijñā, see Traité, pp. 328 – 333. The six are listed at RĀ III, 92 – 97; also Traité, pp. 1809 ff.

121 See Traité, p. 1124 for ṛddhipāda. For the four brahmavihāra, or apramāṇa, ibid., pp. 1239 – 1273; RĀ I, 24; SL 40.

122 These comparisons (āśīviṣa, śūnyagrāma, and vadhaka) are well known. See Vimalakīrtinirdeśa, p. 136, n. 28. *Kāya/parṣad in pāda c (and the commentary's *vedanākāya) is not plausible.

123 The following stanzas (123 – 145) are inspired by the author's study of the Kāśyapaparivarta. References are to sections in the edition of von Staël-Holstein). See loc. cit., § 1. For the ācāryamuṣṭi, see Vimalakīrtinirdeśa, p. 267, n. 19; CPD II, p. 33.

124 Kāśyapaparivarta § 2.

125 Ibid. § 2. For the term puṇyakṣetra, see PED, under puññakkhetta; Śūraṁgamasamādhi, pp. 231–235.

126 This and the following verse should be compared with §§ 3–5.

128 This verse and the following two verses are modeled upon Kāśyapaparivarta § 6. For āryavaṁśa, see references in Traité, p. 1739, n. 4.

131 Ibid. § 8. A bodhisattva who is ṛjuka never tells a lie.

132 Ibid. § 8.

133 Cf. ibid. § 10.

134 This and the three following verses give the four bodhisattvaskhalita; ibid. § 11; see Śikṣāsamuccaya, p. 54; cf. Traité, p. 1846).

137 For the twelve ascetic practices (dhūtaguṇa), see Dharmasaṁgraha § 63; BHSD, p. 286; Vimalakīrtinirdeśa, p. 150, n.

138 The Sanskrit has sarvasattveṣu samacittatā . . . buddhajñānasamādāpanatā . . . samyakprayogatā; cf. Kāśyapaparivarta § 12.

139 See ibid. §§ 15–16.

140 Ibid. § 16. For puṇyakriyāvastu, see verse 14 and the accompanying note.

141 Kāśyapaparivarta § 14. Other kinds of kalyāṇamitra (good friends) are mentioned at SS 212b3.

142 The four kumitra (bad friends) mentioned here and in 143 occur at op. cit. § 13.

144 Ibid. § 17. For apratihatacitta see also Traité, p. 393–394.

145 This verse sums up Kāśyapaparivarta §§ 29–32.

147 The nine āghātavastu are canonical. See the references in the Vimalakīrtinirdeśa, p. 289, n. 18. The twenty "minor matters" (i.e., upakleśa) are, according to the commentary: āśraddhya, āhrīkya, śāṭhya, auddhatya, vikṣepa, pramāda, vihiṁsā, anapatrāpya, kauśīdya, kaukṛtya, styāna, middha, upanāha, mrakṣa, īrṣyā, mātsarya, unnati (or mada?), krodha, vipratisāra (or ālekhya, etc.?), and mūchā (?); cf. Dharmasaṁgraha § 69; VV 7 (svavṛtti); RĀ V, 3–33 *passim*; compare various treatises on Abhidharma under the headings paryavasthāna, upakleśa, and nivaraṇa. For the eight kusītavatthūni, see e.g. Dīgha III, p. 255.

148 Cf. Kāśyapaparivarta § 23.

149 The commentary to this verse is translated in Traité, p. 1228. See also Kāśyapaparivarta §§ 63–65, quoted in Prasannapadā, p. 248.

150 On vandanā and pūjā see Śikṣāsamuccaya XVII.

152 For avetyaprasāda, see Vimalakīrtinirdeśa, p. 99, n. 8; May (1959), p. 219, n. 744. Correct qù in pāda a to fā.

153 This amounts to anupalambhaśūnyatā; cf. Traité, p. 2035.

157 Apparently inspired by the Ratnamegha, cited in SS 183b6–7.

159 For buddhakṣetra, cf. the references in Vimalakīrtinirdeśa, p. 461.

160 This is neatly summarized in RĀ IV, 96: śūnyatākaruṇāgarbham ekeṣāṁ bodhisādhanam (cf. Prasannapadā, p. 360, variant reading).

162 For dharmapūjā, see Vimalakīrtinirdeśa, pp. 377–382.

163 This verse echoes Vimalakīrtinirdeśa, p. 378. See ibid., n. 18 for the meaning of bodhisattvapiṭaka.

164 Here wèi renders vyañjana (one of the four pratisaraṇa). Cf. de Jong's remarks in *Eastern Buddhist* XIII, p. 157.

Concluding Essay: The Unity of Nāgārjuna's Thought

The purpose of the following pages is to present a synthesis of the tenets of Nāgārjuna's philosophy and its presuppositions. Any such attempt must be preceded by a brief sketch of the historical background if the proper perspective is not to be distorted.

Without wishing in any way to appear disparaging of previous efforts to present a survey of Madhyamaka, I do think that two circumstances warrant a novel exposition of the Madhyamaka system forged by Nāgārjuna.[154] First, previous accounts of his thinking have only been based on the testimony provided by a few of Nāgārjuna's works. Second, and to some extent an outcome of the first, these discussions tend to present his philosophy as a series of more or less coherent and sensible ideas concerning various epistemological, logical, or ontological issues.

In my view, however, a careful reading of Nāgārjuna's authentic writings will show that his extraordinary genius succeeded in blending a great mass of inherited moral, religious, and philosophical ideas into a harmonious whole. If we had to condense his system in all its aspects to one single term, we should therefore not choose a term such as śūnyatā or pratītyasamutpāda, but instead should focus on bodhisādhana. By recognizing bodhisādhana (for which puṇyajñānasaṁbhāra can be considered an equivalent) to be the heading under which all Nāgārjuna's various theories and injunctions are unified, we place ourselves in a better position to appraise each of his writings in relation to others and within its own confines.[155]

The Non-Buddhist Background

While Nāgārjuna was, of course, aware of the existence of various 'heretical' darśanas such as the Sāṁkhya, Vaiśeṣika, Jaina,[156] Nyāya,[157] Lokāyata,[158] *Īśvaravāda[159], and probably also many other sectarians, their influence upon the development of his thought amounts to virtually nil. Doubtless his study of Nyāya, and, I suppose, Vaiśeṣika, provoked his endeavor to match the former's notion of apavarga to the Buddhist nirvana and the latter's abhyudaya/naiḥśreyasa to his own sukha/mokṣa.[160] A similar attitude can be seen in his attempt to absorb the deities of popular religion — Brahmā, Indra, Viṣṇu, Rudra, and the rest — by interpreting them as emanations of the Buddha.[161] But we never find any trace of positive influence from any of these sources in Nāgārjuna's authentic writings.

On the other hand it must be conceded that Nāgārjuna could not escape the impact which orthodox Brahmin dialectics (vāda), natural philosophy, arts, crafts, and sciences indirectly exerted upon the Buddhist milieu. Allusions to cikitsā, śilpa, vidyā, kalā and various worldly śāstras (BS 79) indicate the wide scope of his erudition. On the level of 'empirical sciences' he obviously did not hesitate to accept the best of traditional Hindu lore as means conducive to temporal happiness (abhyudaya).[162]

Let us finally not ignore a circumstance so obvious that it may easily be overlooked. From his birth to his death Nāgārjuna must as a member of the community have received an unceasing flow of impressions and convictions, prejudices and superstitions from the Hindu society surrounding him. This forms a part of his background which was never recorded and for an assessment of which no sources are available to us.

The Buddhist Tripiṭaka Tradition

Nāgārjuna's writings give ample evidence of his acquaintance not only with the Sūtras of the Mahāyāna but also with the Sūtras, Vinaya, and Abhidharma of Hīnayāna (or as he invariably puts it, conscious of the distinction among the three vehicles: the Bodhisattvayāna versus the Śrāvakayāna and Pratyekabuddhayāna).

Before considering the features which distinguish Mahāyāna from Hīnayāna it may be useful to recall the fundamentals of the Dharma propounded in the ancient Sūtras.[163]

The historical Buddha himself, once enlightened (buddha), had no other wish than to impart to others a method (mārga) leading to deliverance (mokṣa) from the cycle of birth and death (samsara); i.e. from duḥkha. He shared with numerous contemporary śramanas the conviction that our life in a gati in samsara — without a beginning in time — depends solely upon our previous volitional actions (karma). He shared with many other contemporaries as well the conviction that adherence to such a life was the source of nothing but duḥkha, and the idea that nothing could be deemed more desirable for living beings than to obtain release from samsara; in other words, nirvana.

It was in regard to the path (mārga) devised for escape and surely (if we read between the lines) by virtue of his impressive personality as a "teacher of gods and men" that the Buddha stood out among contemporary teachers with fundamentally the same presuppositions. He did this in such a way as to appeal mainly to the upper strata of society. His was a mārga for āryas, not a popular religion for pṛthagjanas, the common masses.

The Buddha's entire life within society was devoted to teaching the mārga to monks and laymen. He never tired of re-formulating it from new and different angles according to the demands of circumstances and invariably with a keen perception of the capacities and inclinations of his listeners. Though his way of teaching may have altered, the theory behind his teachings remained unchanged throughout his life: It is kleśas that motivate living beings to that karma which keeps the wheel of life turning; above all, the three fundamental kleśas of rāga, dveṣa and moha. These teaching were collected in the Sūtrapiṭaka, the first part of the canonical Tripiṭaka. As the Dharma gradually gained ground and with it the Sangha, rules for the regulation of the daily life of the monks came into demand. Hence the origin of the Vinayapiṭaka, the collection of monastic rules. From a doctrinal point of view the Vinaya adds nothing to the Dharma propounded in the collections of Sūtras, and it is hardly surprising to find that the rules codified in the Vinaya of the various schools vary in several instances due to geographical circumstances and other conditions. The Vinaya referred to by Nāgārjuna seems to have been that of the Mūlasarvāstivādins.

The origins of the third piṭaka is to be sought in the Sūtras themselves; or rather, in my opinion, with the Buddha himself. Abhidharma originally marked an attempt to group all the positive, negative and neutral dharmas familiar from the discourses of the Master systematically so as to present a survey for monks studying in seclusion. Through the exercise and gradual development of his intellectual faculty (prajñā)[164] the monk was thus enabled in a most rationalized manner to become thoroughly conversant with those dharmas to be developed and those to be abandoned. The ingenious device laid down in the Abhidharma had the advantage of forming a kind of highway to mokṣa. In the course of time some of the best Buddhist minds contributed to the vigorous development of Abhidharma, a development which reached its peak about the time of Nāgārjuna with the compilation of the magnificent thesaurus of Buddhist lore, the Mahāvibhāṣā of the Sarvāstivāda.

At the same time, however, the abstract and systematic spirit of the Abhidharma inevitably embodied a tendency to dogmatism. In the end, this attitude was to render it unfaithful to the intention of its founder.

As we shall see, it was profound discontent with the prevailing and somewhat complacent tendency toward dogmatism, or 'clinging', among Ābhidhārmikas that induced Nāgārjuna to adopt the non-dogmatic spirit breathing in the Prajñāpāramitāsūtras and regenerate it, as it were, among the renegades. The fact that, as the Buddha himself phrased it, ayaṁ dhammavinayo ekaraso vimuttiraso[165] also accounts for his characteristic and outspoken opposition to speculative and dogmatic theories not lending themselves to personal experience and ratification. The Buddha's deliberate setting-aside of current 'metaphysical' anta-dvayadṛṣṭi had a decisive impact upon Nāgārjuna.

I will conclude this survey by collecting some of these passages, as well as others from the ancient Sūtras that were to be formative of Nāgārjuna's philosophical thinking.

The Four Noble Truths

It was in his celebrated sermon at Banaras that the Buddha first preached the Four Noble Truths. The life of the individual (the five upādānaskandha) is sheer duḥkha. Its origin (samudaya) is tṛṣṇā, the will to life. (Note that strictly speaking this gives only a simplified 'exoteric' account of duḥkhasamudaya. The real cause is avidyā.) The purpose of human life is its nirodha; i.e., nirvana. The Buddha shows a path (or method) to nirodha: the Noble Eightfold Path, further reducible to śīla, samādhi and prajñā. Here we have the motive, the cause, the purpose, and the method of Buddhism in a nutshell.

I quote here the recension Nāgārjuna is most likely to have known, that of the Mūlasarvāstivādins.[166] The Tibetan and English for his own paraphrase, which occurs at SL 113–115, follows.[167]

> catvārīmāni bhikṣava āryasatyāni; katamāni catvāri? duḥkham ārya-satyam, duḥkhasamudayo duḥkhanirodho duḥkhanirodhagāminī pratipad āryasatyam. duḥkham āryasatyam katamat? jātir duḥkham, jarā duḥkham, vyādhir duḥkham, maraṇaṁ duḥkham, priyavi-prayogo duḥkham, apriyasaṁprayogo duḥkham, yad apīcchan paryeṣamāṇo na labhate tad api duḥkham; saṁkṣepataḥ pañca ime upādānaskandhā duḥkham; tasya parijñāyai āryāṣṭāṅgo mārgo bhāvayitavyaḥ. duḥkhasamudayam āryasatyaṁ katamat? tṛṣṇā paunar-bhavikī nandīrāgasahagatā tatra tatrābhinandinī; tasyāḥ prahāṇāya āryāṣṭāṅgo mārgo bhāvayitavyaḥ. duḥkhanirodham āryasatyaṁ katamat? yad asyā eva tṛṣṇāyāḥ paunarbhavikyā nandīrāgasaha-

gatāyās tatra tatrābhinandinyā aśeṣaprahāṇaṁ pratinisargo vāntībhāvaḥ kṣayo virāgo nirodho vyupaśamaḥ astaṁgamaḥ; tasya sākṣātkriyāyai āryāṣṭāṅgo mārgo bhāvayitavyaḥ. duḥkhanirodhagāminī pratipad āryasatyaṁ katamat? āryāṣṭāṅgo mārgaḥ — tadyathā, samyagdṛṣṭiḥ, samyaksaṁkalpaḥ, samyagvāk, samyakkarmāntaḥ, samyagājīvaḥ, samyagvyāyāmaḥ, samyaksmṛtiḥ, samyaksamādhiḥ; so 'pi bhāvayitavyaḥ. . . .

These are the four Noble Truths, O monks! What are the four? The Noble Truths of suffering, of the origin of suffering, of the cessation of suffering, and the Noble Truth of the method leading to the cessation of suffering. What is the Noble Truth of suffering? Birth is suffering, aging is suffering, disease is suffering, death is suffering. Separation from what is dear is suffering, contact with what is not dear is suffering, not to get whatever one wants is suffering. In short, suffering is these five skandhas of appropriation. In order fully to understand this one must develop the noble Eightfold Path.

What is the Noble Truth of the origin of suffering? Desire leading to rebirth, accompanied by taking delight, passion, and indulging in pleasure here and there. In order to abandon it one must develop the noble Eightfold Path.

What is the Noble Truth of the extinction of suffering? It is the complete abandonment, relinquishing, ejection, destruction, indifference to, cessation, stopping, and extinction of this desire leading to rebirth, accompanied by taking delight and by passion, and by indulging in pleasure here and there. In order to realize this one must develop the noble Eightfold Path.

What is the Noble Truth of the method leading to the cessation of suffering? The noble Eightfold Path: right view, right resolve, right speech, right conduct, right livelihood, right effort, right mindfulness, and right concentration. This must also be developed.

* * *

| yang dag lta dang 'tsho dang rtsol ba dang | | dran dang ting 'dzin ngag dang las mtha' dang | | yang dag rtog nyid lam gyi yan lag brgyad | | 'di ni zhi bar bgyi slad bsgom par bgyi |

| skye 'di sdug bsngal sred pa zhes bgyi ba | | de ni 'di yi kun 'byung rgya chen te | | 'di 'gog pa ni thar pa lags te lam | | de thob 'phags lam yan lag de brgyad lags |

| de ltar 'phags pa'i bden pa bzhi po dag | | mthong bar bgyi slad rtag tu brtson par bgyi | | pang na dpal gnas khyim pa rnams kyis kyang | | shes pas nyon mongs chu bo las brgal bgyi |

The eight members of the path are right view, livelihood, effort, mindfulness, concentration, speech, conduct, and resolve. You must develop them to attain tranquility. This birth is suffering; what is called 'thirst' is the major cause of this [suffering]. Its cessation is tantamount to liberation. The way to achieve it is the noble Eightfold Path. Therefore you must always strive to see the Four Noble Truths, for even laymen dwelling in the lap of prosperity may cross the river of impurity by means of this knowledge.

The twelve-fold chain of dependent origination

No less celebrated but far more intricate is the Buddha's teaching of the dvādaśāṅgapratītyasamutpāda. The purpose of this formula is to explain the genesis (samudaya) of duḥkha. The Buddha himself spoke of it as

> dharmo gambhīro gambhīrāvabhāso durdṛśo duravabodho 'tarkyo 'tarkyāvacaraḥ sūkṣmo nipuṇapaṇḍitavijñavedanīyaḥ . . .
>
> . . . a doctrine that is profound and appears profound, difficult to see, difficult to understand, beyond thought, inaccessible to discursive thinking, subtle, comprehensible only to the wise and intelligent.

It is, so to speak, the 'esoteric' account of duḥkhasamudaya.[168]

Ancient and modern attempts to interpret this enigmatic formula are not lacking.[169] That it was a matter of deep concern to Nāgārjuna is seen most clearly in the Pratītyasamutpādahṛdayakārikā and also in the Śūnyatāsaptati. The significance of the principle of pratītyasamutpāda in its extended general sense is evident from all his writings. MK XXVI and SL 109–112, reproduced here, both present the traditional list of the twelve nidānas, beginning with avidyā and ending with duḥkha:

> . . . idam evaṁ dvādaśāṅgaṁ pratītyasamutpādam anulomapratilomaṁ vyavalokayan, yaduta asmin satīdaṁ bhavati, asyotpādād idam utpadyate—yadutāvidyāpratyayāḥ saṁskārāḥ, saṁskārapratyayaṁ vijñānam, vijñānapratyayaṁ nāmarūpam, nāmarūpapratyayaṁ ṣaḍāyatanaṁ, ṣaḍāyatanapratyayaḥ sparśaḥ, sparśapratyayā vedanā, vedanāpratyayā tṛṣṇā, tṛṣṇāpratyayam upādānam, upādānapratyayo bhavaḥ, bhavapratyayā jātiḥ, jātipratyayā jarāmaraṇaśokaparidevaduḥkhadaurmanasyopāyāsā amī bhavanti; evam asya keva-

lasya mahato duḥkhaskandhasya samudayo bhavati; yaduta asminn asatīdaṁ na bhavati, asya nirodhād idaṁ nirudhyate—yaduta avidyānirodhāt saṁskāranirodhaḥ . . . .[170]

. . . considering thus dependent origination, which has twelve parts—forward and backward; i.e., when this is present that is present, and when this arises that arises—namely: the formations depend on ignorance, consciousness depends on the formations, name and form depend on consciousness, the six organs of sense depend on name and form, contact depends on the six organs of sense, feeling depends on contact, thirst depends on feeling, grasping depends on thirst, becoming depends on grasping, birth depends on becoming, old age, death, sorrow, grief, suffering, distress, and unrest depend on birth. Thus this whole great mass of suffering arises. But when this is absent that is absent, and when this ceases that ceases, namely: when ignorance ceases the formations cease. . . .

* * *

| ma rig pa las las te de las ni | | rnam shes de las ming dang gzugs rab 'byung | | de las skye mched drug ste de dag las | | reg pa kun tu 'byung bar thub pas gsungs |

| reg pa las ni tshor ba kun 'byung ste | | tshor ba'i gzhi las sred pa 'byung bar 'gyur | | sred pas len pa bskyed par 'gyur ba ste | | de las srid pa srid las skye ba lags |

| skye ba yod na mya ngan na rga dang | | 'dod pas 'phongs dang 'chi bas 'jigs sogs kyi | | sdug bsngal phung po shin tu che byung ste | | skye ba 'gag pas 'di kun 'gag par 'gyur |

The Muni has declared: Karma depends on ignorance. From this comes consciousness; from this comes name and form; from these the six organs of sense arise; from these contact arises. From contact arises feeling; based on feeling thirst arises; thirst gives rise to grasping; from this there is becoming; from becoming there is birth. When there is birth there arises the great mass of suffering: sorrow, disease, old age, frustration, fear of death, and the rest. However, when origination ceases, all this ceases.

Nirvana

Nirvana is really nothing but duḥkhanirodha, either with skandhas (= duḥkha) remaining (sopadhiśeṣanirvāṇa) or without skandhas remaining (nirpadhiśeṣanirvāṇa). This amounts to deliverance from future birth. This state of peace in body and mind may, however be considered from various conventional perspectives:[171]

Psychologically, nirvana is kleśakṣaya, barely different from the Stoic ideal of *apateia*. Thus, SS 221a cites the Saṁyuktāgama:

> . . . dge slong dag khyed la mya ngan las 'das pa dang | mya ngan las 'da' bar 'gro ba'i lam bshad par bya'o | | de la mya ngan las 'das pa gang zhe na | 'di lta ste | 'dod chags zad pa dang | zhe sdang zad pa dang | gti mug zad pa'o ||
>
> Monks, I will explain to you nirvana and the way of nirvana! What is nirvana? It is the extinction of desire, the extinction of hate, and the extinction of ignorance . . . .

Compare Saṁyutta IV, p. 371: . . . nibbānañ ca vo bhikkhave desissāmi nibbānagāmiñ ca maggaṁ . . . rāgakkhayo dosakkhayo mohakkhayo . . .

Ontologically, nirvana is a world beyond samsara. A well-known passage from the Udāna (p. 80 in the Pāli edition), describes nirvana:

> . . . atthi, bhikkhave, tad āyatanaṁ yattha neva paṭhavī na āpo na tejo na vāyo na ākāsānañcāyatanaṁ na viññāṇañcāyatanaṁ na akiñcaññāyatanaṁ na nevasaññānāsaññāyatanaṁ nāyaṁ loko na paraloko na ubho candimasuriyā. tatrāpāhaṁ, bhikkhave, neva āgatiṁ vadāmi na gatiṁ na ṭhitiṁ na cutiṁ na upapattiṁ; appatiṭṭhaṁ appavattaṁ anārammaṇaṁ evetaṁ: esevanto dukkhassā ti.
>
> Monks, there is a place where there is neither earth nor water nor fire nor air, no sphere of infinite space, no sphere of infinite consciousness, no sphere of nothingness, no sphere of neither-consciousness-nor-nonconsciousness. This world is not there, the other world is not there, both are not there, moon and sun are not there. I say that there is no coming there, no going, no abiding, no falling, no arising; it is not fixed, it is not moved, it has no base; it is, in fact, the end of suffering.

Nāgārjuna alludes to this passage in SL 105:

> | tshul khrims dag dang shes rab bsam gtan gyis | | mya ngan 'das zhi dul ba dri med pa'i | | go 'phang mi rga mi 'chi zad mi 'tshal | | sa chu me rlung nyi zla bral thob mdzod |

By means of good conduct, wisdom, and concentration you should obtain the peaceful, subdued, and pure state of nirvana—devoid of earth, water, fire, air, sun, and moon—where there is no age, no death, no cessation.

Epistemologically, (sometimes barely distinguished from the abovementioned points of view) one may say that paramaṁ ariyasaccaṁ yadidaṁ amosadhammaṁ nibbānaṁ (Majjhima, III, p. 245; cf. YṢ 35): "The ultimate noble truth is nirvana in its true nature." Nonetheless, nirvana cannot be an object of the senses or of consciousness. On this point, Nāgārjuna alludes twice to a passage that is found in the Pāli Dīghanikāya (I, p. 223), once at YṢ 34, and again at RĀ I, 93–95, in a passage which I present here:[172]

| sa dang chu dang me dang rlung | | ring thung phra dang sbom nyid dang | | dge sogs nyid ni rnam shes su | | 'gag par 'gyur zhes thub pas gsungs |

| rnam shes bstan med mtha' yas pa | | kun tu bdag po de la ni |
| sa dang chu dang me dang ni | | rlung gi gnas thos 'gyur ma yin |

| 'dir ni ring dang thung ba dang | | phra sbom dge dang mi dge dang | | 'dir ni ming dang gzugs dag kyang | | ma lus par ni 'gag par 'gyur |

The Muni has declared that earth, water, fire, and wind, long and short, fine and coarse, good, and so on are extinguished in consciousness. In this invisible, endless and all-powerful consciousness there is no place to be found for earth, water, fire, and wind. Here long and short, fine and coarse, good and bad, here name and form all stop.

Ignorance

The initial nidāna of duḥkha (or the skandhas) is, as we saw, avidyā, which is not merely absence of knowledge but positively, amitravat—more or less a synonym of abhiniveśa, dṛṣṭi, kalpanā or grāha, (cf., for example, the Dhammasaṅgaṇi, p. 213, which Nāgārjuna may have had in mind at ŚS 64). Avidyā may have various objects (see Dhammasaṅgaṇi, p. 190), and according to the Pratītyasamutpādasūtra (quoted in the Prasannapadā, p. 452, *ad* MK XXIII, 1) it also has a cause:

. . . avidyāpi bhikṣavaḥ sahetukā sapratyayā sanidānā. kaś ca bhikṣavaḥ avidyāyā hetuḥ? ayoniśo bhikṣavo manaskāro 'vidyāyā hetuḥ. āvilo mohajo manaskāro bhikṣavo 'vidyāyā hetuḥ. (ity ato 'vidyā saṁkalpaprabhavā bhavati).

> Monks, ignorance also has a cause, a condition, a determining factor. And what, monks, is the cause of ignorance? The cause, monks, of ignorance is superficial attention; the cause of ignorance, monks, is disturbed, deluded attention. . . .

More specifically, avidyā is due to the four viparyāsas, or perverted views (ŚS 10). Canonical passages are scarce, but see Aṅguttara II, p. 52:

> anicce bhikkhave niccan ti saññāvipallāso cittavipallāso diṭṭhivipallāso, adukkhe bhikkhave dukkhan ti saññāvipallāso cittavipallāso diṭṭhivipallāso, anattani bhikkhave attā ti saññāvipallāso cittavipallāso diṭṭhivipallāso, asubhe bhikkhave subhan ti saññāvipallāso cittavipallāso diṭṭhivipallāso . . . .

> Monks, to consider impermanent as permanent is a perversion of ideas, a perversion of mind, a perversion of view; monks, to consider painful as not painful is a perversion of ideas, a perversion of mind, a perversion of view; monks, to consider lack of self as self is a perversion of ideas, a perversion of mind, a perversion of view; monks, to consider not pure as pure is a perversion of ideas, a perversion of mind, a perversion of view. . . .

Compare the Vibhaṅga, p. 376; SL 48; MK XXIII, *passim*; Abhidharmakośa V, p. 21 (with references).

We may have here a clue to one of the most puzzling aphorisms in the ancient canonical texts; namely, the 'Kātyāyanāvavāda', referred to at MK XV, 7. This Sūtra proposes to define samyagdṛṣṭi, or right view. Cf. Saṁyutta II, p. 17:

> . . . dvayanissito khvāyaṁ Kaccāyana loko yebhuyyena atthitañ ceva natthitañ ca. lokasamudayaṁ kho Kaccāyana yathābhūtaṁ sammappaññāya passato yā loke natthitā sā na hoti; lokanirodhaṁ kho Kaccāyana yathābhūtaṁ sammappaññāya passato yā loke atthitā sā na hoti . . . sabbam atthīti kho Kaccāyana ayam eko anto, sabbaṁ natthīti ayaṁ dutiyo anto. . . .[173]

> Kaccāyana, generally this world [mankind] takes two opposite things for granted: existence and non-existence. But, Kaccāyana, when one with true understanding sees the origin of the world as it is, [then] non-existence in the world is not [valid]; when one with true understanding sees the cessation of the world as it is, [then] existence in the world is not [valid]. . . . Kaccāyana, to claim that all exists is one extreme; to say that all does not exist is the opposite extreme . . . .

The teachings suggested in these canonical extracts provided Nāgārjuna with his fundamental philosophical outlook. Duḥkha (the skandhas) is due to avidyā, which in turn is a result of the activity of the viparyāsas. These four are, in the final analysis, founded upon the assumption of asti and nāsti—existence and non-existence. This dichotomy is, as it were, the *prōton pseudos* of samsara.[174]

Nāgārjuna may have arrived at this position from a desire to achieve a consistent exegetical result of his study of the Buddha's doctrine as recorded in the scriptures.[175] In the eyes of Nāgārjuna the Buddha was not merely a forerunner but the very founder of the Madhyamaka system. It would be a rewarding task, but one which would unduly extend the limits of the present inquiry, to consider to what extent his opinion was historically justified.

No Self

Among the four perverted views the third—anātmani ātmā iti—is gravest and most basic. It consists in a vikalpa which imposes a self (ahaṁkāra; Tibetan bdag tu 'dzin pa) upon the five skandhas taken collectively or separately. It is also called satkāyadṛṣṭi and may as such take twenty different forms (cf. SL 49 and notes; Traité, p. 737, n. 3). The following verses are quoted from RĀ I, 31–35 (for a counterpart, see Saṁyutta III, p. 105):[176]

> yathādarśam upādāya svamukhapratibimbakam |
> dṛśyate nāma tac caiva na kiṁ cid api tattvataḥ ||
>
> ahaṁkāras tathā skandhān upādāyopalabhyate |
> na ca kiṁ cit sa tattvena svamukhapratibimbakam ||
>
> evaṁvidhārthaśravaṇād dharmacakṣur avāptavān |
> āryānandaḥ svayaṁ caiva bhikṣubhyo 'bhikṣṇam uktavān ||
>
> (skandhagrāho yāvad asti tāvad evāham ity api |
> ahaṁkāre sati punaḥ karma janma tataḥ punaḥ ||)

> Just as one sees an image of one's own face by means of a mirror, though this [face] is really nothing in itself, so the notion of an ego, based on the [five] skandhas, like the image of one's face, is really nothing in itself. By listening to such ideas the noble Ānanda obtained the eye of Dharma and at once explained it himself to the monks. (As long as one seizes the skandhas one also [believes in] an ego. When there is belief in an ego there is karma, and then rebirth.)

The Prasannapadā makes the point also:

> . . . rūpaṁ nātmā rūpavān nāpi cātmā rūpe nātmā nātmani rūpam . . . evaṁ yāvad vijñānaṁ nātmā vijñānavān nātmā vijñāne nātmā nātmani vijñānam iti . . . tathā anātmānaḥ sarvadharmā iti . . .[177]
>
> The self is not the body, the self does not possess the body, the self is not in the body, the body is not in the self. . . . A similar [argument] applies to [the remaining skandhas], until: The self is not the consciousness, the self does not possess consciousness, the self is not in consciousness, consciousness is not in the self . . . . In this way all dharmas are without a self. . . .

Finally, there are these verses from SL 48-49:

> I mi ni yang dag nyid du mi bde zhing I I mi rtag bdag med mi gtsang rig par bgyi I I dran pa nye bar ma gzhag rnams kyis ni I I phyin ci log bzhir lta ba 'phung bkrol ba I
>
> I gzugs ni bdag ma yin zhes gsung ste bdag I I gzugs dang ldan min gzugs la bdag gnas min I I bdag la gzugs mi gnas te de bzhin du I I phung po lhag ma bzhi yang stong rtogs bgyi I
>
> You must understand that a human being is in truth unhappy, impermanent, devoid of self, and impure; those who fail to bear this in mind are ruined by believing in the four distorted views. It has been declared that the body is not the self, the self does not possess the body, the self is not located in the body, and the body is not situated in the self. In the same way you must also understand that the four other skandhas are empty.

The skandhas

Ancient Buddhism — and the Hīnayāna — denied the existence of a permanent ātman. Instead it acknowledged the five skandhas, which like all other phenomena (dharmas) are characterized by three lakṣaṇas: anitya, duḥkha, and anātman. Mahāyāna went further: In the final analysis the skandhas are no less illusory than the notion of an ātman. Though this was scarcely in accord with the stage of development reached in the ancient Sūtras, these texts nevertheless foreshadowed the advent of Mahāyāna, above all in the following pregnant stanzas of the Saṁyuktāgama (on which BV 12–13 are based):[178]

> phenapiṇḍopamaṁ rūpaṁ vedanā budbudopamā I
> marīcisadṛśī saṁjñā saṁskārāḥ kadalīnibhāḥ I
> māyopamaṁ ca vijñānam uktam ādityabandhunā II

evaṁ dharmān vīkṣamāṇo bhikṣur ārabdhavīryavān I
divā vā yadi vā rātrau saṁprajānan pratismṛtaḥ I
pratividhyet padaṁ śāntaṁ saṁskāropaśamaṁ śivam II

The Kinsman of the Sun has declared that physical form is like a ball of foam, that feeling is like a bubble, that perception is like a mirage, that volitions are like a plantain-trunk and that consciousness is like an illusion. A monk who, full of energy, regards the dharmas thus, being mindful and aware day and night, will comprehend the peaceful place, the blissful extinction of the formations.

The Mahāyāna

Despite an increasing number of modern contributions to the study of Mahāyāna Sūtras, our knowledge of the historical origins of this developed form of Buddhism still remains meager and fragmentary and will, for all one can say, do so for decades to come.[179] Fortunately this circumstance has little effect upon our understanding of Nāgārjuna as an exponent of Mahāyāna.[180] On the contrary, the fact that he is the first individual known to have collected the Sūtras of the new school and systematized their teachings provides us not only with a *terminus ante quem* for more than three score Sūtras, but also with valuable textual and exegetical materials. As we have seen, Nāgārjuna's Sūtrasamuccaya is a collection of extracts culled largely from Sūtras belonging to the Mahāyāna. In addition, the Catuḥstava and *Bodhisaṁbhāra[ka] contain numerous allusions to, or even quotations from, these texts.[181]

In general, one may conclude that Nāgārjuna was thoroughly conversant with the ancient Tripiṭaka as well as the later developed Sūtras of the Mahāyāna. Without ever breaking radically with the ancient tradition, the Mahāyāna scriptures launched new ideas about the nature of the world, such as śūnyatā, and about the foundation of ethical behaviour (karuṇā). In Nāgārjuna they found a staunch supporter. The main source of inspiration for his *magnum opus,* the Mūlamadhyamakakārikā (which bears the subtitle Prajñā), is that group of Mahāyāna scriptures commonly known as the Prajñāpāramitāsūtras.[182] As Yasunori Ejima puts it: "The Madhyamaka-kārikā starts with and aims at nothing other than prajñāpāramitā or perfect wisdom."[183] Nāgārjuna's own words prove that from among the many Prajñāpāramitā texts he knew at least the Aṣṭasāhasrikā, the Saptaśatikā, and the Vajracchedikā.[184]

If one were to condense the tenets of the Prajñāpāramitā literature into a few sentences it would perhaps amount to this: Their view of the world is that fundamentally all phenomena (dharmas) are void of substance; i.e., illusory or empty. Their view of the individual is that as a Bodhisattva gradually recognizing this fact, one should accordingly live in the equanimity of universal emptiness. At the same time, through compassion one should devote oneself to the task of liberating all other beings, not scorning any means for the achievement of that ideal (upāyakauśalya).[185]

Naturally, in the course of time this deepened conception of the world led to novel developments within the field of ontology and epistemology. The widened view of the human situation likewise inspired a flourishing movement in the field of religion and ethics. All this gave room for the work of independent thinkers, and for this reason it often proves advantageous to center study of the Mahāyāna around its individual representatives.

Here, however, we must confine our investigation to Nāgārjuna himself. Several passages in the Ratnāvalī show that he was well aware of the features distinguishing the great yāna from the less comprehensive one, as well as the sustained opposition aroused by such divergences.[186]

First of all, Mahāyāna and Hīnayāna differ in their outlook of the world. They both endorse śūnyatā as one of the three fundamental lakṣaṇas of existence taught by the Buddha. However, according to the Mahāyāna this term indicates 'non-origination'—the fact that all phenomena lack svabhāva—whereas the Hīnayāna simply takes it as a synonym of impermanence. Thus, RĀ IV, 86ab: anutpādo mahāyāne pareṣāṁ śūnyatā kṣayaḥ | ("In Mahāyāna [emptiness means] non-origination; to others it means destruction.") Similarly, MK XIII, 3–4ab.

Second, the ancient scriptures do not mention a number of concepts specific to the Mahāyāna, such as the vows for enlightenment (praṇidhāna), the Bodhisattva's practice (caryā) of the pāramitās, his dedication of the merit thus achieved (puṇyapariṇāmanā) and his extraordinary powers (adhiṣṭhāna; on this term see BHSD). Therefore they do not provide sufficient guidance for the achievement of enlightenment. RĀ IV, 90–91ab:

> na bodhisattvapraṇidhir na caryāpariṇāmanā |
> uktāḥ śrāvakayāne 'smād bodhisattvaḥ kutas tataḥ ||
>
> adhiṣṭhānāni noktāni bodhisattvasya bodhaye |

In the Śravakayāna there is no mention of a Bodhisattva's aspirations, course, and transfer (of merit). How then can one become a Bodhisattva by following it?

Nor do the ancient texts speak of a Bodhisattva's perseverance (pratiṣṭhā = prasthāna; cf. Bodhicaryāvatāra I, 15) in the bodhicaryā. RĀ IV, 93:

bodhicaryāpratiṣṭhārthaṁ na sūtre bhāṣitaṁ vacaḥ ।
bhāṣitaṁ ca mahāyāne grāhyam asmād vicakṣaṇaiḥ ॥

In the [Śravaka] Sūtras not a word has been said about the perseverance of a Bodhisattva, but it has been discussed in the Mahāyāna. Hence the wise must accept [the Mahāyāna].

Again, the notion of puṇya- and jñānasaṁbhāra characteristic of the Mahāyāna is an object of critique or neglect among adherents of the Hīnayāna. RĀ IV, 67; IV, 83:

bodhisattvasya saṁbhāro mahāyāne tathāgataiḥ ।
nirdiṣṭaḥ sa tu sammūḍhaiḥ pradviṣṭaiś caiva nindyate ॥

puṇyajñānamayo yatra buddhair bodher mahāpathaḥ ।
deśitas tan mahāyānam ajñānād vai na dṛśyate ॥

The Tathāgatas have taught [two kinds of] accumulation in the Mahāyāna. Nevertheless, the ignorant and those filled with hate still criticize it.

Due to ignorance one does not acknowledge the Mahāyāna, in which the Buddhas have pointed out that a great path consisting of merit and wisdom leads to enlightenment.

Because of his sense of 'human responsibility' (kāruṇya), a Bodhisattva abstains from entering nirvana in order to help other living beings obtain enlightenment (cf. RĀ IV, 66). This is the very core of Mahāyāna ethics. To abuse it can only be considered a sign of mental depravity. RĀ IV, 78–79:

karuṇāpūrvakāḥ sarve niṣyandā jñānanirmalāḥ ।
uktā yatra mahāyāne kas tan nindet sacetanaḥ ॥

atyaudāryātigāmbhīryād viṣaṇṇair akṛtātmabhiḥ ।
nindyate 'dya mahāyānaṁ mohāt svaparavairibhiḥ ॥

What sensible person would deride the Mahāyāna, in which it has been stated that all results are the effect of compassion and stainless cognition? Due to ignorance, the Mahāyāna is derided because of its extreme sublimity and profundity by people desperate and unripe, enemies of themselves as well as others.

Nor do the eight stages of spiritual progress in the Śrāvakayāna reach as far as the ten bhūmis of the Mahāyāna.[187] The former lead to arhattva; the latter to buddhatva. RĀ V, 40:

> yathā śrāvakayāne 'ṣṭāv uktāḥ śrāvakabhūmayaḥ I
> mahāyāne daśa tathā bodhisattvasya bhūmayaḥ II

> As eight stages of a Disciple have been spoken of in the Śrāvakayāna, so there are ten stages of a Bodhisattva in the Mahāyāna.

Despite such differences, however, one should not simply discard the Śrāvakayāna as useless or unorthodox. On the contrary, this yāna should be regarded as preliminary to the great yāna. It addresses itself to those individuals whose moral and intellectual faculties are still at a lesser stage of development. RĀ IV, 94–96:

> yathaiva vaiyākaraṇo mātṛkām api pāṭhayet I
> buddho 'vadat tathā dharmaṁ vineyānāṁ yathākṣamam II

> keṣāṁ cid avadad dharmaṁ pāpebhyo vinivṛttaye I
> keṣāṁ cit puṇyasiddhyarthaṁ keṣāṁ cid dvayaniśritam II

> dvayāniśritam ekeṣāṁ gambhīraṁ bhīrubhīṣaṇam I
> śūnyatākaruṇāgarbhaṁ keṣāṁ cid bodhisādhanam II

> Just as a grammarian instructs [his students gradually] in the rudiments, so the Buddha expounds the Dharma to those to be trained according to their ability [to understand]: To some he explains the Dharma in order to make them abstain from evil, to others in order to make them achieve merit, [while] to others [he expounds a Dharma] based on opposites. To some [he teaches] a profound [Dharma] terrifying to the fearful; to others the means of enlightenment that has emptiness and compassion as its essence.

Nāgārjuna thus takes into account the fact that the Buddha often varied his teachings according to his audience and circumstances (cf. BV 98–99; MK XVIII, 6, 8; YṢ 33). But this is merely a pedagogical device. In reality there is only one single yāna: Śrāvakayāna and Pratyekabuddhayāna are both encompassed within the Mahāyāna (cf. SS § 10).[188] RĀ IV, 88:

> tathāgatābhisandhyoktāny asukhaṁ jñātum ity ataḥ I
> ekayānatriyānoktād ātmā rakṣya upekṣayā II

The statements of the Tathāgata having a deeper purpose are not easy to understand. Since he spoke of one *and* three vehicles, you must arm yourself with equanimity!

Nāgārjuna's Philosophical System

In discussing Nāgārjuna's own philosophical system, the preliminary question is which of Nāgārjuna's works can be considered authentic.

In a previous work[189] I have attempted to assign all the texts and fragments (to the extent I have come across such in the commentarial literature) attributed to Nāgārjuna to three classes; namely, works correctly attributed, works wrongly attributed, and those which may or may not be genuine.

The following internal and external criteria of authenticity were applied: I took my point of departure in a close study—with careful regard to the commentaries[190]—of the doctrine and the style of the Mūlamadhyamakakārikā,[191] which I axiomatically accept as his principal work, in accord with a unanimous and, so far as we know, reliable Indian, Chinese and Tibetan tradition.[192] Those among the remaining works which agree with the Mūlamadhyamakakārikā in style, scope, and doctrine, and which (turning to external criteria) are also explicitly ascribed to Nāgārjuna by the testimony of 'trustworthy witnesses'; namely, Bhavya (Bhāvaviveka), Candrakīrti, Śāntarakṣita, and Kamalaśīla, I recognize as genuine.[193] Works provable as inauthentic (e.g., if they quote from a source later than Nāgārjuna, always allowing for cases of interpolation) belong to the second class, while texts from which I have tried in vain to extract decisive criteria, external or internal, come within the third.

The works dealt with in this book are those that I concluded must be considered genuine. Decidedly not genuine, on the other hand, are the *Mahāprajñāpāramitopadeśa,[194] Abudhabodhakaprakaraṇa,[195] Guhyasamājatantraṭīkā,[196] *Dvādaśadvāraka,[197] Prajñāpāramitāstotra,[198] and Svabhāvatrayapraveśasiddhi.[199]

The third group; i.e., the dubious texts, may be divided into those that are perhaps authentic: the Mahāyānaviṁśikā,[200] Bodhicittopādavidhi,[201] Dvādaśakāranayastotra,[202] (Madhyamaka-)Bhavasaṁkrānti,[203] *Nirālambastava,[204] Śālistambakārikā,[205] Stutyatītastava,[206] Dānaparikathā,[207] Cittavajrastava,[208] Mūlasarvāstivādiśrāmaṇerakārikā,[209] *Daśabhūmikavibhāṣā,[210] *Lokaparīkṣā,[211] Yogaśataka,[212] Prajñādaṇḍa,[213] Rasavaiśeṣika-sūtra,[214] and Bhāvanākrama;[215] and those most likely not: Akṣara-śataka,[216] Akutobhayā (Mūlamadhyamakavṛtti),[217] Āryabhāṭṭaraka-Mañjuśrīparamārthastuti,[218] Kāyatrayastotra,[219] Narakoddharastava,[220] Niruttarastava,[221] Vandanāstava,[222] Dharmasaṁgraha,[223] Dharmadhātu-garbhavivaraṇa,[224] *Ekaślokaśāstra,[225] Īśvarakartṛtvanirākṛti,[226] Sattva-arādhanastava,[227] *Upāyahṛdaya,[228] *Aṣṭādaśaśūnyatāśāstra,[229] Dharma-dhātustava,[230] Yogaratnamālā,[231] etc.

I turn now to a discussion of Nāgārjuna's thought based on the texts that I do consider to be indisputably genuine. Here we find at the outset an undeniable variety in regard to style, themes and philosophical profundity. One cannot quite rule out the possibility that such diversity is to some extent to be accounted for by assumed personal motives, such as a shift of interests or a development of thinking. However, apart from the fact that the Śūnyatāsaptati and the Vigrahavyāvartanī were certainly written later than the Mūlamadhyamakakārikā, no means of establishing a relative chronology in authorship are at our disposal.

In my view, the decisive reasons for the variety of Nāgārjuna's writings is to be sought in the author's desire, as a Buddhist, to address himself to various audiences at various levels and from various perspectives. This motive would of course be quite consistent with the Mahāyāna ideal of upāyakauśalya (skillful means) (cf. BS 17). Thus, the Mūlamadhyamakakārikā, the Śūnyatāsaptati and the Vigrahavyāvartanī were intended to be studied by philosophically minded monks. The Vaidalyaprakaraṇa was written as a challenge to Naiyāyikas. The Yuktiṣaṣṭikā, the Vyavahārasiddhi, and the Pratītyasamutpādahṛdayakārikā as well are contributions to Buddhist exegesis. The Catuḥstava is a document confessing its author's personal faith in the Buddha's doctrine, while the Sūtrasamuccaya, the Bodhicittavivaraṇa, the *Bodhisaṁbhāra[ka], the Suhṛllekha, and the Ratnāvalī on the whole address themselves to a wider Buddhist audience, monks as well as laymen.

I will thus take it for granted that Nāgārjuna never changed his fundamental outlook essentially, and accordingly look upon his writings as expressions of an underlying unity of thought conceived before he made his debut in writing.

The Suhṛllekha is the most 'elementary' of Nāgārjuna's writings. It was composed in order to arouse the reader's interest in the values of Buddhism in general, and consists mainly of injunctions for laymen. With the exception of a few stray allusions there is nothing here that an adherent of the Śrāvakayāna would be inclined to disavow.

Nāgārjuna's remaining works were written from the higher level of the Mahāyāna, and we must probably take it for granted that he assumed his readers to be well versed in the fundamentals of the Tripiṭaka.[232]

The career of a Bodhisattva; i.e., a gṛhastha (householder) or pravrajita (mendicant) devoted to the ideals of Mahāyāna, is inaugurated the moment he forms bodhicitta, setting his mind on enlightenment. Now he does not merely seek his own nirvana (= kleśaskandhanirodha) but yearns for the bodhi of all beings, himself as well as others. Thus he exhibits a sense of human responsibility or compassion (karuṇā) virtually foreign to the Hīnayāna. Intellectually he will be satisfied with nothing less than the omniscience of a Buddha.[233]

The first manifest expression of a Bodhisattva's new attitude is his regular performance of the anuttarā pūjā, or bodhicittotpādavidhi. RĀ V, 65–87 thus enjoins a Bodhisattva to declare his śaraṇagamana, pūjanā, pādadeśanā, adhyeṣaṇā, yācanā, bodhicittotpāda, and puṇyapariṇāmanā three times a day in front of a buddhapratimā, a stūpa, or any other sacred object.[234] The purpose of this rite is to remind the Bodhisattva of the high ideals to which he has obligated himself. Thus a Bodhisattva embarks on the Mahāyāna by declaring his lofty aspirations (praṇidhāna), thereby, as it were, swearing his allegiance to its principles.

But pious promises and solemn vows will not suffice. In order to become a Buddha a Bodhisattva must personally collect the moral and intellectual outfit (saṁbhāra) conducive for bodhi. In due course an anantapuṇyasaṁbhāra will endow him with a Buddha's physical body (Rūpakāya), adorned with the remarkable thirty-two major and eighty minor marks, whereas an anantajñānasaṁbhāra will put him in possession of the inconceivable Dharmakāya. These two bodies constitute Buddhahood.[235]

But all this depends on fulfilling the two saṁbhāras for bodhi. This is done by practicing—in a spirit of karuṇā—the six pāramitās: dāna, śīla, kṣānti, vīrya, dhyāna and prajñā (cf. SL 8).[236] In RĀ V, 36–38 Nāgārjuna briefly defines these 'perfections' and states their respective effects:

> Liberality is to surrender one's own benefit, good morals are actions beneficial to others, patience is to renounce anger, energy is to strive for merit, meditation is to be concentrated without kleśas, insight is to ascertain the true meaning. Compassion (kṛpā) is an attitude that is the same toward all living beings; namely, love (karuṇā). From liberality comes enjoyment, from good morals happiness, from patience grace (kānti), from energy brilliance, from meditation peace, from insight (mati = prajñā) liberation, and from compassion success in all matters (sarvārtha).[237]

According to the RĀ IV, 81–82, mahāyānārtha is this: dāna and śīla are performed parārtha (for others), kṣānti and vīrya are svārtha (for one's own benefit), and dhyāna and prajñā are mokṣārtha (performed for the sake of liberation). The practice of these perfections is tantamount to bodhisaṁbhāra. According to a later source, dāna, śīla, and kṣānti are equivalent to puṇyasaṁbhāra, while dhyāna and prajñā amount to jñānasaṁbhāra. Vīrya is "a mutual friend" (gñis ka'i grogs).[238]

It would indeed be possible to read the *Bodhisaṁbhāra[ka], the Suhṛllekha, and the Ratnāvalī as expositions of these pāramitās and understand virtually any verse as an instance of one or more of these. This, however, I will leave for the reader himself to undertake.

The gradual process of development which a Bodhisattva undergoes practicing the pāramitās and a large number of other moral and intellectual virtues is minutely depicted in a number of Mahāyāna texts. According to the scheme of the Daśabhūmikasūtra, which is the authority followed by Nāgārjuna (and later Mādhyamikas) in this respect, a Bodhisattva must ascend through ten spiritual stages (bhūmi) before he finally achieves buddhatva.[239] An abstract of the ten bodhisattvabhūmis is given in RĀ V, 41–61:

> The first is pramuditā, [so called] because the Bodhisattva rejoices as he abandons the three saṁyojanas and is born in the Tathāgatagotra. By ripening this, his dānapāramitā becomes eminent. He causes one hundred lokadhātus to tremble and becomes an emperor of Jambudvīpa. The second is called vimalā, because the ten kinds of physical, vocal and mental karma are stainless, since he naturally abides by them. By ripening this, śīlapāramitā becomes eminent. He becomes an altruistic cakravartin, a glorious master of the seven ratnas. He is an expert in making living beings shun bad moral conduct.
>
> The third bhūmi is [called] prabhākarī, because as dhyāna and abhijñā arise and rāga and dveṣa are completely extinguished, the peaceful light of jñāna arises. By ripening this he controls [the pāramitās of] kṣānti and vīrya. Being a clever mahendradevānām, he resists kāmarāga. The fourth is called arciṣmatī, because the light of samyagjñāna arises as he cultivates all the bodhipakṣyas with eminence. By ripening this he becomes a devarāja of [the gods of] Suyāma. He is a master in subduing the attacks of satkāyadṛṣṭi.
>
> The fifth [is called] sudurjayā, because as he becomes skilled in understanding the profound meaning of the Noble Truths and the like it is very difficult for any of the Māras to gain power. By ripening this he becomes a king of the gods residing in Tuṣita. He repudiates the foundations of kleśa [and the] dṛṣṭi of all the tīrthakaras. The sixth is called abhimukhī, for by cultivating śamatha and vipaśyanā he

> comes face to face with the buddhadharmas and advances to obtain nirodha. By ripening this he becomes a king of the gods [of] Sunirmāṇa. Invincible against the Śrāvakas, he pacifies those who have adhimāna.
>
> The seventh [bhūmi is called] dūraṁgamā, because it has passed far beyond all calculation. Moment by moment he there enters nirodhasamāpatti. By ripening this he becomes a master of the Vaśavartin gods. Having realized the Noble Truths he becomes an ācāryamahānṛpa. Likewise the eighth, [also called] kumārabhūmi, is [called] acalā, because it is fathomless, for the range of body, speech, and mind is inconceivable. By ripening this he becomes Brahmā, master of a thousand [worlds]. He cannot be matched in arthaniścaya by Arhats, Pratyekabuddhas, or the rest.
>
> The ninth bhūmi is called sādhumatī. Here, like a crown prince, he obtains the pratisaṁvids and thereby has a fine intellect. By ripening this he becomes Brahmā, the master of two thousand [worlds]. In questions concerning the attitudes of living beings, Arhats and the like cannot surpass him. The tenth is dharmamegha, because the rain of the True Dharma falls as the Bodhisattva is consecrated with light by the Buddha. By ripening this he becomes a master of the Śuddhavāsa gods. A lord of infinite jñāna, he is a supreme maheśvara. Thus these ten are celebrated as the stages of the Bodhisattva . . . .

Subsequently the Bodhisattva becomes a Buddha (ibid., 61–64).

The Role of Prajñā

The majority of Nāgārjuna's writings — the Mūlamadhyamakakārikā, Śūnyatāsaptati, Vigrahavyāvartanī, Yuktiṣaṣṭikā, Catuḥstava, Bodhicittavivaraṇa, and Vaidalayaprakaraṇa — center upon one single pāramitā: prajñā. This is above all an outcome of Nāgārjuna's innate philosophical inclination, but it is also a natural consequence of the fact that prajñāpāramitā is considered the most important of all the pāramitās (cf. BS, 5–7; RĀ, I, 5). It will thus be reasonable to subject it to closer consideration.[240]

Traditionally, prajñā is said to exhibit three degrees: one of śruti, one of cintā and one of bhāvanā. The first consists in the correct understanding of the scriptures (āgama). As far as the writings of Nāgārjuna are concerned, the Sūtrasamuccaya, Pratītyasamutpādahṛdayakārikā, Suhṛllekha, and so forth are designed to serve that need. The second is tantamount to a well-reasoned appraisal of what one has learned from one's study of the scriptures. These two kinds of prajñā are thus of a discursive or rational order and serve a most practical purpose — a correct understanding of Buddhist teaching. The third mode of prajñā gradually unfolds itself by means of bhāvanā and is based on the former two. It consists in meditating upon the results of one's learning and understanding in order to realize them for oneself and integrate them in one's personality.[241]

Taking it for granted that his reader is conversant with this gradation Nāgārjuna does not spend many words discussing prajñā in the abstract. Instead he employs it in its current sense of analytical understanding, or "intellect as conversant with general truths." (See PED, under pañña.) However, his dialectical writings, especially the Mūlamadhyamakakārikā, Śūnyatāsaptati, and Vigrahavyāvartanī, which may in fact be regarded as exercises in the application of this pāramitā, vividly display how he assigns to prajñā a new and major role. Now prajñā is not merely the analytical faculty which allows us to determine the lakṣaṇas and the svabhāva of dharmas at the vyavahāra level with certainty, but is the mediator which conveys its adept from a world of appearance (saṁvṛti) to one of absolute reality (paramārtha).

Here the deep impact that the Prajñāpāramitā texts exerted upon Nāgārjuna is unmistakable. For Nāgārjuna, prajñā is at the outset a critical faculty constantly engaged in analyzing the more or less commonsense notions presented to it by tradition or experience. The more it penetrates them and 'loosens them up', the more their apparent nature vanishes. In the final analysis their true nature turns out to be 'empty'; i.e., devoid of substance or simply illusory. It cannot really be determined as either A or not-A. At this stage, prajñā has also brought to an end its own *raison d'être:* By analyzing its objects away it has also deprived itself of an objective support (ālambaṇa, etc.).[242]

At this moment the analytical understanding suddenly shifts into an intuitive jñāna that has śūnyatā as its 'object'; i.e., that has no object. The culmination of prajñā, then, is jñāna, or intuitive insight into reality (tattva) beyond the duality of asti and nāsti, existence and non-existence. This jñāna is also the suspension of avidyā, which, as we have seen, is based in the final analysis precisely on the wrong assumption of existence and non-existence.[243]

Bodhisattvas who are still far from Buddhahood may enjoy occasional glimpses of tattva, since their prajñā has not yet achieved the perfection of a pāramitā. Only a Buddha has perfected the dhyāna- and prajñāpāramitās (i.e., jñānasaṁbhāra), attaining the unremitting possession of tattvajñāna. Only to him does the epithet sarvajña apply, for he experiences the samatā of all dharmas, their śūnyatā. He knows them all to be the same.[244]

The development of the pāramitās must in other words come about gradually. Again and again one must apply one's prajñā to the 'facts' of experience and tradition. This necessity accounts for the circumstance that Nāgārjuna's dialectical writings are so replete with 'repetitions' of what is essentially a very simple principle indeed. Let us therefore turn our attention to the stage where prajñā plays the principal role.

All conscious beings find themselves living in an extended world of plurality (prapañca). Only the Buddha is beyond prapañca.[245] Now, from the common Buddhist outlook we cannot really distinguish between an 'objective' and a 'subjective' world; we cannot really isolate 'facts' from 'judgments'. This is a most decisive point that should not be left out of account.[246] For this reason prapañca also means *our* expansion of the world, or, as one might say, the world presented to us in and by language. The very *modus operandi* of prapañca is vikalpa, usually to be translated as 'discursive or conceptual thinking' but occasionally also 'objectively' as 'distinctions, differences', and the like. Vikalpas differentiate the world of prapañca into something which is said to exist (astīti) and something which is said not to exist (nāstīti) and hypostatize these respectively as being (bhāva) and non-being (abhāva). These again entail the wrong views of śāśvata- and ucchedadarśana.

These are the basic conscious functions of mind. Subsequently we form ideas (saṁkalpa), assumptions (parikalpa), opinions (kalpanā), theories or dogmas (dṛṣṭi), etc., and this in the end is tantamount to duḥkha. All of them are ultimately based on the uncritical acceptance of being (bhāvābhyupagama; cf. YṢ 46).[247]

Now prajñā performs its task in the systematic intellectual endeavor to demonstrate that the net of prapañca is empty, that it lacks 'objective' foundation (cf. YṢ 25–27, etc.). This is achieved by bringing to light that asti and nāsti — hypostatized by the activity of vikalpa — do not pertain to reality (tattva).

Before we see how prajñā confronts its task, the categories in which vikalpa operates must be ascertained. The things (bhāva) and conceptual phenomena (dharmas) assumed to exist are perforce conceived in terms of hetu/phala, pūrva/apara/saha, kāraka/kriyā/karma/karaṇa, lakṣya/lakṣaṇa, sva/para, dīrgha/hrasva, eka/aneka (i.e., saṁkhyā), and so forth. In short, human understanding invariably presupposes some kind of spatial, temporal, or causal relationship.[248]

At the very base of any such specific relationship lies the principle of identity (ekatva) and difference (anyatva). Without assuming this dichotomy no language, no rational discourse, no world — in a word, no prapañca — is possible.[249]

Now, what Nāgārjuna simply wants to demonstrate is that strictly speaking (i.e. paramārthataḥ) not a single bhāva or dharma can be conceived either as 'one' (eka) — i.e., as an independent unity — or as 'other' (anya) — i.e., as absolutely independent of its correlate (cf. MK II, 21). Why not? Because, obviously, the assumption that anything is eka or anya faces endless absurdities when confronted with the relentless demands of logic (yukti) or experience (upapatti/saṁbhava). It would be of little benefit to depict here how easy it is for Nāgārjuna to demonstrate the inherent conflict in discursive thinking ('reason'). None of the correlates in the above-mentioned categories can be taken as eka or anya. For example, who would maintain that long and short were either identical or absolutely independent! The Mūlamadhyamakakārikā, Śūnyatāsaptati and Vigrahavyāvartanī show this at length, and anyone could — and should, if he follows Nāgārjuna's advice about getting rid of all vikalpas — multiply the instances *ad infinitum*.[250] From this it seems clear that the constructions of vikalpa do not point to any tattva; and I think that in this perspective the meaning of terms like śūnya, vivikta, nirālamba, anālaya, nirāśraya, anāspada, and the like also becomes intelligible. It simply means that there really is no dharma or bhāva to fix one's mind upon as support.

By pointing out that nothing within the domain of experience can be conceived of in and by itself, independent of something else, Nāgārjuna merely intends to call attention to the fact that nothing has svabhāva (or, of course, parabhāva, etc.; cf. MK XV, 3).[251] He displays the absurdities inherent in the assumption of bhāva of any kind whatsoever. Instead of taking things in terms of asti and nāsti one should become aware that all 'entities' are pratītyasamutpanna — without, however, committing the fallacy of conceiving pratītyasamutpāda as a fact in and by itself. Transcending asti and nāsti, it is not apprehensible but elusive, like phantoms, mirages, and dreams. To use a term often employed in Mahāyānasutras: Things are simply anutpanna, or non-arising.[252]

Establishing Non-Arising

From later Madhyamaka sources we learn that there are four main arguments (mahāhetu) in support of anutpāda.[253] As each of these is already applied by Nāgārjuna himself, I advance them here:

1. catuṣkoṭyutpādapratiṣedha. This demonstrates that there is no subject of origination. Examples are provided in ŚS 4; CS I, 13; III, 9; MK XII, 1. The following quotation is from MK I, 6–7:

> naivāsato naiva sataḥ pratyayo 'rthasya yujyate I
> asataḥ pratyayaḥ kasya sataś ca pratyayena kim II

na san nāsan na sadasan dharmo nirvartate yadā I
kathaṁ nirvartako hetur evaṁ sati hi yujyate II

It is not logical that either an existent or a nonexistent thing has a condition. For how can something that does not exist have a condition, and how can something that already exists need a condition? Since neither an existent, a nonexistent, or an existent-nonexistent dharma arises, how can there possibly be an efficient cause?

2. vajrakaṇa. This demonstrates that there is no source of origination. See MK XXI, 12–13; CS I, 13; III, 9. But MK I, 1 is the classic statement:

na svato nāpi parato na dvābhyāṁ nāpy ahetutaḥ I
utpannā jātu vidyante bhāvāḥ kva cana ke cana II

Nothing ever arises in any place, be it from itself, from something else, from both, or without a cause.

3. ekānekaviyoga. This shows that things cannot be established, since they cannot be conceived as identical or different. See ŚS 32; MK XXI, 6; and, above all, MK II, 21:

ekībhāvena vā siddhir nānābhāvena vā yayoḥ I
na vidyate tayoḥ siddhiḥ kathaṁ nu khalu vidyate II

If something cannot be established as one or as many how can it be established at all?

4. pratītyasamutpāda. This points to the fact that 'things' only appear as they do in relation to a correlative and vice versa. See CS III,11–16. MK XIV, 5–7 puts it tersely:

anyad anyat pratītyānyan nānyad anyad ṛte 'nyataḥ I
yat pratītya ca yat tasmāt tad anyan nopapadyate II

yady anyad anyad anyasmād anyasmād apy ṛte bhavet I
tad anyad anyad anyasmād ṛte nāsti ca nāsty ataḥ II

nānyasmin vidyate 'nyatvam ananyasmin na vidyate I
avidyamāne cānyatve nāsty anyad vā tad eva vā II

Something else is something else based on something else: Something else is not something else without something else. Something is not different from that [something] on which it depends. Something else as such is not found in something else, nor is it found in something that is not something else [i.e., in itself]. Since something else [in itself] is not to be found, something else and that [something in relation to which it is something else] certainly do not exist.

See also YṢ 19 and MK XVIII, 10:

pratītya yad yad bhavati na hi tāvat tad eva tat ǀ
na cānyad api tat tasmān nocchinnaṁ nāpi śāśvatam ǁ

Now, first of all, whatever depends on something, is certainly not the [independent entity] it [appears to be]. Moreover, it is not different from that either. So it is neither annihilated nor permanently prolonged.

These proofs are of course conducted at the level of cintāmayī prajñā with the specific purpose of rendering support to the unsystematic statements of anutpāda found in the Prajñāpāramitā scriptures (śrutamayī prajñā). Needless to add, it must be left to the adept himself to attain anutpādajñāna by practicing bhāvanāmayī prajñā. Being aparapratyaya (Tibetan: gzhan las shes pa ma yin) (see MK XVIII, 9), it cannot be communicated by scriptures or arguments.[254]

Thus Nāgārjuna is able to argue — or at least to suggest — that all theories and the like generated through the operations of vikalpa are in the final analysis untenable. For they impose absurd implications (prasaṅga) on the proponent of any kind of bhāva.[255]

But the svabhāvavādin is not prepared to succumb to such allegations. On the contrary, he may accuse the Prāsaṅgika of tacitly endorsing the existence of the very svabhāva he is negating. For how could anyone negate something unless he presupposes its existence as what is to be negated? That would be a glaring inconsistency.

Nāgārjuna, however, is convinced that this is an unwarranted accusation (adhilaya: see MK XXIV, 13; VV 63). Lack of svabhāva is universal and knows no exceptions. For this reason there is really no question of negating it (pratiṣedha). Nāgārjuna merely does his best to suggest its absence. He himself is not really negating or affirming anything at all. True, if he assumed bhāva at the outset and then negated it he might have to plead guilty of the alleged inconsistency. But everything lacks svabhāva, and thus is śūnya (= anutpanna) — his own arguments claim no exception to that rule. Similarly for all the Buddhist dharmas; being pratītyasamutpanna they are certainly śūnya.[256] In the terminology of the Vaiyākaraṇas, Nāgārjuna's 'negations' of svabhāva may be classified as prasajyapratiṣedhas, without any intended affirmation, rather than paryudāsas, implying an affirmative proposition.[257]

If the opponent at this stage has been persuaded to accept Nāgārjuna's arguments — arguments *ad hominem*, in a sense — he should apply himself to bhāvanā in order gradually to become personally convinced of universal emptiness. Doing this, he will obtain anutpattika-dharmakṣānti,[258] patient acceptance of the non-arising of dharmas.

The Doctrine of Two Truths

Living beings who have fully realized universal emptiness — sarvajñatā — are rare indeed. As we have seen, this realization presupposes that the practice of dhyāna and prajñā has been brought to complete perfection (pāramitā), and only Buddhas have gone that far.[259]

This difficulty brings us to Nāgārjuna's celebrated doctrine of two truths (satya), or two levels of reality. The distinction between a saṁvṛti- and a paramārthasatya was not invented by Nāgārjuna: It is found, above all, in the Mahāyānasūtras.[260] And it is worthy of notice that even though the theory of satyadvaya has a cardinal function in his philosophy it does not play a very conspicuous role on the pages of his writings. The *locus classicus* is of course MK XXIV, 8–10:

> dve satye samupāśritya buddhānāṁ dharmadeśanā I
> lokasaṁvṛtisatyaṁ ca satyaṁ ca paramārthataḥ II
>
> ye 'nayor na vijānanti vibhāgaṁ satyayor dvayoḥ I
> te tattvaṁ na vijānanti gambhīraṁ buddhaśāsane II
>
> vyavahāram anāśritya paramārtho na deśyate I
> paramārtham anāgamya nirvāṇaṁ nādhigamyate II
>
> The Dharma teaching of the Buddhas actually presupposes two realities: the relative reality of the world and reality in the ultimate sense. Those who do not understand the distinction between these two truths do not understand the truth in the profound instruction of the Buddha. The ultimate sense cannot be shown without the support of language; without understanding the ultimate sense nirvana remains unapproachable.

Read along with the other pertinent passages (ŚS 1, 69–73; VV 28, YṢ 30–33), these verses provide us with the following important information. In order to achieve nirvana one must understand paramārtha; i.e., pratītyasamutpāda = niḥsvabhāvatā = śūnyatā. But before this is feasible a beginner must as an indispensable prerequisite receive instruction (deśanā) in the Dharma and practice accordingly. Unless his teacher resorts to the conventions of language (vyavahāra) he is unable to impart his instructions. Otherwise the pupil cannot form any correct idea about the lakṣaṇas and svabhāva of the skandhas, dhātus and āyatanas, the true nature of which—śūnyatā—he must gradually realize himself through the exertion of his own prajñā.

Thus conventional worldly truth is an indispensable pedagogical device for one's personal understanding of paramārtha. As Candrakīrti puts it: upāyabhūtaṁ vyavahārasatyam upeyabhūtaṁ paramārthasatyam.[261]

The two truths cannot be regarded as expressing different levels of objective reality, since all things always equally lack svabhāva. They are merely two ways of looking (darśana) at things: a provisional and a definite. The first is, in the unpretentious words of the Akutobhayā *ad* MK XXIV, 8–9, *sarvadharmotpādadarśana; the second is *sarvadharma-anutpādadarśana.[262] This division must be clear. In his characteristic style Bhavya puts it this way:

> tathyasaṁvṛtisopānam antareṇa vipaścitaḥ |
> tattvaprāsādaśikharārohanaṁ na hi yujyate ||[263]

> Surely, without the stair-case of the true relative [reality] a sage cannot ascend to the heights of the palace of true reality.

By adopting this two-truth distinction and taking it as an upāya-upeya relationship, Nāgārjuna is able on the one hand (paramārthataḥ) to maintain that all things are empty, and on the other (saṁvṛtitaḥ) to advocate the practical value of all the various Buddhist teachings about skandhas, pāramitās, and so forth. While there is no ontological justification for satyadvayavibhāga, there is most certainly a didactic (psychological) one. As long as all living beings have not yet become Buddhas the need for dharmadeśanā will remain. But the day that all beings have fulfilled jñānasaṁbhāra by realizing pudgaladharmanairātmya and puṇyasaṁbhāra by perfecting dāna, śīla, and kṣānti, the manifold teachings of Buddhism are rendered superfluous.

We are now able to recapitulate Nāgārjuna's soteriological system. In actuality the entire universe is nothing but emptiness, beyond all conceptions and limitations. However, owing to avidyā we find ourselves confined in a manifold world of duḥkha. The beginning of avidyā cannot be accounted for, but fortunately, as the Buddha has pointed out, it can be abolished by jñāna.[264] Therefore we should strive to arouse ourselves and (not to be forgotten) all others from the nightmare of ignorance. But we shall only obtain 'enlightenment' when we have prepared ourselves morally and intellectually for bodhi. We must unremittingly accumulate an immense amount of puṇyajñānasaṁbhāra before we wake up as Buddhas and recognize that all along we have been dreaming a life in saṁsāra. Then at last we can see (YṢ 5): na saṁsāraṁ na nirvāṇaṁ manyante tattvadarśinaḥ ("Those who see reality believe in neither samsara nor nirvana.")

Such is the basic framework of the Mahāyāna view of the world, and *mutatis mutandis*, of several major ancient Hindu soteriologies as well.[265]

Tracing Nāgārjuna's Influence

It would be a fascinating task to trace the impact of Nāgārjuna's writings on subsequent developments inside and outside the domain of Buddhist thinking. If the present study has to some extent paved the way for such research it will have served a useful purpose. Though it falls outside the limits imposed upon this work, I cannot resist pointing out briefly some instances where the influence of Nāgārjuna (or his school) must be assumed in order to account for the present state of affairs.

Āryadeva was the first important direct pupil of Nāgārjuna.[266] His works must always be read with an eye toward those of his guru. The first four chapters of his *magnum opus*, the Catuḥśataka in sixteen chapters, deal with the means of abandoning the four viparyāsas: nitya-, sukha-, śucigrāha and ahaṁkāra.[267] Nāgārjuna also treats these 'distorted views' in MK XXIII, and, with increasing attention to their basic significance as a source of avidyā, in the Śūnyatāsaptati (10, 62), written later than the Mūlamadhyamakakārikā. Still, Nāgārjuna's discussion is not as extensive as the importance of the topic would warrant. It is therefore natural to regard Catuḥśataka I–IV as a deliberate continuation of the work initiated by Āryadeva's teacher.

The Catuḥśataka IX–XVI seethes with arguments directed against various 'tīrthikas', above all representatives of the Sāṁkhya and Vaiśeṣika schools. The same is true for Āryadeva's *Sataka I–X (found in Chinese, Taishō 1569). As we have seen, Nāgārjuna is aware of these and other tīrthikas (RĀ I, 61), but for some reason he apparently only engaged in a debate with the Naiyāyikas. It is therefore a fair guess to say that he decided to leave the task of refuting other non-Buddhist schools to a talented disciple he could rely on: Āryadeva. It may be added that though Āryadeva proves extremely faithful to the thought of his master, the style in which he clothed his arguments was very much his own.

Outside the Buddhist fold, we have evidence to the effect that Āryadeva's Catuḥśataka in turn was studied by early Jaina philosophers.[268] An interesting instance is provided by Kundakunda's Samayasāra I, 8:

jaha ṇavi sakkam aṇajjo aṇajjabhāsaṁ viṇā u gāheduṁ ।
taha vavahāreṇa viṇā paramatthuvadesaṇam asakkaṁ ॥[269]

Just as you can only communicate with a foreigner in a foreign language, so the ultimate meaning cannot be communicated without the use of language.

This recalls Catuḥśataka VIII, 19:

nānyayā bhāṣayā mlecchaḥ śakyo grāhayituṁ yathā ।
na laukikam ṛte lokaḥ śakyo grāhayituṁ tathā ॥

Just as you can only communicate with a foreigner in a foreign [read nāryayā for nānyayā] language, so you cannot communicate with mankind without using conventional (language).

Similarly Samayasāra I, 7, 11, 12, etc., betray the unmistakable influence of the Mādhyamika theory of the two truths.

In later times, I do not think that it is possible to name one single Mādhyamika in India—Prāsaṅgika or Svātantrika—who does not expressly acknowledge or at least indicate through allusions, quotations, etc. Nāgārjuna as his authority par excellence, second only to Śākyamuni Buddha himself. Whether future research decides to focus on issues such as the development of philosophical prose style, the difference in presenting the mārga, the controversy between Prāsaṅgikas and Svātantrikas, or the debates between Madhyamaka and Yogācāra — to mention only a few vital approaches — it will be imperative to take one's starting-point in the extant writings of Nāgārjuna.

Finally, though traces of Madhyamaka influence may now and then also be detected in Jaina and Cārvāka sources (see especially the Tattvopaplavasiṁha), it would be no exaggeration to claim that it penetrated deepest in early Advaita Vedānta, and subsequently in affiliated Hindu literature. This link is nowhere more manifest than in the Gauḍapādīyakārikās, a fact noted by several modern scholars.[270] But the close affinity between Madhyamaka and Vedānta was recognized by some of the ancient Buddhist authors too. The first to do so seems to have been Bhavya, the author of the Madhyamakahṛdayakārikā.[271] In his Madhyamakālaṁkāravṛtti, Śāntarakṣita (ca. 725–788) also quotes some stanzas from what is now known as the Gauḍapādīyakārikās,[272] including II, 31–32, 35:

svapnamāye yathā dṛṣṭe gandharvanagaraṁ yathā ।
tathā viśvam idaṁ dṛṣṭaṁ vedānteṣu vicakṣaṇaiḥ ॥

na nirodho na cotpattir na baddho na ca sādhakaḥ I
na mumukṣur na vai mukta ity eṣā paramārthatā II

vītarāgabhayakrodhair munibhir vedapāragaiḥ I
nirvikalpo hy ayaṁ dṛṣṭaḥ prapañcopaśamo 'dvayaḥ II

As a castle of gandharvas and dreams and illusions are seen, thus this entire universe is seen by the wise in Vedānta.

There is no cessation, no origination; no person is bound, realizes, strives for liberation, or is liberated. This is the state of ultimate meaning.

This non-dual, non-discursive cessation of the expanded world is [only] recognized by Sages fully conversant with the Veda and free from attachment, fear, and anger.

To this, Śāntarakṣita exclaims, and not without a certain indignation, "de dag gis gang brjod pa de ni bde bar gshegs pas gsungs pa": ("What they state has already been said by the Sugata!").

Let these brief observations suffice to indicate that an extensive and rewarding task awaits future research within the field of Madhyamaka studies.

NOTES AND APPENDICES

Notes

1 Suffice it to mention Murti (1966); Robinson (1967); Streng (1967). General bibliographical surveys may be found in Potter (1970), pp. 480–484; Regamey (1950), pp. 55–58; Streng (1967), pp. 237–245; Nakamura (1977), pp. 77–94. Good selective bibliographies in May (1959), pp. 23–45; Lamotte (1970), pp. lxi–lxviii; (1976), pp. xvii–xix; (1980), pp. xii–xv. The most recent survey of Madhyamaka is by May in *Hōbōgirin*, pp. 470–493, under Chūgan. [Publisher's note: see now the more recent survey by Ruegg, cited in the bibliography.]

2 Namely, the Mūlamadhyamakakārikā, Vigrahavyāvartanī, Pratītyasamutpādahṛdayakārikā, and in part the Ratnāvalī. See below.

3 The Chinese translations are conveniently registered in the *Fascicule annexe* to *Hōbōgirin*, Tokyo, 1978; the Tibetan in e.g. the index volume to the *Tibetan Tripiṭaka*, Peking edition, Tokyo, 1962. [Publisher's note: see also the *Research Catalogue and Bibliography of the Nyingma Edition of the sDe-dge bKa'-'gyur and bsTan-'gyur*, Berkeley, 1983.]

4 Here I have only pointed out a few instances where the influence of Nāgārjuna is obvious. See the Concluding Essay in Part III.

5 Lamotte, *Vimalakīrtinirdeśa*, pp. 40–51 and May, *TP* LIV, pp. 339–342 (cf. *Hōbōgirin* under Chūgan, p. 474) have attempted to summarize "la position du Mādhyamika" in six fundamental theses, or essential elements. Since many of Nāgārjuna's authentic works have not been taken into account, full justice has not been done to the ethical, epistemological, and psychological (religious) aspects of his thought, nor has an attempt to demonstrate the inherent unity of these aspects been made. In my saṁkṣepa I take it for granted that a philosopher faces four fundamental problems: the ontological, the epistemological, the psychological, and the ethical. This division reflects a distinctly occidental approach, one that, historically speaking, ultimately traces to Xenocrates' partition of philosophy into logic, cosmology, and ethics (according to Sextus Empiricus, *Adv. Mathematicos* VII, 16). I am mainly indebted to the clear exposition by H. Høffding, *Filosofiske Problemer*, Copenhagen, 1902 (English translation: *The Problems of Philosophy*, New York, 1905), and *Den menneskelige Tanke, dens Former og dens Opgaver*, Copenhagen, 1910 (German translation: *Der menschliche Gedanke, seine Formen und seine Aufgaben*, Leipzig, 1911). These two are not at all outdated; the latter may even claim to be one of the most substantial philosophical works ever written in Danish. In the Concluding Essay in Part III, I have set myself to describe the unity of Madhyamaka vistareṇa.

6 To Nāgārjuna the theory of satyadvaya is above all a pedagogical device. I have collected the most instructive texts on this theme in an article: "Atiśa's Introduction to the Two Truths, and its Sources," in *JIP* IX, pp. 161–214.

7 SL 104; RĀ I, 4.

8 RĀ III, 12–13; YṢ 60.

9 VV 22; MK XXIV, 18; YṢ 19, etc.

10 CS II, 3; III, 37–39; YṢ 1; MK XXV, 24; RĀ I, 98, etc.

11 MK XXII, 11; XXIV, 18; cf. May (1959), p. 161, n. 494 (ref.).

12 SŚ 73; MK XVIII, 5; XXV, 2.

13 CS I, 1 (and accompanying notes in Part III of this book); MK XXVII, 30.

14 RĀ III; BS, *passim*.

15 RĀ IV, 81, 99, etc.

16 RĀ IV, 81, etc.

17 RĀ I, 6; III, 12.

18 RĀ I, 24; IV, 98; I, 4; III, 30.

19 Nāgārjuna hardly defines prajñā (cf. RĀ V, 37) and jñāna and their mutual relationship. However, it seems fairly consistent with his usage (and Buddhist usage in general) to claim that prajñā is a discursive, intellectual understanding presupposing the analysis or experience of phenomena, whereas jñāna is the intuitive knowledge gradually developed by exercising prajñā. Thus a Buddha hardly employs prajñā, but always enjoys jñāna of everything (cf. also May [1959], p. 104, n. 252, with references). In brief, prajñā is sādhana, jñāna is sādhya.

20 RĀ I, 4, 45; III, 30.

21 RĀ III, 12.

22 RĀ IV, 96: śūnyatākaruṇāgarbham ekeṣāṁ bodhisādhanam. Cf. Prasannapadā, p. 360; Bu ston I, p.111. These two aspects of bodhicitta form the theme of the Bodhicittavivaraṇa.

23 For 'biographical' accounts of Nāgārjuna, see Ramanan (1966), pp. 25–30; K.S. Murty, *Nāgārjuna*, New Delhi, 1978, pp. 38–67; M. Walleser, *The Life of Nāgārjuna from Tibetan and Chinese Sources*, Delhi, 1979 (reprint); May, *Chūgan*, p. 478 (with references); É. Lamotte, "Der Verfasser des Upadeśa und seine Quellen," *Nachrichten der Akademie der Wissenschaften in Göttingen. I. Philologisch-historische Klasse.* 1973[2], pp. 3–5. I can only subscribe to the Belgian master's statement that "Dieser Mischung an sagenhaften Überlieferungen, in denen sich unterschiedslos Wahres, Falsches, und Zweifelhaftes widerspiegeln, steht die moderne Kritik ratlos gegenüber. Sie hat nur einige Arbeitshypothesen vorbringen können." (Ibid., p. 4.) Accordingly, I shall only take these traditions into account when they coincide with the evidence, however scanty, to be gleaned from the author's own writings, above all the Ratnāvalī.

24 The strange question posed by A.K. Warder, "Is Nāgārjuna a Mahāyānist," in M. Sprung (ed.), *The Problem of Two Truths in Buddhism and Vedānta*, Dordrecht, 1973, pp. 78–88, has been given a reply by May, *Chūgan*, p. 473. One may add that the term gandharvanagara (MK VII, 34; XVII, 33; XXIII, 8) does not occur in the ancient āgamas (cf.Traité, p. 370, n. 1). Moreover, MK XIII, 8 is inspired by Kāśyapaparivarta (cf. Traité, p. 1227), and MK XXIV, 8 by the Akṣayamatinirdeśa (cf. P.L.Vaidya, *Études*

sur Āryadeva et son Catuḥśataka, Paris, 1923, p. 21, n. 6). So even in the Mūlamadhyamakakārikā alone the Mahāyāna background is indisputable.

25 It is noteworthy that on the vyavahāra level Nāgārjuna endorses polymathy; see BS 79, 103.

26 We have no reason to believe that such attempts proved very successful. Whatever the reason—perhaps lack of time or interest—it was left for Nāgārjuna's most brilliant pupil, Āryadeva, to refute the doctrines of Sāṁkhya and Vaiśeṣika (cf. RĀ I, 61 and Laṅkāvatārasūtra X, 723).

27 The Śūnyatāsaptati and Vigrahavyāvartanī are, as Candrakīrti observes (cf. *IIJ* XXIII, p. 177, n. 4), elaborations respectively of MK VII, 34, and I, 3. It is in fact only in this perspective that the motives behind the objections raised and the topics introduced become quite intelligible. Along with the Yuktiṣaṣṭikā and possibly the Vyavahārasiddhi these writings are intended to establish the ontological and epistemological tenets of Mahāyāna by way of yukti.

28 Perhaps a Śātavāhana; see É. Lamotte, *Histoire du bouddhisme indien*, Louvain, 1958, p. 379; K.S. Murty (1978), pp. 62–65. Also S. Dietz, "Der Autor des Suhṛllekha," in *Proceedings of the Csoma de Körös Symposium, Velm/Vienna, Sept. 13th–19th, 1981.*

29 Ibid.

30 Ibid., p. 64; K.K. Murthy, *Nāgārjunakoṇḍā: A Cultural Study*, Delhi, 1977. References to caityas, stūpas, vihāras, Buddha images, etc. can be found in RĀ II, 77; III, 31–41, 92; IV, 10–11, 17; V, 65; BS 111, 113, 136, 150–151. It would certainly be worthwhile to compare this evidence closely with the archaeological remains of Nāgārjunakoṇḍā and Amarāvatī. See also BS 79, 103 (śilpa).

31 His verses are usually simple as far as syntax, meter, vocabulary, and style are concerned. They differ distinctly from those of a predecessor such as Aśvaghoṣa or a successor such as Āryadeva or Mātṛceṭa. His prose seems modeled on that of Patañjali's Mahābhāṣya (see L. Renou, *Histoire de la langue sanskrite*, Paris, 1956, p. 135; K. Bhatttacharya, et. al., *The Dialectical Method of Nāgārjuna*, Delhi, 1978, p. 8). It differs totally from, e.g., that of the Arthaśāstra of Kauṭilya (cf. Renou, loc. cit., p. 136).

32 For the list and on Buddhist hymns in general see D. Schlingloff *Buddhistische Stotras aus ostturkistanischen Sanskrittexten*, Berlin, 1955, n. 16.

33 The earliest reference to the Catuḥstava (in Tibetan, the bsTod pa bzhi pa) as a whole with which I am familiar is to be found in Vairocanarakṣita's Bodhisattvacaryāvatārapañjikā, Pek. 5277, Sha, at fol. 169a2 and 174b8. Prajñākaramati's Bodhicaryāvatārapañjikā (ed. La Vallée Poussin) twice gives the form Catuḥstava (pp. 420, 488), while Candrakīrti speaks of the Saṁstuti (cf. n. 80 below). In most cases the individual hymns are quoted without mention of source.

34 The various options have been summarized by de Jong, "Emptiness," *JIP* II, pp. 11–12. Professor Hahn kindly forwarded me a copy of S. Sakai: "On the Four Hymns Ascribed to Nāgārjuna," *The Journal of the Nippon Buddhist Research Association* XXIV, pp. 1–44, which contains a revised edition of CS II and IV and a Japanese version of the two other hymns with accompanying notes.

35 See below. Copies of these were courteously put at my disposal by the authorities of the Akademia Nauk (Leningrad), Dr. M. Hara (Tokyo), and Dr. V.V. Gokhale (Poona). I am particularly grateful to Dr. Gokhale, who originally planned to edit the Catuḥstava himself (see *Festschrift Kirfel*, Bonn, 1955, p. 102, n. 3).

36 Edited by G. Tucci, *Minor Buddhist Texts* I, Rome, 1956, pp. 235–246. Tucci also edited and translated CS II and IV (Niraupamya- and Paramārthastava) in "Two Hymns of the Catuḥstava of Nāgārjuna," *JRAS* (1932), pp. 309–325. Cf. *MCB*, III, p. 374. The manuscripts at my disposal require these emendations in Tucci's text: CS II, 1b: read niḥsvabhāvārthavedine; 2d, tattvārthadarśinī; 3a, boddhavyam; 4d, padam; 23b, īkṣyase; CS IV, 5a, harin māñjiṣṭho; 5b, nopalabhyate; 5c, pītaḥ kṛṣṇaḥ śuklo (cf. *IIJ* II, p. 168, n. 12); 9a, evaṁ stute. A version in French of these two hymns was published by L. Silburn, *Le bouddhisme*, Paris, 1977, pp. 201–209; an Italian (including the Lokātīta- and Acintyastava, from the Tibetan) by R. Gnoli, *Nāgārjuna, Le stanze del cammino di mezzo . . .*, Torino, 1961, pp. 157–179.

37 See the conspectus testium. Though far from exhaustive it shows that the hymns exerted a considerable influence.

38 Discussing the authenticity of the Catuḥstava, Gnoli says (op. cit., p. 12): "L'unica obiezione contro la loro autenticità, può concernere, semmai, uno solo di essi, l'Acintyastava o 'Laude dell'Inconcepibile', il terzo e più lungo della raccolta, che, per l'eccessiva concisione di alcune parti, per l'oscurità di altre (forse imputabile, d'altronde, alla versione tibetana), per certi bruschi passagi e certe ripetizioni, non è, in realtà, escluso che sia una compilazione posteriore. Specialmente sospette, in questo senso, le stanze 43–44 [45–46 in my Sanskrit edition], nelle quali è un'evidente allusione alla scuola dei Vijñānavādin o dell' Idealismo buddhistico, considerata, per tradizione, posteriore a Nāgārjuna. Ma la data di Nāgārjuna é poi sicura?" But these arguments do not carry much weight: The stylistic features noticed by Gnoli are, in fact, also known from the Śūnyatāsaptati and the Yuktiṣaṣṭikā, the authenticity of which cannot be impeached. The allusions to Vijñānavāda — or more precisely to the Vijñānavāda found in the Laṅkāvatārasūtra (see note to CS III, 45), generally held to be posterior to Nāgārjuna — are quite consistent with the fact that Nāgārjuna also refers to this Sūtra elsewhere (compare, e.g. MK XVIII, 7 with Laṅkāvatāra, III, 9; XXI, 11 with X, 37; XVII, 33 with X, 279; YṢ 3 with X, 466; SS 222b2–3 equals X, 640, etc.). These hymns (as seen in the very titles) show Nāgārjuna's 'conception' of the Buddha consistent with MK XXII, 15: . . . buddhaṁ prapañcātītam avyayam. Some of the verses in CS II and IV were discussed by D.S. Ruegg, "Le Dharmadhātustava de Nāgārjuna," *Études Tibétaines dédiées à la Mémoire de Marcelle Lalou*, Paris, 1971, at pp. 454–463.

39 The main theme of CS I and III is pudgala- and dharmanairātmya. The composition is — like that of the Yuktiṣaṣṭikā — not structurally strict. Though CS I first refutes sattva and then the skandhas, first in general, then in particular, it is none the less on the whole a loose collection of aphorisms about anutpāda, like CS III, teeming with allusions to Mahāyānasūtras.

40 See the information on sources in Part II. Regarding the manuscript housed in Tokyo, cf. S. Matsunami, *A Catalogue of the Sanskrit Manuscripts in*

the Tokyo University Library, Tokyo, 1965, p. 122, no. 340. I also collated the two manuscripts of CS I listed in this work on p. 149 (No. 419, III, 153 = fol. 292b4–294a5; No. 420, XI, 5 = fol. 10b5–21a4), but not to encumber the apparatus needlessly I have not given the numerous *voces nihili* found.

41 Cf. however, n. 206 below.

42 Some glimpses of how and when hymns and other texts were chanted we get from RĀ V, 65; Bhāvanākrama III, p.13; Ratnapradīpa 355a; J. Takakusu (tr.), *A record of the Buddhist religion as practised in India and the Malay archipelago (A.D. 671–695), by I-tsing*, London, 1896, pp. 152–166.

43 As expressed in the pariṇāmanā at the end of each hymn. Note that the purely dialectical works do not contain any such puṇyapariṇāmanā.

44 Cf. the remarks on buddhamāhātmya, RĀ IV, 84–87.

45 Cf. Bu ston II, p. 126; J. Naudou, op. cit. n. 88, p. 187. (Note that two verses quoted by Bu ston at I, p. 133 as from the Ratnāvalī are in fact BV 91–92.) The Bodhicittavivaraṇa is seldom referred to by modern authors, though P. Patel has identified some quotations from it in *IHQ* VIII, pp. 790–793. See also my article in *WZKS* XXVI (1982).

46 Ibid.

47 Both quote the celebrated verse 20, see ibid.

48 Verses 12, 13a, 20, 25, 27, 45, 46, 52ab, 57, 98, 99.

49 Cf. n. 38 for evidence regarding Nāgārjuna's acquaintance with the Laṅkāvatārasūtra.

50 CS I, 10; III, 50; ŚS 56–57.

51 B has smon pa (praṇidhi, or prārthanā); A has smon lam (praṇidhāna). For bodhicitta in general, see *Encyclopedia of Buddhism* III, pp. 184–189; Har Dayal (1932), pp. 58–64; RĀ III, 86.

52 See verse 71 for this equivalence: tathatā = bhūtakoṭi = ānimitta = paramārtha paramabodhicitta = śūnyatā. Cf. ŚS 69; CS I, 27; III, 41, 45. Also Siddhi, pp. 757–761.

53 To be sure, Pek. ed. 2666, vol. Gi, fol. 48a–50b (Narthang ed. 665), a Bodhicittavivaraṇa ascribed to Nāgārjuna, is a brief prose commentary on the verse sarvabhāvavigatam . . . from the Guhyasamājatantra, which it quotes (loc. cit., 49b6); cf. note 56 below. It does not seem unlikely that the author of this tract is one and the same with the author of the Guhyasamājatantraṭīkā referred to below (n. 196). Taishō No. 1661, the Pú tí xīn lí xiàng, also ascribed to Nāgārjuna, is in fact nothing but a Chinese prose paraphrase of the Bodhicittavivaraṇa. Dr. Eric Grinstead, who carefully compared it with my version of the Bodhicittavivaraṇa, succeeded in identifying all 112 verses (in some cases only slight traces) including the prologue. Consequently the title should be taken as rendering Sanskrit Bodhicittavivaraṇa, not *Bodhicittanimittarahita (?) as Robinson (1967), p. 27 has, or *Lakṣaṇavimuktabodhihṛdayaśāstra, as Ramanan (1966) p. 35 suggests. For strictly philological purposes it has proved to be of no avail.

54 For the full list of translators for A as well as a few other details see *Encyclopedia of Buddhism* III, p. 190.

55 I have refrained from editing A, as it would take up too much space without contributing in the least to a better understanding of the sense intended by the author of the Bodhicittavivaraṇa. On the other hand a comparison of A and B would (especially if carried out as meticulously as done e.g. in N. Simonsson, *Indo-tibetische Studien,* Uppsala, 1957) cast some light into the workshop of the translators and revisors.

Note that in the critical apparatus A, B, and C indicate the *consensus* of the Peking and Narthang editions. My collation of these two editions of B has revealed remarkably few variants: 5d brten P : rten N; 19c ni P : na N; 74e bzo P : bza N.

56 This introduction calls for some remarks. The initial stanza is, as C 455b4 notes, from the Guhyasamāja (see ed. Bhattacharya, p. 12, where it is printed as if prose): sarvabhāvavigataṁ skandhadhātuāyatanagrāhyagrāhakavarjitam | dharmanairātmyasamatayā svacittam ādyanutpannaṁ śūnyatābhāvam ||. It also occurs in the Bodhicittavivaraṇa (Pek. ed. 2666, Gi, fol. 48a4), also ascribed to Nāgārjuna (corresponds to Taishō 1661). The corresponding Sanskrit text is reproduced in P. Python, *Vinaya-viniścaya-Upāli-paripṛcchā, 'Hors-texte',* fol. 10a3 (not 10b as the editor assumes; cf. de Jong, *IIJ* XIX, p. 131) with the variant in d śūnyatāsvabhāvam. How we are to account for the fact that a verse from a tantric text occurs in Bodhicittavivaraṇa I am not to say. Since, however, the Bodhicittavivaraṇa otherwise has nothing tantric about it (cf. v. 1), nor has this verse taken in itself, it should not, I think, induce us to regard the author of the Bodhicittavivaraṇa as being identical with, for example, the author of the Pañcakrama. Moreover, the verse is also found in the Bodhicittotpādavidhi, which is pure Mahāyāna. See note 201.

There are two aspects of bodhicitta (not the same as those of Bodhicaryāvatāra I, 15). The relative is merely the desire or quest (prārthanā) for bodhi. It is expressed in a praṇidhāna, here alluding to Aṣṭasāhasrikā, p. 215 (cf. Har Dayal (1932), p. 65; see also the Śatapañcāśatka, p. 40, which like the Bodhicittavivaraṇa presupposes the reading atīrṇān, etc. for tīrṇāḥ, etc.). The absolute is simply bodhi, see BV 45 ff. This passage is also quoted in F. D. Lessing and A. Wayman (1968), p. 334; Guenther (1959), p. 131. I have corrected B's snying po byang chub (a simple transposition) to byang chub snying po (thus A and C, *bodhimaṇḍa; cf. BHSD, p. 402).

Text C 460b4 explains sngags (not gsang sngags as given in A and B): de la sngags ni shes skyob ste | rnam par mi rtog pa'i ye shes dang snying rje'i rang bzhin sangs rgyas nas bzlas pa'i phyir ro ||. I thus take *mantramukha as the equivalent of dhāraṇīmukha; see BV 100 and Traité, p. 1854 et. seq. for a full explanation.

57 Also known as the Mādhyamikasūtra or Mādhyamikaśāstra (cf. May [1959], p. 7), or, particularly among Tibetans, as the rTsa ba shes rab, *Mūla-prajñā, or *Mūlaprakaraṇa (given thus, for example, in the Śūnyatāsaptativṛtti, Pek. ed. 5268, Ya, fol. 309a, 312a, 325a, 329a, etc.). The standard edition is that of La Vallée Poussin (see n. 191), supplemented by de Jong, "Textcritical notes on the Prasannapadā," *IIJ* XX, pp. 25–59, 217–252. As no satisfactory English version of the kārikās alone exists one must refer to those incorporated in one of the commentaries (cf. May [1959], pp. 8–10; notes 190–191 below), or R.

Gnoli, op. cit. n. 36, pp. 39–139. A Danish version (with Sanskrit) can be found in my *Nāgārjunas filosofiske Værker*, Copenhagen, 1982.

58 Along with the ŚS,VV, VP, VS and YṢ, the Mūlamadhyamakakārikā may, to adopt the convenient Tibetan "classification tripartite, qui est à la fois formelle et synchronique" (D.S. Ruegg, op. cit. n. 38, p. 449) be said to form the *yuktikāya, in which it is its 'backbone'. The hymns, of course, form the *stavakāya; the remaining texts the *kathākāya (expositions or sermons, mainly but not exclusively yathāgamam).

59 As edited by La Vallée Poussin with the addenda of J.W. de Jong; see n. 57.

60 See n. 190 for the list. The titles of the twenty-seven prakaraṇas are identical in the Akutobhayā, Buddhapālitavṛtti, Prajñāpradīpa and Prajñāpradīpavṛtti, and they have been adopted here.

61 The Prasannapadā differs thus: II: gatāgata°; III: cakṣurādi°; VII: saṁskṛta°; XI: pūrvāparakoṭi°; XIII: saṁskāra°; XV: svabhāva°; XVIII: ātma°; XX: sāmagrī°. As far as the number of verses is concerned, Prasannapadā III, 7 (cf. *IIJ* XX, p. 40); XII, 6; and XXIII, 20 are absent in the four other commentaries. So unless it is supposed that Candrakīrti had access to better manuscripts than his predecessors — which I find unlikely — these three verses as well as the titles of the eight chapters mentioned are probably Candrakīrti's own innovations. Clearly it influenced the separate Tibetan version of the kārikās (Pek. ed. 5224).

I append some remarks on a few kārikās. Comparing the commentaries there seems to be only one really significant variant reading (in XXVII, 19d). I, 3: hi is used as a technical term to indicate something logically or empirically obvious, in no need of further elaboration; cf. I, 7; II, 6, 19, 22; III, 2; VI, 3, 4; VII, 9, 10, 28, 30; VIII, 7, 8; IX, 2; XI, 1; XII, 2, 7, 8, 10; XV, 2, 3, 4, 8; XVII, 22; XVIII, 7, 10; XIX, 1; XX, 14, 19; XXI, 3, 4, 5, 14, 15; XXIII, 1, 4, 23, 24; XXIV, 21, 34; XXV, 4, 5, 6, 8, 12; XXVI, 6; XXVII, 3, 6, 9, 10, 15. It provides the saṁvṛti basis for arguments paramārthataḥ. For pratyayādiṣu cf. XXIII, 9 and Pāṇini III, 3, 37. I, 4: cf. XXI, 6. I, 5: kila (as in Abhidharmakośabhāṣya, etc.) indicates an opponent's opinion considered to be only provisionally acceptable; cf. RĀ IV, 50. II, 1: tāvat always indicates the first of two (equally absurd) alternatives. II, 2d: Buddhapālita read yasya for yataḥ, for which Bhavya rightly criticizes him. III, 6d: Buddhapālita takes te as tava (hardly convincing). VII, 13d: for jāte cf. niruddhe, I, 9d. VII, 29c: perhaps tadaiva for tadaivaṁ? VII, 31cd: same dṛṣṭānta in the apparatus to Mahābhārata XII, 173, 27. XII, 5d: Candrakīrti has kutaḥ and in 8d (= 7d) katham. The other commentators vice versa. XIII, 6c: read kasyātha for kasya cid. The manuscripts read kasyārtha. XVI, 6 (and XXVI, 2): atha is also left untranslated in the Tibetan. XX, 7d: read yac for yaś. XXI, 7b: all Tibetan versions point to °syāpi rather than °syāsti. XXI, 8: Candrakīrti reverses the order of pādas ab and cd against the previous commentators (Prasannapadā, p. 417, 1 is a quotation from Akutobhayā 91b3). XXI, 11: nearly verbatim Laṅkāvatārasūtra, X, 36. XXI, 12: identical with Catuḥśataka, XV, 14. XXIII, 8cd = XVII, 33cd. XXIII, 10c: Candrakīrti has pratītya śubham, but the previous commentators read pratītyāśubhaṁ. XXIII, 11c: again Candrakīrti has pratītyāśubhaṁ against pratītya śubhaṁ. XXIII, 13cd: Candrakīrti has nānityaṁ . . . viparyayaḥ against na nityaṁ . . . 'viparyayaḥ. XXIII, 14a: Candrakīrti has anitye nityam, in b as in 13b, in c anityam against anitye 'nityam in a, in b as in 13d and in c nānityam, in d perhaps aviparyayaḥ (or naviparyayaḥ) for na viparyayaḥ. XXIV, 18: Professor Wayman's interpretation of this important verse in *JAOS*, LXXXIX, pp. 141 ff. does not make any sense. XXV, 13b, 14b: Candrakīrti reads katham but the previous commentators read yadi (cf. 11b, 12b). XXVII, 19d: Candrakīrti's saṁsāraḥ seems to be a gloss. The previous commentators have rtag par gyur na; i.e. śāśvataḥ. (The wording of the kārikās included in the various commentaries was also discussed by S. Yamaguchi, *Chūkan Bukkyō Ronkō*, Tokyo, 1965, pp. 3–28, which was, however, not available to me.) I have edited the Mūlamadhyamakakārikā anew in *Indiske Studier* II.

62 An account of the textual transmission of the Mūlamadhyamakakārikā, etc. (along the lines, *mutatis mutandis*, of e.g. L.D. Reynolds & N.G. Wison, *Scribes and Scholars*, Oxford, 1974, or H. Hunger et. al., *Die Textüberlieferung der antiken Literatur und der Bibel*, Zurich, 1961) would certainly prove highly instructive. However, the paucity of sources, at least as far as early Mādhyamika is concerned, warrants no such attempt. Still we may note that at least the kārikās, then as now, were meant to be learned by heart, cf. svādhyāya, PK 5. But naturally in the case of Sūtras, commentaries, etc. the oral transmission was supported by a written; cf. RĀ III, 38: thub dbang gsung dang des byung ba'i I I gzhung rnams bri dang glegs bam ni I I snag cha dag dang smyu gu dang I I sngon du 'gro ba sbyin par mdzod II. Cf. Traité, p. 752; Upālipariprcchā, p. 95. Our knowledge of how books (pustaka) were copied, corrected, circulated, preserved, and quoted is regrettably quite fragmentary. However, the fact that the Mūlamadhyamakakārikā was transmitted virtually without variants or corruptions for many centuries within the body of different commentaries, the earliest of which, the Akutobhayā, is hardly more than a century later than the Mūla, must surely inspire us with confidence in the text as received. Though I believe that this rule on the whole also applies to the twelve other clearly authentic works, it is by no means universal: Texts such as the Bhavasaṁkrānti and the Mahāyānaviṁśikā are in many cases so contaminated or hopelessly corrupt that we can never hope to reconstruct an archetype but only, at best, one intelligible recension among others in their own right.

63 Here I confine myself to a summary of the observations set forth at some length in the introduction to my Danish translation of the Mūlamadhyamakakārikā (cf. also *IIJ* XXIII, pp. 153–154). The Mūla is addressed to monks thoroughly conversant with the Abhidharma of the most influential of all contemporary schools: Sarvāstivāda. Other less influential schools are occasionally introduced and criticized (see May [1959], p. 111, n. 278). It would be misleading to claim, as some modern authorities have done, that Nāgārjuna also had non-Buddhists (Sāṁkhya, Vaiśeṣika) in mind, though, of course, many of his arguments also indirectly apply to them (as Bhavya more than other commentators is never reluctant to point out). The purpose of the Mūla (as well as the Śūnyatāsaptati and the Vigrahavyāvartanī) is to train Ābhidhārmikas in prajñāpāramitā; i.e., to make them realize pudgaladharmanairātmya by understanding the Buddha's doctrine of pratītyasamutpāda in the sense of

śūnyatā, through cintā and bhāvanā. (The first aspect of prajñā, śruti, Nāgārjuna treats in the Sūtrasamuccaya, the Suhṛllekha, and so forth.) The twenty-seven chapters are arranged in a number of 'clusters'. I–VII refute the fundamental notions of Abhidharma: I–II those of causality and movement; III–V sarvaṁ yad asti; namely, the skandhas; VI sahabhāva; VII saṁskṛtalakṣaṇa, with an excursion against the Sāṁmitīya. VIII–X refute various aspects of pudgalavāda. XI–XIII may have been intended to refute the notion of bhāva in a more general sense. XIV–XVII elaborate on II, VI, and specific Buddhist notions not discussed previously. XVIII is in a sense the culmination; here for once the author reveals his own opinion about tattva and tattvāvatāra. XIX–XXI abruptly return to the criticism of Sarvāstivāda. They elaborate I. XXII–XXV show that all Buddhist concepts are empty *in the ultimate sense.* Not even the most sacred is spared. The final chapters, XXVI–XXVII, dealing with traditional Buddhist ideas in a *relative* sense, may at first seem to form a curious anticlimax. In my opinion the author appended them with a very specific purpose; namely, in order to show the orthodoxy of his śūnyavāda: One can only understand the dvādaśāṅga and the warnings against dṛṣṭis by means of śūnyatā.

64 Thus, according to Nāgārjuna, the Saddharma was taught sarvadṛṣṭiprahāṇāya: MK XXVII, 30. Similarly, XIII, 8; CS I, 23; III, 52, etc. All dṛṣṭis being due to astīti/nāstīti (cf. MK XV, 10) they can only be abolished by realizing their parasparāpekṣikī siddhi, or śūnyatā.

65 Not only is Nāgārjuna intent on being an orthodox Buddhist (BS 130), but in the cases where he writes according to āgama and we are able to check his use of sources he proves to represent them very meticulously. See, above all, SL, BS and SS, *passim.*

66 A number of 'axiomatic aphorisms' scattered more or less at random in the Mūlamadhyamakakārikā indicate the logical premises from which Nāgārjuna reduces his opponent to an absurd position: MK I, 1, 3; II, 1, 21; IV, 6, 8, 9; V, 8; VI, 4; VII, 34; IX, 5; X, 10, 11, 16; XI, 1; XIII, 1, 8; XIV, 4cd, 5, 6, 7; XV, 1, 2, 10; XXI, 6, 12; XXII, 12, 15, 16; XXIII, 1; XXIV, 8, 9, 10, 11. They were later formulated as the four mahāhetu (cf. CS I, 13; III, 9 and the acccompanying notes); see also the concluding essay in Part III of this book.

67 On this term see May (1959), p. 124,
Absolute in the Madhyamaka School," *JIP* II, pp. 2–3.

68 RĀ I, 72: vināśāt pratipakṣād vā syād astitvasya nāstitā . . . .

69 See e.g. the initial stanzas of MK; also RĀ IV, 86. For anutpāda in Mahāyāna Sūtras, see Vimalakīrtinirdeśa, pp. 408–413; *Hōbōgirin,* under Chūdō.

70 Cf. n. 79. Quotations in Ratnapradīpa 345a, 355a, 363a, 364b.

71 Cf. n. 90. Quotations in e.g. Madhyamakāvatāra, pp. 228, 232.

72 Madhyamakālaṁkāravṛtti, 72b, 75b, 76a, 76b, 79b, 82a.

73 From these sources about twenty percent of the Yuktiṣaṣṭikā has been saved in Sanskrit; see my notes for details. As virtually every later Mādhyamika cites Yuktiṣaṣṭikā now and again, the references could easily be multiplied, but I have confined myself to a few of textual import.

74 The Tibetan version of the kārikās (with the variants of Candrakīrti's vṛtti) was edited with the Chinese version and translated into Japanese by S. Yamaguchi, *Chūkan Bukkyō Ronkō,* Tokyo, 1965, pp. 29–110. See also

Nakamura (1977), p. 81, n. 23. In Sanskrit only 19ab and 39 were known to Yamaguchi. The Chinese version is usually too inaccurate to be of any philological value. A certain idea of it may be had from P. Schaeffer, *Yukti-ṣaṣṭikā, die sechzig Sätze des Negativismus, nach der chinesischen Version übersetzt*, Heidelberg, 1923. Few are the verses that say what Nāgārjuna actually had in mind!

75 In the translation of the kārikās given in Part I, I have strictly adhered to Candrakīrti's commentary. I have refrained from discussing the Chinese version; cf. n. 74.

76 I have given some of the references in the notes.

77 Cf. Yuktiṣaṣṭikāvṛtti 2b: rig(s) pa drug cu pa 'di ni dbu ma bzhin du 'dir yang gtso bor rten cing 'brel par byung ba dpyad pa las brtsams te byas pa'i phyir dbu ma las 'phros pa lta bu ni ma yin no ||. Thus it is an independent text as compared with the Śūnyatāsaptati and the Vigrahavyāvartaṇi.

78 Above all, verses 46–48 are instructive. They are often quoted. Thus bhāvābhyupagama→dṛṣṭi→kleśa→vivāda.

79 Ratnapradīpa 33a: dbu ma'i rtsa ba rtsod pa bzlog | | stong nyid bdun cu rigs drug cu | | rnam par 'thag pa la sogs pas | | dngos rnams skye med shes par bya ||.

80 *Madhyamakaśāstrastuti (ed. de Jong), 10: dṛṣṭvā Sūtrasamuccayaṁ parikathāṁ Ratnāvalīṁ Saṁstutīr abhyasyāticiraṁ ca Śāstragaditās tāḥ Kārikā yatnataḥ | Yuktyākhyām atha Ṣaṣṭikām sa Vidalāṁ tāṁ Śūnyatāsaptatiṁ yā cāsāv atha Vigrahasya racitā Vyāvartanī, tām api ||

81 v. 58 is quoted in the Madhyamakālaṁkāravṛtti, 72b.

82 vv. 19–21 are quoted with indication of source at 90b.

83 v. 8 is quoted (very freely) from the *Saptatiśāstra at 160a22, and v. 19 without indication of source at 164b27.

84 Bodhipathapradīpa (ed. Eimer) 1.205.

85 See my remarks on his prose at n. 31. It differs markedly from that of e.g. the Akutobhayā, tediously dull as this work often is, or the Akṣaraśatakavṛtti (cf. n. 216 below), already more condensed in its style. On the other hand it is very close to that of Buddhapālita. The verses of the Śūnyatāsaptati were āryās, as Parahita states *ad* 18–20, 32, 36–37, 54–55, 63, and 68–69.

86 See above, n. 27. Having stated that the Śūnyatāsaptati and Vigrahavyāvartanī both are dbu ma las 'phros pa, Candrakīrti continues by quoting MK VII, 32 and adds that stong pa nyid bdun cu pa ni de la brgal ba dang lan btab par gyur pa'i phyir de las 'phros pa yin par mngon no (Yuktiṣaṣṭikāvṛtti, Pek. ed. 5265, Ya, fol. 2b). This is, incidentally, also the opinion of the Śūnyatāsaptativivṛtti, (Pek. ed. 5269, Ya, fol. 381b).

87 Thus v. 29 is a summary of MK XIX, vv. 33–44 elaborate MK XVII, and 45–54 supplement MK IV. These are only the most obvious instances beyond all doubt. According to C 306a, the Śūnyatāsaptati is a *saṁkṣepa of the Mūlamadhyamakakārikā.

88 For information about the Indian and Tibetan translators I must refer to J. Naudou, *Les bouddhistes kaśmīriens au Moyen Âge*, Paris, 1968. Possibly the

Sanskrit text of Candrakīrti's commentary (C) is still extant, see G.N. Roerich, *The Blue Annals,* Calcutta, 1949, p. 342. (Note that C does not include verses 53 and 67, but P has all 73 stanzas.)

89 The variants are of some interest for the light they shed on the technique of translating Sanskrit into Tibetan. As they hardly ever affect the sense, and a separate edition of C is expected, I have only referred to C occasionally. P has not been of much use for the present purpose. V does not seem to have been known to C and P.

90 See my Danish translation (based on the Peking, Narthang, and Derge editions), referred to at n. 6. I regret that the Japanese translation (*Daijō Butten* XIV) by Ryūshin Uryūzu was not accessible to me.

I may add here that having collated K and V in the Derge edition, I deemed that the variant readings, disregarding scribal errors, may be accounted for as results of emendation and contamination. Hence they have been eliminated from the apparatus. A similar editorial licence has clearly affected the transmission in the case of the Vigrahavyāvartanī and the Yuktiṣaṣṭikā. I have not collated the other texts in the Derge edition.

Reprinted in Part II of this book is the critical edition of the vṛtti that first appeared in *Filosofiske Værker*. It is based on the Narthang, Derge, and Peking editions. No critical apparatus has been given, as a full critical edition with all variants, etc. is expected soon from Mr. Felix Erb, Hamburg. Here, however, it should be noted that the order of the commentary to verses 52 and 53 in the Tibetan editions has been changed and restored as follows (Peking edition): 136a1–136a3; 135b5–136a1; 135b1–135b5; 135a5–135b1; 135a2–135a5; 135a1–135a2. Verse 53 found at 134b8 should be deleted (~135b8). The edition contains several valuable conjectures suggested to me by Mr. Ole Holten Pind.

91 In my view it would be very naive to interpret the introduction of e.g. śraddhā in the Śūnyatāsaptati (cf. RĀ I, 4–6; SS 175b ff.) or the stress laid on vāda in the Vigrahavyāvartanī as signs of a development in the thought of Nāgārjuna. Of course, facing new charges he had to lend new nuances to his standpoint, but I do not think that his fundamental belief in śūnyatā, once formed, ever underwent any decisive change.

92 See n. 79.

93 See n. 80; Prasannapadā, pp. 16, 29, 59; Yuktiṣaṣṭikāvṛtti 2b.

94 Madhyamakālaṁkāravṛtti 72b (quotes VV 70).

95 E.g., Atiśa's Pañjikā to the Bodhipathapradīpa, pādas 205–208 (translated in my article referred to at n. 6).

96 Too many repetitions and too much spelling out. On the other hand this serves to prevent misunderstandings among vaineyas about the author's doctrine. Thus the style may to a certain extent be dictated by the notion of upāyakauśalya (see BS 17).

97 The critical edition of E. H. Johnston and A. Kunst was recently reprinted with a (revised) English translation by K. Bhattacharya: *The Dialectical Method of Nāgārjuna (Vigrahavyāvartanī),* Delhi, 1978. (This supersedes K. Bhattacharya's previous rendering and notes, *JIP* I, pp. 217–261 and V, pp. 237–241.)

98 The Chinese version (Taishō 1631) was translated by G. Tucci in *Pre-Diṅnāga Buddhist Texts on Logic from Chinese Sources,* Baroda, 1929. The

Tibetan version (also edited by Tucci) was translated into French by S. Yamaguchi: "Traité de Nāgārjuna: Pour écarter les vaines discussions," *JA*, CCXV, pp. 1–86, with useful notes. A good Italian version by R. Gnoli, op. cit. n. 36, pp. 139–156 (kārikās only). A partial version by E. Frauwallner in *Die Philosophie des Buddhismus*, Berlin, 1969, pp. 200–204. Several modern discussions, most recently by M. Siderits: "The Madhyamaka Critique of Epistemology," *JIP* VII, pp. 307–335.

99 MK XXIV, 10 cited at VV 28.

100 See n. 27.

101 See the brief "Glossary of the significant Nyāya technical terms used in the Vigrahavyāvartanī" given by Bhattacharya, op. cit., p. 51 (cf. *JIP* V, pp. 240–241). In the opinion of Bhattacharya (ibid., p. 38, n. 2) Nāgārjuna's opponent is a "Naiyāyika realist," and in his article "On the Relationship between Nāgārjuna's Vigrahavyāvartanī and the Nyāyasūtra-s," *JIES* V, pp. 265–273 (cf. op. cit., p. 4, n. 15 [not n. '51']) he has discussed this question, criticizing some of the views expressed by G. Oberhammer, "Ein Beitrag zu den Vāda-Traditionen Indiens," *WZKSO* VII, pp. 63–103. It is true that the Vigrahavyāvartanī and Nyāyasūtra are "interdependent" (to use Tucci's expression, op. cit., p. xxvii) but it is wrong to regard the 'opponent' in the Vigrahavyāvartanī as a Naiyāyika (i.e., an exponent of the Nyāyasūtra in some form). In my opinion he must be seen as an Ābhidhārmika — following, of course, the rules of debate prescribed in some Buddhist work on logic such as the *Upāyahṛdaya. My main arguments are: a) Together with MK and ŚS, VV forms a unity addressed to the same audience (cf. above, n. 63); namely, Ābhidhārmikas; b) In VV the Buddhist term āgama (the third pramāṇa) is invariably used, not the corresponding Nyāya term śabda; c) The udāharaṇas VV 23 and 27 can only be acceptable to a Buddhist opponent; d) The svavṛtti to VV 54, 55, and 70 only makes sense if the opponent is a Buddhist; e) Nāgārjuna devoted a special work to his controversy with Nyāya: the Vaidalyaprakaraṇa (see Kajiyama, "On the Relation between the Vaidalyaprakaraṇa and the Nyāyasūtra," *IBK* V, pp. 192–195). Future discussions concerning the relationship between VV and NS are bound to take into account not only the Vaidalyaprakaraṇa but also the pertinent evidence found in the *Śataśāstra or *Śataka (Taishō 1569), and *Upāyahṛdaya (see note 228).

102 Thus, verses 1–20 give the objections of the Buddhist opponent, real or imaginary. Verses 21–26 are Nāgārjuna's replies saṁvṛtitaḥ following the common rules of debate, giving a pratijñā, etc. Verses 27 ff. give Nāgārjuna's standpoint paramārthataḥ. The āgama background of this is, I think, the Laṅkāvatārasūtra, pp. 166–169 (. . . pratijñā na karaṇīyā . . .). The decisive shift of argumentative level (i.e., between saṁvṛti and paramārtha) is indicated by "athavā" (VV 28a), which often has a strong adversative force in Nāgārjuna, as well as in Āryadeva. Often it must (like its short form 'atha') be rendered by "on the other hand," or better by the Latin *immo vero* or *sin autem* (see e.g. VV 2a, 10a, 12a, 15a, 19a, 27a, etc.) Apparently this crucial point has escaped modern translators of the Vigrahavyāvartanī and consequently obscured the inherently clear structure of that work. The fact that Nāgārjuna is thus ready to argue at both levels also renders Candrakīrti's criticism launched at Bhavya

(Prasannapadā, p. 16) in the words of VV 29–30 taken out of context somewhat perfidious.

103 S. Mookerjee has offered an exposition of the standpoint set forth in VV in *The Nava-Nalanda-Mahavihara Research Publication*, I, Nalanda, 1957, pp. 7–41. It also contains a reprint of the Sanskrit text of Johnston and Kunst. A new edition "with slight but obvious improvements" of Rāhula Sāṅkṛtyāyana's *editio princeps* is given by P.L. Vaidya, *Madhyamakaśāstra of Nāgārjuna*, Darbhanga, 1960, pp. 277–295. (As is also the case for the Mūlamadhyamakakārikā, the version of VV offered by F.J. Streng, *Emptiness: A Study in Religious Meaning*, Nashville, 1967, pp. 221–227, is full of mistranslations).

104 I follow S's svabhāvaḥ san (in 20d) against R and T but in accordance with C (loc. cit., 14a11; 17c7), without actually subscribing to the view of the editors that "C's reading . . . is unquestionably correct as giving the opponent's final conclusion."

105 If we are to believe Nāgārjuna, negation of existence differs *toto caelo* from indication of absence. The former implies previous affirmation of existence (cf. RĀ I, 72); the latter does not. See the verse from the *Lokaparīkṣā (below, n. 211) to the same effect. I assume that Nāgārjuna would regard astitvapratiṣedha as an upādāya prajñapti (see MK XXIV, 18); i.e. as an indication, a concept borrowed (from common parlance; cf. the usual Japanese rendering as kemyō, "borrowed name;" see May, "On Mādhyamika Philosophy," *JIP* VI, p. 240). For according to Nāgārjuna himself there is really no astitva to negate. On prajñapti/paññatti, see *JIP* VIII, pp. 2–14.

106 See CS I, 22 (with references in the accompanying note); MK XXIV, 18; XXVII, 30. Note that the Śūnyatāsaptati and VV have no independent initial stanzas of homage like the Mūlamadhyamakakārikā (as Candrakīrti observes: Yuktiṣaṣṭikāvṛtti 2b) and that only the Mūla and VV have final stanzas of homage (which seem to supplement one another well).

107 I have consulted Pek. ed. 5226 (sūtras) as well as 5230 (the prakaraṇa proper), both of which were edited (also collating the Narthang and Derge editions) by Y. Kajiyama in *Miscellanea Indologica Kiotensia* VI–VII, pp. 129–155. Kajiyama also discussed VP and translated it into Japanese. See Nakamura (1977), p. 81, n. 24.

108 See note 79.

109 See note 80.

110 It is without compare the most lively and amusing of all texts ascribed to Nāgārjuna, full of sophistries as it is. Historically speaking its quotations from the Nyāyasūtra are important; see note 101. Some useful remarks can be found in a review by P.M. Williams, *JIP* VI, pp. 287–290. One may here note that an English translation is forthcoming in Indiske Studier.

111 rtog ge shes pa'i nga rgyal gyis | | gang zhig rtsod par mngon 'dod pa | | de yi nga rgyal spang ba'i phyir | | zhib mo rnam 'thag bshad par bya ||. Similarly the initial lines of the *Upāyahṛdaya, see below, n. 228.

112 The following text is an analysis and paraphrase intended to expose the line of arguments (or sophisms). The notes are confined to a minimum. The number of sūtras follows Kajiyama.

113 The Tibetan rendering of s. 8 (. . . 'jig rten spyod pa po . . .) must be wrong; cf. NS I, 1, 25: laukikaparīkṣakānām . . . ; read instead: 'jig rten dang dpyod pa po . . . .

114 Cf. NS II 1, 8–15; Laṅkāvatārasūtra X, 779; see also the articles by Bhattacharya and Oberhammer referred to at n. 101. It certainly seems that Nāgārjuna, both here (s. 12) and at VV 20 is aware of the boomerang in NS, II, 1, 12, *pace* Oberhammer (op. cit., p. 70) who concludes: "Es kann daher mit Sicherheit gefolgt werden, dass die traikālyasiddhi-Diskussion von NS II 1, 8–15 Nāgārjuna nicht vorgelegen hat." Possibly Nāgārjuna only knows an earlier recension of NS than the text as we have it.

115 The verse on homonyms also occurs in the Abhidharmakośabhāṣya (ed. P. Pradhan), p. 81 (with the variant reading upadhārayet in d); Nyāyabhūṣaṇa (ed. S. Yogīndrānanda), p. 341: vāgdigbhūraśmivajreṣu paśvakṣisvargavāriṣu I navasv artheṣu medhāvī gośabdam avadhārayet II.

116 The same argument as *Dvādaśadvāraka 26. The fact that Nāgārjuna's sophistic reply follows immediately after "chala" lends it a particular finesse (which is of course lost in its Tibetan garb).

117 Nāgārjuna's conclusion is worth citing (Kajiyama, p. 154): gcig nyid dang gzhan nyid dang gnyi ga med pa'i phyir dngos po thams cad med par khas blangs pa yin no I I de lta bas na dngos po med par mngon par brjod par bya ba dang I mngon par brjod pa yang med pa yin no I I de'i phyir mya ngan las 'das pa dang byang grol zhes bya ba dag don gzhan nyid ni ma yin no II. Cf. MK II, 21; XVIII, 7; ŚS 2.

118 I have edited PK and discussed its authenticity in my "Adversaria Buddhica," *WZKS* XXVI (1982). For further biographical details, see C. Dragonetti, "The Pratītyasamutpādahṛdayakārikā and the Pratītyasamutpādahṛdayavyākhyāna of Śuddhamati," *WZKS* XXII, pp. 87–93; also Nakamura (1977), p. 83, n. 40; V.V. Gokhale in collaboration with M.G. Dhadphale, "Encore: The Pratītyasamutpādahṛdayakārikā of Nāgārjuna," in M.G. Dhadphale (ed.), *Principal V.S. Apte Commemoration Volume*, Poona, 1978, pp. 62–68 (with a plate).

119 To be sure, the Chinese jìng (usually viśuddha, śuddha, also svaccha, nirañjana, śubha, etc.) cannot be taken as an exact rendering of the Sanskrit corresponding to Tibetan bzang po (usually bhadra, su-, but also śubha, praṇīta, etc.; see e.g. Lokesh Chandra, *Tibetan-Sanskrit Dictionary*, New Delhi, 1961, p. 2094). However, recalling on the one hand how free Bodhiruci's renderings often are, and on the other that Indo-Tibetan and Chinese tradition otherwise ascribe PK (and its commentary) to Nāgārjuna (or *Sumati), I do not hesitate to deem the external evidence unanimous.

120 See above all May's annotated version of MK XXVI, op. cit., pp. 251–276, with references by La Vallée Poussin in *MCB* 2, pp 7–26.

121 For trivartman in Abhidharma see e.g. J. van den Broeck (tr.), *La saveur de l'immortel (A-p'i-t'an Kan Lu Wei Lun)*, Louvain-la-Neuve, 1977, p. 131, n. 2; Abhidharmakośa III, p. 68; Traité, p. 349; Bodhicaryāvatārapañjikā, p. 351 (based on Daśabhūmikasūtra); Triṁśikābhāṣya (ed. S. Lévi), p. 28.

122 See Bu ston I, 51. The Tibetan is found in Lokesh Chandra (ed.), *The Collected Works of Bu-ston* (Śatapiṭaka Series LXIV), Ya, fol. 670: don dam par rang bzhin med kyang kun rdzob tu 'jig rten gyi tha snyad 'thad cing

grub par ston pa tha snyad grub pa dang drug yin no zhe gsung ngo ll (excerpts due to Mr. Per K. Sørensen).

123 E.g. F.D. Lessing and A. Wayman, *Mkhas grub rje's Fundamentals of the Buddhist Tantras*, The Hague, 1968, p. 87.

124 Pek. ed. 5285, Sa, fol. 69b, quoted and translated in the text below.

125 Pek. ed. 5286, Sa, fol. 123a–124b. For Kamalaśīla's reliability as a witness see E. Steinkellner, "Zur Zitierweise Kamalaśīla's," *WZKSO* VII, pp. 116–150.

126 Compare in particular MK XXIV, 36: sarvasaṁvyavahārāṁś ca laukikān pratibādhase l yat pratītyasamutpādaśūnyatāṁ pratibādhase ll. (Note that Bhavya [Prajñāpradīpa 292b–293a] and Avalokitavrata [Prajñāpradīpaṭīkā 293b] connect 36ab with the previous lines and take 36cd as introductory to the following verses, whereas Candrakīrti [Prasannapadā, p. 513] subordinates 36cd to 36ab by taking yat as a kriyāviśeṣaṇa. The Akutobhayā [here adopted by Buddhapālita] and Zhōng lùn [loc. cit., 34b14–17] are similar.)

127 For further evidence see the notes and comments to the verses.

128 See Kamalaśīla *ad* (5); CS II, 21.

129 Cf. n. 80; Madhyamakāvatāra, p. 402.

130 In Bodhi[sattva]caryāvatāra V, 106. Discussion and references found in A. Pezzali (1968), pp. 80–97. I prefer Śānt*a* deva to Śānt*i* deva, as the former is invariably the transcription given in our earliest source, Atiśa's Bodhimārgadīpapañjikā (Pek. ed. 5344, Ki, fol. 288b5, 288b7, 299b7, 329a2, 329a7). Derge ed. *item*.

131 In G. Tucci (ed.), *Minor Buddhist Texts* III, Rome, 1971, pp. 22, 25, 27. (Having collated the Leningrad manuscript of Bhāvanākrama III, I have found these misreadings in Tucci's text: p. 2, 6, read nirūpayed; p. 2, 16, °paryantādhi°; p. 7, 19, śūnyāni [clear]; p. 11, 19, kālaṁ vā; p. 27, 12, °ratnacūḍe [not °kūṭe].)

132 Pek. ed. 5330; Taishō 1653. Sanskrit fragments are available not only from Sūtras still extant in Sanskrit and quoted by Nāgārjuna (see the list, items 7, 18, 23, 25, 27, 37, 46, 47, 48, 51, 64) but also in later compilations or other works quoting from SS; e.g. the Śikṣāsamuccaya. (I regret that M. Ichishima: "Sūtrasamuccaya [Kyōshū] no bonbun danpen," in *Tendai gakuhō* XIV, pp. 165–169 was not available to me.) Reference to an English version of SS in *IIJ* XXIII, p. 326.

133 This list is a critical revision of A. Banerjee, "The Sūtrasamuccaya," in *IHQ* XVII, pp. 121–126.

134 This is a lengthy and very interesting section treating the ethical aspects of the bodhisattvacaryā of a gṛhastha. It would certainly deserve to be carefully compared with the corresponding passages in the Ratnāvalī, Suhṛllekha, and *Bodhisaṁbhāra[ka].

135 From the philosophical point of view this is essentially the most interesting paragraph in the Sūtrasamuccaya. Here we find various scriptural sources dealing with the fundamental notions of Nāgārjuna's philosophy as seen in the Mūlamadhyamakakārikā and elsewhere:

śūnyatā, vimokṣamukha, anutpāda, prajñāpāramitā, etc. Like section eight, this portion of the Sūtrasamuccaya deserves a separate treatment.

136 The main source here is the Vimalakīrtinirdeśa: IV, 17, 20; XII, 17 (in Lamotte's translation).

137 See Vimalakīrtinirdeśa V, 20.

138 Tarkajvālā, Pek. ed. 5256, Dza, fol. 145a (= RĀ V, 35–39).

139 Cf. n. 80. Also Madhyamakāvatāra, pp. 7, 8, 20, 21, 22, 23, 29, 184, 224; Prasannapadā, pp. 135–188, 275, 245, 346, 347, 359, 360, 413, 458, 460 (= RĀ II, 48–49), 496, 549. Cf. de Jong, *IIJ* XX, p. 137.

140 Madhyamakālaṁkāravṛtti 75a (= RĀ I, 60), 83a (= RĀ IV, 79).

141 I, 1–77 was edited and translated by G. Tucci, *JRAS* (1934), pp. 307–324 (reprinted in *Opera Minora*, II, Rome, 1971, pp. 321–366); II, 1–46 and IV, 1–100 in *JRAS* (1936), pp. 237–252, 423–435. Tucci's edition was twice reprinted: by P.L. Vaidya, *Madhyamakaśāstra of Nāgārjuna*, Darbhanga, 1960, pp. 296–310, and by H. Chatterjee Sastri, *The Philosophy of Nāgārjuna as Contained in the Ratnāvalī*, Calcutta, 1977, pp. 83–100, without any significant changes. Partial versions by E. Frauwallner, *Die Philosophie des Buddhismus*, Berlin, 1969, pp. 204–217; K.S. Murty, *Nāgārjuna*, New Delhi, 1978, pp. 87–103. Complete versions by J. Hopkins et al., *The Precious Garland and The Song of the Four Mindfulnesses*, London, 1975, and by myself in *Nāgārjuna: Juvelkæden og andre skrifter*, Copenhagen, 1980. See de Jong in *IIJ* XX, pp. 136–140; Nakamura (1977), p. 83, n. 44 for works in Japanese. Some of my emendations to the Sanskrit text will appear in the forthcoming edition of the Ratnāvalī (Sanskrit-Tibetan) by M. Hahn.

The first chapter contains several allusions to the ancient Sūtras: 5: cf. Saṁyutta I, p. 214; 10: see Majjhima III, 22; 14–19: see Majjhima III, p. 203 ff.; 26: see Majjhima I, p. 40; 31: see Saṁyutta III, p. 105; 34: see Saṁyutta III, p. 132 ff.; 52–56: cf. Saṁyutta III, p. 141; 80: cf. Majjhima III, p. 31; 93–96: see Dīgha I, p. 223. (Many of these are of course repeated elsewhere in the Canon, to which other locations Nāgārjuna might equally well be referring.)

142 Note that Pek. ed. 5428: Ratnāvalyudbhavasaptāṅgavidhigāthāviṁśaka and Pek. ed. 5928: Rājaparikathānāmodbhavapraṇidhānagāthāviṁśaka — both ascribed to Nāgārjuna — are extracts from RĀ V, 66–85.

143 Originally I had worked out a list of the fifty-seven doṣas giving the Tibetan with references to Chinese and suggested Sanskrit originals. Then, quite recently, the Sanskrit text of RĀ V, 1–55 and 79–100 was published by S. Dietz in *Journal of the Nepal Research Centre* IV, pp. 189–220, and just a few days ago (March 2, 1981) I received a paper: "On a Numerical Problem in Nāgārjuna's Ratnāvalī" from Prof. Michael Hahn (Bonn). The work of Dr. Dietz and the courtesy of Prof. Hahn have enabled me to correct a number of the Sanskrit terms originally proposed by me. Though I do not quite agree with all Prof. Hahn's views concerning numbers and readings I am sincerely grateful for having had the opportunity to consult his very valuable critical notes. I am also very glad to learn that he is now preparing a critical edition of RĀ I–V (Tibetan and extant portions of the Sanskrit) (letter 28.1.1981).

144 Apart from several partial versions, three complete English ones are known to me: L. Kawamura, *Golden Zephyr: Instructions from a Spiritual Friend*, Emeryville, CA, 1975 and Ven. Lozang Jamspal et. al., *Nāgārjuna's Letter to King Gautamīputra*, Delhi, 1978 supersede the pioneering version of H. Wenzel: "Friendly Epistle," *JPTS* (1886), pp. 1–32. Further biographical information in Kawamura, loc. cit., pp. 114–117. (Dr. S. Dietz is now preparing a critical edition of the Tibetan.) For a Danish version (from Tibetan) see *Indiske Studier* I.

145 For the identity of this monarch, see Kawamura, loc. cit., p. 4 (with references); de Jong, *IIJ* XX, p. 137. See also n. 28. See more recently, S. Dietz, *Die buddhistische Briefliteratur Indiens*, Bonn, 1980, I, pp. 36–39.

146 In the celebrated words of his Chinese translator, I-tsing (tr. Takakusu, op. cit. n. 41, pp. 159–160): "The beauty of the writing is striking, and his exhortations as to the right way are earnest. His kindness excels that of kinship, and the purport of the epistle is indeed manifold . . . ."

147 See Mi pham's and Sa skya paṇḍita's scholastic and elaborate "tables of content" in Kawamura, loc. cit., pp. 96–113.

148 Only very few allusions or quotations were traced to their canonical sources by Wenzel. As a rule the Tibetan commentators were either ignorant of Nāgārjuna's sources (most of them never having been translated into Tibetan), or (being devout Buddhists) simply not inclined to assess their sacred texts from a historical point of view. To a large extent this is also true for Indian commentators of the Madhyamaka lineage. These circumstances tend to obscure how 'traditional' Nāgārjuna really was in such works as the Suhṛllekha, the Bodhisaṁbhāra[ka], etc.

149 Otherwise Bu ston may have based his description on the Indian oral tradition. Anyhow, one or two quotations would not warrant any such generally correct classification of BS. There is a Japanese translation of BS: see Nakamura (1977), p. 83, n. 39 (not seen). In the West BS has remained virtually unnoticed.

150 For the other quotation see v. 64 (and the accompanying note).

151 See note to v. 26 of the text.

152 Cf. Ramanan (1966), p. 340, n. 61; Vimalakīrtinirdeśa, p. 76.

153 A particular debt of gratitude is due to Prof. de Jong, who went carefully through the version which I myself and Dr. Grinstead had already revised thoroughly at least four times. Finally, Prof. S. Egerod, Copenhagen, also offered some remarks.

154 For previous expositions see n. 1; also La Vallée Poussin: "Réflexions sur le Madhyamaka," *MCB* II, pp. 1–59; P. Tuxen, *Indledende bemærkninger til buddhistisk relativisme*, Copenhagen, 1936.

155 For some remarks on this see the discussion of Nāgārjuna's philosophical system in the text below. Here much remains for 'higher criticism'.

156 See RĀ I, 61. For an extensive critique of these schools one has to turn to the writings of Āryadeva.

157 In the Vaidalyaprakaraṇa (ed. Kajiyama, p. 148), Nāgārjuna refers to the spokesmen of this school as the rigs pa phra ba'i phyogs su lhung ba. I think that they are identical with the *Naya-sauma known from Chinese

sources; see Tucci (1929), p. xxviii; Ui (1917), p. 55, n. 3. (Surely the Chinese xiū mó corresponds to Tibetan phra ba, which is probably the Sanskrit sūkṣma.)

158 RĀ III, 68 refers to Lokāyata (or Lokāyatika, Tibetan 'jig rten rgyang pan). They are frequently criticized in the Laṅkāvatārasūtra; see Suzuki's *Index*, p. 150. Their identity is not very clear.

159 Cf. CS III, 34 (with references in the accompanying note); also in Suzuki's *Index*, p. 45.

160 See VP (ed. Kajiyama), p. 155; RĀ I, 3–4; III, 30.

161 BV 77–78; YṢ 28.

162 In endorsing traditional Hindu learning at the level of saṁvṛtisatya, Nāgārjuna is in fact merely following an ideal generally advocated in Mahāyāna scriptures. Cf. the Buddhāvataṁsakasūtra, cited at SS 251b, and BS 79 (with references in the accompanying note).

163 This survey is an attempt to give the gist of the Tripiṭaka, and is above all based on the testimony of the Sūtras. In the majority of cases I refer to the Pāli Canon, as it is the most convenient to consult. Nāgārjuna, of course, used a Sanskrit recension.

164 For the trividhā prajñā, see Dīgha III, p. 219; see also Vibhaṅga, p. 324; Dharmasaṁgraha § 110. See also PED, under paññā ("intellect as conversant with general truths").

165 Aṅguttara IV, p. 203; Udāna, p. 56; Vinaya II, p. 239.

166 Cited from R. Gnoli, *The Gilgit Manuscript of the Saṅghabhedavastu*, Rome, 1977, pp. 137–138. (This edition is in need of numerous corrections.)

167 Pek. ed. 5682, 289a–289b (also Pek. ed. 5409, with minor variants).

168 Gnoli, op. cit., p. 128; cf. Traité, p. 35, n. 2. The two different canonical accounts of duḥkhasamudaya are, in my view, not to be regarded as more or less inconsistent or incompatible. The former, or 'exoteric', is usually given to an audience unacquainted with the Buddha's Dharma; the latter, or 'esoteric', to monks well versed in the Dharma. Thus they are simply expressions of the Buddha's skillful means.

169 See references in May, op. cit., p. 251, n. 1, and the late F. Bernhard: "Zur Interpretation der Pratītyasamutpāda-Formel," *WZKSO* XII–XIII, pp. 53–63.

170 Gnoli, op. cit., p. 127. SL 109–111 is cited from the Pek. ed. 5682, 289a (also Pek. ed. 5409 with insignificant variants).

171 Cf. recently R.E.A. Johansson, *The Psychology of Nirvana*, New York, 1970; G.R. Welbon, *The Buddhist Nirvāṇa and its Western Interpreters*, Chicago, 1968; J.W. Boyd: "The Theravāda View of Samsara," in *Buddhist Studies in Honour of Walpola Rahula*, London, 1980, pp. 29–43. SL 105 is cited from the Pek. ed. 5682, 288b–289a (also Pek. ed. 5409 with slight variants).

172 Pek. ed. 5658, 133a–133b. Note that the Pāli sabbatopaha (see PED, p. 448 and Majjhima I, p. 329) is rendered by Tibetan kun tu bdag po. But -paha is surely -prabha, as often in Buddhist Hybrid Sanskrit. (Cf. also J. W. de Jong, *Buddhist Studies*, Berkeley, 1979, p. 49.)

173 For further references and a discussion of this passage see *Hōbōgirin*, under Chūdō, especially p. 459. Also Dhammasaṅgaṇi, p. 16.

174 Cf. YṢ 1; MK XV, 10; RĀ I, 38; etc. See also the discussion on the fourteen avyākṛtavastūni in Murti (1960), pp. 36–54. Also May, (1959) p. 277, n. 1015. In the final analysis they are based on the assumption of asti or nāsti.

175 This is quite decisive. Nāgārjuna is not a 'freethinker' but primarily a Buddhist patriarch with uncompromising faith in the Dharma. Cf. BS 61–62, 123–127.

176 Cf. BV 61–62; PK 5.

177 Prasannapadā, p. 355; see also Subhāṣitasaṁgraha (ed. Bendall), p. 394; Dhammasaṅgaṇi, p. 220; Mahāvyutpatti, § CCIX. The verses from the Suhṛllekha are quoted from Pek. ed. 5682, 285b (also Pek. ed. 5409 without significant variants).

178 Frequently cited; here from Prasannapadā, p. 41. On śūnyatā in the ancient Sūtras see Traité, pp. 1079–1081; 2140–2144 (with references). In the Pāli, Saṁyutta III, p. 142. Cf. above all the Akṣayamatinirdeśa, vol. Bu, fol. 125a6–126a6.

179 Very useful is H. Nakamura: "A Survey of Mahāyāna Buddhism with Bibliographical Notes. Part I: Mahāyāna Sūtras," in *Journal of Intercultural Studies* III, pp. 60-145 [publisher's note: now reprinted in revised form in H. Nakamura, *Indian Buddhism: A Survey with Bibliographical Notes*, Osaka, 1980]. Speaking of Har Dayal, *The Bodhisattva Doctrine in Buddhist Sanskrit Literature*, Nakamura says: "Probably the best critical study of the textual evidence dealing with the career of the Bodhisattva." I agree.

180 It would, of course, be most interesting to ask: Is Nāgārjuna a faithful exponent of the Mahāyāna? But this is impossible to answer at present.

181 I have done my best to locate these, but much remains to be done.

182 In this field we are indebted to the work of the late Edward Conze. See his useful bibliography in *The Prajñāpāramitā Literature*, Tokyo, 1978. See also, L. Lancaster (ed.), *Prajñāpāramitā and Related Systems: Studies in Honor of Edward Conze*, Berkeley, 1977.

183 Y. Ejima, *Chūgan-shisō no tenkai, Bhāvaviveka kenkyū*, Tokyo, 1980, p. 495.

184 He quotes from these in the Sūtrasamuccaya. Consult the list of sources given in the discussion of that text above: items 37, 48, and 64.

185 Conze, op. cit., p. 15 presents a summary: "The thousands of lines of the Prajñāpāramitā can be summed up in the following two sentences: 1) One should become a Bodhisattva (or Buddha-to-be); i.e., one who is content with nothing less than all-knowledge attained through the perfection of wisdom for the sake of all living beings. 2) There is no such thing as a Bodhisattva, or as all-knowledge, or as a 'being', or as the perfection of wisdom, or as an attainment. To accept both these contradictory facts is to be perfect." Cf. ibid. for "new ideas" in these Sūtras (tathatā, upāyakauśalya, and punyapariṇāmanā).

186 See text below and BS 24–27. Cf. Har Dayal, op. cit., pp. 1–29.

187 The eight Śrāvakabhūmis are the same as the eight āryapudgalas. See Saṁyutta V, p. 202. For these stages and their relationship to the bhūmis of the Mahāyāna, see the Śūraṁgamasamādhisūtra, pp. 246–251.

188 On ekayāna, see Siddhi, p. 673 and p. 724 (The verses translated at this location are from Candrakīrti's Triśaraṇasaptati, 45–47.) References in the Mahāyānasaṁgraha, p. 63*; Vimalakīrtinirdeśa, p. 214, n. 144. Also F. Kōtatsu: "One Vehicle or Three," *JIP* III, pp. 79–166. On upekṣā, see Akṣayamatinirdeśa, Bu, fol. 140b1–141b6.

189 Nāgārjuna: Ægte og Uægte. Copenhagen, 1978 (unpublished). It is superseded by the present work.

190 Namely, the Akutobhayā (Pek. ed. 5229), Buddhapālitavṛtti (Pek. ed. 5242), Prajñāpradīpa (Pek. ed. 5253) by Bhavya, Prajñāpradīpaṭīkā (Pek. ed. 5259) by Avalokitavrata, and Prasannapadā (ed. La Vallée Poussin) by Candrakīrti. I have only resorted to the commentaries extant in Chinese (Taishō 1564, 1567) occasionally, as they are seldom of much use from a philological point of view.

191 Sanskrit text in *Mūlamadhyamakakārikās (Mādhyamikasūtras de Nāgārjuna avec la Prasannapadā Commentaire de Candrakīrti,* published by Louis de La Vallée Poussin, St. Petersburg, 1902–1913. There is a separate edition of *Nāgārjuna, Mūlamadhyamakakārikāḥ* by J.W. de Jong, Adyar, 1977. As the modern versions of the MK (by Inada and Streng) are most unreliable, one still has to consult the text as translated together with the Prasannapadā by Stcherbatsky, Schayer, Lamotte, de Jong, and May. See de Jong, *IIJ* XX, p. 25. A recent attempt by M. Sprung, *Lucid Exposition of the Middle Way: The Essential Chapters from the Prasannapadā of Candrakīrti,* London, 1979, again suffers from the author's insufficient philological outfit.

192 I.e., colophons as well as the testimony of Indian commentators and Chinese and Tibetan "historians."

193 Buddhapālita is not included on this list, as he refers only to the Mūlamadhyamakakārikā (cf. my remarks in *IIJ* XXIII, p. 154). I have consulted all the extant works of Candrakīrti (for a brief account of which see *Acta Orientalia* XL, pp. 87–92) and Bhavya (see *WZKS* XXVI [1982]). Among the many works of Śāntarakṣita and his pupil Kamalaśīla, the former's Madhyamakālaṁkāravṛtti and Tattvasiddhi and the latter's Madhyamakālaṁkārapañjikā, Madhyamakāloka, and Bhāvanākrama I and III have proved most helpful. True, we cannot prove that these authorities possessed any objective means of deciding what Nāgārjuna wrote and what he did not write. However, we do know that all of them were very learned and meticulous in dealing with their texts, and that even a slight misquotation or the like on their part would be certain to expose them to the censure of lurking svayūthyas. On the other hand, I have never accepted the testimony of other (usually later) authors unless its credibility can be established independently.

194 Cf. May, *Chūgan*, p. 482.

195 Pek. ed. 5238. This is a small but very readable prakaraṇa demonstrating pudgaladharmanairātmya. It betrays itself by quoting (without attribution of a source) Catuḥśataka XIII, 2; BV 18; MK V, 6; PK '7'; Bhavasaṁkrānti '8'. An Abodhabodhaka ascribed to Advayavajra (Pek. ed. 3145) is another recension of the very same text.

196 As pointed out by G. Tucci, *Opera Minora* I, p. 214, a quotation from Maitreya occurs in this ṭīkā. I find it quite likely that the author of this work is identical with the author of the Pañcakrama (ed. La Vallée Poussin, Gand, 1896), a work which is already cited in the Madhyamakaratnapradīpa, composed ca. 570 A.D. (see *WZKS* XXVI [1982]). As a mere working hypothesis I would at present suggest that this 'Nāgārjuna II'; i.e., the tāntrika or siddha, flourished ca. 400 A.D. He may also have been responsible for numerous sādhanas and other more or less tantric works transmitted under the name of Nāgārjuna (see e.g. B. Bhattacharya, *Sādhanamālā* I–II, Baroda, 1968). As a discussion of this complex question has no direct bearing on the 'real' Nāgārjuna, it must await further research.

197 Usually referred to as the Dvādaśanikāyaśāstra, Dvādaśamukhaśāstra, or Dvādaśadvāraśāstra (Taishō 1568), but there is seldom any reason to attach much weight to the Chinese lùn in titles, etc. For some observations on the text see May, *Chūgan*, pp. 488–489; Robinson (1967), p. 32. Cf. also sTong pa nyid kyi sgo bcu gnyis pa, no. 595 in the lDan-dkar-ma Catalogue. While there can be no doubt that (nearly) all the verses were originally composed by Nāgārjuna (MK and ŚS) there are in my opinion good reasons for maintaining that the author of the commentary (most probably identical with the compiler of the verses) is *not* Nāgārjuna but rather *Piṅgala. I postpone further remarks to a future occasion.

198 See *IIJ* XXIII, p. 182, n. 94.

199 Edited and translated by La Vallée Poussin, *MCB* II, pp. 147–161. First of all the doctrine of svabhāvatraya (already attested in the Laṅkāvatāra) is refuted by Nāgārjuna at BV 28. Moreover, the existence of paratantrasvabhāva endorsed in the Svabhāvatrayapraveśasiddhi (also called the Trisvabhāvanirdeśa) is repeatedly refuted by Bhavya, Candrakīrti, and by others, who never quote this work, which is sometimes and perhaps correctly ascribed to Vasubandhu.

200 The Sanskrit text was edited and translated by G. Tucci, *Minor Buddhist Texts, Part I*, pp. 195–207. Further references in Nakamura (1977), p. 83, n. 38. I have come across quotations from this work that are ascribed to Nāgārjuna in the Caryāmelāyanapradīpa (Pek. ed. 2668, 95a) and in the Tattvasārasaṁgraha (Pek. ed. 4534, 92a, 100a). Atiśa also ascribes this work to Nāgārjuna in the Bodhimārgadīpapañjikā (Pek. ed. 2668, 95a), but Bhavya, etc. never quote it. Still, it does show great similarity to the Yuktiṣaṣṭikā, Ratnāvalī, and Bodhicittavivaraṇa as far as style and doctrine are concerned, so it may be authentic. Here are some emendations to Tucci's edition made in light of the Tibetan and Chinese translations: 3a, read pārāvāram ivotpannaḥ; cf. CS III, 11 (note that Tibetan wrongly has tshul bzhin for tshu bzhin). 6a, Tucci has ṣaḍgatir yaś ca saṁsāraḥ svargaś, which is impossible; read with the Tibetan and Chinese ṣaḍgatayaś ca saṁsāre svarge. 6d, Tucci has jarāvyādhir apīyatām, with the note that the manuscript has °rapībhyatām or rapītyatām; however, as the Tibetan and Chinese show, this is not to be counted as 6d but as 7b—due to haplography (originally 6c and 7a must have ended with duḥkham) the scribe left out two pādas. In 7b we find . . . mi rtag nyid, so Tucci's manuscript apparently has anityatām. '11a', read bhāvato. '12b', Tucci reads karuṇādhīramānasāḥ, but the Tibetan has snying rje'i dbang gyur, a common idea (cf. CS I, 1; II, 1, etc.), so read karuṇādhīnamānasāḥ (Tucci probably misread the manuscript). '14',

read of course tattvārtha°, following the Tibetan and Chinese. '15a', Tucci reads tena ("therefore"), but with the Tibetan de dag read te na; cf. YṢ 5. '17a', read māyāvī, and in '18b' perhaps māyākārasamutthitam; cf. Caryāmelāyanapradīpa, loc. cit.: sgyu ma'i rnam par yang dag 'byung.

201 A brief but interesting ritual text (Pek. ed. 5361, 5405—the two are nearly identical). It prescribes a sevenfold rite for a Bodhisattva (cf. Upālipariprcchā, p. 98, n. 7; BS 48 with references in the notes): vandanā, pāpadeśanā, puṇyānumodanā, śaraṇagamana, ātmatyāga, bodhicittotpāda, and pariṇāmanā. The final paragraph is noteworthy as it alludes to the same āgama as the prose introduction to the Bodhicittavivaraṇa. Moreover, it ends with three praṇidhānas, the first of which is identical to RĀ V, 83, while the second recalls RĀ V, 80. A Danish translation of this text can be found in C. Lindtner, et. al., *Buddhismen,* Copenhagen, 1982, pp. 102–105.

202 Only extant in Tibetan (Pek. ed. 2026) in fourteen stanzas. Clearly a Madhyamaka text (speaks of puṇyajñānasaṁbhāra, upāyakauśalya, etc.), relating the Twelve Acts of the Buddha; cf. BV 91–92; CS II, 23. Perhaps the same author as the Aṣṭamahāsthanacaityastotra, see H. Nakamura, *Indianisme et bouddhisme,* Louvain-la-Neuve, 1980, pp. 259–265.

203 The edition by N.A. Sastri, while useful, remains far from definitive. The transmission of this text is more complex than that of any other work ascribed to Nāgārjuna. Apart from the versions published by Sastri one must consult the Bhavasaṁcara ascribed to Nāgārjuna and the Nirvikalpaprakaraṇa ascribed to Āryadeva, both of which contain many similar or identical verses. Verse '6' is attributed to Nāgārjuna in Bhavya's Madhyamakaratnapradīpa 352a. Incidentally, the same verse is discussed in Williams, *JIP* VIII, p. 27. In Sanskrit I have come across a quotation (no source given) in the Ādikarmapradīpa (ed. La Vallée Poussin), p. 196: dānaśīlakṣamāvīryadhyānādīn sevayet sadā | acireṇaiva kālena prāpyate bodhir uttamā ||; cf. RĀ II, 25; IV, 80, 98–99.

204 Known from a quotation in Dharmendra's Tattvasārasaṁgraha, Pek. ed. 4534, 102b: bsam byed bsam gtan bsam bya dag | | spangs pa bden pa mthong ba yin | | 'di kun rtog pa tsam nyid do | | gang gis rtogs pa de grol 'gyur ||. Atiśa ascribes this verse to Nāgārjuna in the Bodhimārgadīpapañjikā, Pek. ed. 5344, 329b: kun tu rtog pas ma btags shing | | yid ni rab tu mi gnas la | | dran med yid la byed pa med | | dmigs med de la phyag 'tshal lo || The three verses found in the Pañcakrama (ed. La Vallée Poussin), p. 36, ending in nirālamba namo 'stu te, may be from the same source (note that the previous verses are extracted from CS II, 18–19).

205 Only in Tibetan (Pek. ed. 5466 and 5485). Seventy verses, originally probably anuṣṭubh. 47d is missing in the Pek. ed. This is simply a faithful versification of the Śālistambasūtra, one of Nāgārjuna's basic āgamas; cf. svavṛtti to VV 54; May (1959), p. 267, n. 967. According to Ratnapradīpa 342a, Nāgārjuna is the author of a Sa lu ljang pa'i mdo'i grel pa (*Śālistambhasūtravṛtti); possibly this refers to these kārikās. In any case, it is hardly likely to refer to the Śālistambhasūtraṭīkā, also attributed to Nāgārjuna, as this must be a rather late work, inasmuch as it deals with the four anubandhas, not attested in early Madhyamaka.

206 Only in Tibetan (Pek. ed. 2020). A Sanskrit reconstruction was presented by Patel, *IHQ* VIII, pp. 689–705. Apart from Catuḥstava I and III, the most philosophical of all the hymns attributed to Nāgārjuna. I have not seen any quotations from this hymn, which is quite possibly authentic.

207 Only in Tibetan (Pek. ed. 5661). A collection of thirteen verses in various meters forming a sermon on one of the distinctive pāramitās of an upāsaka often praised by Nāgārjuna (BS, SL, RĀ , SS, *passim*). It belongs to the same genre as several other products of the early Madhyamaka school; e.g., Mātṛceṭa's Caturviparyayakathā. No quotations are known to me. Cf. also Traité, p. 650–769. The Svapnacintāmaṇiparikathā, in thirty-two verses, also belongs to this group of dubious texts.

208 The Tibetan version was edited with a French translation by La Vallée Poussin in *Le Muséon,* N.S. XIV, pp. 14–16. I have found v. 3 in the Ādikarmapradīpa, p. 200: cittena labhyate bodhiś cittena gatipañcakam | na hi cittād ṛte kiṁ cil lakṣaṇaṁ sukhaduḥkhayoḥ || (Tibetan rim thob must be corrupt.)

209 Only in Tibetan (Pek. ed. 5629). Fifty kārikās based on the Vinayavibhaṅga on the Bhikṣuprātimokṣasūtras of the Mūlasarvāstivādins. Recalling how influential the Vinaya of this school must have been in the early centuries A.D. (cf. Traité III, p. xviii) in the Madhyamaka milieu, it is not at all unlikely that Nāgārjuna should have compiled a *summa* of monastic rules. It would tally excellently with RĀ V, 1, 34, and also be consistent with the samuccaya genre, a favorite of Nāgārjuna's. There is a possible allusion to this work in Ratnapradīpa 350a, which speaks of the śikṣās . . . slob dpon klu sgrub kyi zhal snga nas ji ltar bkod pa pa rnams . . . .

210 Only in Chinese (Taishō 1521); cf. Vimalakīrtinirdeśa, p. 76; Ramanan (1966), p. 340, n. 61; Nakamura (1977), p. 82; Traité III, p. xliv (with references). Like the *Mahāprajñāpāramitopadeśa, this commentary is apparently unknown to the Indo-Tibetan tradition, but there are in my opinion several reasons to consider it authentic: the very early Chinese evidence, quotations from the *Bodhisaṁbhāra[ka], the correspondence between the Amitābha doctrine set forth here and that in SL 121 (cf. RĀ III, 99), and the fact that the Daśabhūmikasūtra is known to have been used by Nāgārjuna elsewhere (PK; RĀ V, 41–60; SS 249b). All this certainly deserves a discussion more thorough than I am prepared to undertake at present. Cf. J. Eracle, *Le Chapitre de Nāgārjuna sur la Pratique Facile, suivi du Sūtra qui loue le Terre de Pureté,* Brussels, 1981 (not seen).

211 Only known to me from a quotation in Prajñāpradīpa 114b: 'di ni yod nyid 'gog pa ste | | med nyid yongs su 'dzin pa min | | nag po min zhes smras pa na | | dkar po yin zhes ma brjod bzhin |. According to Avalokitavrata (op. cit., Zha, fol. 96a), its source is Nāgārjuna's 'Jig rten brtag pa zhes bya ba'i gtan (read: bstan) bcos, *Lokaparīkṣā. To paraphrase, astitvapratiṣedha does not necessarily imply nāstitvaparigraha. Thus, one can deny that something is black without necessarily affirming that it is white. In other words (see Avalokitavrata, loc. cit.), a Mādhyamika is allowed to express paramārthataḥ a prasajyapratiṣedha of astitva, without advocating nāstitva by way of a paryudāsa. Other verses attributed to Nāgārjuna also occur; e.g. Ekasmṛtyupadeśa (Pek. ed. 5389, 26a),

Madhyamakālaṁkāravṛtti (Pek. ed. 5285, 72b = Pek. ed. 5274, 383a), Caryāmelāyanapradīpa (Pek. ed. 2668, 95a). These are only a few of the most interesting verses that I have failed to identify in the extant works.

212 A summary of therapeutic formulas (yoga) composed in various meters and closely following the classical doctrine of medicine (aṣṭāṅga). Recently two useful editions (including the Tibetan) have appeared: B. Dash, *Tibetan Medicine with special reference to Yoga Śataka*, Dharamsala, 1976; and J. Filliozat, *Yogaśataka: Texte médical attribué à Nāgārjuna*, Pondicherry, 1979. (Note that there are two manuscripts in The Royal Library, Copenhagen, not collated: Rask and Tuxen collections.) The Yogaśataka is commonly but not exclusively ascribed to Nāgārjuna. See Filliozat, op. cit., pp. iv–xix, where the question of authenticity is discussed. Here I call attention to three pieces of evidence in favor of authenticity: a) RĀ III, 46, speaking of triphala, trikaṭuka, ghṛta, madhu, añjana, etc. has the following: 'bras bu gsum dang tsha ba gsum I I mar dang sbrang rtsi mig sman dang I I dug sel chu rar bzhag bgyi zhing I I grub pa'i sman dang sngags kyang bgyi II. b) BS 79 and SS 251b recommend that a Bodhisattva cultivate vidyāsthāna, etc., which include cikitsā. c) The Ratnapradīpa (337b) reports that Nāgārjuna mastered gso-ba (cikitsā). For other medical texts, see Dash (1976), pp. 9–17.

213 The Tibetan version (260 verses, in various meters) was edited and translated by W. L. Campbell, *The Tree of Wisdom*, Calcutta, 1919. Recently a translation of 255 verses appeared in *Elegant Sayings*, Emeryville, CA, 1977. Note that verses 76, 108, and 196 recall RĀ II, 41; IV, 49, 8. Atiśa's Satyadvayāvatāra 25 is nearly identical with 140. The Prajñādaṇḍa and other texts ascribed to Nāgārjuna in Tibetan versions have been discussed by S.K. Pathak, *The Indian Nītiśāstras in Tibet*, Delhi, 1974.

214 Contrary to what one might expect, this is not an alchemic tract but rather a 'biochemical' one. See N.E. Muthuswami (ed.), *Rasavaiśeṣikasūtram Narasiṁhakṛtabhāṣyopetam*, Trivandrum, 1976. Filliozat (1979), pp. x–xiii has discussed the question of authenticity.

215 Only in Tibetan (Pek. ed. 5304), in 55 anuṣṭubh. The most salient feature of this text, which advocates full-fledged māyāvāda, is that a large number of its stanzas also occur in the Laṅkāvatārasūtra (e.g. 1–4 ~ X, 7-10; 53–55 ~ X, 255–257), with a number of interesting variants. The third verse is quoted in the Tattvasārasaṁgraha 102b as being from Nāgārjuna's *Nirālambastava (see n. 204), while the fourth also occurs as Madhyamakabhavasaṁkrānti '15'. This text certainly deserves separate treatment, preferably together with the many other (if not always unambiguous) points of agreement between early Madhyamaka and the Laṅkāvatārasūtra.

216 Only in Tibetan and Chinese. See *Encyclopedia of Buddhism* I, p. 360; V.V. Gokhale, *Akṣaraśatakam. The Hundred Letters*, Heidelberg, 1930. The Chinese (Taishō 1572) attributes it to Āryadeva, the Tibetan (Pek. ed. 5234 [sūtra] and 5235 [vṛtti]) and Atiśa (Bodhimārgadīpapañjikā 324a) to Nāgārjuna. If the sūtras and the vṛtti have the same author, as is most likely the case, and if the quotation of Sāṁkhyakārikā 9 in the vṛtti (see W. Liebenthal, *Satkārya in der Darstellung seiner buddhistischen Gegner*, Stuttgart-Berlin, 1933, p. 25) is not simply a late interpolation, then the text

cannot possibly have been composed by either Nāgārjuna or Āryadeva. Liebenthal instead suggests 'Vasu', perhaps correctly. See also Robinson (1967), p. 33. A new edition by Mr. Holten Pind will appear in *Indiske Studier* V.

217 See Nakamura (1977), p. 78 and May (1979), p. 481. May summarizes some of the arguments against the authenticity of the Akutobhayā. In my opinion the same Sanskrit original must be supposed to lie behind both the Tibetan version (Pek. ed. 5229) and the Chinese (Taishō 1564). The latter is quite free in its rendering of the verses as well as commentary. In spite of the fact that there is a good Indian tradition in support of Nāgārjuna as the author of the Akutobhayā (see *IIJ* XXIII, p. 212, n. 18; *WZKSO* VII, p. 37; Bodhimārgadīpapañjikā 324b; Akutobhayā 114a), I consider it spurious, not just because its prose compares rather poorly with that of the svavṛttis to VP, ŚS,and VV, but especially because Āryadeva's Catuḥśataka VII, 9 is quoted *ad* MK XXVII, 24, in the Tibetan version as well as the Chinese (so correct Robinson's remark that XXVII, 25 has "no counterpart in the Sanskrit:" It must have had, not in the root text, but in the vṛtti quoting the Catuḥśataka). At present we must accept the obscure *Piṅgala as the author of the commentary. Cf. May (1979), p. 481. He was certainly not identical with Āryadeva.

218 Pek. ed. 2023. Another recension of the Paramārthastava (CS IV).

219 Four verses in the sragadharā meter. See A. von Staël Holstein, "Bemerkungen zum Trikāyastava," *Bulletin de l'Académie des sciences de St. Petersbourg* XI, pp. 837–835; G.N. Roerich, *The Blue Annals*, Calcutta, 1949, pp. 1-2; D.S. Ruegg (1969), p. 49. Ascribed to Nāgārjuna in Jñānaśrīmitra's Sākārasiddhiśāstra, p. 503, but the trikāya doctrine is hardly compatible with the kāyadvaya of YṢ 60 and RĀ III, 10, 12. Moreover, the style is very loose, rather unlike Nāgārjuna. There are several extracts in *JRAS* (1906), pp. 943–977.

220 I have edited and translated this hymn in *Acta Orientalia* XL, pp. 146–155. It has nothing to do with Nāgārjuna. (Corrigenda: 4c: yās°; 6a: °rūdha; 15a: °rājā. Professor de Jong kindly makes the following suggestions: 1a: read dāridrya°?; 2b: is anātha° an old corruption for ananta°?; 4: cf. Dharmasamuccaya XIII, 13; 13c: seems corrupt—read rājāhaṁ me tadā mānas?)

221 Only in Tibetan (Pek. ed. 2021). Eight verses, too poor to be genuine.

222 Only in Tibetan (Pek. ed. 2027). Also eight poor verses.

223 Cf. Murti (1960), p. 91, n. 5. Though certainly a Mahāyāna text, there is nothing particularly Nāgārjunian about it.

224 Pek. ed. 5602. Discussed and reconstructed into Sanskrit by S.K. Pathak, *IHQ* XXXIII, pp. 246–249. Cf. the note to vv. 59–63 of the Bodhicittavivaraṇa.

225 A literal version of the Chinese (Taishō 1573) is found in L. de La Vallée Poussin, *Catalogue of the Tibetan Manuscripts from Tun-huang in the India Office Library*, London, 1962, no. 595; rang gi ngo bo nyid myi rtag I I de bzhin ngo bo ngo bo myed I I rang bzhin ngo bo nyid myed pas I I de phyir stong dang myi rtag gsungs II

226 Also called Viṣṇor ekakartṛtvanirākaraṇam. Discussed and translated by G. Chemparathy, "Two early Buddhist refutations of the existence of Īśvara as the creator of the universe," *WZKSO* XII–XIII, pp. 85–100 (with references). Text and translation also in H.C. Gupta (tr.), *Papers of Th. Stcherbatsky*, Calcutta, 1969, pp. 3–16.

227 Nine verses in Tibetan (Pek. ed. 2017) and Sanskrit (vasantatilakā) edited by S. Lévi and ascribed to Aśvaghoṣa in "Autour d'Aśvaghoṣa," *JA* CCXV, pp. 264–266. According to the Tibetan colophon (which ascribes the text to Nāgārjuna), it is a bsdus pa of a part of the Bodhisattvapiṭaka called tshwa chu klung. The style of this nice little hymn recalls Mātṛceṭa more than anyone else.

228 There is a Chinese version (Taishō 1632) 'retranslated' into Sanskrit by G. Tucci, *Pre-Diṅnāga Buddhist texts on logic from Chinese sources*, Baroda, 1929. Its authenticity was impeached by H. Ui; cf. Nakamura (1977), p. 85. At least two circumstances render it dubious to my mind. First, it appears unlikely that Nāgārjuna, whose predilection for arguing merely by way of prasaṅga is well-known, should recommend conventional rules of debate in order to vindicate the Dharma. And again, why does the *Upāyahṛdaya never figure in the subsequent Svātantrika–Prāsaṅgika controversy in which its tenets would certainly have entitled it to play a decisive role, if it was authentic? If, on the other hand, we assume that it fell into oblivion at an early date, it is quite possible that Nāgārjuna composed it "from a desire to defend the Saddharma" (loc. cit., 23b19–20); i.e., on the saṁvṛti level (see ibid., 25a4 ff., where a satyadvaya theory is implicit). Moreover, we find here the same disdainful attitude toward vāda usually motivated by various kleśas (ibid., 23b6 ff. Here the pūrvapakṣa is of course rhetorical).

229 See the arguments advanced by Ramanan (1966), p. 34.

230 Extant in Tibetan (101 verses; Pek. ed. 2010) and also in Chinese (87 verses; Taishō 1675). They are not different works (as Nakamura, op. cit., p. 84 apparently thinks), the Chinese being merely a free version. Discussed and paraphrased by D.S. Ruegg, "Le Dharmadhātustava de Nāgārjuna," *Études Tibétaines dédiées à la Mémoire de Marcelle Lalou*, Paris, 1971, pp. 448–471. It is attributed to Nāgārjuna by Bhavya, quoting vv. 91–96 and 101 (op. cit., 358a and 361a). It must also be noted that several Sūtras asserting the existence of dharmadhātu or tathāgatagarbha as nitya, dhruva, śiva, and śāśvata (cf. CS II, 22) are also known from quotations in Nāgārjuna's Sūtrasamuccaya. In this stava (or stotra) we also find a *prima facie* 'positive ontology': dharmadhātu is niyatasthāna (1), saṁsārahetu (2), anutpanna, aniruddha (8), prabhāsvara, viśuddha (9), sāra (15), bīja (17), anātman (24, here 'without gender'), dhruva (35), etc. It is not merely śūnya (22). It would be a glaring inconsistency for the author of the MK, ŚS, VV to express himself thus paramārthataḥ. On the other hand, we cannot wholly exclude the possibility that Nāgārjuna wrote this hymn saṁvṛtitaḥ, or neyārtha (cf. CS III, 57), with the motive sattvāvatārataḥ (cf. CS II, 21–22).

231 See most recently P. Kumar (ed.), *Nāgārjuna's Yogaratnamālā*, Delhi, 1980. It is a verse collection dealing with matters such as vaśīkaraṇa, vidveṣakaraṇa, uccāṭana, piśācīkaraṇa, āveśavidhāna, vandhyāputrajanma, dīpena kāṇīkaraṇa and similar whimsical—not to say criminal—devices

that in Nāgārjuna's opinion would certainly secure their author a place of honor in Avīci Hell. Worthy of a more serious interest are the extracts from Rasaratnākara, edited by P.C. Ray, *A History of Hindu Chemistry*, Calcutta, 1909, vol. II, pp. *3–*17. The author of this work is an alchemist with a high opinion of his sacred vocation (III, 4): prajñāpāramitā niśīthasamaye svapne prasādīkṛtam I nāmnā tīkṣṇamukhaṁ rasendram amalaṁ nāgārjunaproditam II. Perhaps this line, which apparently does not belong to the Rasaratnākara but rather to the Kakṣāpuṭa (sometime ascribed to Nāgārjuna; cf. Tucci, op. cit., p. 214) reveals the true identity of this unknown namesake: śrīsailaparvatasthāyī siddho nāgārjuno mahān I sarvosattvopakārī ca sarvabhāgyasamanvitaḥ II (ibid., p. *12). On the Rasaratnākara compare also M. Eliade, *Yoga: Unsterblichkeit und Freiheit*, Frankfurt, 1977, p. 430 [publisher's note: in English, *Yoga: Immortality and Freedom*]; Traité, p. 383.

The remaining works ascribed to Nāgārjuna are mainly sādhanas and the like, or other texts the form or content of which, at least from a first perusal, appear to me too insipid and unworthy of the author of the thirteen works I consider established as genuine.

232 Thus the Mūlamadhyamakakārikā and Śūnyatāsaptati cannot be read without a basic knowledge of the Abhidharma. Verses such as RĀ III, 35; BS 62, 97, 119, 147; SL 27, 53, etc. presuppose the reader's acquaintance with some of the Sūtras. RĀ V, 34 and SL 53 refer to Vinaya rules.

233 On bodhicitta, see Har Dayal (1932), pp. 50–79; BV, passim; RĀ II, 74–75; Siddhi, p. 727; A. Bareau in *Die Religionen Indiens*, Stuttgart, 1964, p. 147 (with references at p. 146, n. 3).

234 RĀ V, 65. See also the note on BS 48. Recently B.C. Beresford has translated the Triskandhakasūtra (cf. Upālipariprcchā, p. 107, n. 4) in his *Mahāyāna Purification: The Confession Sūtra and the practice of Vajrasattva*, Dharamsala, 1978. In addition, this book includes some excerpts from the Bodhyāpattideśanāvṛtti (Pek. ed. 5506), ascribed to Nāgārjuna. Even if the authorship of this very interesting commentary remains questionable, there can be no doubt that it originated in the 'circle' of early Madhyamaka. It is closely related to Mātṛceta's Sugatapañcatriṁśatstotra and other early texts on bodhisattvavidhi; for example, the Bodhyākarapraṇidhāna (Pek. ed. 5930), also ascribed to Nāgārjuna. It would certainly prove a rewarding task to deal with all these early ritual texts collectively.

235 RĀ III 12–13. On the mahāpuruṣalakṣaṇa see RĀ II, 76–96; Traité, pp. 271–281 (with references). For the anuvyañjanas, see the list in the Mahāyānasaṁgraha, pp. 56*–58* and the references ibid., p. 54*; Konow (1941), pp. 57–81.

236 On the pāramitās, see Har Dayal, op. cit., pp. 165–269; Traité, pp. 650–1113; Siddhi, pp. 620–638.

237 Pek. ed. 5658, 149a–149b; cf. the quotation in the Tarkajvālā referred to above, n. 138.

238 Commentary to BV 96 (Pek. ed. 2694, 480b).

239 On the ten bhūmis see, above all, Har Dayal, op. cit., pp. 270–291; Siddhi, pp. 721–742; Traité, pp. 2372–2445; Śūraṁgamasamādhisūtra, pp. 155–158.

240 On the relationship between prajñā and the other pāramitās, see Murti (1960), p. 267 and pp. 209–227; Traité, pp. 2365–2371.

241 See n. 164 above; Vimalakīrtinirdeśa, pp. 420–425; Bhāvanākrama I (ed. Tucci), pp. 198–205; Pañcaskandhaprakaraṇa (my ed.), pp. 16–27; Ratnapradīpa VII.

242 As Āryadeva puts it (Catuḥśataka VIII, 5): bhavaḥ saṁdehamātreṇa jāyate jarjarīkṛtaḥ (". . . a bit of critical sense . . ."). I cannot refrain from giving Dharmakīrti's celebrated verse to the same effect (Pramāṇavārttika II, 209): yathā yathārthāś cintyante viśīryante tathā tathā. (To the references given in the edition by Miyasaka may be added in addition: Madhyamakālaṁkāravṛtti, Pek. ed. 5285, 65b; Syādvādamañjarī [ed. Dhruva], p. 117; Siddhiviniścayaṭīkā [ed. Jain], p. 92; Nyāyāvatāravivṛtti [ed. Upadhye], p. 31 [printed as prose].)

243 Cf. on jñāna in Nāgājuna: samyagjñāna (YṢ 10; RĀ II, 22); jñānacakśus (YṢ 54; CS I, 1); viviktajñāna (CS I, 1); asamajñāna (CS III, 1); tattvajñāna (CS III, 19, 47); śūnyatājñāna (BV 90). See also MK XXVI, 11; XVIII, 12; BS 46. For (a-)parijñāna, YṢ 4, 6, 47, 48; RĀ I, 28, 39; II, 22, etc. See *Hōbōgirin*, under Chie.

244 Traité, pp. 1743–1755; *Hōbōgirin*, under Byōdō (samatā); Vimalakīrtinirdeśa, *passim*; RĀ I, 74; II, 6, 8.

245 On prapañca see May (1959), p. 175, n. 562; also L. Schmithausen, *Der Nirvāṇa-Abschnitt in der Viniścayasaṁgrahaṇī der Yogācārabhūmiḥ*, Vienna, 1969, pp. 137–142.

246 This ambiguity is decisive in key words such as artha, ('object' or 'meaning'), upalabdhi ('exist' or 'perceive'), prapañca ('the universe' or 'language'), satya ('reality' or 'truth'), sad ('real' or 'good'), saṁbhava ('occurence', 'possibility') — to mention only a few at random. I think that in a certain sense La Vallée Poussin was quite right when he claimed: "Indians do not make a clear distinction between facts and ideas, between ideas and words; they never clearly recognized the principle of contradiction." (quoted in de Jong's review in *JIP* I, p. 401). On the other hand this need not always be a drawback! Cf. also the most interesting book by the late R.E.A. Johansson, *The Dynamic Psychology of Early Buddhism*, London, 1979.

247 On pari-, vi- and saṁ-kalpayati, etc. see May, op. cit., p. 64, n. 64.

248 This list is culled from MK and ŚS, *passim*, and from the 'table of categories' given at RĀ I, 91–92.

249 Cf. MK II, 21 (quoted in text below); also Catuḥśataka XIV, 19: tasya tasyaikatā nāsti yo yo bhavaḥ parīkṣyate | na santi tenāneke 'pi yenaiko 'pi na vidyate || (often cited in later literature). Similarly Pramāṇavārttika II, 360: bhāvā yena nirūpyante tadrūpaṁ nāsti tattvataḥ | yasmād ekam anekaṁ vā rūpaṁ teṣāṁ na vidyate ||. Ejima (1980), p. 254.

250 See the exhortations occuring at intervals in MK (but not in any of the author's other works!): III, 8; IV, 7; VIII, 13; X, 15 and XIX, 4 (note that the verses in Prasannapadā, p. 384 already appear in Prajñāpradīpa *ad loc.*!).

251 On the interpretation of svabhāva, see May, op. cit., p. 124, n. 328; de Jong, *JIP* II, p. 2–3. Cf. also Steinkellner, *WZKSO* XV, pp. 179–211.

252 See, for example, Vimalakīrtinirdeśa, pp. 39–51.

253 They have been discussed by Atiśa in his Pañjikā to the Bodhipathapradīpa, 189–208 and translated in my "Atiśa's Introduction to the two Truths, and its sources," in *JIP* IX, pp. 206–212. The nomenclature is probably originally Bhavya's.

254 See also the ref. in CPD, under apara(p)paccaya. The Chinese version of aparapratyaya in MK XVIII, 9 is quite explicit: zì zhī, 'personally known'.

255 For prasaṅga, see Murti, op.cit., pp. 131 ff.; Ramanan (1966), p. 152.

256 All this is discussed at length in the Vigrahavyāvartanī.

257 Cf. e.g. K.V. Abhyankar and J.M. Shukla, *A Dictionary of Sanskrit Grammar*, Baroda, 1977, pp. 244, 373. In Madhyamaka, as known, the Svātantrikas argued paramārthataḥ by way of prasajyapratiṣedha; cf. especially Ejima, op. cit., pp. 113—25; Y. Kajiyama, *An Introduction to Buddhist Philosophy*, Kyoto, 1966, n. 62. Nāgārjuna never uses these terms but may have known them; cf. the fragment from *Lokaparīkṣā above, n. 211, and Tarkajvālā 213a.

258 BS 28–30, 47; Śūraṁgamasamādhisūtra, p. 160, n. 119 (anutpattikadharmakṣānti is obtained at the eighth bhūmi [acalā]).

259 SL 8, etc.

260 On this subject see my article, mentioned at n. 253, which gives some of the most interesting Indian sources.

261 Madhyamakāvatāra VI, 80 (some references in *Acta Orientalia* XL, p. 89, n. 12).

262 Pek. ed. 5229, 102b.

263 Madhyamakahṛdayakārikā III, 12; see Ejima's ed., p. 271; see also my edition of Atiśa's Satyadvayāvatāra, 20 (in the article cited at n. 253).

264 MK XXVI, 11; XI, 1 : Being based on avidyā, samsara has no beginning (anavarāgro hi . . .), but the attainment of jñāna brings it to an end.

265 Due to considerations of space I must abstain from drawing parallels to cognate Indian darśanas or to Western philosophers. See, however, Conze's "Buddhist Philosophy and its European Parallels" and "Spurious Parallels to Buddhist Philosophy," *PEW* XIII, pp. 9–23, 105–115 (both reprinted in his *Thirty Years of Buddhist Studies*. Oxford, 1968). More recently, N. Katz (ed.), *Buddhist and Western Philosophy*, New Delhi, 1981 (not seen).

266 Bibliographies of Āryadeva appear in Traité III, pp. 1370–1375, and most recently J. May, "Āryadeva et Candrakīrti sur la permanence," in *Indianisme et boudhisme. Mélanges offerts à Mgr. Étienne Lamotte*, Louvain-la-Neuve, 1980, pp. 215–232. For three new fragments see my note 22 in *IIJ* XXIII, p. 178. There are three more verses in Śāntarakṣita's Madhyamakālaṁkāravṛtti, Pek. ed. 5285, 61a. I postpone further remarks on Āryadeva and his works to my edition of the Catuḥśataka, to appear in Indiske Studier VII.

267 For the titles of the individual chapters see V. Bhattacharya, *The Catuḥśataka of Āryadeva*, Calcutta, 1931, pp. xx–xxi. On the four viparyāsas cf. SL 55, with references in the notes.

268 Catuḥśataka XI, 18, quoted in the Dvādaśāraṁ Nayacakram (ed. Jambūvijayajī), p. 73; Anekāntajayapatākā (ed. Kāpadīā) I, p. 233; II,

p. 202. Hastavālaprakaraṇa 1 (if authentic) is cited at Dvādaśāraṁ Nayacakram, p. 93.

269 Cited from A. Chakravarti, *Samayasāra of Śrī Kundakunda*, New Delhi, 1971, p. 17. (For Kundakunda's date, see E.H. Johnston, *Early Sāṁkhya*, p. 14.)

270 cf. e.g. La Vallée Poussin, *MCB* II, p. 35: "Le bon interprète de la pensée de Nāgārjuna serait Gauḍapāda, le maître de Śaṁkara. . . . Armé des arguments et des expressions de Nāgārjuna, faisant sien tout le nihilisme de Nāgārjuna, Gauḍapāda introduisit dans l'archaïque Vedānta la doctrine de l'irréalité du contingent (māyāvāda), la doctrine rigoureuse de l'unité et du caractère 'impensable' de l'Être." More recently, see Murti (1980), pp. 109-117; F. Whaling: "Śaṅkara and Buddhism," *JIP* VII, pp. 1-42; T. Vetter: "Die Gauḍapādīya-Kārikās: Zur Entstehung und zur Bedeutung von (a)dvaita," *WZKS* XXII, pp. 95-131; also T. Vetter, *Studien zur Lehre und Entwicklung Śaṅkaras*, Vienna, 1979, pp. 27-74; Tuxen (1936), pp. 22-24. This is not the place to discuss the decisive impact the satyadvaya-theory has exerted upon the śabdādvaitavāda of Bhartṛhari, though this fact and its far-reaching implications seem to have escaped the notice of the modern interpreters of the Vākyapadīya. This point will be dealt with in a forthcoming work by Mr. Torvald Olsson (Lund).

271 Pointed out by M. Walleser, *Der ältere Vedānta: Geschichte, Kritik und Lehre*, Heidelberg, 1910, p. 18; cf. V.V. Gokhale: "The Vedānta-Philosophy described by Bhavya in his Madhyamakahṛdaya," *IIJ* II, p. 175.

272 Cf. Walleser, op.cit., p. 20. But Walleser's list is not complete, as Śāntarakṣita also cites III, 31-32. His quotation of II, 31-32, 35 occurs in the Madhyamakālaṁkāravṛtti, Pek. ed. 5285, 81b.

Abbreviations

BHS	Buddhist Hybrid Sanskrit
BHSD	Buddhist Hybrid Sanskrit Dictionary
BST	Buddhist Sanskrit Texts
CPD	Critical Pāli Dictionary
IBK	Indogaku Bukkyōgaku Kenkyū
IHQ	Indian Historical Quarterly
IIJ	Indo-Iranian Journal
JA	Journal Asiatique
JAOS	Journal of the American Oriental Society
JIES	Journal of Indo-European Studies
JIP	Journal of Indian Philosophy
MCB	Mélanges Chinoise et Bouddhique
NS	Nyāyasūtra
PED	Pāli English Dictionary
PEW	Philosophy East and West
Siddhi	Vijñāptimātratāsiddhi
TP	T'oung Pao
Traité	Mahāprajñāpāramitopadeśaśāstra
WZKS(O)	Wiener Zeitschrift für die Kunde des Süd- (und Ost)asiens

For a list of abbreviations for the principal works dealt with in this book, see page xix; for abbreviations for texts listed as citing the Catuḥstava, see page 237.

Parallel Citations

Peking	*Ny/Derge*	*Peking*	*Ny/Derge*	*Peking*	*Ny/Derge*
2010	1118	5227	3827	5330	3934
2012	1120	5228	3828	5344	3948
2017	1125	5229	3829	5361	3966
2019	1128	5230	3830	5389	3928
2020	1129	5231	3831	5405	3966
2021	1130	5232	3832	5409	4182
2023	1132	5238	3838	5428	5054
2026	1135	5242	3842	5466	3985
2027	1136	5253	3853	5470	1800
2658	1793	5254	3854	5485	3985
2664	1799	5256	3856	5506	4005
2665	1800	5259	3859	5512	4011
2666	1801	5265	3864	5552	4051
2668	1803	5266	3865	5602	4101
2694	1829	5268	3867	5629	4127
3145	2297	5269	3868	5658	4158
4531	3708	5274	3873	5659	4159
4532	3709	5277	3875A	5661	4161
4534	3711	5282	3880	5682	4182
5224	3824	5285	3885	5690	4190
5225	3825	5286	3886	5928	4388
5226	3826	5287	3887	5930	4385
		5304	3908		

Bibliography

This bibliography is selective. Usually it does not repeat a reference already given once or twice in full in the text. It lists some standard works which I have found indispensable for Madhyamaka and allied studies, as well as a few other books that I have consulted. Extensive bibliographical information is provided in the following works:

Hanayama, S., *Bibliography of Buddhism,* Tokyo 1961.

Nakamura, H., *Indian Buddhism: A survey with Bibliographical Notes,* Osaka 1980.

Potter, K. H., *The Encyclopedia of Indian Philosophies,* Delhi 1970.

A good selective bibliography is given in

Regamey, C., *Buddhistische Philosophie,* Bern 1950.

Bibliographies with particular regard to Madhyamaka may be found in the works of May (1959); Murti (1960); Ramanan (1966); Streng (1967) and several others listed below. Also in D. S. Ruegg, *The Literature of the Madhyamaka School of Philosophy in India,* Wiesbaden 1981 (which I received too late to make use of).

Throughout the book, references to works in Pāli are to the editions of the Pāli Text Society. For Tibetan texts I have referred to Suzuki, D. T. (ed.), *The Tibetan Tripiṭaka. Peking edition,* Kyoto 1955–1961 (abbreviated Pek. ed.). References to the Narthang edition are to the copy belonging to the Royal Library (Copenhagen). I have also referred to modern critical editions when these exist. The recent Japanese reprint of the Derge edition (Madhyamaka section) reached me too late for me to take it fully into account, nor did I have the opportunity to consult the *Nyingma Edition of the sDe-dge bKa'-'gyur and bsTan-'gyur,* Berkeley 1981. All Chinese texts are quoted or translated from Takakusu, J. and Watanabe, K. (eds.), *Taishō Shinshū Daizōkyō,* Tokyo 1924–1929.

Edited Sanskrit texts have been listed below. Mahāyāna Sūtras and śāstras are occasionally quoted from Vaidya, P. L. (ed.), *Buddhist Sanskrit Texts,* Darbhanga 1958, unless otherwise indicated.

Abhyankar, K. V. & Shukla, J. M., *A Dictionary of Sanskrit Grammar*, Baroda 1977.

Bendall, C. (ed.), *Śikṣāsamuccaya. A compendium of Buddhistic teaching*, St. Petersburg 1897–1902.

Bendall, C. (ed.), 'Subhāṣitasaṁgraha', *Le Muséon*, IV–V, Louvain 1903–1904.

Broeck, J. van den, *La saveur de l'immortel (A-p'i-t'an Kan Lu Wei Lun)*, Louvain-la-Neuve 1977.

Carelli, M. E. (ed.), *Sekoddeśaṭīkā*, Baroda 1941.

Conze, E., *Materials for a Dictionary of the Prajñāpāramitā Literature*, Tokyo 1973.

Conze, E., *The Large Sūtra on Perfect Wisdom*, Berkeley 1975.

Conze, E., *The Prajñāpāramitā Literature*, Tokyo 1978.

Dayal, H., *The Bodhisattva Doctrine in Buddhist Sanskrit Literature*, London 1932.

Edgerton, F. *Buddhist Hybrid Sanskrit Dictionary*, New Haven 1953.

Eimer, H. (ed.), *Bodhipathapradīpa*, Wiesbaden 1978.

Ejima, Y., *Chūgan-shisō no tenkai . . . Bhāvaviveka kenkyū*, Tokyo 1980.

Frauwallner, E., *Geschichte der indischen Philosophie*, Salzburg 1953–1956.

Frauwallner, E., *Die Philosophie des Buddhismus*, Berlin 1969.

Guenther, H. V., *The Jewel Ornament of Liberation*, London 1959.

Hattori, M., *Dignāga. On Perception*, Cambridge, MA 1968.

Hikata, R. (ed.), *Suvikrāntavikrāmiparipṛcchā Prajñāpāramitā*, Fukuoka 1958.

Hirano, T., *An Index to the Bodhicaryāvatārapañjikā, chapter IX*, Tokyo 1966.

Jaini, P. S. (ed.), *Abhidharmadīpa with Vibhāṣāprabhāvṛtti*, Patna 1977.

Jhalakīkar, B., *Nyāyakośa or Dictionary of Technical Terms of Indian Philosophy*, Poona 1978.

Jolly, J., *Indian Medicine*, New Delhi 1977.

Johnston, E. H. (ed.), *The Saundarananda of Aśvaghoṣa*, Lahore 1928.

Jong, J. W. de, *Cinq chapitres de la Prasannapadā*, Paris 1949.

Kajiyama, Y., *An Introduction to Buddhist Philosophy. An annotated translation of the Tarkabhāṣā of Mokṣākaragupta*, Kyoto 1966.

Kasawara, K. et al. (eds.), *Dharmasaṁgraha*, Oxford 1885.

Kiyota, M. (ed.), *Mahāyāna Buddhist Meditation: Theory and Practice*, Honolulu 1978.

Konow, S., *The two first Chapters of the Daśasāhasrikā Prajñāpāramitā*, Oslo 1941.

Kunst, A., *Probleme der buddhistischen Logik in der Darstellung des Tattvasaṁgraha*, Cracow 1939.

Kværne, P. (ed.), *An Anthology of Buddhist Tantric Songs*, Oslo 1977.

Lamotte, É. (ed.), *Saṁdhinirmocanasūtra*, Louvain 1935.

Lamotte, É. (ed.), "Karmasiddhiprakaraṇa," *MCB* IV, Brussels 1936.

Lamotte, É., *La Somme du grand véhicule d'Asaṅga (Mahāyānasaṁgraha)*, I–II, Louvain 1938.

Lamotte, É., *Le Traité de la grande vertu de sagesse de Nāgārjuna (Mahāprajñāpāramitāśāstra)*, I–V, Louvain 1949–1980.

Lamotte, É., *Histoire de bouddhisme indien, des origines à l'ère Śaka*, Louvain 1958.

Lamotte, É., *La concentration de la marche héroïque (Śūraṁgamasamādhisūtra)*, Brussels 1965.

Lancaster, L. (ed.), *Prajñāpāramitā and Related Systems*, Berkeley 1977.

La Vallée Poussin, L. de, *Bouddhisme. Études et matériaux. Ādikarmapradīpa, Bodhicaryāvatāraṭīkā*, London 1898.

La Vallée Poussin, L. de (ed.), *Bodhicaryāvatārapañjikā*, Calcutta 1901–1914.

La Vallée Poussin, L. de (ed.), *Mūlamadhyamakakārikās de Nāgārjuna avec la Prasannapadā*, St. Petersburg 1903–1913.

La Vallée Poussin, L. de (ed.), *Madhyamakāvatāra par Candrakīrti. Traduction tibétaine*, St. Petersburg 1907–1912.

La Vallée Poussin, L. de, *Théorie des douze causes*, Gand 1913.

La Vallée Poussin, L. de, *L'Abhidharmakośa de Vasubandhu*, I–VI, Louvain 1923–1931.

La Vallée Poussin, L. de, *Vijñaptimātratāsiddhi. La Siddhi de Hiuan-tsang*, I–III, Paris 1928–1948.

La Vallée Poussin, L. de, "Le Joyau dans la main," *MCB* II, Brussels 1933.

Lévi, S. (ed.), *Vijñaptimātratāsiddhi: deux traités de Vasubandhu, Viṁśatikā et Triṁśikā*, Paris 1925.

Lindtner, C. (ed.), "Candrakīrti's Pañcaskandhaprakaraṇa," *Acta Orientalia* XL, Hauniae 1979.

Malvania, D. (ed.), *Ācārya Jinabhadra's Viśeṣāvaśyakabhāṣya,* I–III, Ahmedabad 1966–1968.

Matsunami, S., *A Catalogue of the Sanskrit Manuscripts in the Tokyo University Library,* Tokyo 1965.

May, J., *Candrakīrti Prasannapadā Madhyamakavṛtti,* Paris 1959.

Mimaki, K., *La réfutation bouddhique de la permanence des choses (sthirasiddhidūṣaṇa) et la preuve de la momentanéité des choses (kṣaṇabhaṅgasiddhi),* Paris 1976.

Miyasaka, Y. (ed.), *Pramāṇavārttikakārikā (Sanskrit and Tibetan),* Naritashi 1972.

Murti, T. R.V., *The Central Philosophy of Buddhism,* London 1960.

Nagao, G. M. (ed.), *Madhyāntavibhāga-Bhāṣya,* Tokyo 1964.

Nakamura, H., "A Survey of Mahāyāna Buddhism with Bibliographical Notes," *Journal of Intercultural Studies,* III–IV, Osaka 1976–1978.

Nanjio, B. (ed.), *Laṅkāvatārasūtra,* Kyōto 1923.

Naudou, J., *Les bouddhistes kaśmīriens au Moyen Age,* Paris 1968.

Obermiller, E., *Bu ston: History of Buddhism,* I–II, Heidelberg 1931–1933.

Obermiller, E. (ed.), *Ratnaguṇasaṁcaya,* The Hague 1960.

Pezzali, A., *Śāntideva, mystique bouddhiste des VIIe et VIIIe siècles,* Florence 1968.

Pradhan, P. (ed.), *Abhidharmakośabhāṣyam of Vasubandhu,* Patna 1975.

Python, P. (ed.), *Vinaya-viniścaya-Upālipariprcchā,* Paris 1973.

Rahder, J. (ed.), *Daśabhūmikasūtra,* Louvain 1926.

Rahder, J., *Glossary of Sanskrit, Tibetan, Mongolian and Chinese versions of the Daśabhūmikasūtra,* Paris 1928.

Rahula, W., *Le compendium de la super-doctrine (philosophie) (Abhidharmasamuccaya) d'Asaṅga,* Paris 1971.

Ramanan, K. V., *Nāgārjuna's Philosophy as presented in the Mahāprajñāpāramitāśāstra,* Tokyo 1966.

Randle, H. N., *Indian Logic in the Early Schools,* Oxford 1930.

Ritter, J. et al. (eds.), *Historisches Wörterbuch der Philosophie,* Basel 1971.

Robinson, R. H., *Early Mādhyamika in India and China*, Madison 1967.

Ruben, W., *Die Nyāyasūtra's*, Leipzig 1928.

Rubow, P., *Den kritiske Kunst. En afhandling om filologisk litteraturforskning*, Copenhagen 1938.

Ruegg, D. S., *La théorie du Tathāgatagarbha et du Gotra*, Paris 1969.

Samtani, N. H. (ed.), *The Arthaviniścaya-sūtra and its commentary (Nibandhana)*, Patna 1971.

Sakaki, R., *Mahāvyutpatti*, Kyoto 1916–1925.

Sastri, N. A. (ed.), *Śālistamba Sūtra*, Adyar 1950.

Schiefner, A. (ed.), *Tāranāthae de doctrinae buddhicae in India propagatione*, St. Petersburg 1868.

Schmithausen, L., *Der Nirvāṇa-Abschnitt in der Viniścayasaṁgrahaṇī der Yogācārabhūmiḥ*, Vienna 1969.

Shackleton Bailey, D. R., *The Śatapañcāśatkastotra of Mātṛceṭa*, Cambridge 1951.

Staël-Holstein, A. von. (ed.), *Kāśyapaparivarta*, Shanghai 1926.

Streng, F., *Emptiness: A Study in Religious Meaning*, Nashville 1967.

Suali, L. (ed.), *Ṣaḍarśanasamuccaya by Haribhadra with Guṇaratna's commentary Tarkarahasyadīpikā*, Calcutta 1905.

Suzuki, D. T., *An Index to the Laṅkāvatārasūtra*, Kyoto 1934.

Takakusu, J., *The Essentials of Buddhist Philosophy*, Honolulu 1956.

Takasaki, J., *A study on the Ratnagotravibhāga (Uttaratantra)*, Rome 1966.

Thakur, A. (ed.), *Jñānaśrīmitranibandhāvalī*, Patna 1959.

Tripāthī, C. (ed.), *Fünfundzwanzig Sūtras des Nidānasaṁyukta*, Berlin 1962.

Tucci, G., "Studi Mahāyānici, I: La versione cinese del Catuḥśataka de Āryadeva confrontato col testo sanscrito e la traduzione tibetana," *Rivista degli Studi Orientali* X, Rome 1925.

Tucci, G., *Pre-Diṅnaga Buddhist texts on Logic from Chinese Sources*, Baroda 1929.

Tucci, G. (ed.), *Minor Buddhist Texts*, I–III, Rome 1956–1971.

Tucci, G., *Opera Minora*, I–II, Rome 1971.

Tuxen, P., *Yoga*, Copenhagen 1911.

Tuxen, P., *Indledende Bemærkninger til buddhistisk Relativisme*, Copenhagen 1936.

Ui, H., *Vaiśeṣika Philosophy, according to the Daśapadārthaśāstra*, London 1917.

Vetter, T., *Studien zur Lehre und Entwicklung Śaṅkaras*, Vienna 1979.

Walleser, M., *Die Mittlere Lehre des Nāgārjuna*, Heidelberg 1912.

Wayman, A., *Calming the Mind and Discerning the Real. Buddhist Meditation and the Middle View. From the Lam rim chen mo of Tsong-kha-pa*, New York 1978.

Weller, F., *Zum Kāśyapaparivarta*, Leipzig 1965.

Yamaguchi, S., *Chūkan Bukkyō Ronkō*, Tokyo 1965.

Yamaguchi, S., *Index to the Prasannapadā Madhyamaka-vṛtti*, I–II, Kyoto 1974.

Glossary

Sanskrit Terms and Lists

Ālayavijñāna in some Buddhist teachings, the fundamental consciousness, ground for all other forms of consciousness and for all experience; also referred to as the storehouse consciousness

Ānantarya five wrongful misdeeds of the utmost gravity, which bear the immediate consequence of a rebirth in the hell realms

Arhat one who attains realization by breaking through the bondage of the emotional obscurations

Bhagavat an epithet for the Buddha or other advanced spiritual masters; sometimes translated as 'Lord' or 'Sir'

Bodhi enlightenment or awakening: the state of perfect realization attained by the Buddha (literally, one who has awakened)

Bodhicitta a mind dedicated to enlightenment, consisting in one aspect of the intention to liberate all beings and in the other of the direct realization of śūnyatā

Bodhisattva one who bases his practice on bodhicitta, generating the intention to lead all beings to enlightenment

Caitya a monument containing holy relics

Cakravartin a universal ruler; a king or emperor whose domain extends to the farthest known limits

Dhāraṇī literally, 'that which bears the meaning': a formula that contains the essence of an aspect of the teachings; meant to be memorized and recited

Dharma the teaching of the Buddha; also a term for truth or reality, or (lower case) for an element or phenomenon of experience

Dharmacakra literally, 'Wheel of the Dharma': An aspect of the teaching promulgated or 'set in motion' by the Buddha

Dhyāna a general term for meditation

Eightfold Path right vision, right conception, right speech, right action, right livelihood, right effort, right mindfulness, right samādhi

Four Applications of Mindfulness mindfulness of body, feeling, mind, and dharmas

Four Bases of Miraculous Power will, mind, effort, analysis

Four Restraints cutting off the non-virtuous and abandoning it; producing the virtuous and maintaining it

Five Powers faith, effort, mindfulness, samādhi, prajñā

Five Strengths faith, effort, mindfulness, samādhi, prajñā

Gandharvas beings that live in the desire realm in cloud-like cities

Jina literally, 'Conqueror': an epithet of the Buddha

Kāya literally, 'body' or 'embodiment': an aspect of the Buddha's manifestation to benefit all beings

Karma voluntary action, producing consequences that determine the conditions and circumstances of sentient beings

Kleśa a form of obscuration based on emotion and ignorance: The three fundamental kleśas are greed, hatred, and delusion

Mahāyāna the great vehicle of realization, followed by all Buddhas

Māra the lord of illusion, ruler of the desire realm, whom the Buddha defeated before attaining enlightenment

Mantra syllables and words whose sounds can communicate the nature of tantric deities, grant supernormal powers, or lead to purification or realization

Marga a path or method for achieving a goal

Muni an epithet of the Buddha, sometimes translated as Sage.

Nāga a powerful, long-lived serpent-like being that inhabits bodies of water and often guards great treasure

Nirvana the extinction of samsara; the corresponding Tibetan means 'passing beyond misery'

Pāramitā an action or practice that leads beyond the limitations of conventional ways of being and toward enlightenment; sometimes translated as 'perfection'

Piṭaka a collection of Buddhist teachings: the Tripiṭaka consists of Vinaya, Sūtra, and Abhidharma

Prajñāpāramitā the teaching of complete omniscience; the heart of the Buddha's realization, known as the Mother of the Tathāgatas.

Pratyekabuddha one who practices the Dharma without a teacher, investigating the laws of existence for himself

Samādhi meditative or concentrative absorption in which the ordinary workings of mind are transformed

Samsara ordinary reality; an endless cycle of frustration and suffering generated as the result of karma based on ignorance

Śāstra a commentary on a root text or treatise that illuminates an aspect of the teaching

Seven Branches of Enlightenment mindfulness, investigation of truth, effort, joy, refinement, samādhi, equanimity

Six destinies rebirth in the realm of the gods, the jealous gods, human beings, animals, hungry ghosts, or creatures of the hell realms

Skandha one of the five 'aggregates' into which the Buddha divided the realm of human experience, which together encompass the whole range of existence

Śrāvaka one who practices on the basis of having heard the teachings, focusing on the reality of suffering inherent in samsara and the non-existence of an independent self

Sumeru the mountain said in Buddhist cosmology to be at the center of a world system: a world axis; also referred to as 'Meru'.

Śūnya the quality of being 'empty'

Śūnyatā the 'emptiness' of all elements of existence: their conditioned nature and lack of own-being, so that nothing remains fixed, determined, or limited

Sūtra a discourse of the Buddha; in some contexts, simply a short, aphoristic saying

Tathāgata the perfectly realized being; an epithet for the Buddha meaning literally 'thus-come' or 'thus-gone'

Tīrthika a follower of extreme views such as nihilism or eternalism that do not accord with the teachings of the Buddha and are not conducive to enlightenment

Tuṣita the most pleasing of all the heavens in the desire realm; the abode of the Buddha when he was a Bodhisattva, immediately before his final birth into the human realm

Upāya 'skillful means' employed by Bodhisattvas and enlightened beings in order to lead other to liberation: a direct response perfectly suited to the circumstances, based on wisdom and compassion

Vajra the diamond scepter or thunderbolt, indestructible and dynamic in working toward enlightenment

Vāsanā a tendency, pervasive flavor, or habit pattern that colors experience and limits possibilities, arising on the basis of past conduct and thoughts

Vijñānāvāda a Buddhist philosophical school that made the path of consciousness fundamental to practice and realization

Yakṣa a being of the desire realm, usually benevolent, that inhabits trees and mountains

Yāna a vehicle or path of realization

Yogācāra a Buddhist philosophical school linked to mentalism and experiential realization

Sanskrit — Tibetan — English

KA

sarvajña	kun mkhyen	omniscient
saṁkalpa	kun (tu) rtog	conception
parikalpita	kun brtags	imagined
saṁvṛti	kun rdzobs	convention
ālayavijñāna	kun gzhi rnam shes	~
kṣudh	bkres pa	hunger
pratyaya	rkyen	condition
kṣaṇika	skad cig	instant
pipāsā	skom	thirst
āyatana	skye mched	sense-fields
utpāda	skye ba	origination; birth; arising
anutpanna	skye ba med	unborn; non-arising
jana	skye bo	people
janaka	skyed pa	creator
anutpāda	skyed med	non-origination

KHA

dhātu	khams	element
viśeṣa	khyad pa	difference
viśiṣṭa	khyad 'phags	excellent
ākāśa	mkha'	space
paṇḍita; vicakṣaṇa	mkhas pa	learned person; wise man
cakra	'khor lo	wheel

GA

anuttarapada	go 'phang bla med	unsurpassed stage
siddha	grub pa	proved

nagara	grong khyer	city
mokṣa	grol ba	liberation
gaja	glang po	elephant
śubha; kuśala	dge ba	positive; good; merit
bhikṣu	dge slong	monk
kāryārtham	dgos pa'i don	practical purpose
nirodha	'gags pa	destruction
nirodha	'gog pa	annihilation; extinction
ṣaḍgati	'gro drug srid pa	six destinies
jara	rga ba	decay; grow old
jinaputra	rgyal ba'i sras	sons of the Buddha
hetu	rgyu	cause
saṁtāna	rgyun	continuity
vyavaccheda	rgyun chad pa	disintegrated
māyā	sgyu ma	illusion
māyāpuruṣa	sgyu ma'i skyes bu	phantom; apparition
śabda	sgra	sound
samāropa	sgro 'dogs	attribution
bhāvana; bhāvanā	bsgom pa	meditational development
nivṛta	bsgribs	enveloped

NGA

niyata	nges par	necessarily
svabhāva	ngo bo nyid	own-being
vastu	dngos	substance; thing
bhāvātmaka	dngos bdag can	positivistic attitude
artha; bhāva	dngos po	thing; entity; fact
sāmagrī	dngos po thams cad	totality
bhāvagraha	dngos po 'dzin pa	materialism
vasturūpa	dngos po'i ngo bo	the mode of an entity
bhāvagraha	dngos po'i gdon	fever of positivism
abhāva	dngos med	non-being
pratyakṣa	mngon sum	evident
bherī	rnga	drum
pūrva	sngon	first

CA

yugapat	cig car	at once; simultaneous
itara	cig shos	contrary
eka	gcig	one
akṛtrima	bcos ma yin	absolute

CHA

aṁśa	cha shas	part
vairāgya	chags bral ba	indifference
uccheda	chad	destruction
ucchedavāda	chad pa	advocate of annihilation or nihilism
kadalī	chu shing	plantain (tree)
dharma	chos	principle; phenomenon; attribute
dharmin	chos can	subject
sāmagrī	chos rnams kun	totality
vaidharmya	chos mi mthun	heterogeneity

JA

naṣṭa; vināśa; bhaṅga	'jig pa	destroyed; destruction
loka	'jig rten	world; worldly
lokanātha	'jig rten mgon po	protector of the world
abhidāna; abhidhāna	brjod pa	designations; expression
abhidheya	brjod par bya ba	expressible

NYA

śrāvaka	nyan thos	~
doṣa	nyes pa	faults
kleśa	nyon mongs	~
advaya	gnyis med	non-duality

sama	mnyam pa	moderate
samatā	mnyam pa nyid	equality
durlabha	rnyed par dka'	rarely met with
lokavyavahāra	snyad	convention
karuṇā	snying rje	compassion
sāra	snying po	core; heart
lokavyavahāra	bsnyad	convention

TA

samādhi	ting (nge) 'dzin	~
sadā	rtag tu	constantly
nitya; śāśvata	rtag pa	permanent; eternal
śāśvata	rtag pa nyid	eternalism
pratītyasamutpāda	rten cing ('brel bar) 'byung ba	dependent co-arising
dvādaśāṅga	rten 'byung yan lag bcu gnyis	twelve dependently arising members
kalpanā	rtog pa	abstraction; notion
bodhya	rtog bya	knowable
bodhaka	rtog byed	knower
dṛṣṭi	lta ba	dogma; view
apekṣate	ltos pa	dependent
śūnya	stong pa	empty
śūnyatābhāva	stong pa nyid kyi rang bzhin	in essence empty
kalpanā	brtags	imagination
pratītyasamutpāda	brten nas byung ba	dependent co-origination
āśraya	brten pa	support
deśanā	bstan pa	doctrine; teaching

THA

vyavahāra	tha snyad	conventional
anta	tha ma	last
khala	tha shal	base
mokṣa	thar pa	liberation

kṛṕtmaka	thugs rje'i bdag nyid	compassionate
muni	thub pa	~
munīndra	thub dbang	an epithet of the Buddha
viruddha	'thad ma yin	inconsistent

DA

śraddhā	dad pa	faith
sat	dam pa	a good
viṣa	dug	poison
paśu	dud 'gro	beasts
kāla	dus	time
kālatraya	dus gsum	the three times
tattva(taḥ)	de (bzhin) nyid	reality
artha	don	thing; object; value; meaning
neyārtha	don kun rdzob	provisional meaning, requiring interpretation
paramārtha	don dam	the absolute; ultimate meaning
arthasama	don mtshungs pa	similarity to objects; similar in meaning
gandharva	dri za	~
prajñapti	gdags pa	designation
vaṁśa	gdung	lineage
ātman	bdag	self
ātmasthāna	bdag gi gnas pa	substantial foundation
mahātman	bdag nyid che	great soul
mahātman	bdag nyid chen po	magnanimous
ātmagraha	bdag tu 'dzin pa	belief in a self
nairatmyā	bdag med	selfless(ness)
nairātmyarūpa	bdag med ngo bo	lacking substance
ahaṁkāra	bdag 'dzin	I-making
māra	bdud	Māra
sugatidurgati	bde 'gro dang ngan 'gro	good and bad rebirth

sukha	bde ba	happiness; pleasure
satya	bden pa	true
paṅka	'dam	mud
atīta	'das pa	past
saṁskṛta	'du byas	compound; conditioned
saṁskāra	'du byed	formative forces; karma-formations
samjñā	'du shes	apprehension; perception
asaṁskṛta	'dus ma byas	non-composite; unconditioned
rāga	'dod chags	passion
aṇu; paramāṇu	rdul	atom; form-atom
duḥkha	sdug; sdug bsngal	pain; suffering

NA

antaḥ	nang	internal
śakta	nus pa	efficacious
ratna	nor	jewel
sthāna; sthita	gnas	standpoint; abiding
sthiti	gnas pa	duration
anāspada; asthita	gnas (pa) med	homeless; unfixed
āśrayaparivṛtti	gnas yongs gyur nas dag pa'i sems	mind purified by a transformation in position
avīci	mnar med pa	a hell realm
vikalpa	rnam rtog	construct; discrimination
vimokṣa	rnam thar	liberation
viveka; vivikta(tā)	rnam par dben (pa)	void; separation
vicāryamāṇa yuktyā	rnam dpyad	analyzed logically
vipāka	rnam smin ngo bo	maturation
vijñāna	rnam shes	consciousness
yogācārin	rnal 'byor spyod pa	~
citra	sna tshogs	manifold world; varied
darśana	snang ba	appearance; manifestation

PA

vicāra	dpyad pa	analysis
caryā	spyod pa	course

PHA

hitaiṣin	phan par bzhed	solicitous
anyonya; parasparasiddha	phan tshun	correlation; mutually established
skandha	phung po	~
namaḥ	phyag 'tshal	obeisance
bāhya	phyi rol	external
viparyāsa	phyin ci log	perverted views
pakṣa	phyogs	thesis
ārya	'phags pa	noble

BA

vāsanā	bag chags	potentiality
bodhi	byang chub	enlightenment
mahābodhicitta	byang chub chen por thugs bskyed	thought of Great Enlightenment
bodhimaṇḍa	byang chub snying po	heart of enlightenment
kṛtaka	byas pa	composite; created
bāla	byis pa	simple-minded; fool
kriyā	byed pa	efficacious
kārakatva	byed pa po nyid	creator
kāraka(tva)	byed po	agent; creator
buddhi	blo	mind; understanding
vaśāt	dbang	force; power
indriya	dbang po	sense [organ]; faculty; power
indriyavijñāna	dbang shes	sense consciousness
vivikta	dben pa	void

bheda	dbye ba	part
prayatnena	'bad pa	effort
mahābhūta	'byung chen; 'byung ba che	great elements
phala	'bras bu	fruit; effect
sarpa	sbrul	snake

MA

anupādāya	ma brten pa	unconditioned
anāgata	ma 'ongs	future
avidyā	ma rig pa	ignorance
aneka	mang po	many
anitya	mi rtag	impermanent
aniṣṭa	mi 'dod	unacceptable
acala	mi g·yo	unswerving
avisaṁvādi	mi bslu ba	indisputable
samjñā	ming	concept
koṭi	mu	category
tīrthika	mu stegs can	~
agni	me	fire
ādarśa	me long	mirror
asat	med	non-being
nāstitā	med nyid	non-being
nirvāṇa	mya ngan 'das	nirvana
aṅkura	myu gu	sprout
hīna	dman pa	inferior; lesser; low
ālambana	dmigs pa	support; object of perception
nirālamba	dmigs pa yod ma yin	non-objective
niraya	dmyal ba	hell
svapna	rmi lam	dream
mūḍha; moha	rmongs pa	confused; confusion; delusion; stupidity
amūḍha	rmongs med	unperplexed
auṣadha	sman	medicine

marīci	smig rgyu	mirage
prārthanā	smon pa	aspiration
praṇidhāna	smon lam	aspiration

TSA

mātra	tsam	mere
śuci	gtsang ma	pure
cāraka	btson ra	prison
nirmūla	rtsa ba med	rootless
vivāda	rtsod pa	contentions; contentious
ārambha	rtsom pa	beginning

TSHA

naya	tshul	principle
sāmagrī	tshogs	totality
vedanā	tshor ba	feeling
lakṣaṇa	mtshan	mark
nimitta	mtshan ma	signs
animitta	mtshan ma med	indeterminable; signless
lakṣya	mtshan gzhi	the marked

DZA

grāha	'dzin	belief
grāhaka	'dzin pa	subject
dravya	rdzas	real; material thing
mṛṣā	rdzun	false

ZHA

śānta	zhi ba	calm; peace; quieted; tranquil
naṣṭa	zhig pa	dissolved

parabhāva	gzhan dngos	other-being
parahita	gzhan don	altruism; welfare of others
parapakṣa	gzhan phyogs	opposing thesis
paratantra	gzhan dbang	dependent; relative
āśraya, ālaya	gzhi	basis
anālaya	gzhi med	baseless

ZA

kṣīṇa	zad pa	exhausted; extinguished; spent
rūpa	gzugs	form
rūpākāra	gzugs kyi rnam pa	the aspect of form
rūpa	gzugs nyid	matter
pratibimba	gzugs brnyan	reflection
arūpin	gzugs med	immaterial
grāhya	gzung	object

YA

aṅga	yan lag	spoke (of a wheel); member; limb
tattva	yang dag	truth
bhūtakoṭi	yang dag mtha'	real limit
samyagjñāna	yang dag ye shes	full knowledge
akṣara	yi ge	syllable; word
preta	yi dags	ghost
manas	yid	mind
viṣaya	yul	object
jñāna	ye shes	cognition; knowledge
jñānacakṣuḥ	ye shes kyi mig; ye shes spyan	eye of knowledge
parijñānāt	yongs shes pa	thorough knowledge

parinișpanna	yongs su grub pa	absolute
bhāva; sat	yod pa	being
astivādin	yod par smra ba rnams	advocates of being
cala	g·yo ba	fickle; wavering

RA

svacitta	rang gi sems	mind in itself
svabhāva	rang dngos	own-being
svārtha	rang don	selfishness
prakṛtyā; svabhāva	rang bzhin	own-being; substance; by nature
vedya	rig bya	(known) object
vedaka	rig byed	(knowing) subject
yukti	rigs pa	argument
krameṇa	rim	gradual
asa	ro	elixir; taste

LA

mārga	lam	method; path
karma	las	deed; action
karmaphala	las 'bras	fruit of one's deeds
deha	lus	body
sopādāna	len bcas	appropriator
mithyā	log pa	false
bhoktṛ	longs spyod pa	enjoyer

SHA

sūkṣma	shin tu phra ba	most subtle
jñeya	shes pa	cognition; knowledge
jñātṛ	shes bya rtog pa	knower
prajñāpāramitā	shes rab pha rol phyin	perfect wisdom

SA

bhūmi	sa	stages
bīja	sa bon	seed
siṁhanāda	seng ge'i sgra	lion's roar
citta	sems	mind
sattva	sems can	living being
cittomohana	sems rmongs pa	illusion
cittamātra	sems tsam po	pure consciousness
svapratyātmagati	so so rang rig	specific knowledge of itself
pṛthagjana	so sor skye bo	common people
bhava; bhāva	srid pa	existence
trailokya	srid pa gsum	three worlds
tṛṣṇā	sred pa	craving
tuccha	gsog pa	vain
puṇya	bsod nams	merit
puṇyarāśi	bsod nams phung po	mass of merit
puṇyajñānasaṁbhāra	bsod nams ye shes tshogs bsags	provisions of merit and knowledge
moṣadharman	bslu ba'i chos	fraudulent

Index

Subject Index to Translations

Canonical Texts Cited

Śrī Vaiśravaṇa